D. H. Lawrence's Nightmare

D. H. LAWRENCE'S

NIGHTMARE

The Writer and His Circle
in
the Years of the Great War

BY

PAUL DELANY

Basic Books, Inc., Publishers

NEW YORK

Library of Congress Cataloging in Publication Data

Delany, Paul.
   D. H. Lawrence's nightmare.

   Includes bibliographical references and index.
   1. Lawrence, David Herbert, 1885-1930.
2. Authors, English--20th century--Biography.
3. European war, 1914-1918--Literature and the war.
4. European war, 1914-1918--Great Britain.
5. Great Britain--Intellectual life--20th century.
I. Title.
PR6023.A93Z6235547   823'.9'12 [B]   78-54998
ISBN 0-465-01641-3

For Lisa Berland

I see Van Gogh so sadly. If he could only have set the angel of himself clear in relation to the animal of himself, clear and distinct but always truly related, in harmony and union, he need not have cut off his ear and gone mad. But he said, do you remember—about "in the midst of an artistic life the yearning for the real life remains"—*"one offers no resistance, neither does one resign oneself"*—he means to the yearning to procreate oneself "with other horses, also free." This is why he went mad. He should either have resigned himself and lived his animal "other horses"—and have seen *if his art would come out of that*—or he should have resisted, like Fra Angelico. But best of all, if he could have known a great humanity, where to live one's animal would be to create oneself, *in fact, be the artist creating a man in living fact* (not like Christ, as he wrongly said)—and where the art was the final expression of the created animal or man—not the be-all and being of man—but the end, the climax. And some men would end in artistic ut-terance, and some wouldn't. But each one would create the work of art, the living man, achieve that piece of supreme art, a man's life.

D. H. Lawrence
letter to Lady Ottoline Morrell, 1915

FOREWORD

ANYONE who writes on Lawrence's life must be uncomfortably aware that the classic and probably unsurpassable biography is the collection of memoirs and letters by Edward Nehls, *A Composite Biography*—a book that has no coherent author, and perhaps no coherent subject either. For Lawrence combined, in an extraordinary way, both a hermetic egotism and an empathy so forceful that his intimates felt their own identities being stirred together with his; this was never an entirely comfortable sensation, and it often led to confused and violent reactions against Lawrence once his spell was broken. Even for critics who never knew Lawrence in the flesh, this uneasy complicity between the observed and the observer has persisted: one cannot write about Lawrence without in some measure writing about oneself, and insofar as all views of him remain personal and fragmentary, the ideal of a just and stable assessment of Lawrence's place in modern British culture remains elusive. To borrow one of his own phrases, you may nail him to the floor, but he gets up and walks away with the nail.

I do not claim, then, to have captured that will-o-the-wisp, a definitive estimate of Lawrence; I have attempted no more than to make a detailed and thoughtful study of four critical years in Lawrence and Frieda's life. The years are those of the Great War, when Lawrence's romantic and self-creating impulses encountered the strongest resistance from an implacable and fearsome social reality. I have no wish to argue yet again the vexed issue of the relevance of literary biography—the predominant mode of this book—to critical interpretation; but I have tried to show how frequently and easily the events of day-to-day life, as they affected Lawrence's moods, doctrines, or personal relationships, could move him to revise those artistic projects that ran parallel to his mundane experience and often could scarcely be separated from it. Lawrence, furthermore, rarely scrupled to sacrifice the consistent development of a work, or its initial form, if he wanted to accommodate new and more pressing concerns. The radical break between *The Rainbow* and *Women in Love* is only the most striking of many such shifts of perspective; their persistence reflects Lawrence's longing for a personal transformation that would be an adequate response to the destruction of Europe's traditional values in the holocaust of the Western Front. It should neither be denied nor condoned that Lawrence saw potential solutions to this crisis in the restoration of male dominance and authoritarian rule; nonetheless, I have tried to show that his quest for a salvationist philosophy during the unhappy years of the war was much more than a mindless lapse into protofascism. So profound a confrontation of his own darkest desires cannot be dismissed in a pat formula, as Bertrand Russell did in claiming that Lawrence's ideas "led straight to Auschwitz."

Detained in England by the outbreak of war, Lawrence defined his life over the next four years as an unsought, purely adventitious reunion with his native culture. He struggled desperately to preserve his ideals, which were exogamous, individualistic, and cosmopolitan, against the claims on him of English state and society. Without being a doctrinal pacifist, he was nonetheless completely alienated from his country's war effort; if I have not referred in my narrative to Paul Fussell's admirable *The Great War and Modern Memory,* it is only because Lawrence tried so hard to stay aloof from the world of trench warfare and the myth-making that it engendered. His refusal to mention the war in *Women in Love*—though in a sense that book is one of the most remarkable war novels in English—reflected his determination to keep up a one-man imaginative boycott of the popular consciousness. He had already begun to slough off his English origins before the war; but what started as a positive project of sexual and cultural emancipation degenerated, in the bitterness of the war years, into a savage hacking at his own roots. I disagree with much of F. R. Leavis's interpretation of Lawrence, but share his regret that Lawrence's quarrel with England should have led him to a posture of contemptuous dismissal; and I cannot help feeling that Lawrence's artistic achievement might have been greater, and more useful to his successors, if that dismissal had been less harsh and complete.

Foreword

In Lawrence's orphaned condition, there could be only one agent of reconciliation between him and the English Establishment; this was the social circle, affiliated with the Bloomsbury Group, that was headed by Lady Ottoline Morrell and Bertrand Russell. The disastrous outcome of Lawrence's relations with this circle confirmed, for him, the hopelessness of any rapprochement with his country's intellectual and artistic elite; on the other hand, his disappointment and pique achieved an artistic expression in *Women in Love,* probably his greatest novel. I have therefore tried to give as full and nuanced an account as possible of Lawrence's connection with the Morrell circle, and to examine the crucial roles in the debacle of the three people closest to him at the time: Frieda, John Middleton Murry, and Katherine Mansfield. Though *Women in Love* proclaims that the social world is well lost for the higher claims of love and comradeship, it nonetheless concedes that those intimacies may still be racked by conflicts; and these conflicts suggest that personal intimacy cannot be so easily severed from the "false" societal life as Lawrence had claimed, or hoped.

Requirements of space have prevented me giving full recognition of my debts to fellow workers on Lawrence; but I am aware that this book is only a small part of a large collective enterprise, and would like to mention the particular contributions to Lawrence scholarship of George Zytaruk, Mark Kinkead-Weekes, Emile Delavenay, G. M. Lacy, Charles Ross, H. T. Moore, Martin Green, Jeffrey Meyers, and James Cowan and Hebe Bair of *The D. H. Lawrence Review* (where a section of Chapter III first appeared). I regret that P. N. Furbank's magisterial biography of E. M. Forster appeared too late for me to take account of it.

For moving and indispensable experiences of "the spirit of place" I would like to thank the present occupants of Lawrence's wartime dwellings, especially Mrs. Joan Harrison of Greatham, Mrs. M. A. Rowe of Porthcothan House, and Lea Cammack of Higher Tregerthen. David Garnett recaptured the past for me in the charmed ambiance of his own home at Montcuq. Others who helped me gain access to primary sources or answered queries include Warren Roberts and David Farmer at the Humanities Research Center, University of Texas, Kenneth Blackwell of the Bertrand Russell Archives, McMaster University, and Penelope Bullock of King's College, Cambridge; also Sandra Jobson Dar-

Foreword

roch, F. A. Lea, Mrs. Mary Murry, Julian Vinogradoff, Donald Gallup, Perdita Schaffner, Carole Ferrier, Enid Hilton, John Bishop, Meredyth Proby, Marion Brown, K. C. Gay, W. Forster, and Patricia Palmer. The generosity of Michael Black of Cambridge University Press and Gerald Pollinger, acting for the Lawrence estate, made it possible for my work to appear in its present form.

This book could not have been written without the encouragement and financial support provided by fellowships from the Canada Council and the John Simon Guggenheim Memorial Foundation. Erwin Glikes at Basic Books supported my project before I had written a line; Midge Decter, Julia Strand, and Mary-Stuart Garden helped it into print. The office of the Dean of Arts, Simon Fraser University, made my task easier at every stage; for their various services I owe thanks to Sam Smith, Jock Munro, Lorraine Stobie, Phyllis Hawkins, Eileen Stevens, and Sheila Roberts. Reneé Gormley and Peg Kelley did invaluable work on background research.

Any author is most in debt to those who live with him and bear the inconveniences of his peculiar trade; the last word, then, should go to Peg and Jerry Kelley, Charles Watts, my sons Nicholas and Lev, and to the person named in the dedication.

Vancouver, British Columbia
August, 1978

ACKNOWLEDGMENTS

Permission to reprint the following material is gratefully acknowledged:

Laurence Pollinger Ltd., for the estate of Mrs. Frieda Lawrence Ravagli, for permission to reprint material of D. H. Lawrence and Frieda von Richthofen. Copyright the Estate of Mrs. Freida Lawrence Ravagli.

The Provost and Scholars of King's College, Cambridge University, for E. M. Forster's published and unpublished works.

Bertrand Russell Archives, McMaster University, for letters of Bertrand Russell and Lady Ottoline Morrell.

Houghton Library, Harvard University, for letters from D. H. Lawrence to Amy Lowell.

Humanities Research Center, the University of Texas at Austin, for letters of E. M. Forster and Bertrand Russell.

The Society of Authors, for Mrs. Mary Murry, for letters of Katherine Mansfield and John Middleton Murry. © 1978 Estate of Katherine Mansfield, © 1978 Estate of John Middleton Murry.

Mrs. B. Van Dieren for letters of Philip Heseltine to Viva Smith and Lady Ottoline Morrell.

Marjorie Kostenz for the letter of Mark Gertler to Lady Ottoline Morrell.

Julian Vinogradoff for the letters of Lady Ottoline Morrell.

CONTENTS

Contents

Contents

CHAPTER VI

ZENNOR: The Making of *Women in Love*

CHAPTER VII

ZENNOR: The Buried Life

Contents

CHAPTER I

LONDON

Prologue: Lawrence in Italy

FIASCHERINO in 1914 was a cluster of brightly painted peasant houses set among olive groves near Lerici on the Gulf of Spezia; the hills dropped so steeply to the sea that the village could be reached only by boat or by footpath. The beauty of that coast was so startling as to be almost theatrical, a worthy backdrop to the death of Shelley for which it was famed. Lawrence and Frieda had discovered the region in October 1913, and were soon urging their young friends John Middleton Murry and Katherine Mansfield to abandon literary London and live with them there. For two pounds a week, Lawrence told Jack and Katherine, they could have food, a house by the water, and a servant. Moreover, the local peasants would greet them respectfully as "Signoria," not knowing or caring whether they were actually married. In England, on the other hand, both couples had been dogged by scandal; for Frieda was still legally bound to Ernest Weekley, a fiftyish philologist who taught at Nottingham University, and Katherine to George Bowden, an itinerant tenor whom she had left the day after their wedding. But since Jack had no means of making a living in an Italian hamlet he and Katherine refused Lawrence's invitation. Within a year it would be renewed and, with fateful consequences, accepted.

At Fiascherino Lawrence could feel that his new life with Frieda was solidly founded at last, after a year and a half of struggle. Apart from the simple problem of survival—Lawrence was poor and Frieda had little money of her own—Frieda had suffered attacks of profound guilt at having abandoned Weekley, a diligent and respected academic, and their three young children. Furthermore, after thirteen years of confining domesticity she wanted to sow some wild oats with men less priggish and demanding than Lawrence: she had had at least three casual affairs in the first year they were together, and made sure that Lawrence knew about them.[1] Meanwhile they were pursued by Weekley's frantic letters; he swore indiscriminately that he would kill the lovers or kill himself, that he would take Frieda back and forgive all, that he would make sure she never saw their children again. These histrionics still had power to disturb her, till finally he so overplayed his role as the outraged husband that he became an "old figurehead" whom both Frieda and Lawrence scorned. In the midst of this turmoil Lawrence had completed *Sons and Lovers* and sent it out to the world, thereby bidding farewell to his neurasthenic and irresolute youth.

His next novel, to be called successively "The Sisters," "The Wedding Ring," and *The Rainbow,* confronted the thorn in his flesh of Frieda's "God-almightiness": her maddening alternation between the roles of "devouring Mother" and carefree sensualist. Lawrence had fled England with a woman who seemed to offer him, by the immediate and spontaneous gift of herself, freedom at one stroke from the passional constraints of life in the mining country. Her openess and exoticism had given him his manhood, striking off the oedipal shackles of his youth. But deeper acquaintance showed that Lawrence had achieved only a partial escape. If Frieda was a green-eyed hoyden who struck down his inhibitions, she was also a woman six years his senior whose motherhood was only too apparent in her pining for her children, and who expected to retain something of the domestic ease and dignity that were the prerogatives of her aristocratic birth. Frieda revealed to him, Lawrence told an old Eastwood friend, that "life can be great—quite godlike";[2] but she also made him serve her as a goddess—not just physically, by cooking and cleaning, but also by accepting her as his muse and coequal creator.

The Rainbow was to be a "novel about Love Triumphant" that would "do [Lawrence's] work for women, better than the Suffrage."[3] But under Lawrence's identification with woman's struggle to claim her rights lay a deep fear of her implacable power, as he knew it from infancy. The futurist Marinetti had pronounced the resistance of armor plate to a bullet more passionate than "the laughter or tears of a woman"; Lawrence was struck by the image, but argued that the two forces were not really so different: "What is interesting in the laugh of the woman is the same as the binding of the molecules of steel or their action in heat; it is the inhuman will . . . that fascinates me."[4] Though Lawrence's later chauvinism toward women has rightly been called to account, we should recognize that in his demands for female submission there is something of primitive man's quest for incantations to control the tempest and the flood. "Mrs. Weekley is afraid of being stunted and not allowed to grow," he informed her desolate husband, "so she must live her own life. Women in their natures are like giantesses; they will break through everything and go on with their own lives."[5]

By the spring of 1914 Lawrence was convinced that in *The Rainbow* (called at that time "The Wedding Ring") he had resolved his conflicts with Frieda. "It is a big and beautiful work . . ." he told his literary mentor Edward Garnett, reader for the publishing firm of Duckworth, "you will find her and me in the novel, I think, and the work is of both of us."[6] But Garnett did not share Lawrence's enthusiasm. As he read successive drafts of the novel he was dismayed to see Lawrence moving away from the style of *Sons and Lovers* toward a more rhapsodic and incantatory mode, which dissolved the outlines of individual characters. From Fiascherino Frieda announced to Garnett that the credit for her husband's change of style belonged to her:

> I don't really believe in *Sons and Lovers;* it feels as if there were nothing *behind* all those happenings as if there were no *"Hinterland der Seele,"* only intensely felt fugitive things. I who am a believer though I don't know in what, to me it seems an irreligious book. It does not seem the deepest and last thing said; if for instance a man loves in a book the pretty curl on the neck of "her," he loves it ever so intensely and beautifully, there is something behind that curl, *more* than that curl; there is *she,* the living, striving *she.* Writers are so beside the point, not *direct* enough. I am going to throw myself into the novel now and you will see what a *gioia* it will be. There is one triumph for us women, you men can't do things alone.[7]

This letter preceded by some four months Lawrence's famous response to Garnett's criticisms, in which he renounced "the old stable *ego*—of the character" and observed that "that which is physic—non-human, in humanity, is more interesting to me than the old-fashioned human element—which causes one to conceive a character in a certain moral scheme and make him consistent."[8] For Lawrence this was still simply a fascinating aesthetic question; he had yet to realize how radically his new style would undermine his standing with the reading public, and how much scandal would be provoked among his friends by Frieda's growing influence on his work.

When preparing *Sons and Lovers* for publication Lawrence had given Edward Garnett a free hand to revise the manuscript. But with the new novel he was standing firm: partly from conviction that he had made an artistic breakthrough, partly because two prominent literary agents, Curtis Brown and J. B. Pinker, were eager to place the novel elsewhere if Duckworth would not make a good offer for it. Pinker seemed a specially attractive ally: he was the most successful agent in London—his clients included H. G. Wells, Henry James, Arnold Bennett, and Joseph Conrad—and he had been wooing Lawrence for more than a year. In the spring of 1914 he promised Lawrence that he could get an advance of three hundred pounds for *The Rainbow,* a tempting offer because Duckworth's advance of one hundred pounds for *Sons and Lovers* had yet to be covered from the book's sales. Lawrence wanted to assure his solvency because he was determined never to be a teacher again, but to live abroad on his earnings from writing— and also to support Frieda, who had neither skille nor inclination to support herself.

The Lawrences had another reason for coming to England that summer: Ernest Weekley had finally agreed to give Frieda a divorce, which was granted on 28 May 1914. Lawrence, who "believed tremendously in marriage," wanted to seize this opportunity to become a married man himself; he and Frieda hoped also that once they had stopped "living in sin" she might be able to gain visiting rights with her children, who had been closely sequestered from her since she eloped. They decided, therefore, to come to London in June, then return in early autumn to their beloved villa at Fiascherino, where Lawrence could work on his next novel. The pattern of their life seemed set: happily married, Lawrence a successful novelist and poet, they would move as the spirit took them between the Mediterranean, London, and Bavaria—where Frieda had relatives prominent among the liberal intelligentsia. To take possession of these fortunate prospects they left Fiascherino on 8 June to reach England by different routes, since Frieda wanted first to spend two weeks with her parents at Baden-Baden while Lawrence planned a short walking tour in the Alps.

Twenty days later another intense, consumptive young man from the provinces cut across the line of their future, and of every other European: Gavrilo Princip, a high-school student and Serbian nationalist, shot the archduke Franz Ferdinand of Austria at Sarajevo. Lawrence's summer excursion became an enforced return to the country he never expected to live in again. Two and a half years later, still detained in England, he summed up his condition for a friend living in Egypt:

> I have not a friend in the world, nor an acquaintance, I have the honor to say. Neither have I any money at all, I have the dishonor to say. Neither have I much in the way of health: I seem to have spent a great deal of my time in bed, lately. Really, one looks through the window into the land of death, and it *does* seem a clean good unknown, all that is left to one ... I am so weary of mankind.[9]

In the intervening period Lawrence had completed *The Rainbow* and *Women in Love,* his two greatest novels, while struggling with the most protracted personal crisis of his life and with the damage inflicted on him by the world-historical crisis of Europe. His passage through that crisis—in his novel *Kangaroo* he called it simply "The Nightmare"—is the subject of this book.

Return to London

UNTIL his health broke down in the 1920s, Lawrence was a formidable walker. On this occasion he crossed the Grand St. Bernard pass from Aosta, staying overnight at the famous monastery, then went on to Zermatt and Interlaken; his companion was an English engineer named Lewis. He probably joined Frieda at Baden-Baden, for they arrived in England together on 24 June. There they stayed at the Kensington house of Gordon Campbell, a successful young lawyer who dabbled in the arts; he was a close friend of Jack Murry and Katherine Mansfield, through whom the Lawrences had met him the previous summer.

Lawrence's first concern was to place *The Rainbow.* He went to see Gerald Duckworth on the twenty-seventh and told him of Pinker's guarantee of a three hundred pound advance; when Duckworth refused to match the offer Lawrence promptly signed up with Pinker—much to the delight of Frieda, who was eager for some ready money. William Heinemann had published Lawrence's first novel, *The White Peacock,* but then rejected his next two, saying of *Sons and Lovers* that it was "one of the dirtiest books he had ever read."[10] Duckworth had helped Lawrence out of this fix and its reader, Edward Garnett, subsequently became a loyal friend as well as an astute literary adviser. So Lawrence felt somewhat ashamed of taking *The Rainbow* elsewhere; but he was nettled by Garnett's criticisms and wanted a better income for his works.* Pinker's offer was made on behalf of Methuen, a more dynamic and wealthier firm than Duckworth. Methuen had prospered with authors of conservative or imperialistic views— Kipling, Belloc, Chesterton, Conrad—and was willing to back a few dark horses like Lawrence in the hope that one of them might turn into a best seller. Lawrence assumed that by giving him a big advance Methuen was backing him to the hilt; but they had not even read *The Rainbow* and were simply relying on Pinker's recommendation. Furthermore, they were only advancing one hundred pounds on signature of the contract, and Pinker would take 10 percent of this as his fee; another fifty pounds would be paid when the manuscript was delivered in acceptable form, and the remaining one hundred and fifty pounds on actual publication of the novel. Lawrence soon discovered that the rest of his advance would not be easily gained.

Gerald Duckworth himself, fortunately, was not deeply offended by Lawrence's agreement with Methuen. He was still eager for his house to publish a collection of Lawrence's short stories, which had appeared singly over the last few years. In the first two weeks of July Lawrence assembled the texts of about fifteen stories, of which twelve were finally included in the collection published as *The Prussian Officer* at the end of November. As usual, he could not resist tinkering with the stories before hand-

---

* Garnett, however, was neither surprised nor offended by Lawrence's move; according to his son David, "he had seen it coming" (conversation with the author).

ing them over: "Lord, how I've worked again at those stories," he told a friend, "—most of them—forging them up. They're good, I think."[11] He revised with extraordinary speed in the brief time available, working into the stories some of the new themes and techniques that had evolved as he composed *The Rainbow*. One story, "Vin Ordinaire," was substantially rewritten and given a new title, "The Thorn in the Flesh." As soon as this was done Lawrence turned to another project, a short book on Thomas Hardy's characters commissioned by an obscure publisher named Bertram Christian. Christian promised fifteen pounds on delivery of the manuscript, and Lawrence thought he could write it in a few weeks while he and Frieda were visiting Ireland in August as guests of Campbell and his wife, Beatrice.

No doubt Lawrence felt that by boosting his career he would get his marriage off to a good start. The ceremony took place on the morning of 13 July at South Kensington registry office. In the wedding photograph Lawrence looks unusually dapper with a new boater, wing collar, and a flower in his buttonhole. Frieda stands solid and unperturbed while Jack and Katherine have the enigmatic half-smiles they habitually assumed for the camera.* Indeed, their pleasure in the occasion was mixed with envy since they could not themselves marry until George Bowden agreed to give Katherine a divorce.† No wedding party was held, nor did any of Lawrence's family or other friends attend; the mundane ceremony was as far removed as could be from the exuberant revels at the marriage of Anna and Will Brangwen in *The Rainbow*. By marrying a divorced woman and a foreigner Lawrence had severed his ties to that England, the intimate rural community of Hardy and George Eliot. Yet he still hovered on its fringes, long after he had become a cosmopolitan and an intellectual, as if unwilling to admit how much he had deracinated himself.

During that summer of 1914 the Lawrences found themselves in the thick of the other England, the literary and intellectual society of London. They met everyone from Wyndham Lewis—who had

---

* I assume this was taken before the wedding because the background is the garden of Campbell's house at 9, Selwood Terrace, and the angle of the shadows shows that it was taken around mid-morning (the wedding took place at 10:30). The photographer would have been the third witness, Gordon Campbell. See illustrations following p. 204.

† When they were able to marry, they went to the same registry office; so did James Joyce and Nora Barnacle in 1931, after living together for twenty-seven years.

just published *Blast,* proclaiming "No Old Pulp. End of the Christian Era"—to Lady St. Helier, a hostess who collected fashionable writers and artists. The impresario of many of these contacts—with Rupert Brooke and J. M. Barrie, for example—was Winston Churchill's private secretary, Eddie Marsh, effete in his manners but sensible and generous underneath. Marsh was the patron of innumerable struggling artists and writers; he had a weakness for young men with exquisite profiles like Brooke, but had taste enough to help also those who lacked that distinction, like Lawrence or Stanley Spencer.[12] Lawrence was ideally placed to advance his fortune, for literary London would readily adopt talented outsiders if they were at all presentable socially. But Lawrence was restive in these fashionable circles; he might buy a dress suit for a party given by H. G. Wells, but it would not sit easily on his shoulders. The knowledge that Wells, now a great "swell," had origins similar to his own may have added to his discomfort. He was happy to leave London in July whenever he could: to stay at the Garnetts' country house, to visit his family in the Midlands, and to go on a walking tour of the Lake District.

The only lasting friends Lawrence made in this period were not people of fashion. One was Catherine Carswell Jackson, a divorced woman of Frieda's age. Lawrence appreciated her physical charm (though there was no sexual tension between them), and he also liked Scots on principle. Carswell was writing a novel, which he was glad to help her with, and she became a lifelong supporter of Lawrence and his reputation. Then, on 30 July, Lawrence met the Aldingtons, a young literary couple. Richard, only twenty-one, was already a published poet; his wife, Hilda, six years older, was also becoming known under her nom de plume of "H.D." They all were guests at a dinner given by Amy Lowell, a wealthy and contentious Boston poet, who had recently quarreled with Ezra Pound, her more talented associate in the "Imagiste" group, and was shopping around—literally, one might say—for new recruits.* Aldington has given a lively account of that fine summer evening at the Berkeley Hotel: the entry of Lawrence, whose "vivid, flame-like spirit" gleamed from his "bril-

---

* Lawrence was willing to accept Amy's patronage, but he did not join her feud against Pound since he was grateful to him for past favors (though he seems to have considered him an affected ass: CL 516).

For a list of bibliographic abbreviations, see p. 397.

liant blue eyes," and, as a climax, the appearance on a newsstand opposite of two posters: "Germany and Russia at War" and "British Army Mobilised." [13]

The flaw in the anecdote is that these events had not yet happened, although the threat of a European war had become imminent. Yet Lawrence was sufficiently unperturbed by the war rumors that he left Frieda the next day to spend a week walking through the Lake District. Characteristically, he chose to sally off to the mountains with three nobodies when through his friendships with Eddie Marsh and Lady Cynthia Asquith (the prime minister's daughter-in-law) he could have been a close and privileged observer of the European crisis. His companions were Lewis, the Vickers engineer who had crossed the Alps with him, a friend of Lewis's named Horne, and Samuel Solomonovich Koteliansky, a Russian-Jewish political refugee; the two latter worked for the Russian Law Bureau, a Gogolesque office whose main function seemed to be the drinking of tea and the eating of sardines. Horne soon disappeared from Lawrence's life but "Kot," as he was familiarly called, became a prickly, stubborn, devoted friend.

One reason for Lawrence's readiness to escape was the friction during July over Frieda's children. Marriage had brought her no closer to gaining visitation rights; instead there were grotesque scenes like one Lawrence reported to Edward Garnett: "Frieda has seen . . . the little girls being escorted to school by a fattish white unwholesome maiden aunt who, when she saw their mother, shrieked to the children—'Run, children, run'—and the poor little things were terrified and ran." [14] Weekley still held a legally unassailable position, and he wished to punish Frieda to the limits of his power. From this ugly deadlock Lawrence was glad to flee to the moors, where he garlanded himself with lilies, sang songs, and imitated music-hall turns in the rain with the sheep looking on. But then came the inevitable descent, from Wordsworth's England to the realm of Moloch:

We came down to Barrow-in-Furness, and saw that war was declared. And we all went mad. I can remember soldiers kissing on Barrow station, and a woman shouting defiantly to her sweetheart—"When you get at 'em, Clem, let 'em have it," as the train drew off—and in all the tramcars, "War." Messrs. Vickers-Maxim call in their workmen—and the great notices on Vickers' gateways—and the thousands of men streaming over the bridge. Then I went down the coast a few miles. And I think of the amazing sunsets over flat sands and the smoky sea . . . and a French onion boat coming in with her sails set splendidly in the morning sunshine—and the electric suspense everywhere—and the amazing, vivid, visionary beauty of everything, heightened by the immense pain everywhere.[15]

So Lawrence recalled the shock of the Great War; but he did so six months after it began, when Europe had begun to realize the magnitude of the struggle. At the time, how could even the most sensitive and prescient observer guess what lay ahead? Since the eighteenth century Europe had become accustomed to wars of movement: in 1870 it took the Germans a mere two months to defeat the French army in the field and lay siege to Paris, which capitulated four months later. In August 1914 no one expected that the war would last over four years, that the machine gun and massed artillery would lead to a death toll of ten million soldiers (the entire German army in 1870 was only about 250,000 strong), that the whole form of life in Europe would be radically changed. Nor, in England, was it appreciated how many traditional liberties would be stripped away; wars were for professional soldiers to fight, and intellectuals like Lawrence could have no inkling at the outset how hard the issue of conscription would press on them two years later.

Lawrence, then, did not cut short his trip even after the declaration of war. But when he returned to London four days later, on 8 August, he received a shock that exposed the uncertain foundations of his career as a novelist. Methuen, having now read *The Rainbow*, had returned the bulky manuscript to its author with a letter saying that the novel "could not be published in its then condition."[16] Lawrence was afraid that the first installment of his advance—which Pinker had already given him from his own funds—might not be paid, though Pinker reassured him that it was safe. Methuen's rejection of the manuscript was undoubtedly because of its insistent eroticism. Six months later, when Lawrence had completely rewritten the story, he told Pinker to assure Methuen that there would be "no very flagrant love-passages in it."[17] Now, however, he could not envisage what to do with the novel, nor was it possible for him and Frieda to return to their home at Fiascherino. He knew only that his golden prospects had suddenly dissolved, and that he must go to earth.

CHAPTER II

CHESHAM

Gone to Earth

AS A MINER'S SON, familiar with injuries, strikes, and layoffs, Lawrence recognized what he must do when Methuen rejected *The Rainbow*. "I shall try to get a tiny cottage somewhere," he told Pinker, "put a little bit of furniture in it, and live as cheaply as possible."[1] Within six days he had done just that. "The Triangle," at Bellingdon near Chesham, Buckinghamshire, was a block of three farm laborers' cottages, buried in thickly wooded country some thirty miles from London; the novelist Gilbert Cannan and his wife, Mary, lived nearby and it was probably through them that the Lawrences found the place. Their cottage had the standard two small rooms down and two up; it rented for six shillings a week. The drift away from the land during the nineteenth century had caused many such cottages to fall vacant, and then to be snapped up by the bohemian fringe of the middle classes. Lawrence and Frieda lived in a series of them, as did many of their friends. It was a mildly picturesque way of life, and much cheaper than London; but as a rule these places lacked indoor sanitation or hot water, and were heated only by a large kitchen stove. Shops might be far away and transportation—the railway, since there was no rural bus service yet—even farther.

Lawrence's health was so precarious that such living conditions might literally bring him to the brink of death each winter. Yet later, after four years of wartime privation, he still affirmed his faith in a spartan rural life:

> Every time we turn on a tap to have water, every time we turn a handle to have fire or light, we deny ourselves and annul our being. The great elements, the

earth, air, fire, water are there like some great mistress whom we woo and struggle with, whom we heave and wrestle with. And all our appliances do but deny us these fine embraces, take the miracle of life away from us. The machine is the great neuter. It is the eunuch of eunuchs. In the end it emasculates us all.[2]

This was not mere rhetoric, for Lawrence was surely the first major English writer to look after his own material needs, rather than being cared for by servants or wife. Frieda was not entirely idle, but neither was she inclined to go out of her way to be busy; and before she left Weekley she always had servants. So it fell largely to Lawrence to decorate and furnish the houses he and Frieda found in odd corners of Europe; he also cooked, washed, mended, put up preserves, and gardened, all the while producing hundreds of pages each year.

Even so modest a life as the Lawrences led at Chesham required a small income, which was now uncertain. Frieda had occasional gifts from her family, but help from this quarter was blocked by the war. Lawrence's main hope had to be placed on Pinker, whom he jeered at privately as a "little parvenu snob of a procureur of books."[3] Pinker was indeed easy to jeer at, a beady-eyed little Scotsman who rose from obscurity to become an inveterate fox-hunter and proprietor of a coach-and-pair. When Methuen said *The Rainbow* was "unpublishable," Pinker could simply have dropped Lawrence but, to his credit, he stood by his client and provided him with enough to live on over the next year until Methuen finally paid him the rest of its advance. He was to do a great deal more on Lawrence's behalf in the course of the war, though not the one thing Lawrence most wanted: to convince publishers to buy his writings at a rate he could live on.

If he was not able to depend on his writings for money, Lawrence could still have some expectation of patronage and was not shy of seeking it. His most visible target was Amy Lowell: Lawrence invited himself to tea with her when he returned from the Lake District and soon after she descended on Chesham, in her chauffeur-driven car, to inspect his cottage. Such maneuvers did not abash Lawrence, since he preferred to solicit money from his rich acquaintances rather than from his poor friends; but he was less skillful at the game than James Joyce, who had been trained from childhood in the hard school of Dublin. Though Miss Lowell was shocked by the poverty and discomfort of the cottage at Chesham, she assumed that Lawrence "would not accept charity."[4] Certainly he did not *like* to accept charity, but he took it when he had to. On returning to America in September Miss Lowell sent him a typewriter, which at least saved him money on preparing his manuscripts. Lawrence kept up a steady correspondence with her, and later in the war years she sent him what he really needed—large sums of ready cash.

Meanwhile Mary Cannan, who had many contacts from her former life as the wife of Sir James Barrie, set about pulling some strings on behalf of her new neighbors. She got her friend Alfred Sutro, a successful dramatist, to give Lawrence ten pounds and persuaded the novelist Maurice Hewlett to recommend Lawrence to the Royal Literary Fund, which provided relief for "authors of some published work of approved literary merit, who shall be in want or distress." On the official form Lawrence listed his "Present Means of Support" as "Money owed by *English Review* for an article, a sum on account from Methuen at a date uncertain and £3"; to "Cause of Distress" he answered succinctly "The War."[5] The application was supported by Harold Monro, who described Lawrence as a "fine writer, and one who promises to do better and better"; by Gilbert Cannan; and by Eddie Marsh, who both praised Lawrence on his own account and regretted that James Barrie could not be reached. "He would certainly have supported the application," Marsh wrote, "as he told me that he thought *Sons and Lovers* the best novel that he had ready by any of the younger men."[6] In mid-October Lawrence was granted fifty pounds from the Fund. "There is no joy in their tame thin-gutted charity," he complained to Amy Lowell. "I would fillip it back at their old noses, the stodgy, stomachy authors, if I could afford it. But I can't."[7] Still, the money would keep him through the winter, along with twenty-five pounds for the sale of "Honour and Arms" (later called *The Prussian Officer*) to an American magazine.

Though he now had settled his practical affairs, Lawrence had still to confront difficulties that were deeper and more intransigent. He had to find a new direction for his career after Methuen's humiliating rejection of *The Rainbow;* to absorb the shock of the war; to set the terms of his married life with Frieda; and to reconcile himself to being confined in England. He could neither ignore these problems, nor resolve them; over the next four years they continually tormented him, bringing both his physical health and his sanity to the verge of breakdown. This was the real "nightmare" of the war years; the threat of conscription, so central in *Kangaroo,* was only part of Lawrence's agony. Yet the ordeal was not without its Dead Sea fruit, that strained and disjointed masterpiece *Women in Love.* To create a novel of such magnitude, while suffering the harsh conditions of life in wartime England, demanded a more absolute commitment of his vital energies than he would ever again be able to afford.

The War

DURING 1914 the war was one of movement, with surprises and reverses for both sides, and Lawrence's feelings about it were equally volatile. He opposed the war from the start, of course, but somewhat blindly and perversely; he attacked Frieda for supporting the German cause, yet he himself sympathized with the *style* of German actions, if not with their ultimate aims. "I alternate between hating [Germany] thoroughly, stick, stock & stone," he wrote Amy Lowell, "and yearning over it fit to break my heart. I can't help feeling it a young and adorable country—adolescent—with the faults of adolescence."[8] "So," he argued in the *Study of Thomas Hardy,* "let there be an end of this German hatred. We ought to be grateful to Germany that she still has the power to burst the bound hide of the cabbage. Where do I meet a man or a woman who does not draw deep and thorough satisfaction from this war?"[9] Yet he also feared being drawn into the vortex of nationalistic passions and saw a clear departure from Europe as the safest escape. When Harriet Monroe, editor of *Poetry,* offered a prize for the best war poem, Lawrence refused to compete. "The nearest I could get to it," he replied, "would be in the vein of 'The owl and the pussycat went to sea/ In a beautiful pea green boat'—and I know you wouldn't give me the hundred dollars."[10] Lear's poem is about sailing away to a desert island with "plenty of money" and Lawrence's offhand jest pointed to a real intention of doing just that. The project, to which he gave the name of Rana-nim,* was to be a recurrent obsession during the war years and after. At other times he faced the sober reality that the war promised to be long and bitter, and that everyone must bear the slowly festering effects. He had already sensed this threat in August, when he told Eddie Marsh "The War is just hell for me . . . I can't get away from it for a minute: I live in a sort of coma, like one of those nightmares when you can't move. I hate it—everything."[11]

So long as the war of movement continued, Lawrence could at least hope for a quick end to the torment; but on 18 October the Western Front reached the Channel at Nieuport, in Belgium, without any sign of an early decision. For the next three weeks the Germans tried vainly to penetrate the British front at Ypres, some thirty miles to the south. Their failure proposed a lesson that leaders on both sides seemed determined to ignore: that in trench warfare the advantage lay heavily with the defense. By the winter of 1914–15 trenches ran without a break from Switzerland to the North Sea and despite the deaths of millions, the line would not vary by more than a few miles until the summer of 1918. One segment of it between Ypres and Verdun, some 150 miles as the crow flies, remained for four years the killing-ground of Europe; on each side, whole nations mobilized to keep pouring men and ordenance into the holocaust.

The long enmity of Germany and France had prepared them morally for total war: both proclaimed conscription and mobilized five and four million men, respectively, in the opening days. But England's leaders still believed that the old traditions of civility and personal freedom could be preserved by an invincible navy and a professional army of only three-quarters of a million. The first battle of Ypres (October–November 1914) taught them otherwise. The full weight of the German offensive fell on the British Expeditionary Force and though it absorbed the shock, two-thirds of the defenders were killed or wounded. If England were to remain in the land war, she must raise a civilian army; at first of volunteers but ultimately, it was clear, of conscripts. It was also clear that those on the Home Front—as the civilian sector was euphemistically renamed—would suffer regimentation and surveillance more severe than England had ever known. The war was

---

*Apparently a Hebrew word that Lawrence interpreted as "let us rejoice" and picked up from Koteliansky's chanting of psalms on their walking tour.

only a few days old when the Lawrences were questioned by three sets of detectives after they were overheard speaking German at a dinner party given by David Garnett. Hundreds of Germans were denounced as spies, many were arrested and interned. As a naturalized British subject Frieda should have been safe from this; but public opinion was volatile, and the Lawrences probably were encouraged to move to Chesham by the belief that they would be safer in the country than in London—a false hope, as it turned out.

By mid-November, then, Lawrence was feeling the full burden of the war; he could neither observe it coldly nor move to some part of the world where it might affect him less. "The war-atmosphere has blackened here," he wrote Amy Lowell, "it is soaking in, and getting more like part of our daily life, and therefore much grimmer."[12] Abandoning his earlier claim that the war had not changed his beliefs or visions, he now chose to go forward into the destructive element: "The war is dreadful. It is the business of the artist to follow it home to the heart of the individual fighters ... it's at the bottom of almost every Englishman's heart—the war—the desire of war—the *will* to war—and at the bottom of every German's."[13] But for the artist to "follow home" the war meant that he must himself swallow Europe's poison of hatred, blood lust, and grief; and Lawrence was sorely vulnerable to their inner wounds. Jack Murry, late in 1914, was given a glimpse of these:

> ... There was a knock on the door of the shed where I worked and Lawrence came in. He said nothing, but sat in a chair by the stove, rocking himself to and fro, and moaning. . . . Suddenly [he] had been overwhelmed by the horror of the war and had made his way across in the dark. That was all. I can see him now, in his brown corduroy jacket, buttoned tight up to the neck, and his head bowed, radiating desolation.[14]

That winter at Chesham Lawrence endured the first crisis of his wartime ordeal, and emerged from it a different man. His conflicts with Frieda played a large role in this transformation, for they had settled into a domestic war of attrition that was, in its own fashion, as debilitating to Lawrence as the struggle across the Channel.

"The Trouble with the Children"

EARLIER in 1914, as we have seen, Frieda had hoped that once she had married Lawrence she would be granted visitation rights to her children; but Weekley was as implacable as before. Nonetheless, Frieda simply could not accept the fact that she had lost her motherhood by throwing in her lot with Lawrence. In July she asked her formidable mother to come to England and tackle Weekley, a confrontation that Lawrence anticipated with relish: "I *do* hope that old Baroness will turn up in a state of indignation. Then we shall see sparks fly round the maggoty Weekley household—curse the etiolated lot of them, maggots."[15] But the war scotched the plan, and in any case Weekley held all the legal trumps; he even threatened to have Frieda arrested if she kept on trying to contact her children.

In December Frieda got into Weekley's house in Nottingham by giving a false name; Lawrence sent a wry report to Amy Lowell:

> Frieda: I came to see you about the children.
> Quondam Husband: Aren't you ashamed to show your face where you are known! Isn't the commonest prostitute better than you?
> Frieda: Oh no.
> Quon. Husb.: Do you want to drive me off the face of the earth, Woman? Is there no place where I can have peace?
> Frieda: You see I must speak to you about the children.
> Quon. Husb.: You shall *not* have them—they don't want to see you.[16]

And so it continued. But Frieda was not the type to give up easily, and the proximity of the children—they were living with relatives in Hampstead—kept the issue inflamed. By all accounts, Lawrence showed little sympathy for Frieda's grief (David Garnett recalls that he "was an absolute beast with her about the children").[17] At Chesham Lawrence was backed up by Jack and Katherine, and by Koteliansky, who told Frieda, "You have left your children to marry Lawrence. You must choose either your children or Lawrence—and if you choose Lawrence, you must stop complaining about the children."[18] Logical advice, perhaps, but rather glib when offered by people who, not being parents, failed to appreciate Frieda's depth of feeling.

Lawrence himself was far from insensitive; rather, he contested Frieda's mother love because he knew how powerful and exclusive an emotion it could be. Gertrude Morel, in *Sons and Lovers,* discards her husband and lives only through her sons. In a poem ("She Looks Back") about their first weeks together, Lawrence confessed that he feared a similar abandonment if Frieda's children were restored to her:

> You looked into my eyes, and said: "But this is joy!" . . .
> But the shadow of lying was in your eyes,
> The mother in you, fierce as a murderess, glaring to England,
> Yearning towards England, towards your young children,
> Insisting upon your motherhood, devastating . . .
> I have learned to curse your motherhood,

Another poem, "Rose of all the World," argues that in sex the lovers' fullness of being is more important than procreation:

> How will you have it?—the rose is all in all,
> Or the ripe rose-fruits of the luscious fall?
> The sharp begetting, or the child begot?
> Our consummation matters, or does it not?

The poem carries on a debate with Frieda, who apparently wanted children by Lawrence to compensate for those she had lost. Jack Murry has claimed "that Lawrence was incapable of begetting children and that at one time he was deeply distressed by it."[19] The time referred to would most likely be late 1914, since before then the two couples had not been in close and continuous contact. Though Lawrence suffered from impotence toward the end of his life, that was probably not the problem at Chesham; one would assume, rather, that Lawrence and Frieda stopped using contraception after they were married, but no pregnancy followed.[20]

This failure would inevitably arouse jealousy of Weekley, who still regularly offered to take Frieda back, and who had fathered her three children. Lawrence admitted this rivalry in "Meeting Among the Mountains," where the poet, encountering a brown-eyed peasant driving a bullock wagon, is reminded of Weekley; he feels himself a Judas who has bought his pleasure at the price of another man's destruction. The poem also recalls Oedipus' murder of his father, Laius, who tried to drive his son out of the way of his carriage. But in Lawrence's poem there is no struggle for passage, only a dead weight of guilt laid on the younger man. He is "frozen" and his lungs "turned to stone," as if Lawrence himself were subconsciously accepting impotence and tuberculosis as condign punishments for ousting Weekley from Frieda's affections.* We have seen Lawrence jeer at Weekley as a music-hall cuckold; but he was actually a successful academic and author, and a dangerous legal adversary. Moreover, he had risen to his modest eminence from a background only a little more privileged than Lawrence's—he too was a talented scholarship boy. In Lawrence's struggle with Frieda over the children, Weekley's role as an irritant should not be minimized, especially since from time to time Frieda was still moved to address him as a suppliant.

The aftereffects of Frieda's first marriage thus continued to damage her relation to Lawrence at this time, exacerbating his ingrained oedipal difficulties.† In "Both Sides of the Medal" he tried to rationalize his fierce quarrels with her:

> And because you love me,
> think you you do not hate me?
> Ha, since you love me
> to ecstasy
> it follows you hate me to ecstasy.

But no poem could do much to moderate their battles, or make them easier to bear. Frieda was temperamentally without rancor, resilient, and free of self-doubt; she could easily shake off hurts that Lawrence took deeply to heart. More than once that winter they came close to separation.

---

*Lawrence may also have drawn on his rivalry with Weekley in the story "The Old Adam." Edward Severn, a young, slender intellectual, lodges with Mr. and Mrs. Thomas. His attraction to Mrs. Thomas leads to an unacknowledged rivalry with her husband, and finally to a fistfight. The husband's name suggests his phallic superiority over the less robust Severn; he is also a father, which Severn is not. However, the story may have been composed before Lawrence met Ernest and Frieda Weekley: see PL 136 and Delavenay 111, 196.

† An entry in J. M. Murry's journal for 18 November 1914 gives another glimpse of this: "L _____ accused me of a lack of [the sensuous nature], which is probably right. . . . I feel certain that that part of me was terribly stunted by my Father. It worries me profoundly that it may have been irreparable. But Lawrence surprised me by a far more passionate indignation against my Father than I had ever been able to summon up myself." BTW 315.

The Chesham Circle

AT CHESHAM the Lawrences lived quietly and saw only a small circle of friends. All were people of talent, though not yet widely known; compared to the notables with whom the Lawrences mingled before and after Chesham they were outsiders—and, despite their later achievements, they generally remained so. Perhaps for this reason, the Lawrences stayed intimate with many of them after more fashionable acquaintances had fallen away or been driven off.

When the Lawrences arrived the Cannans were already settled at Cholesbury, two miles away. Gilbert Cannan was thirty, a year older than Lawrence, and had already published several fluent but superficial novels. His career was a watered-down version of Lawrence's own: from a modest background he had gone to Cambridge, then made some impression on intellectual society by his writings and his agreeable manner. He was also handsome enough for Lytton Strachey to try a mild flirtation though he soon withdrew, finding Gilbert "very very dull . . . an empty bucket, which has been filled up to the brim with modern ideas—simply because it happened to be standing near that tap."[21] Cannan's chief claim to notice was that he had taken advantage of his position as assistant to Sir James Barrie by wooing away his wife. Mary Barrie was an actress of fading appeal and her husband, though rich, was impotent. Her preference for Gilbert was understandable since he was charming, apparently talented, and twenty some years younger than she. Barrie, moreover, was gallant enough to provide his errant wife with a substantial income. The Cannans lived in an arty cottage attached to a spindly, phallic windmill that had been converted into a study for Gilbert.

Whatever the eccentricities of the Cannan household, they were an agreeable couple who bore the same stigma of divorce as the Lawrences.* They also had interesting visitors who helped break the tedium of rural life; notably Mark Gertler, a graduate of the Slade School who was already, at twenty-two, an accomplished artist. He had been taken up a year earlier by Eddie Marsh, who

---

* In 1914 only 856 divorces were granted in England and Wales.

ingenuously described his find to Rupert Brooke as "a beautiful little Jew, like a Lippo Lippi cherub."[22] Gertler came from a poor immigrant family and his English was imperfect, but this only added to his appeal for people like Eddie or Gilbert (who told him he "was extremely fortunate to live in the East End amongst *real* people").[23] He was mercurial, fun-loving, and very attractive to women; though the only one he deeply loved, his fellow student Dora Carrington, tormented him by her evasiveness.* Lawrence appreciated Gertler's charm and his artistic gifts from the beginning; later he borrowed some of his traits in portraying the decadent sculptor, Loerke, in *Women in Love*.

Through the Lawrences Gertler met Koteliansky, and the two became lifelong friends. Kot tended to be critical of everyone except a chosen few to whom he was meticulously loyal. These included Lawrence, Gertler, and Katherine Mansfield, the creative artists of the group; but he looked askance at Frieda and Jack as hangers-on who were unworthy of their partners. Lawrence made use of Kot's devotion, asking him to forward supplies from London and to type manuscripts, but tried to shield him from the more inflammatory entanglements within the circle. Sustained by this unusual diplomacy on Lawrence's part, their friendship remained intact until Lawrence's death; it was also strengthened by Lawrence's early recognition of a solidity of character in Kot that not even he would be able to shift.

Another frequent visitor to the Chesham circle was Gordon Campbell, the same age as Lawrence but already well launched on a career at the bar and in Irish public affairs. Hospitable, literary, and sensitive to Ireland's ancient wrongs, he fitted in with the others for a while; Murry in particular was strongly attached to him as a companion in his convoluted, mystical self-explorations. But Campbell was only sprinkled with the waters of the spirit—not immersed in them, as Murry was. Early in 1915 he would return to a more conventional frame of mind, leaving Murry lonely and disillusioned. Thereafter Lawrence too looked on Campbell as little more than a well-placed acquaintance who might help him with practical difficulties.

---

*The course of her troubled relationship with Gertler may be traced in Holroyd, in MGL, and in *Carrington: Letters and Extracts from her Diaries*, ed. D. Garnett, (London: Jonathan Cape, 1970). According to Garnett (conversation with the author), Lawrence disliked Carrington for provoking Gertler's desire without satisfying it.

The group was rounded out in mid-October when Katherine and Jack, after staying with the Lawrences for ten days, were induced to rent a vacant cottage three miles away at The Lee. The war had cut down Jack's income from journalism, so they preferred to live in the country rather than in cheap lodgings in London. The cottage, however, proved inconvenient and they found it a strain to be in close daily contact with the Lawrences. Still, the three neighborhood couples, with the regular visits of Kot, Gertler, and Campbell, formed a little society that provided mutual defense against the miseries of the war. Except for Campbell they all hovered on the fringes of respectability, yet were not fully bohemians or outcasts. They had close ties to many people of real power and wealth, such as Eddie Marsh and Katherine's father, Harold Beauchamp, who gave her just enough to live on and whom she derided as "the richest man in New Zealand, and the meanest."[24] Frankie Birrell, who came to visit in November, was the son of a cabinet minister; and the year before Lawrence had struck up a friendship with Herbert Asquith, son of the Liberal prime minister, and his wife, Lady Cynthia.

The position of the Chesham circle was therefore ambiguous. They were well connected, yet shadowed by marital scandal, lack of regular occupations, and by their origins. Katherine, Kot, and Frieda were foreigners; Kot and Gertler evidently Jewish. That Lawrence was the son of a miner was, inevitably, the most distinctive thing about him to his upper-class acquaintances; Murry's father was a shabby-genteel civil servant, and Mary Cannan's mother had been a seaside landlady—yet Mary had risen to marry the most successful playwright of the age. They were all people who had been welcomed into "society" because of their good looks, charm, or artistic talent; but they were not well rooted in the Establishment world, and could be discarded as easily as they had been taken up. Nor, on the other hand, were they true bohemians who rejected bourgeois values regardless of personal hardship or ostracism. Murry made this clear in a later comment to Frieda about Dylan Thomas's self-destruction by alcohol: "So appallingly *ignoble*. Well, we may have had our failings, but that kind of disaster was inconceivable for us."[25] Living modestly in the country they kept the distractions of fashionable artistic society at arm's length and got on steadily with their own productions. Lawrence was especially wary of losing favor with publishers and reviewers, so he preferred to shave expenses and always have enough money for a few months ahead.

The Chesham group had a special cause for concern in 1914: none of the men were doing much for the war effort, and most were outspoken pacifists. For the time being this meant only that they were vaguely under suspicion. But already Lawrence and Gertler felt constrained in their relations with Eddie Marsh, who strongly upheld Britain's war policy. As the war intensified, official disapproval of those who held back from serving moved steadily toward a policy of outright compulsion, while the pacifists banded together more tightly to resist the government's pressure. In 1914–15 they formed a political and social group centering on the Liberal M. P. Philip Morrell, his wife, Lady Ottoline, and her lover Bertrand Russell. It was natural that Lawrence and his friends should be drawn into that orbit, since they were not strong enough to stand alone; but they were different enough from the Morrell circle, in rank and outlook, that the alliance, when it came, was sure to be an uneasy one.

Christ and Crisis

BY ELOPING with Frieda to the Continent Lawrence had rejected his exiguous place in English society as an invalided schoolteacher and assumed a new identity as a pioneer of eroticism. But his return to the narrow confines of Chesham felt like a falling back into isolation and eclipse. The conflicts that followed his marriage to Frieda in July marked the end of the "all for love" phase of their relationship; lovers they still might be, but married lovers, with a lengthening history of mundane disputes. In completing *The Rainbow* during that winter, Lawrence must have seen his celebration of Ursula's exuberant femininity as a phase of consciousness that already lay behind him. From now on he would view the relations between men and women as more deeply contradictory, and place a higher value on manly self-reliance. At Chesham he sought, therefore, to renew his identity by a spiritual descent into the underworld, as he had done in 1911 after his mother's death.

A visible sign of change was the beard he grew in October and kept to the end of his life. On recovering from a long spell of bronchitis he decided to keep his invalid's beard, not because he liked the look of it but because it was "so warm and complete, and such a clothing to one's nakedness."[26] He had spat blood the year before and usually spoke of his lung troubles as being centered in his "bronchials," as if his throat and upper chest were his weakest spots.[27] One could use a beard for concealment, too: behind his he would "take as much cover as [he could], like a creature under a bush. . . . a wise rabbit [in a] little hole . . . much too valuable a creature to offer myself to a German bullet."[28] But his beard was also a gesture of self-assertion: soldiers had to be short-haired and clean shaven, so Lawrence was deliberately rejecting the military style (he also wore his hair longer than before). The worst case of such defiance, in the popular mind, was the outrageously epicene and hairy pacifist Lytton Strachey; for Lawrence, though, the beard was an aggressively masculine adornment, and perhaps a sign of identification with his father, who was impressively bearded. Reacting against the "devouring mother" in Frieda, he was taking the first steps in his long quest for an emotionally satisfying "masculine mystique."

Finally, Lawrence's beard linked him with Christ and the prophets, those stern voices "crying in the wilderness." He found in Christ's story a pattern of his own psychic death and transfiguration. After the first weeks of trying to stay emotionally detached from the war, Lawrence took Europe's suffering into himself. He was part of the body of mankind, and was wounded with it in spirit, if not literally: "The War finished me," he told Cynthia Asquith, "it was the spear through the side of all sorrows and hopes . . . my soul [at Chesham] lay in the tomb—not dead, but with a flat stone over it, a corpse, become corpse-cold." By sharing vicariously in the myriad deaths in Flanders and then rising to a renewed fullness of life, Lawrence hoped to stand as an example of salvation for agonized Europe. The war showed that men must know death before they could choose life; though "the killed soldiers [would] have to wait for the last trump."[29]

These themes find expression in what he called his "war poem," "Eloi, Eloi, Lama Sabachthani?"[30] In this poem, first called "Ecce

Homo," he wonders why his vision of erotic liberation has been shattered by the perverse eroticism of violence:

> Why should we hate, then, with this hate incarnate?
> Why am I bridegroom of War, war's paramour?
> What is the crime, that my seed is turned to blood,
> My kiss to wounds?
> Who is it will have it so, who did the crime?
> And why do the women follow us satisfied,
> Feed on our wounds like bread, receive our blood
> Like glittering seed upon them for fulfilment?

The only answer Lawrence can give is that the war is an act of expiation for an "unknowable crime," whose effects will end after he has offered his brother to death:

> I walk the earth intact hereafterwards;
> The crime full-expiate, the Erinnyes sunk
> Like blood in the earth again; we walk the earth
> Unchallenged, intact, unabridged, henceforth a host
> Cleansed and in concord from the bed of death.

Lawrence's poem took a view of the war that was beyond politics: that was both its strength and its weakness. He assumed that the ostensible causes of the war—Serbian nationalism, disturbance of the balance of power, and so on—were mere excuses. What really mattered were the deep currents of emotion in the masses of all European countries that made them eager to join in. Fundamentally, this had to be a collective desire for death—one's own as much as the enemy's—caused by some hidden morbidity of European civilization. Here Lawrence parted company with the socialist humanism of the Hopkins, his early political mentors: the masses had not been betrayed into war by secret diplomacy or a corrupt ruling class, but had gladly taken to arms in revulsion against a way of life that thwarted and made rotten their vital instincts. In 1915 this belief would precipitate Lawrence's famous quarrel with Bertrand Russell over how the war should be opposed.

Lawrence identified with Christ because he found in the Passion an image of individual participation in the war's immeasurable suffering, and also the hope that man could be reborn out of destruction. The symbol of the Phoenix, which he adopted around this time, was another way of signifying his psychic death and resurrection.[31] Moreover, the deep historical roots of the Christ image made it a talisman that could reassure Lawrence when he was attacked by fears of having lost his sense of his own reality. Events in the outer world were so overwhelming, and Frieda's power over his feelings apparently so complete, that his identity seemed pulled out of him and dispersed among the stronger realities outside.[32] This nightmarish experience he described a few months later in "New Heaven and Earth":

> When I gathered flowers, I knew it was myself plucking my
>   own flowering. . . .
> When I heard the cannon of the war, I listened with my own
>   ears to my own destruction.
> When I saw the torn dead, I knew it was my own torn dead body.
> It was all me, I had done it all in my own flesh.
> I shall never forget the maniacal horror of it all in the end
>   when everything was me. . . .

Faced with such horror, the vicarious death inflicted on him by the war's slaughter comes as a relief. Though Lawrence believed that men and women could only find their deepest selves in the consummation of true marriage, he recognized also that to cast oneself utterly into the being of another person was a kind of death. It followed that marriage must be redefined according to Lawrence's developing sense of his relation with Frieda, and his contact with other couples such as Jack and Katherine. For recent events convinced Lawrence that unless men were secure in their own identities they would all too readily throw themselves into the crucible of war, out of pure revulsion from living the social and marital lie. These were the problems that would shape the violent intellectual and physical encounters of *Women in Love*.

Study of Thomas Hardy

WHEN Methuen rejected *The Rainbow* Lawrence could not at first face the task of reshaping it into an acceptable offering in the literary marketplace. Instead, he took up the little potboiler on

Thomas Hardy that he had planned to write in July. But now it had changed its nature; Lawrence told Pinker that he had begun to write it out of "sheer rage" against the "colossal idiocy" of the war, and that it would be about "anything but Thomas Hardy . . . queer stuff."[33] This was hardly the right mood for dashing off something to pay the rent; the book produced no money and could not even find a publisher until after Lawrence's death. No matter; he wrote it for himself, really, as a "Story of My Heart, or a *Confessio Fidei.*"[34] He wanted to explore his own "inhuman will," rather than that of his fictional characters: to take stock of his unexpected predicament and contact the subterranean impulses that should guide his response. As he composed the *Study of Thomas Hardy* Lawrence arrived at answers to these questions that implied fundamental changes in his personal and artistic vocations.

"Because the novel is a microcosm," he wrote in the *Study,* "and because man in viewing the universe must view it in the light of a theory, therefore every novel must have the background or the structural skeleton of some theory of being, some metaphysic."[35] His first effort in this line was the unpublished Foreword to *Sons and Lovers,* a murky disquisition on The Word, Flesh, and Woman.[36] Then, at Chesham, the intrusive philosophizing of Hardy's novels moved Lawrence to expound the beliefs that underlay his own. He wanted to put himself "more in order" intellectually, but a definitive statement of his principles always seemed to elude him; after the *Study* he wrote a long series of speculative works, from *The Crown* in 1915 to *A Propos of Lady Chatterley's Lover* in 1929. Though many of these books have been considered only minor or even embarrassing fragments of the Lawrence canon, he himself valued them highly as contributions to the true purpose of philosophy: to aid man in his "mighty struggle to feel at home on the face of the earth."[37]

The Wessex novels were therefore no more than a point of departure for the *Study of Thomas Hardy,* though Lawrence used them intermittently to illustrate his beliefs. Setting aside, then, chapters 3 and 9—those on Hardy's novels—the work falls into two parts. The first, roughly chapters 1 to 6, is a rambling argument for individualism in the personal life and anarchism in social life. The second, chapters 7 to 10, is Lawrence's attempt to explain nature and history in terms of polarities, such as male and female, motion and rest, knowing and being; he ends by defining life as a continuously shifting balance between these great absolutes.

Lawrence's basic individualism is first given a systematic form in the *Study*. From his first years he was conscious of being set apart from the general run of miners' children—who, for their part, derided him as "mardy-arsed" (fearful and effeminate). He found that by excelling in his school work he could escape from grimy Eastwood into a more spacious world of culture and refinement, though this talent also confirmed his status as an outsider, marked out for another fate than going "down pit" at fourteen. Yet a scholarship boy left the working-class world for one that was in its way equally limited and rule-bound: that of the red-brick university, the training course, the hierarchy of the teaching profession. Lawrence's clever young friends at Eastwood and Croydon reached this level of society—the progressive, educated segment of the lower middle class—but hardly any went beyond it. In early 1912 he took a far more radical step with his fourfold revolt against convention: he decided at a single stroke to abandon his teaching career, to elope with a married woman, to live abroad, and to support himself by writing. This was a real breaking of the mould, all the more courageous in one who had just been warned by two doctors that his chest was too weak for him to consider marriage.

Over the next two years Lawrence's experience was nicely calculated to establish a mood of confident self-assertion: his difficulties provoked his native contentiousness, but were not so great as to crush his initiative or to turn his independence of the herd into a full-blown misanthropy. In Germany, for example, he and Frieda were arrested for making love *al fresco*,[38] but they were also given shelter by such pillars of the Establishment as Alfred Weber and Edgar Jaffe; in Italy Lawrence could feel free of his homeland while also being sought out by Eddie Marsh and other literati. He thought it no great feat to ignore the taboos of English respectability, so he was quite ingenuously disappointed when Jack Murry refused in 1913 to abandon his fledgling literary career in England and live with Katherine in Fiascherino. Lawrence had done it, and survived; why could not his friends do so too? Before 1915, when he began to feel the range of sanctions that could be invoked against those whose individualism threatened the state, he believed that the first and last stage of emancipation from society was just to turn one's back on it. In the *Study* he imagined society as a mere dead weight of repression: "All that matters is that each human being shall *be* in his own fulness. If something obstructs us, we break it or put it aside, as the shoots of the trees break even through the London pavements." By June 1915 Lawrence would use a more realistic metaphor in warning Bertrand Russell against showing his pacifism too openly: "One must take care of the pack. When they hunt together they are very strong. *Never* expose yourself to the pack. . . . Be rather their secret enemy."[39]

The *Study* expresses, therefore, a naive individualism. Lawrence had not yet realized that his break with English convention had coincided with the last moments of the era that upheld the "liberty of the subject" as the highest value. In fact, that era had ended on 8 August, when Lawrence returned to London from his hike in the Lake District. The House of Commons passed that day, after five minutes of discussion, the Defence of the Realm Act ("DORA"), whereby "the traditional freedoms of Britons were signed away at the stroke of a pen."[40] But few people appreciated at once the full significance of the act; only after Lawrence had been given a taste of official compulsion did he understand the power of the opponent he had so blithely defied before the war.

Lawrence's philosophy in the *Study of Thomas Hardy* was founded on a distinction between "self-preservation"—man's care for the social enterprise—and "excess"—his transcending this basis of subsistence to achieve a "maximum of being":

> The final aim of every living thing, creature, or being is the full achievement of itself. This accomplished, it will produce what it will produce, it will bear the fruit of its nature. Not the fruit, however, but the flower is the culmination and climax, the degree to be striven for. Not the work I shall produce, but the real Me I shall achieve, that is the consideration; of the complete Me will come the complete fruit of me, the work, the children.[41]

Man is split because he cannot help being aware that he could do much more than just preserve his race, but up to now few men have been able to fulfill this potential; only the aristocrat "could afford to *be,* to be himself, to create himself, to live as himself. That is his eternal fascination."[42] Lawrence assumes that society could be reorganized to give everyone an adequate living for two or three hours of work a day; then, unyoked from the great economic machine, men would have no excuse for not realizing *themselves* to the full. About the machine itself the *Study* says little. Lawrence's polemic against the industrial system is carried on elsewhere, notably in the portrait of the mining engineer, Tom Brangwen, in *The Rainbow,* and in "The Industrial Magnate," a chapter in *Women in Love.* Both these passages were probably composed after the *Study of Thomas Hardy,* as a more detailed and wary examination of industrialism than Lawrence's somewhat facile dismissal of it in the earlier work.[43] At first he saw the war as a self-explanatory sign of the European crisis; not till later, when it had become settled and institutionalized, did he trace its deeper roots in the social structure.

When the Germans shelled Scarboro in December 1914 Lawrence commented sardonically "the whole country is thrilled to the marrow, and enjoys it like hot punch."[44] This universal love of destruction existed, in his view, because men had chosen to be "sex-degraded and . . . money-degraded":

> We are each one of us a swamp, we are like the hide-bound cabbage going rotten at the heart. And for the same reason that, instead of producing our flower, instead of continuing our activity, satisfying our true desire . . . we hang back, we dare not even peep forth, but, safely shut up in bud, safely and darkly and snugly enclosed, like the regulation cabbage, we remain secure till our hearts go rotten, saying all the while how safe we are.
>
> No wonder there is a war.

Sexuality has been reduced to a mere adjunct of the lower system, of self-preservation; but when love ceases to be discovery it becomes sensationalism, "the repeating of a known reaction." Caught in this mechanical process, man becomes like the flower that "if it cannot beat its way through into being, will thrash destruction about itself."[45]

Individualism, for Lawrence, demands a constant testing of one's boundaries, since knowledge of oneself is inseparable from knowledge of what is not oneself. The crucial mode of self-realization is therefore the sexual act when undertaken as a radical confrontation between one's own subjectivity and that of the alien other: "I go to a woman to know myself, and knowing myself, to go further, to explore in to the unknown, which is the woman, venture in upon the coasts of the unknown."[46] In the second part of the *Study* Lawrence links sex to the fundamental polarities in the universe. "Why do we consider the male stream and the female stream as being only in the flesh?" he asks; ". . . . The physical, what we call in its narrowest meaning, the sex, is only a definite indication of the great male and female duality and unity. . . . There is female apart from Woman, as we know, and male apart from Man." Borrowing perhaps from Otto Weininger's *Sex and Character,* he posits that a normal person would have a roughly equal mixture of male and female; a totally male man would not be an ideal, but a freak.[47] Between man and woman a perfect complementarity of qualities will therefore be rare and transient. More commonly, "a man must seek elsewhere than in woman for the female to possess his soul, to fertilize him. . . . And the female exists in much more than his woman. And the finding of it for himself gives a man his vision, his God."[48]

Lawrence's belief that the life process consists of a continual interplay of opposing forces has an obvious kinship with such concepts as the Hegelian dialectic, or the contrast between anabolism and catabolism in biology. But he made difficulties for his readers by defining his dualisms in a highly personal way. In his philosophical works he made up his systems as he went along (and continually revised them), while in his novels his characters were often governed by an underlying moral scheme that often, to the uninitiated, seemed quite arbitrary. *Sons and Lovers* had been mainly a traditional novel about the formation of its hero's character by family and society; but after 1914 Lawrence conceived of character as little more than the external signs of the deep forces swaying a person—and those signs might be only scanty indicators of the turmoil beneath the surface. Knowing his own emotional lability, and seeing also the mass irrationality of the war unfolding before him, Lawrence was convinced that he must go deeper into the sources of human feeling if his art as a novelist was to advance beyond his predecessors. Critics had condemned Hardy's philosophy as too intrusive and mechanical; but it seemed to Lawrence that his fault lay rather in not taking his philosophy seriously enough. Hardy was always losing his nerve and striking down those of his characters who were struggling toward a new way of being, while allowing the conventional to inherit the spoils. For his part Lawrence determined to draw out and systematize his intuitions, and it mattered little to him if they appeared dark and dif-

(35)

fuse to outsiders. "It seems to me it was the greatest pity in the world, when philosophy and fiction got split," he wrote in a later essay.[49] At Chesham, he took it upon himself to reunite them.

So, late in November, he completed the first draft of the *Study of Thomas Hardy* and again took up the manuscript of *The Rainbow*. He had by now survived the worst of his psychological crises at Chesham, and in mid-November he had come to terms with the war, for the time being at least, by writing "Eloi, Eloi, Lama Sabachthani?" The poem ended with the hope that destruction might lead to purgation and renewal; certainly Lawrence's personal energies were reviving. On 3 December he reported to Kot that he was "working *frightfully* hard—re-writing my novel";[50] two days later he sent Pinker the first hundred pages of the new draft, and a month after he sent two hundred more. He was again filled with self-confidence about the novel and about its eventual reception. "I am glad of this war," he said, "it kicks the pasteboard bottom in of the usual 'good' popular novel. People have felt much more deeply and strongly these last few months, and they are not going to let themselves be taken in by 'serious' works whose feeling is shallower than that of the official army reports. . . . I am glad of the war. It sets a slump in trifling."[51] This idea of the war—as a necessary purge for a sick society—was one to which he clung until it became evident that Europe was suffering from a cure far worse than any disease that might have afflicted it before 1914.

The Circle Broken

IN EARLY DECEMBER the Lawrences went to the Midlands for Freida's futile confrontation with Weekley; then, after a day with Lawrence's sister Ada in Derbyshire, they visited David Garnett in London. Such engagements scarcely checked the rush of work on the final version of *The Rainbow*. Shortly before Christmas *The Prussian Officer*, Lawrence's first collection of stories, was published. Reviews were mixed and he had no great hopes for the book; moreover, Edward Garnett had irritated him by changing the name of the title story (Lawrence had called it "Honour and Arms") in an unsuccessful attempt to make the book topical. The most important consequence of *The Prussian Officer*'s publication was Lawrence's friendship with Lady Ottoline Morrell; but this did not happen at once.

Meanwhile Christmas was approaching, and Lawrence decided to spend it with his friends at Chesham rather than with his family. After the hard months of war, sickness, and depression he felt "like kicking everything to the devil and enjoying [himself] willy-nilly—a wild drunk and a great and rowdy spree.[52] Two Christmas parties came off, with the same nine friends at each: the Lawrences, the Cannans, Jack and Katherine, Gertler, Koteliansky, and Gordon Campbell (Beatrice was away in Ireland). The first was held on Christmas Eve at the Lawrences' little cottage, where everyone feasted happily and got drunk. Then they danced and sang songs; Katherine, in one of her impish moods, revelled in music-hall gloom:

> I am an unlucky man,
> I fell into a coalhole
> I broke my leg,
> And got three months for stealing coal.

This was a parody of the way she had been feeling for the past two months, stuck in a cold and damp cottage while Jack agonized through another bout of contorted self-analysis. But she also had a bawdy little song in her repertoire—which Lawrence thought "fast" and forbade Frieda to sing:

> Ton sirop est doux, Madeleine,
> Ton sirop est doux.
> Ne crie pas si fort, Madeleine,
> La maison n'est pas à nous.[53]

The song hinted at a daydream that Katherine had been cherishing for some time: of having a runaway affair with Francis Carco, a writer and close friend of Jack's whom she had met a year before in Paris, and who was now in the French army. In the sodden winter of Buckinghamshire, Carco held the promise of escape into southern warmth and sensuality (like herself, he had been born in the Southern Hemisphere—in New Caledonia, only a thousand miles from New Zealand). Later, when she was disillusioned with him, she put him in a story, where he takes inventory of his own charms:

> I am little and light with an olive skin, black eyes with long lashes, black silky hair cut short, tiny square teeth that show when I smile. My hands are supple and small. A woman in a bread shop said to me: "You have the hands for making fine little pastries." I confess, without my clothes I am rather charming.[54]

Carco, a naively egotistical personage, approved of this fictional portrait of himself—apparently unaware of the malice with which he had been sketched.

Frieda, a connoisseur of such affairs, seems to have encouraged the infatuation. A week before Christmas Katherine determined to leave Murry and go to Carco, who had been wooing her by mail from his training camp at Gray, near Dijon. She felt that her love for Jack was girlish rather than a real passion, and that to him she was little more than "a gratification and a comfort." "What we have got each to kill—is my *you* and your *me*," she wrote in her *Journal,* "That's all. Let's do it nicely and go to the funeral in the same carriage, and hold hands hard over the new grave, and smile and wish each other luck."[55] At the Christmas dinner given by the Cannans both were striving to be civilized about their forthcoming separation. But the centerpiece of the meal, a roast suckling pig, caused a fiasco when no one could carve it. Everyone got drunk and Jack was moved to stage a charade about "the actual situation between Katherine and me, and in which Mark Gertler . . . was cast for the part of my successor."[56] At the end Katherine rejected Jack's scenario, in which she was reconciled with him, and instead acted out her intended affair, all too vividly. Gertler reported the dénouement to Lytton Strachey: "I got so drunk that I made violent love to Katherine Mansfield! She returned it, also being drunk. I ended the evening by weeping bitterly at having kissed another man's woman and everybody trying to console me. . . . So interesting was [the party] that all the writers of Cholesbury feel inspired to use it in their work."[57] But Lawrence was outraged; once again, he felt, Jack had acted spinelessly and deserved Katherine's contempt.*

"Fortunately, the next day everybody decided to take it as a

---

* A year earlier, Lawrence had warned Jack: "She must see if she really *wants* you, wants to keep you and to have no other man all her life. . . . You must say, 'How can I make myself most healthy, strong, and satisfactory to myself and to her?' . . . Be more natural, and positive, and stick to your own guts. You spread them on a tray for her to throw to the cats" (CL 238).

joke," Gertler told Carrington, "the Lawrences were the last to come to this decision, as they were most anxious to weave a real romance out of it. Seeing that Katherine's man and myself were just as friendly afterwards, they *had* to take it as a joke. They were very disappointed."[58] Nonetheless, the web of friendship among the Chesham circle was beginning to unravel. Lawrence, preaching his ideal of an island colony far from "this world of war and squalor," wanted them to go forward into a closer and more demanding group relationship, but several members were planning to go off in irreconcilable directions. Katherine would join Carco in France as soon as she could find the means to do so. Kot was, as usual, prickly and suspicious of his acceptance by the group. He and Frieda had settled into an antagonism that would make it impossible for him to live at close quarters with the Lawrences; with the Murrys, conversely, he idolized Katherine and mistrusted Jack. Gertler, for his part, was moving toward independence rather than community. He had been using his parents' home in the East End as a base, while staying regularly with Eddie Marsh in London or with Gilbert Cannan; but he wanted his own establishment, and in January 1915 he rented a studio near Hampstead Heath. He liked to be free to withdraw from social contact altogether, and he was still mired in his unhappy affair with Dora Carrington. Gordon Campbell, finally, was planning to devote more of himself to his family and his career and less to his long-drawn-out lucubrations with Jack.

As these various crosscurrents threatened the circle, Lawrence pressed on them his scheme of moving to some idyllic setting where there could be a deeper intimacy and mutual reliance between them all. An island, he thought, would be ideal for the purpose. During January he held long planning sessions at Chesham, and also broached the idea to Willie Hopkin, his old Eastwood friend:

> I want to gather together about twenty souls . . . and found a little colony where there shall be no money but a sort of communism as far as necessaries of life go, and some real decency. It is to be a colony built up on the real decency which is in each member of the community. A community which is established upon the assumption of goodness in the members, instead of the assumption of badness.[59]

Lawrence even wrote a formal constitution for Campbell to study, "believing him to have the organizing capacity and the capital to work the scheme."[60] But Campbell was too much a man of the world to see in it anything more than an agreeable pipe dream. The constitution has been lost though we can get some idea of it from the "laws" that Lawrence proposed four years later to his friend Dr. Eder, who was going to join the Zionist settlers in Palestine:

> First Law: there shall be no laws: every man shall hold up his hand in token that he is self-responsible and answerable to his own soul.
> Second Law: Every man shall have food, shelter, knowledge and the right to mate freely—every man and woman shall have this, irrespective of any other claim than that of life-necessity: and every man who enters, and every woman, shall hold up a hand to signify that in these two principles we are at one.
> Then everything else can be done by arrangement, not by law. There are many deep and bitter and sweet things to know and learn, afterwards. But in accepting the first two principles, we put ourselves, like beginners, into the state of pure attention, like acolytes. And so our State begins.[61].

In its first conception Rananim appealed to Lawrence as an escape from wartime England into a miniature anarchist community. Before the war he and Frieda had already been living for most of the year in cheap and picturesque corners of the Continent. The only drawback to such places was their isolation, and as soon as he arrived in one Lawrence would fire off letters to his friends urging them to come and stay. Always he pursued the dream he had confided to Jessie Chambers when he was seventeen or eighteen:

> . . . he said to me how fine it would be if some day he could take a house, say one of the big houses in Nottingham Park, and he and all the people he liked could live together. I was dubious and suggested that his friends might not agree if they all lived together. But he brushed my objection aside; it would be all right, he was sure, and wouldn't it be fine?[62]

Rananim would be such a long-term gathering of his friends: to write, to discuss, and to share a common domestic life. It is unlikely that Lawrence envisioned any sexual sharing within the group: both he and Jack had monogamous ideals while Katherine and Frieda, though they took lovers from time to time, did so usually as brief diversions. Practical arrangements for ten or twenty people to live together would have been awkward, but Lawrence's housekeeping talents could probably have coped with the challenge. The real problems lay elsewhere. First, Lawrence wanted the support of friends to compensate for the pain and humiliation often inflicted on him by Frieda; but the friends tended to shy away precisely because they did not wish to be too deeply involved in the Lawrences' embattled marriage. Second, people were always being drawn into Lawrence's circle by his extraordinary vitality and gift for intimacy, but once there they were likely to find themselves at odds with the other members. After the war this situation degenerated into the pursuit of a disgruntled Lawrence by a band of mutually suspicious disciples. In 1914 and 1915, however, his friends were mostly strong-minded persons of independent talent; when push came to shove, they would go their own ways rather than submerge their personalities in his. The exception was Murry who, as Katherine drifted away from him, became an enthusiastic sharer in Lawrence's plans for Rananim. But it was not wise to rely too heavily on Murry's enthusiasms and protestations of loyalty, as Lawrence was to learn again and again.

In any case, Campbell's unwillingness to put up the money meant that Rananim would have to be postponed until some other sponsor turned up. Lawrence was much downcast, though Frieda took the setback calmly. "I did not oppose his colony plan," she wrote long afterward, "my reason: I never believed in it."[63] Meanwhile Chesham seemed more and more a dead end: in addition to sickness, cold, and damp the Lawrences had to endure the suspicion of the police and local residents. Sometime in December they had been offered by Viola Meynell the use of a cottage in her family colony at Greatham, near Pulborough, Sussex. On 5 January Lawrence was still wary of accepting; he had doubts about being cast into the bosom of "the whole formidable and poetic Meynell family." But within a few days, swayed by poor health and Frieda's eagerness to move, he had decided to leave their "miserable little cottage" for one at Greatham that was "more comfortable, not so depressing and misfitting."[64] On 19 and 20 January they had farewell dinners at Jack and Katherine's and at the Cannans'; the weather was bad the second night so the Murrys stayed over with the Lawrences rather than walk home across the fields. Katherine noted in her *Journal* "Very untidy—newspapers and faded mistletoe. I hardly slept at all, but it was nice."[65] In the morning the Murrys returned home while Lawrence and Frieda set out to spend two days in London, before going down to Sussex. After five months of retreat in Buckinghamshire they were beginning a year—the only one of Lawrence's life—in which they would be right at the center of English intellectual society. Lawrence's mood was outgoing and cheerful, as it usually was at the prospect of a move. Moreover, they were going to have dinner in London with Lady Ottoline Morrell, whose home in Bloomsbury welcomed all the most advanced artists and thinkers. Lawrence looked forward to becoming intimate with some of them; he did not foresee that within a year he would again be eager to bury himself in the remote countryside and call down fire and brimstone on the world he had left.

CHAPTER III

GREATHAM

Interlude at Bedford Square

ON THE LAST DAY of 1914 Lady Ottoline Morrell wrote to her lover Bertrand Russell about *The Prussian Officer,* which she had read on his recommendation:

> I am amazed how good it is—quite wonderful some of the Stories—He has great passion—and is so alive to things outward and inward—a far better writer than Cannan and quite different from that muddled stuff of Woolfe— Did you ever read "Sons and Lovers" by him? It has been a comfort reading anything so real. All the Nottinghamshire Stories seem very familiar to me. Didn't you think "The Vicar's Daughters" very good?[1]

The previous August Lawrence had attended a party Lady Ottoline gave at 44, Bedford Square, and had offended Katherine Mansfield, also a guest, by being "perceptibly over-eager in aristocratic company."[2] Ottoline had not read his books then and their acquaintance did not "take," though she probably heard of his fortunes at Chesham through their mutual friend Gilbert Cannan. But now, full of enthusiasm for *The Prussian Officer,* she wrote the author (as was her custom), asking him to visit her. On 3 January Lawrence sent a grateful acceptance, thus entering into one of the crucial relationships of his life.

Lawrence and Lady Ottoline had spent their childhood years some twenty miles apart, yet in utterly different circumstances. When Lawrence was born in 1885, in a tiny, mean house at the center of the mining village of Eastwood, Ottoline Cavendish Bentinck was a girl of twelve living with her widowed mother at Welbeck Abbey, the hereditary seat of her half brother, the sixth duke of Portland. The Cavendishes and the Bentincks had been counted among the great families of England since the seventeenth century. They were politically influential—there had been a prime minister in each family—and immensely wealthy; their holdings included large parts of the Nottinghamshire coalfields where Lawrence's father worked at the pit face. Ottoline moved to Welbeck when she was six at the death of her second cousin, the fifth duke. This half-crazed peer had for some twenty years lived alone in four or five scanty rooms of the vast mansion, consumed by a pathological fear of his fellow beings. He engaged hundreds of miners to excavate a network of underground rooms and tunnels, the largest of them over a mile long and wide enough for two carriages to pass each other. Another tunnel allowed him to go underground from the main house to the gardens and stables; it was paralleled by a separate one for servants, since he "did not wish to meet anyone walking in the same tunnel as himself."[3]

Ottoline's mother ran the household of her son the sixth duke until his marriage in 1889. She tried to make Welbeck habitable and even cheerful, though this was an almost hopeless task in such a monument to paranoia. Ottoline's brothers were apparently not affected by the atmosphere; they were conventional young men, fond of hunting, shooting, and fishing. But Ottoline became an awkward and lonely child who hankered after the warmth of life among the common people. Her brother the duke once lectured her for riding in a crowded third-class carriage on the train to Welbeck; thereafter she changed from third to first as she neared home. She was too self-conscious to fit into the social life of a young woman of her class; the others in her set sniggered at her appearance—she was tall, with aquiline features and marmalade-colored hair, and dressed unconventionally—while she responded with "passionate disapproval" of their frivolity. Thomas a Kempis' *The Imitation of Christ* inspired her (like Maggie Tulliver in *The Mill on the Floss*) to live by an ideal of strict self-denial, and she was plagued all her life by physical and nervous ailments.

Ottoline gradually emancipated herself from her painful childhood, but her personality never lost its impress. In her late twenties she was still "under the spell of some tyranny which forbade me to enjoy freely, or to drink deeply of the cup of life in my hand."[4] She married Philip Morrell, a lawyer of less exalted background than her own, in 1902, and supported his career as a Liberal M. P. By the time Lawrence met her she had turned her back on traditional aristocratic society and had become London's leading intellectual hostess. This eminence was remarkable for one without any creative gift in the arts, and scanty formal education (her spelling and syntax were wildly erratic); though no woman of her time was more widely lampooned, none could have done what she did without extraordinary forces of character and intuitive intelligence. Her salons at Bedford Square and later at Garsington included almost everyone in England of original talent in the arts.

Some might sneer that Ottoline was always looking for fresh recruits, since she often became sexually infatuated with her protégés; a more friendly estimate would note her willingness to help artists and writers while they were still struggling and little known. Lawrence, anyway, was as eager to join Ottoline's circle as she was to have him. Nor, in replying to her letter of praise for *The Prussian Officer,* did he neglect to mention that "the thermometer of [his] wealth [was] nearly at zero."[5] After all, it was his policy to take money from the rich rather than from friends or relatives; and fashionable London looked especially glittering when viewed from a laborer's cottage down a flooded lane in Buckinghamshire. Lawrence was not a snob in the sense of avoiding social contact with ordinary people, but he was certainly susceptible to the glamor of rank and title, especially in a woman. Jessie Chambers claimed, with some malice, that "Frieda's rank was of tremendous significance to Lawrence in the days when he first met her"; and from his first letter to Ottoline he showed that she need fear no proletarian chip on his shoulder: "I am no democrat, save in politics. I think the state is a vulgar institution. But life itself is an affair of aristocrats."[6]

Their early relations were thus shaped by the attraction of opposites that has been typical of the English class system. Lawrence, Ottoline recalled, "liked to talk of my family in Nottinghamshire, for he had a romantic feeling for them. He used to please me by saying that the 'Bentincks were always looked up to as being disinterested.' " On her side there lingered a youthful fascination with the miners:

> I would feel excited and even a little nervous when I met groups of colliers on their way home from the pits. These men, tall, black and mysterious, appeared rather fierce and yet full of laughter and fun, joking together as they hurried pell-mell along the dark roads. . . . How I wished I could talk to these

men, or share their good solid tea, and so bridge the gulf that lay between us, these men whose lives were lived in a world that I knew nothing of.[7]

Lawrence charmed Ottoline by showing her the miners' world from within and talking to her in the Nottinghamshire dialect. Yet at the same time, paradoxically, they longed to meet in a realm that was *beyond* class; for each had sought emancipation by denying their origins. One observes the same impulse in Mark Gertler's delight at the prospect of leaving his parents' home in the East End (they were poor fur sewers) and moving into a Hampstead studio: "There, I shall be free and detached—shall belong to no parents. I shall be neither Jew nor Christian and shall belong to no class. I shall be just myself."[8] In a remarkable letter to E. M. Forster Lawrence explained how the whole system of social distinction had become a dead letter to him:

> I don't belong to any class, now. As for your class, do you think it could tempt me? If I'm one of any lot, I'm one of the common people. But I feel as if I'd known all classes now, and so am free of all. Frieda is a German of good family—in Germany she thinks herself very aristocratic. I have known Lady Ottoline's servants—gate keepers and cooks—at home, who have served in Welbeck. Now I know Lady Ottoline. And whether I sit at tea with Mrs. Orchard, who had been an under servant at Welbeck, and who had erysipelas in her hands, and who was glad when I sat and talked to her for hours, when I was a lad—and she didn't light the gas, for economy's sake, but we looked into a red, low fire—she with her hands wrapped up, and her curious servant's face 'glotzend' in the firelight, and her eyes fixed and her mouth talking, talking about the Duke and Lord Henry and Lady Ottoline—or whether I sit with Lady Ottoline and talk about the war, or about people—what is it, after all? One is only going down different avenues to the same thing. One is only tracking down the secret of satisfaction for the individual—the naked, intrinsic, classless individual. What is class, at its best, but a method of living to one's end? It doesn't *really* alter the end. And for each class, the other class seems to held the secret of satisfaction. But no class holds it.[9]

Lawrence thus believed that he could mingle freely with anyone; but those he met persisted in viewing *him* as a particular social type. As with many of his convictions, once he had worked something through to a conclusion he found it difficult to appreciate that others might think differently.

On 21 January 1915 the Lawrences left Chesham for two crowded days in London before going down to Sussex. They stayed at the home of Dr. David Eder and his wife, Edith, in Hampstead Garden suburb; Mrs. Eder was an aunt of Ivy Low, who had spent six weeks at Fiascherino the previous spring. But the Lawrences must have been in Bloomsbury for most of this visit. On the first evening they had dinner with Ottoline at Bedford Square; the other guests were David Garnett and E. M. Forster. Perhaps Ottoline thought Forster would be sympathetic to Lawrence because his last novel, *Howards End* (1910), had dealt with the obstacles to friendship between persons of different class. The motto of the book was the famous "Only Connect," and because of his superiors' failure to do so the young clerk Leonard Bast meets with disappointment and death. Forster and Lawrence tried conscientiously enough to find common ground, but Lawrence seems to have detected a tinge of condescension in Forster, who was six years older. At the same time, he mistrusted Forster's progressive, mildly Fabian temperament; he preferred that the superior classes should have the nerve or talent to *be* superior, and felt that Forster, with his cultured upper-middle-class background, had an unrealistic idea of the lower classes. Still, he was willing to develop his acquaintance with Forster in the succeeding weeks.

After dinner other guests came for dancing, including Gertler, Carrington, and Duncan Grant, a painter of Lawrence's age whom David Garnett had taken a liking to; he hoped Lawrence and Grant would be as fond of each other as he was of each separately. Grant did his bit by inviting the Lawrences, Forster, and Garnett to have tea at his studio the next day and see his paintings. The viewing, however, turned into a painful fiasco. Grant was an accomplished professional painter; but had not Lawrence won prizes for art in his youth? and did not chapter 7 of the *Study of Thomas Hardy* propose a comprehensive theory of the evolution of Western art since the Middle Ages? Lawrence dissected Grant's paintings with brutal vigor and found them wanting. Grant was experimenting with compositions of related geometrical shapes, which roused Lawrence's dislike of modernism and abstraction in art. He praised Grant for seeking "a whole conception of the existence of man. . . . It is an Absolute we are all after."[10] But the Absolute, Lawrence felt, should be built up from the "concrete Units" that precede the abstraction; it should be inclusive and particular, not a "ready stated" abstraction such as a circle or a triangle.

Lawrence was putting forward a valid critique of Grant's paintings; but he did so in a dogmatic tone that reduced the normally affable Grant to unresponsive dismay. Forster, who hated such scenes, quietly slipped away, and Garnett sadly realized that his new friends in the younger circle of Bloomsbury could never be on easy terms with Lawrence. His distaste for Grant's art was enough in itself to keep them apart; but there was a further cause of tension that would influence all his future relations with Bloomsbury. In writing to Ottoline about Grant, Lawrence professed to like him "very much" but added, presumably in response to something she had told him, "He looks as if he dissipates, and certainly he doesn't enjoy it. Tell him to stop."[11] The word "dissipates" looks like an oblique reference to Grant's sexual proclivities, which were complex. Within the homosexual circle that grew out of the Cambridge secret society "The Apostles," his charm and good looks had gained him the love of Lytton Strachey (a cousin), Maynard Keynes, and others. By the time Lawrence met him he had become bisexual. He lived in the same Bloomsbury house as Keynes and Clive and Vanessa Bell; with Vanessa, who was sexually estranged from her husband, he had begun a life-long intimacy. All of this would have been anathema to Lawrence; an affair with a married woman was bad enough, but worse yet was its admixture with the homosexuality that linked many members of the Bloomsbury set. Lawrence's evident prejudice against it coexisted with an awareness that he himself had strong homosexual impulses which he felt morally bound to repress. The conflict created one of his most painful and frustrating emotional dilemmas over the next few years.

Lawrence and Forster: First Skirmish with Bloomsbury

AFTER LAWRENCE'S DEATH, Forster paid him tribute as "the greatest imaginative novelist of our generation."[12] In life, though, their relations had been uneasy and unfulfilled. From their first meeting over dinner at Ottoline's Lawrence expounded his cherished plans for Rananim, and hinted broadly that Forster would be welcome to join the colony. Forster's response was politely noncommittal, but he was at least willing to correspond with the Lawrences about it and to send them some books to read at Greatham: *Howards End, The Celestial Omnibus* (a collection of his stories), and his friend Virginia Woolf's first novel, *The Voyage Out*.[13] To become a suitable candidate for Rananim, Forster would have had to transform his mild, ironic, and retiring nature; though Lawrence saw no great difficulty in that, nor was he deterred by Forster's seniority or his established reputation as a novelist. "I'm glad you're not really Buddhistic," he wrote, "—everybody said you were. I want somebody to come and make a league with me, to sing the *Chanson des Chansons—das hohe Lied*—and to war against the fussy Mammon, that pretends to be a tame pet now, and so devours us in our sleep."[14]

Lawrence probably knew that Forster had a substantial private income that could help put Rananim on a sound economic footing. But money was only secondary to the higher, metaphysical aims of the colony:

> It is time for us now to look all round, round the whole ring of the horizon—not just out of a room with a view. . . . In my Island, I wanted people to come without class or money, sacrificing nothing, but each coming with all his desires, yet knowing that his life is but a tiny section of a whole—so that he shall fulfil his life in relation to the whole. . . . But I can't find anybody. Each man is so bent on his own private fulfilment. . . . And they make me tired, these friends of mine. They seem so childish and greedy, always the immediate desire, always the particular outlook, no conception of the whole horizon wheeling round.[15]

These reservations about his friends—Jack Murry and Katherine Mansfield, Gordon Campbell, Koteliansky, and the rest—point to a major shift in Lawrence's thinking. Two years earlier he had proclaimed to Ernest Collings his "belief in the blood, the flesh, as being wiser than the intellect," from which he concluded that morality consisted in simply "being a good animal.":

> "To be or not to be"—it is the question with us now, by Jove. And nearly every Englishman says "Not to be." So he goes in for Humanitarianism and suchlike forms of not-being. The real way of living is to answer to one's wants. Not "I want to light up with my intelligence as many things as possible" but "For the living of my full flame—I want that liberty, I want that woman, I want that pound of peaches, I want to go to sleep."[16]

By early 1915, however, Lawrence was struggling toward a more complex philosophy: one that would embody his sense of the ambivalence of all passions, his need for a long-term purpose that could be shared with others and, finally, his search for an understanding of the nightmare of contemporary history. He therefore demanded of Forster that he also should be in progress toward some goal: "What do you want for yourself? You used to want the fulfilment of the natural animal in you—which is after all only an immediate need. So you made an immediate need seem the Ultimate Necessity—so you belied and betrayed yourself. I don't know where you've got to after *Howards End*."[17]

Indeed, the great theme of Forster's earlier fiction was the struggle to break through inhibition and social duty, into true intimacy with a kindred spirit; and the reader often wonders what the next step could be. What Forster now needed, Lawrence insisted, was to look toward the realm that lay beyond sensual fulfillment:

> I do feel every man must have the devil of a struggle before he can have stuffed himself full enough to have satisfied all his immediate needs, and can give up, cease, and withdraw himself, yield himself up to his metamorphosis, his crucifixion, and so come to his new issuing, his wings, his resurrection, his whole flesh shining like a mote in the sunshine, fulfilled and now taking part in the fulfilment of the whole.[18]

We can easily recognize here Lawrence's own recent history; but Forster did not admit that this paradigm fitted his own quite different case. Lawrence's dependence on Frieda, for example, made him so uncomfortable that when she added a friendly postscript to the above letter he replied that he would "have no dealings with a firm"! Lawrence, having just read Forster's "Story of a Panic," volleyed back: "You with your 'Only Connect' motto, I must say that you reach the limit of splitness here. You are bumping your nose on the end of the cul-de-sac."[19]

One would expect that after this there would be nothing more to say, but Forster was still willing to come down to Greatham for a visit from 10 to 12 February. Lawrence had just met Bertrand Russell and now was full of plans for social revolution; he at once tried to convert Forster to this new cause. But he found his friend hard to mobilize. First, as he complained to Mary Cannan, "his life is so ridiculously inane, the man is dying of inanition"; second, his sexuality was blocked. After such a grim diagnosis it is not surprising that both physician and patient stayed "on the edge of a fierce quarrel" all through the visit; yet both men were *trying* to like each other, even though each thought the other totally misguided.[20]

Lawrence attributed Forster's "inanity" to the frustration of his desire to work for humanity. But, as Lawrence explained to Russell in analysing Forster's case, this "social passion" could only be valid if it was indeed the ultimate desire; no man should try to be a philanthropist before he has satisfied his own immediate needs, particularly his sexual passion. When the two passions are split, both are vitiated. A typical result, Lawrence argued, was homosexuality, the literal uselessness of sexual passion in a paralyzed society. "I believe a man projects his own image on another man," he wrote in 1913, "like on a mirror. But from a woman he wants himself re-born, re-constructed. . . . And one is kept by all tradition and instinct from loving men, or a man—for it means just extinction of all the purposive influences."[21] He admitted, however, that most heterosexual Englishmen were in no better state, since in their sexual life they were

> not going for discovery or new connection or progression, but only to repeat upon [themselves] a known reaction.
>
> When this condition arrives, there is always Sodomy. The man goes to the man to repeat this reaction upon himself. It is a nearer form of masterbation [*sic*]. But still it has some *object*—there are still two bodies instead of one. A man of strong soul has too much honour for the other body—man or woman—to use it as a means of masterbation. So he remains neutral, inactive. That is Forster.[22]

So much for Forster: he was moribund, if not yet expired.

The heart of the matter, of course, was Forster's homosexuality; but he would hardly have discussed it with someone he had met only three weeks before. Yet Lawrence had intuited the essentials of Forster's emotional dilemma. In September 1913 he had become friendly with Edward Carpenter, who was a disciple of Whitman, an advocate of preindustrial socialism, and a homosexual. On Forster's second or third visit George Merrill, Carpenter's "comrade," touched Forster on the backside "—gently and just above the buttocks. I believed he touched most people's. The sensation was unusual and I still remember it, as I remember the position of a long vanished tooth. It was as much psychological as physical. It seemed to go straight through the small of my back into my ideas, without involving my thoughts." This rather

Lawrentian sensation inspired Forster to write his openly homosexual novel *Maurice,* which he completed in July 1914.[23] But he could not publish it, and told only a few trusted friends of its existence. So the future author of *Lady Chatterley's Lover* would not have known that his guest at Greatham had written a novel whose protagonist, frustrated by the emotional sterility of upper-class society, finds sexual happiness by eloping with a gamekeeper. However, Forster himself had achieved fulfillment only in imagination; for a man of thirty-five his actual experience of sex was pathetically meager.

Forster, then, had no stomach for the draconian remedies that Lawrence urged on him to restore his vitality. But Lawrence's broadside attack severely rattled him. Lawrence reported to Mary Cannan that his guest "was very angry with me for telling him about himself";[24] and Forster, not wishing to be told more, sent off to Greatham on his return home an uncharacteristically violent snub:

> Dear Lawrences
>   Until you think it worth while to function separately, I'd better address you as one. . . . As for coming again to Greatham, I like Mrs. Lawrence, and I like the Lawrence who talks to Hilda and sees birds and is physically restful and wrote *The White Peacock,* he doesn't know why; but I do not like the deaf impercipient fanatic who has nosed over his own little sexual round until he believes that there is no other path for others to take: he sometimes interests and sometimes frightens and angers me, but in the end he will bore [me] merely, I know. So I cannot yet tell about coming down.[25]

Forster did not visit the Lawrences again, though he became more amiable once he had taken a safe distance. Lawrence forwarded Forster's letter to Ottoline, asking her if Forster was trying to "put him in his place"; her reply has not survived, but there is a note eight days later from Forster to Ottoline that allows us to guess its purport:

> Dear Lady Ottoline
>   The rest must be left to boil itself clear, but it would be very kind of you if you could convey to him that I do not despise him. It's annoying enough that he should think this—it's worse he should think it's the contempt of the semi-detached villa for the cottage: I've looked up to the class that produced him for many years now.[26]

Publication of Forster's homosexual writings has shown that his belief in connections across class lines was closely related to his particular sexual inclinations. A short story he wrote in 1939, "The Obelisk," gives an almost algebraic demonstration of his outlook.[27] Ernest, an elementary schoolmaster, is dissatisfied with his wife, Hilda, and she with him; their sex life has failed from the start, and Ernest also resents his wife for being slightly less genteel than himself. Then they meet two sailors at a seaside resort. One is from a cultured upper-class background; Hilda is so thrilled by his style that she allows him to make love to her in the undergrowth. When she guiltily rejoins Ernest she realizes that he has done the same thing with the other sailor—a crude, bumptious plebeian. Frigid with each other, Hilda and Ernest have been revitalized by lovers from a class either above, or below, their own.

Some modern theorists of sex would see in Forster an extreme case of the rule that no one can be sexually aroused without a "script": we respond physically to another person, it is argued, only if they seem to fit our ruling fantasies, which are essentially private and fetishistic.[28] Forster was entirely clear-sighted about this side of his nature: "I want to love a strong young man of the lower classes," he wrote in a personal memorandum, "and be loved by him and even hurt by him. That is my ticket."[29] Lawrence's view of sex was quite opposite. He believed that the person we desire acts as a kind of lightning rod that transmits to us the alien and impersonal sexual energy of the universe. We do not attribute sexuality to others by an act of will; rather, they bring it to us from somewhere beyond.

Forster's reticence made it impossible for him and Lawrence to work out their disagreements over the nature of sex. But the modern reader may detect a paradox in Forster's ideas about class. He wanted people to "connect" by recognizing their common humanity; yet it was precisely the *differentness* of the lower classes that attracted him—he mythologized them into vital and exotic strangers. For one of his temperament, a truly classless society would become a flat and colorless sexual wasteland; whereas Lawrence hoped that it might lead to the free flow of sexual energy. He reiterated this ideal after Ottoline's mediation had patched up his friendship with Forster: "I only want you to stick to the idea of a social revolution, which shall throw down artificial barriers between men, and make life freer and fuller. Any big vision of life must contain a revolutionised society and one must fulfil ones visions, or perish."[30] In theory, Forster should have continued and deepened his intimacy with Lawrence for the sake of that openness he so much admired in his mentor Goldsworthy Lowes Dickinson: ". . . most of us . . . do not link up within us such gifts as we have. With him, one had the experience of contact with a person who had allowed no internal barriers to survive, so that on whatever side one touched him there was the same impression of unity."[31] Lawrence's character had a similar integrity; but it was far more alien and provocative to Forster than Dickinson's, and burned with a much hotter flame. In 1927 Forster praised Lawrence as "the only living novelist . . . who has the rapt bardic quality, and whom it is idle to criticize." Yet we can discern that the bruises from Forster's single visit to Greatham were still tender: "Nothing is more disconcerting than to sit down, so to speak, before your prophet, and then suddenly to receive his boot in the pit of your stomach. 'I'm damned if I'll be humble after that,' you cry."[32] And suppose one were to yield to this moral bullying and put oneself in the prophet's hands, what then? "To 'let oneself go' under the stress of emotion is all very well," Forster wrote elsewhere, "but, O my brethren, in which direction? Towards 'Kingless continents sinless as Eden'? or down into a uniform orgy where anything is everything, and blackberries and pismires indistinguishable from Socrates? Escape is only the first step towards salvation. It is useless, unless we take the right turning after opening the door."[33]

Certainly Forster in 1915 needed to escape, though not in the direction Lawrence pointed to. The war had destroyed the intellectual foundations of his humanism and "spoiled everything" for him with its grisly sacrifice of Europe's young men; later in the year he left England for the duration to work with the International Red Cross in Alexandria. Like Lawrence, his creative powers would be applied during the twenties to subjects more exotic and vital than England could provide; indeed, Lawrence highly praised *A Passage to India* even though its premises were quite different from his own.

The pattern of relations between the two men did not vary after February 1915: Lawrence continually renewed invitations and friendly gestures, Forster remained evasive. But Lawrence always kept his respect for Forster, which was unusual with friends who had disappointed him. He told the Italian critic Carlo Linati that Forster was "about the best of my contemporaries in England," while to Forster himself he sent what must be the final word on their uneasy friendship: "To me you are the last Englishman. And I am the one after that."[34]

First Days at Greatham

VIOLA MEYNELL first became aware of Lawrence's works through her friend Ivy Low, soon after the publication of *Sons and Lovers* in May 1913. She was one of the numerous children of Wilfred Meynell, then a well-known man of letters, and his wife, Alice, a poet and convert to Catholicism. Alice had become famous for playing the Good Samaritan to the wayward poet Francis Thompson, who had died of tuberculosis in 1907, and Lawrence seems to have been wryly aware that he might be cast for the role of Thompson's successor. The Meynells had established a family settlement at Greatham, a tiny hamlet four miles from Pulborough. There was a large old farmhouse, with several cottages set around it; though it was not far from the foot of the Downs, the country nearby resembled that of *The Rainbow*, low-lying meadows threaded with streams and ditches. Viola Meynell's cottage was a long, narrow, single-story building, a few feet from the main house. The Lawrences accepted her offer of it sight unseen; anything to escape Chesham, where in wet weather they were now trapped behind an overflowing duck pond.

When they arrived at Greatham they at once found the change to be for the better. The cottage was "rather fine," Lawrence told E. M. Forster, "—a bit monastic—it was a cattle shed—now it is like a monks' refectory—the whole establishment is cloistral."[35] The atmosphere at Greatham was, indeed, somewhat oppressively Catholic and pious; the Meynells had even hoped to build a family chapel there, until they were deterred by the expense. Still, the older Meynells were usually away in London, and Lawrence enjoyed the spaciousness and religious severity of his cottage, with its timbered ceiling and oak furniture. Moreover, it was "really comfortable—even a bath with beautiful hot water,"[36] and for a semi-invalid like Lawrence this was a major convenience. Having moved to the heart of fashionable Sussex, he was now able to invite his upper-class friends to visit and so widen his acquaintance with his country's intellectual and political elite. "Here it is rather beautiful," he wrote Pinker. ". . . in fact very beautiful, and I am getting better. I was seedy in Bucks, and so black in spirit. I can even hope beyond the war now."[37]

The Lawrences' first visitor at Greatham was Lady Ottoline, who came down for the day on the first of February. Once she became "interested" in one of her artists she tended to concern herself with everything about him, down to the smallest details of how he would live and work. This could easily be jeered at as an eagerness to dominate, and Lawrence later did pillory Ottoline for this trait in *Women in Love;* but there was much real kindness and generosity in her, and in the early stages of becoming her friend it could often seem that one's fairy godmother had suddenly arrived. Lawrence certainly felt warmed by her enthusiasm for his work after his months "in the tomb" at Chesham. On her side, she was captivated by a personal charm that had not yet been obscured by accumulated bitterness, and was always at its most brilliant when inspired by a woman of grace and intelligence:

> It was impossible not to feel expanded and stimulated by the companionship of anyone so alive, so intensely interested in everyone and everything as [Lawrence] was. . . . He who became so vehement in his writings was nearly always—certainly with me—gentle and tender in personal contact. Indeed, I felt when I was with him as if I had really at last found a friend, that I could express myself without reserve, and without fear of being thought silly. He felt the wind and the flowers with the same vividness that I did. He seemed to open up the way into a holy land by his gospel of instinctive development.[38]

From Ottoline's rhapsodic account Frieda is conspicuously absent. Lawrence intrigued Ottoline by being so different; but Frieda bluntly demanded equal status with Ottoline as an aristocrat, and with her husband as an artist. Still, if Frieda was an aristocrat she was nonetheless, in worldly terms, down on her luck, which Ottoline was not; and Frieda did see in her eminent new acquaintance a chance of manipulating Weekley. On 10 February, then, while Lawrence had gone off to Pulborough station to meet Forster, Frieda wrote to Ottoline asking for help in gaining access to her children.[39] Whether Lawrence knew of Frieda's initiative is not known; but by the next day he certainly was active in the plot.

The blatant opportunism of his letter to Ottoline can be condoned, if not excused, by the long misery this problem had inflicted on him and Frieda:

> Do you think you might write to Professor Weekley, and say that you are a friend of Mrs. Lawrence, and that you would like to see him, to ask him if the children might come to tea at your house, and meet their mother there for an hour. . . . I will get Forster to send you the *Romance of Names* [one of Weekley's books] . . . Then you might say to him it had interested you. God grant it may.
>
> I wish you could tell him you are Lady Ottoline—the sister of the Duke of Portland. . . .
>
> I shall trust your cleverness to make a letter to him. Do keep a copy, for me to preserve for ever. And if he fights shy—I don't think he will, somehow, because I think he would like you to know his children—but if he is a mere churl, you will still be the great lady.

Lawrence perhaps realized at this point that he had revealed more about his own social climbing than about Weekley's. Yet he plunged in deeper, whether from sheer embarrassment or in the hope that Ottoline's appetite for flattery was indeed gross:

> It *is* rather splendid that you are a great lady. Don't abrogate one jot or tittle of your high birth: it is too valuable in this commercial-minded, mean world: and it *does* stand as well for what you really are. Because, of what other woman could we ask this?—of what other woman of rank?
>
> I really do honour your birth. Let us do justice to its nobility: it is no mere accident. I would give a great deal to have been born an aristocrat.[40]

Whatever Ottoline may have thought of this, she agreed to approach Weekley: "Rather a difficult Task," she observed to Russell, "but I will do my best."[41] For a further token of good will, she presented Lawrence with an opal. Frieda, in turn, felt that she had gained a genuine confidante and ally:

> It is so terrible to have to hurt a man as I did, because after all he did his best according to his own lights, my first husband I mean and that everybody turned against me is only natural—but it has been so killing and desperate when I felt everybody against me, even Lawrence, who was always quite genuine, but could not bear it, when I was unhappy because of the children—Even they turned against me. . . . —and now I am no longer alone in this battle, you have given me a generous helping hand and I am so grateful to you that I could sing—[42].

But after all this, Weekley held firm against Lady Ottoline's blandishments. Frieda still had no visitation rights, and "the trouble with the children" dragged on.

Murry Derelict

WHILE Lawrence cherished new hopes during his first weeks at Greatham, Murry was sinking down into loneliness and despair. As Katherine became absorbed in planning her affair with Carco, Jack clung more tightly to his friendship with Gordon Campbell. They were both writing novels (though Campbell's was never published), and would spend whole weekends discussing Dostoevsky and working themselves into a peculiar state of intellectual ecstasy. Campbell, however, had another life in the world of affairs and on 23 January—two days after the Lawrences left for Sussex—he rebuffed Jack by failing to turn up for a promised weekend. Jack poured out his disappointment in an unposted letter, full of what Lawrence called his "wriggling self-abuse":

> It's a curious thing for a person like me when he comes to the knowledge that he is absolutely alone. . . . It seems to me now that I asked too much of you—. . . . I can see that I must have loved you as one man seldom loves another. I look back at myself and find that I would have given you anything. I had very little to give, I know, but all that I did give you, or tried to give.
>
> (All the while I am writing, I stop, to see whether I am exaggerating, being sentimental. I don't know. It may be. I can't see these things plainly now.)
>
> Then I feel I am writing to two persons in you: one that loved me, one that will say—what the hell's happened because I couldn't come down for a weekend. . . . don't let the second you answer; it would hurt me, and I find I have an amazing capacity for being hurt. . . . I seem to have served up too much of my naked soul to the world—it has always been trodden on, but this was the most unkindest cut of all.[43]

Lawrence, meanwhile, tried to prop Jack up from a distance. Soon after leaving Chesham he got word of Jack's troubles with Katherine; he asked Kot to "Look after the Murrys a bit—their condition is I think crucial," and told Campbell that "the Murrys . . . seem a bit upset. Please be decent to them, and don't be tiresome."[44] But both Katherine and Campbell were determined to separate themselves from Jack: Katherine because he gave her too little, Campbell because he demanded too much. Katherine was sick and despondent in Bucks after the Lawrences left; she was only waiting for the means to get to Carco at Gray, in the *zone des armées* or restricted area. In early February her brother, Leslie

("Chummie") Beauchamp, arrived from New Zealand with his army detachment, and lent her the money she needed for the trip. She planned for a while to borrow a pillow and a maternity dress from Beatrice Campbell, thinking that it would be easier to get through checkpoints thus attired; fortunately she gave up the scheme when she realized what serious trouble she would be in if found out. But a good deal of the attraction of the escapade for her seemed to stem from its mildly clandestine and disreputable quality. At Ottoline's, the night before she left for France, she tried to get Beatrice Campbell to play the game of imagining "that we are two prostitutes and that this is the first time we have ever been in a decent house."[45]

Katherine left for France on 16 February; Jack, believing she had the right to her freedom, saw her off without complaint. He expected a long separation. The Lawrences had invited him to come down to Greatham, but he could not go there at once because Lady Cynthia Asquith was staying overnight. After a token day of independence at the cottage near Chesham he went down to Sussex. He walked the last four miles to Greatham in the dark, over flooded roads, then promptly collapsed with influenza and had to be nursed by Lawrence for two days. As soon as he began to mend, Lawrence set about "crucifying" him: breaking down his old habits and beliefs in order to turn him toward a new life. He told him Campbell was right to withdraw from their murky probings into the absolute, and that Katherine had left because she felt Jack and Campbell excluded her from their intimacy. For good measure, he wrote Campbell telling him he was "very sound and healthy not to want [Jack's] close love."[46] At the same time, Lawrence condemned Katherine's infidelity and offered Jack an intimacy with himself that could restore part of what he had lost.

Jack's emotional needs were, on the face of it, simple enough. He had been abandoned by the woman he had loved for three years, and by Campbell, his closest friend; now he needed a replacement who would satisfy his craving for love. Lawrence, he felt, could draw on a reserve of "unconscious strength from a social and instinctive solidarity with his 'people,' " the close-knit miners' community he had grown up in; but Jack himself had been uprooted at the age of eleven by winning a scholarship to Christ's Hospital, a public school with a famous literary tradition. Though he wore the school's archaic uniform proudly, it set him apart from his friends in the shabby-genteel suburbs where he was raised, and his cold, rigid parents did nothing to save him from isolation. When grown up, he sought compulsively the "intense exclusive affection" that Lawrence—on the basis of his own experience with stifling mother love—denounced as "deadly."[47]

With Katherine, Jack was diffident and sexually immature. Though she was a woman of wide sexual experience she preferred him to remain uninitiated; she also led him to believe that it was his fault they had not been able to have a child, when the true cause was complications from an abortion she had before they met. Her escapade with Carco might have become an opportunity for her and Jack to rebuild their relationship on sounder foundations. Instead, Jack delivered himself into Lawrence's hands—a transaction in which both were cheated. Jack was eager to enter Rananim because he imagined that there he "should have had no need to fear," surrounded by an ideal family of friends who would salve the hurts inflicted on him by his unloving parents. Lawrence, however, under the influence of his budding friendship with Bertrand Russell, was now full of grandiose plans to make Rananim a revolutionary base from which all of England could eventually be transformed. He was eager for recruits, and not at all deterred by Jack's confession that he was "completely lacking in personal initiative";[48] he argued that when Jack *did* bestir himself, his effort would be "purer"—because he would be rolled along by a power greater than himself, rather than spurred into action by his conscious will as Lawrence was. Nor did Lawrence have any doubt that Jack would come into his own very soon. "He is one of the men of the future," he told Ottoline, "—you will see. He is with me for the Revolution. He is just finishing his novel—his first—*very* good. At present he is my partner—the only man who quite simply is with me—One day he'll be ahead of me."[49] Lawrence did not admit that he was in fact imposing his own will on his friend; he had argued that a "greater, inhuman will" really determined human action, but failed to see that this force scarcely existed in Jack, except as a mere instinct for warmth and self-preservation. Nor did Lawrence yet understand the paradox that he wanted to *recruit* someone to be his *comrade.* The cause of revolution in England should be sustained, he argued, by "the melting-down of personality in surrender to some great and all-inclusive religious purpose";[50] but most of his disciples, and especially Murry, were attracted by his personal charm, for the sake of which they would pretend interest in the "impersonal" cause that Lawrence was promoting. The actual situation, therefore, was the precise opposite of the ideal he preached.

Some three years after Murry's visit to Greatham Lawrence made fictional use of it in the chapter "Low-Water Mark" in *Aaron's Rod*. The account is colored by changes in their relationship during the intervening period, but it raises an issue that was probably starting to preoccupy Lawrence at the time of Jack's first abandonment by Katherine. Jack has recalled that in speaking of Katherine's affair Lawrence "veered about between blaming me and blaming her";[51] when Lawrence took the latter side there was the further implication that both he and Jack had been let down by their women, and should find comfort in their own intimacy as a substitute. In the novel Rawdon Lilly, a surrogate for Lawrence, is temporarily alone, his wife having gone to visit relatives in Norway. He finds his friend Aaron Sisson sick with influenza and insists on taking him home to nurse him, though Aaron has lost his will to live after abandoning his wife and daughters some months before.

The doctor comes, and blames Aaron's condition on a "toxin in the blood" which is poisoning his heart; when Lilly urges him to pull himself together he only becomes "more gloomily withheld, retracting from life. . . . in a sort of semi-stupor of fear, frustrated anger, misery and self-repulsion: a sort of interlocked depression." Because he is constipated the toxin stays in his body and festers and so Lilly must save his friend's life, even against his will, by rubbing him with oil "as mothers do their babies whose bowels don't work":

> Quickly he uncovered the blond lower body of his patient, and began to rub the abdomen with oil, using a slow, rhythmic, circulating motion, a sort of massage. For a long time he rubbed finely and steadily, then went over the whole of the lower body, mindless, as if in a sort of incantation. He rubbed every speck of the man's lower body—the abdomen, the buttocks, the thighs and knees, down to his feet, rubbed it all warm and glowing with camphorated oil, every bit of it, chafing the toes swiftly, till he was almost exhausted.

Having thus given himself up to Lilly's ministrations, Aaron soon recovers. His yielding contrasts with his marriage, where he "withheld the central core of himself" from his wife's "passional soul" and in retaliation she set her will hard against his. Falling into the hands of Lilly, Aaron must either die of the accumulating poisons, or save himself by submitting; he chooses to submit and also, significantly, to enlist in Lilly's crusade against female egoism and against parenthood.

We do not know if Lawrence actually massaged Jack in the way described in *Aaron's Rod* but he was certainly beginning to seek a special intimacy with a male comrade, sealed by some physical ritual. Yet it would have to be distinct from overt homosexuality, which Lawrence still feared and despised. In 1914–15 he feared that his relation with Frieda was hardening into irreconcilable strife; his solution was to try and advance in three sexual realms, more or less simultaneously. One was his cult of woman as priestess or muse, embodied in Lady Ottoline and Lady Cynthia Asquith. Another was his search, in fiction and perhaps in real life, for an ultimate heterosexual experience that would bring together in sex creation and destruction, the angel and the animal, the genital and the anal. The last was his hope of male comradeship as a fulfillment separate from marriage, but complementary to it. He had scarcely begun to explore this possibility with Jack when Katherine, disillusioned with Carco after six days in his company, telegraphed that she was returning to England; Jack at once went up to London to meet her. Lawrence's demand on him for comradeship was to be continually renewed over the next several years, and Jack's ultimate rejection of his alliance created the most deep and lasting bitterness of Lawrence's life.

Ottoline, Russell, and Revolution

LAWRENCE'S Messianic phase—the time when he imagined himself a prophet called to save England, and to build a new Jerusalem on the ruins of the old—lasted nine months, from late January to late October 1915 and was closely linked with his intimacy with Bertrand Russell. Afterward he lived in England only because he was refused permission to leave. Though he was sufficiently discreet to stay out of prison, he was utterly hostile to the state and to the general will of his countrymen. *The Rainbow*, which he completed in March 1915, ended with a vision of the regeneration of his native land; but *Women in Love*, written mainly in the following year, moved away from England to the icy Alps and even, one might say, beyond humanity altogether. It is easy to point out that Lawrence's hopes of social change were grandiose and naive from the start, that he understood nothing about political organization, and that he was always inclined to will the end without willing the means. But Russell, who was far more politically sophisticated, also found himself by 1917 with only two alternatives: acquiescence to government policy, or prison. The war first evoked from Lawrence, as from other men of vision, plans for social improvement on a grand scale; the imperatives of total war brought all such plans to nothing.

As soon as she "discovered" Lawrence Ottoline was eager to share him with Russell, her closest friend. They had become lovers in March 1911, when she was thirty-eight and he thirty-nine. Russell promptly separated from his wife, Alys, but Ottoline did not wish to abandon her husband, nor to give up her comfortable way of life and become a figure of scandal. Philip Morrell knew of their relationship from the beginning, and tolerated it so long as the external form of his marriage to Ottoline was preserved; when she began her affair with Russell she asked Philip to sleep alone.* Though Ottoline and Russell met frequently, usually at his rooms in London, they were never able to live together; when apart they exchanged some four thousand letters, often several in one day.

How much Lawrence knew of Russell before they met is uncertain. Certainly he knew the public figure, the "Philosophic—and Mathematics man—a Fellow of Cambridge University— F. R. S.†—Earl Russell's brother"—and was somewhat intimidated by his reputation.[52] But his letters do not reveal whether or not he knew Russell was Ottoline's lover. One would expect Gilbert Cannan to know, and probably to tell; another possible source was Helen Dudley, who in November 1914 was a guest of the

---

* "Do not let your imagination work," she told Russell, "—Philip and I are devoted friends—*Not more*" (29 March 1911, BRA).

† Fellow of the Royal Society.

Lawrences for two days. She had had an affair with Russell the previous May when he visited her parents in Chicago. Russell planned to marry her, but by the time she arrived in England in August he had changed his mind. He found her less, and Ottoline more, attractice than previously; and he wished to avoid a scandalous divorce that might undermine his criticism of the war. Miss Dudley became importunate; she would arrive uninvited and ring Russell's bell repeatedly while he lurked within. Ottoline, who had known about the affair from the start, relieved him of this embarrassment by arranging for Helen to be introduced around London. She was grateful for Ottoline's interest, not suspecting the connection between her sponsor and the lover who had rejected her. The Lawrences were drawn into this tangled web, worthy of a Henry James novel; they even recommended Miss Dudley to their eligible young friend David Garnett. One suspects, then, that by the time Lawrence became friendly with Ottoline he knew of her relation with Russell. Partial evidence for this is the way he avoids comment on Russell's personality when writing to Ottoline, or vice versa; his reticence is in such contrast to his very free aspersions on Ottoline's other friends that it seems the result of deliberate policy.

That Lawrence and Russell ultimately fell out is hardly surprising; given the popular stereotypes of each, one wonders rather how they ever became friends. In *Women in Love* Lawrence makes Russell ("Sir Joshua Malleson") into a dry, stiff, intellectual marionette—a queer leftover from the Age of Reason. Indeed, this was Russell's public face for most of his life, and only since the publication of his autobiography and of Ronald Clark's *Life,* has this image of him as a "disembodied mind"[53] been replaced by a less one-dimensional view. Russell's nature, we now see, was turbulent and divided against itself. He was in fact tremulously susceptible to extreme passions; one of the benefits Ottoline gave him, he recalls, was to gradually cure him of "the belief that [he] was seething with appalling wickedness which could only be kept under by an iron self-control."[54] He became more relaxed and genial, but still depended on her love to preserve some balance in his character.

When war broke out Russell knew at once that he must oppose it, but his personal stability was more threatened than ever. "I seem to feel all the weight of Europe's passion," he wrote Ottoline at the beginning of August 1914, "as if I were the focus of a burning-glass—all the shouting angry crowds, Emperors at balconies appealing to God, solemn words of duty and sacrifice to cover red murder and rage. It seems as if one must go mad or join the madmen. . . . I am fixing some things in my mind . . . not to hate any one, not to apportion praise or blame, not to let instinct dominate. The force that in the long run makes for peace and all other good things is Reason, the power of thinking against instinct."[55] These were worthy resolutions; but by Novemember, when it had become clear that the war was going to be far bloodier than any previous conflict, Russell was forced to take a view of human nature much closer to Lawrence's:

> It is strange how many illusions have been shattered by this war; I find myself growing cynical, full of pitiless insight into the hidden springs of beliefs and faiths and hopes, more and more impressed by the biological instinctiveness of man. Thought seems a mere bubble—no part of the stream, but a surface thing thrown up by the stream and showing its direction. Underneath I still have some faith in human possibilities, but it is slight—I feel very much as if I had been dropped from another planet into an alien race.[56]

This was written a week before the publication of *The Prussian Officer* which, as we have seen, Russell read with enthusiasm and recommended to Ottoline. He had organized a branch of the Union of Democratic Control, the leading antiwar organization, at Cambridge;* but this was not an adequate outlet for his feelings. On the one hand he felt despair, helplessness, and a sense that London itself was unreal; against this was his love for Ottoline, which had gained new strength in reaction from a tepid affair he had with his secretary, Irene Cooper-Willis:

> I can't tell you the depth and wildness and vastness of my love to you. . . . You give what the greatest music yearns for, what made the Sunflower be weary of time, what makes one's life a striving and straining and struggling after Heaven—all that, you gave last night. . . . I must and will live for you . . . I *cannot* do anything else. You hold me by a power that is fate.[57]

Russell, then, was in a crisis at the time he met Lawrence: the war had shattered his principles, his private life was turbulent, his emotions scattered and unfulfilled. He was susceptible, as often happened in his life, to the influence of someone whose personality seemed to him more creative, natural, and unified than his

---

* The U.D.C. was a relatively mild, liberal organization that called for a speedy end to the war by open diplomacy; later in the war Russell switched his allegiance to the more radical No-Conscription Fellowship.

own. Wittgenstein, his most brilliant student, had played such a role before the war but he was now in the Austrian army; for a time, Russell seemed to find in Lawrence his successor. He placed all the more weight on such attachments because of his lack of close family ties. At forty-three he had neither enjoyed parental love—both his parents were dead by the time he was four—nor become a parent himself, though he longed for children; and he was in love with a woman he could not hope to marry. When Lawrence offered a key to these emotional problems, and help in opposing the war also, Russell became infatuated with him: not sexually, to be sure, but with all the rest of his being.

Russell accompanied Ottoline on her second visit to Greatham on 6 February. Lawrence expounded his hopes for Rananim but what had previously been an escape from England now became a means for transforming it. His visitors were responsible for the change, he told Kot: ". . . they say, the island [of Rananim] shall be England, that we shall start our new community in the midst of the old one, as a seed falls among the roots of the parent."[58] Nonetheless, the main impetus seems to have come from Lawrence as he exulted in "a new birth of life" after the physical and spiritual agonies of Chesham, though Ottoline was eager to answer such a call. Two years previously she and Philip had bought Garsington Manor, a charming Tudor country house near Oxford, because they had been told by doctors that their daughter, Julian, must live in the country. They were now preparing to take possession in May, giving up their house in Bloomsbury. Garsington was conceived as an intimate and leisured residential salon for England's best talents. Though it would be much derided by the recipients of its hospitality, Garsington did in fact succeed in these aims better than any English country house before or since; and the credit was Ottoline's. She made a place where one might find frolicking together on the lawn Mark Gertler, a Jew from the East End, Aldous Huxley, scion of one of the great intellectual families, and Dorothy Brett, daughter of Viscount Esher; or where the flagitious pacifist Bertrand Russell might emerge naked from the pond to encounter the prime minister, out for a stroll.* True, it often seemed more a carnival than a community, for not even Ottoline's powerful will could yoke her

---

* ABR II, 15; in earlier years Asquith had sought Ottoline's favors, and he remained a regular visitor to her house even though it was the headquarters of intellectual opposition to his war policies.

motley guests to a common purpose. But when Lawrence first proposed to her that Garsington should be the nucleus of a new way of life she could not yet know just how fractious and unruly her guests would prove to be.

For Ottoline, Lawrence conjured up the vision of a mystical community founded on a contemptuous rejection of the existing order:

> This present community consists, as far as it is a framed thing, in a myriad contrivances for preventing us from being let down by the meanness in ourselves or in our neighbours. But it is like a motor car that is so encumbered with non-skid, non-puncture, non-burst, non-this and non-that contrivances, that it simply can't go any more. I hold this the most sacred duty—the gathering together of a number of people who shall so agree to live by the *best* they know, that they shall be *free* to live by the best they know. . . . Every strong soul must put off its connection with this society, its vanity and chiefly its fear, and go naked with its fellows, weaponless, armourless, without shield or spear, but only with naked hands and open eyes. . . .
>
> It is communism based, not on poverty but on riches, not on humility but on pride, not on sacrifice but upon complete fulfilment in the flesh of all strong desire, not in Heaven but on earth. We will be the Sons of God who walk here on earth, not bent on getting and having, because we know we inherit all things. We will be aristocrats, and as wise as the serpent in dealing with the mob. For the mob shall not crush us nor starve us nor cry us to death. We will deal cunningly with the mob, the greedy soul, we will gradually bring it to subjection.[59]

This plan of a separate life for the happy few had been Lawrence's line from the beginning of his friendship with Ottoline. It grew naturally from his early alienation from the working class, his decision to live as an artist at the fringe of society, and his contempt at seeing the masses of Europe rush pell-mell into war. One is amazed, therefore, to encounter in Lawrence's first letter to Russell, on 12 February, an impassioned call for socialism in England:

> There must be a revolution in the state. It shall begin by the nationalising of all industries and means of communication, and of the land—in one fell blow. Then a man shall have his wages whether he is sick or well or old—if anything prevents his working, he shall have his wages just the same. So we shall not live in fear of the wolf—no man amongst us, and no woman, shall have any fear of the wolf at the door, for all wolves are dead. . . .
>
> Something like this must be done. It is no use saying a man's soul should be free, if his boots hurt him so much he can't walk. All our ideals are cant and hypocrisy till we have burst the fetters of this money.[60]

This is the prelude to seventeen pages of analysis of the relation between individual fulfillment—still Lawrence's ultimate concern—and the structures of collective life. It is a remarkable anticipation of positions later developed on the "Freudian left" by Wilhelm Reich and his successors. How, Lawrence asks, can vital spontaneity be preserved, how can man be a "good animal," when he is a slave of the great industrial mechanism? Having seen the degradation of his father's nature during his long years in the pit—a downward spiral that is movingly described in *Sons and Lovers*—Lawrence envisioned no way of palliating or evading such a decline. Man must break the machine, or it will break him:

> There comes a point when the shell, the form of life, is a prison to the life. Then the life must either concentrate on breaking the shell, or it must turn round, turn in upon itself, and try infinite variations of a known reaction upon itself. . . .
> But we shall smash the frame. The land, the industries, the means of communication and the public amusements shall all be nationalised. . . .
> Then, and then only, shall we be able to *begin* living.[61]

This is no less than a sudden and complete change of heart by Lawrence on the social question. When he wrote in January to his socialist friend Willie Hopkin he gave no indication of a political rapprochement and in the letter to Ottoline of 1 February he attacked the idea of social security, for reasons he had already stated in the *Study of Thomas Hardy*:

> This is what we have made of Christ's Commandment: "Thou shalt love thy neighbour as thyself"—a mirror for the tears of self-pity. How do we love our neighbour? By taking to heart his poverty, his small wage, and the attendant evils thereof. . . . [his] labouring in the grip of an unjust system of capitalism. Let me look at him, let my heart be wrung, let me give myself to his service. . . . So I lie to myself and to him. For I do not care about him and his poverty: I care about my own unsatisfied soul.[62]

What moved Lawrence to address Russell in a spirit so opposite to his previous convictions? Forster's visit on 10 to 12 February can hardly have contributed: he was gentle and humanitarian, but a firm opponent of collectivism. Lawrence's own financial difficulties probably had something to do with his change of views: he had written Pinker on 7 February, lamenting that he had almost no money left. None of his friends seemed willing to back Rananim with hard cash, and Methuen's coldness toward *The Rainbow* had blighted his future prospects. It was all the more irritating that he should be so poor just when he was being favorably received by Ottoline and Russell, with all the possibilities that connection opened up. Perhaps he felt it was really time for him to confront the economic issue and kill "the wolf at the door" once and for all; and, by a characteristic feat of mental gymnastics, he assumed that what had become a pressing concern for him would be equally pressing to everyone else. Alternatively his turn toward socialism may have been a temporary acceptance of the role that people like Russell would be inclined to see him in: as a genius whose vitality depended on his working-class roots.

Whatever his reasons, Lawrence's mood was one of loving concern toward his fellow men—for almost the last time in his life. "It was so beautiful on the downs today," he told Ottoline, "with the sea so bright on one hand, and the downs so fresh, and the floods so blue on the other hand, away below, washing at the little villages. I don't know why, but my heart was so sad, almost to break. A little train ran through the floods, and steamed on so valiant into the gap. And I seemed to feel all humanity, brave and splendid, like the train, and so blind, and so utterly unconscious of where they are going or of what they are doing."[63] Here the blindness of the masses is felt by Lawrence as pathetic; but the events of 1915 would give their blindness a more sinister meaning. Lawrence would come to despise humanity for its mindless self-destruction, and to fear that it would destroy him too if he tried to turn it aside from its Gadarene descent.

One cause of disillusionment quickly declared itself in Russell's tepid response to his socialist manifesto. Probably Lawrence had overestimated Russell's radicalism; even under the stress of war he had not yet moved far away from his liberal beliefs, and when invited to join the Independent Labour Party he refused, saying "I am not a socialist, though I think I might call myself a syndicalist." Then, as he explained to Ottoline, he was dismayed by Lawrence's callowness: "I have had a long, long letter from Lawrence—saying it is no good to do *anything* till we get Socialism—and thinking (as the young do) that because *he* sees the desirability of Socialism it can be got by a few years' strenuous work. I feel his optimism difficult to cope with—I can't share it and don't want to discourage it. He is extraordinarily young."[64] Lawrence soon detected that he was being humored, and in some degree patronized. Once a false note had been struck, their relationship became problematic, and though Lawrence continued for a while to defer to Russell, he built up an increasing charge of resentment at his refusal to declare himself a wholehearted convert. Lawrence certainly was impressed by the intellectual and social power of Russell and Ottoline; but his instinct was to hammer at them as hard as he could, just as he did with his less eminent friends. This created a veiled tension in the early stages of their acquaintance, then progressed to open attacks when Lawrence no longer cared to conceal his true feelings.

During February, however, he was still making a conscious effort to "manage" Ottoline and Russell, allotting them different roles in his agenda for 1915. Ottoline was to provide for himself and Frieda a more secure base than Greatham, where they remained only on sufferance as long-term guests. On her first visit Ottoline offered to renovate some "monkish buildings" at Garsington into a future home for the Lawrences. At first all went smoothly, with the Lawrences "most excited thinking of the cottage." "I don't want actually to own it," he told Ottoline, "—ownership always makes me sad, there is something so limited and jealous in it—but I want to call it mine." [65] As a compromise, it was agreed that the Lawrences would pay an annual rent of 6 or 10 percent of the cost of renovations—which were first estimated at two hundred pounds. For weeks the planning continued, though with some differences of opinion: Ottoline wanted the accommodation to be charming and dramatic whereas the Lawrences were more concerned that it be practical. But the main responsibility lay with Ottoline, since she was to retain ownership; later Lawrence was to give a different twist to the situation in chapter 12 of *Women in Love,* where Hermione's interest in the furnishing of Birkin's rooms is made to seem a gratuitous intrusion.

Before his disillusion with Ottoline, however, Lawrence saw her move to Garsington as an opportunity to create a sacred precinct of the "new life," with herself as it oracle:

> Why don't you have the pride of your own intrinsic self? Why must you tamper with the idea of being an ordinary physical woman—wife, mother, mistress. Primarily, you are none of these things. Primarily, you belong to a special type, a special race of women: like Cassandra in Greece, and some of the great woman saints. They were the great *media* of truth, of the deepest truth. . . . It is necessary for this great type to reassert itself on the face of the earth. It is not the *salon* lady and the blue stocking—it is not the critic and judge, but the priestess, the medium, the prophetess. [66]

This was perhaps a backhanded compliment, implying that Ottoline had failed in her relations with Philip; with her daughter, Julian; and with Russell. But it suited Lawrence to posit two great opposed types of femininity, the sacred Diana and the profane Aphrodite. He thus provided separate yet complementary roles for the two women with whom he wanted to be intimate, Ottoline and Frieda. Unfortunately for him, neither woman was content to remain in her allotted sphere, each choosing rather to follow her own possessive and combative instincts.

While Ottoline cultivated her inner gift of prophecy, Russell was to step forward as Lawrence's comrade in the external struggle. Together they would diagnose the condition of England, make the right intellectual alliances, then move forward to open political agitation. Unfortunately, when Lawrence gave his first blast of the trumpet—the letter on socialism—Russell proved reluctant to sally forth. Nonetheless, he still admired Lawrence enough to invite him to Cambridge to meet some of the more progressive dons, and perhaps rouse some of them to revolutionary action. Privately, Russell may have cherished a different hope: that Lawrence would recognize his own limitations through contact with some of the finer university intellects, and scale down his plans accordingly. He did not yet know Lawrence well enough to realize how unlikely such an outcome was. Even before the visit, which was set for 6 to 8 of March, Lawrence sent Russell a reaffirmation of his letter on socialism, as a kind of agenda for discussion with the fellows of Trinity College:

> I have only to stick to my vision of a life when men are freer from the immediate material things, where they need never be as they are now on the defence against each other, largely because of the struggle for existence, which is a real thing, even to those who need not make the struggle. So a vision of a better life must include a revolution of society. And one must fulfil one's vision as much as possible. And the drama shall be between individual men and women, not between nations and classes.[67]

Lawrence told Russell he had written a book about all this—the *Study of Thomas Hardy,* though here he calls it "Le Gai Savaire"[68]— which he now wanted to rewrite "and publish it in pamphlets, weekly or fortnightly, and to start a campaign for this freer life." But he was not able to put this plan into effect until the autumn, by which time he was preaching a different message.

(73)

As Lawrence prepared to launch his revolutionary campaign at Cambridge he also tried to recruit some of his older friends, like Gordon Campbell:

> You see we are no longer satisfied to be individual and lyrical—we are growing out of that stage. A man must now needs know himself as his whole people, he must live as the centre and heart of all humanity, if he is to be free. It is no use hating a people or a race or humanity in mass. Because each of us is in himself humanity. . . . I know that *I* am the English nation—that *I* am the European race—that this which exists ostensibly as the English nation is a falsity, mere cardboard. L'Etat c'est moi. It is a great saying, and should be true of every man.

On the face of it, Lawrence recognized, this might look like megalomania; but he sought to make himself a medium for the aspirations of humanity, rather than to tyrannize over them. It was the old idea of the poet as unacknowledged legislator of mankind, now translated into a metaphor of organic unity between poet and people:

> You see it really means something . . . this feeling that one is not only a little individual living a little individual life, but that one is in oneself the whole of mankind, and one's fate is the fate of the whole of mankind, and one's charge is the charge of the whole of mankind. Not *me*—the little, vain, personal D. H. Lawrence—but that unnameable me which is not vain nor personal, but strong, and glad, and ultimately sure, but so blind, so groping, so tongue-tied, so staggering. You see I *know* that if I could write the finest lyrical poetry or prose that ever was written, if I could be put on the pinnacle of immortality, I wouldn't. I would rather struggle clumsily to put into art the new Great Law of God and Mankind—not the empirical discovery of the individual—but the utterance of the great racial or human consciousness, a little of which is in me. And if I botch out a little of this utterance, so that other people are made alert and active, I don't care whether I am great or small, or rich or poor, or remembered or forgotten.[69]

The question remained, however, whether mankind would welcome Lawrence's word as the voice of "the whole," or turn a deaf ear to it. For Lawrence was not one who would accept the latter verdict with equanimity.

The Rainbow Completed

ALL THROUGH the last part of his stay at Chesham and the first weeks at Greatham Lawrence was rewriting "The Wedding Ring," whose title he had now definitely changed to *The Rainbow.* In his outer life he was intensely active: moving house, dealing with Jack's crisis, and becoming intimate with three striking personalities—Ottoline, Forster, and Russell. Yet he wrote continuously, with astounding speed and fertility of invention. Starting in late November, he had done three hundred pages in longhand by 7 January; at that point he decided the novel was too "unwieldly," and had better be split into two volumes. *The Rainbow* would end with Ursula's separation from Skrebensky, leaving her future uncertain; her relation with Birkin would be the subject of the second volume, eventually to be called *Women in Love.* By 1 February Lawrence had completed 450 pages, and on the twenty-fourth he told Pinker he was "very, very near the end"; as he wrote, Viola Meynell was typing out the whole manuscript from the beginning. On 2 March he exultantly sent her the last installment, making 707 pages in all: "I have finished my *Rainbow,* bended it and set it firm. Now off and away to find the pots of gold at its feet." [70]

The gold, however, still depended on Methuen's willingness to reconsider their rejection of the earlier version of the novel. On 1 February Lawrence had assured Pinker that "there shall be no very flagrant love-passages in it (at least to my thinking)." [71] But he was then just starting to describe Ursula's affair with Skrebensky, and it was between that point and the final revision of the manuscript in May that Lawrence wrote most of the passages that would cause trouble after publication. By 24 February he was already becoming more anxious. "Do you think Methuen is ready to back up this novel of mine? he asked Pinker, "He must make some fight for it. It is worth it, and he must do it. It will never be popular. But he can make it known what it is, and prevent the mean little fry from pulling it down." [72] Lawrence now had come to expect difficulties with the publisher before each of his books appeared, and hostility from most of the critics afterward; but he did not realize how much worse the reception of his works could become.

The subject matter of *The Rainbow* was still essentially prewar, drawn from Lawrence's youth in the Midlands and from Frieda's girlhood. We cannot have full knowledge of the changes made from "The Wedding Ring" and earlier drafts, because only fragments of those manuscripts have survived. But we know that in *The Rainbow* Lawrence made a major subtraction from "The Wedding Ring," the last section of about eighty pages relating to Birkin, and two major additions: he gave more prominence to the Christian and cosmic system of imagery that he had described in the *Study of Thomas Hardy,* and he attributed to Ursula at the end of the novel the revolutionary visions that preoccupied him in February 1915.[73] This new ending has a special relevance to the facts of Lawrence's life at the time.

The central theme of *The Rainbow* is the development from a rural, organic and largely unconscious community to the emancipated and consciously modern individualism of Ursula. So the breakdown of Ursula's relation with Skrebensky makes a natural climax to the conflict between two modes of being in the novel: Skrebensky aspires to be "just a brick in the whole great social fabric," whereas Ursula feels that "to be oneself was a supreme, gleaming triumph of infinity." Ursula's vision of a *social* transformation at the very end of the book is therefore inconsistent with what has preceded it—one might say that she has been converted to her author's way of thinking. The concluding panorama of a regenerated England under the sign of the rainbow derives from Lawrence's sudden shift into a mood of concern for the whole of humanity early in 1915—his announcement to Campbell, for example, that "we are no longer satisfied to be individual and lyrical." I quoted earlier his image of blind humanity, the train in the floods; he actually transfers this scene almost verbatim into Ursula's consciousness.[74] The grafting is skillfully done, and it creates a fervid set piece with which to conclude (always a difficult task for Lawrence); but it cuts across the main flow of the novel up to that point. Furthermore, it would lead to a fundamental disunity in the "Brangwensaga" that Lawrence had conceived on such a massive scale. By the time he began writing *Women In Love* his social outlook had again reversed itself, from the vision of a regenerated community to the savage misanthropy proclaimed by Birkin, and from the historicism of the first novel to the eschatology of the second. Instead of making a single great integrated work of fiction, Lawrence bitterly rejects in the sequel to *The Rainbow* what had previously nourished his imagination. But by then the course of his life seemed to leave him no alternative.

Lawrence at Trinity

RUSSELL'S POSITION at Trinity College was curiously marginal: as a F. R. S. and coauthor of the *Principia Mathematica* he was one of its intellectual stars, but he held only a five-year appointment as lecturer and was thus excluded from the governing body of fellows. His fringe status came partly by his own choosing, for though he loved the purity of mathematical speculation he considered himself a more vital and worldly man than most of the dons, and was often irritated by their cloistered conservatism. Yet Trinity held at that time a remarkable band of creative thinkers. The older fellows included Alfred North Whitehead, Russell's friend and collaborator on the *Principia;* A. E. Housman; and Sir James Frazer, whose anthropological classics had considerably influenced Lawrence. But Russell especially wanted Lawrence to meet some fellows who were closer to him in age, and more open to new ideas: the philosopher G. E. Moore, the mathematician G. H. Hardy, and the young economist J. M. Keynes (of King's College). These were certainly three of the most brilliant and enlightened intellects that the university world could offer; though Lawrence, bearing his diploma from Nottingham University College as a chip on his shoulder, was not inclined to be deferential. He would probably have been even more wary had he known that all three men, and his host too, were "Apostles"—members of a secret club called "The Society" to which only a handful of Cambridge undergraduates were added each year, remaining bound to it thereafter for life (Forster also belonged, as did Lytton Strachey and Leonard Woolf).

The predominant influence in "The Society" in recent years had been G. E. Moore, who had created around himself a cult atmosphere of taciturnity, celibacy, emotional reticence, unworldliness, and purity of intellect. Moore was famous for deflating enthusiasts by asking them "What exactly do you mean by that?" His great passions were music and subtle issues of philosophy; on contemporary questions his stance is well conveyed by Lytton Strachey's anecdote:

> When I last saw [Moore] I asked him whether the war had made any difference to him. He paused for thought, and then said—"None. Why should it?" I asked whether he wasn't horrified by it—at any rate at the beginning. But no; he had never felt anything about it at all.[75]

Moore's ethical philosophy, which had great appeal for a generation in revolt against the strenuous pieties of their Victorian forebears, was summed up in the famous sentence from *Principia Ethica:* "By far the most valuable things, which we know or can imagine, are certain states of consciousness, which may be roughly described as the pleasures of human intercourse and the enjoyment of beautiful objects."

When Lawrence dined in the hall of Trinity on 6 March he was seated next to Moore—who found nothing to say to him; nor, given the natures of the two men, can we imagine that Lawrence had anything to say to Moore. With Hardy things went better; they had a lively conversation, and Russell later told Ottoline that "Hardy was *immensely* impressed by him—after seeing him, he went round to Winstanley [another Fellow] to tell him everybody here was utterly trivial, and at last he had met a real man."[76] Lawrence reciprocated by inviting Hardy to Greatham, but the initiative was never followed up. Still, the failure with Moore was more typical of Trinity's response to Lawrence, and his to Trinity: "He can't stand the lack of vitality and force in the dons," Russell noted sadly.[77] With Keynes, however, matters were more complicated. He was only three years older than Lawrence, ambitious, worldly, and with a prodigious talent for financial analysis. No one was better equipped than he to direct the economic revolution that Lawrence was calling for—except that he was dedicated to upholding the social frame rather than smashing it. In four years he would publish *The Economic Consequences of the Peace,* a plea for leniency toward Germany; he argued that if the Allies extorted enormous reparations they would inflict such damage on the German social order that the consequences would be highly destructive and unpredictable (as proved to be the case). Keynes was never a socialist, but rather the chief intellectual architect of the "mixed economy" or "welfare capitalism" that now prevails in all advanced Western societies. When Lawrence met him he was on the verge of scandalizing his friends in the Bloomsbury group—who all opposed the war—by entering government service; at the Treasury he would make a major contribution to Allied victory through his innovative economic policies.

Keynes's social theories were therefore quite inconsistent with radical changes in English life, but they scarcely mattered in comparison with something about his personal presence that caused Lawrence to tell David Garnett: ". . . when I saw Keynes that morning in Cambridge it was one of the crises of my life. It sent me mad with misery and hostility and rage."[78] The root of this outburst was Keynes's homosexuality. Lawrence had come to Cambridge to advance a philosophy whose cardinal tenet was that "the great living experience for every man is his adventure into the woman. . . . [he] embraces in the woman all that is not himself, and from that one resultant, from that embrace, comes every new action."[79] But the emotional atmosphere he encountered at Cambridge ranged from the celibate to the frankly homoerotic. Moore married late, and Hardy never; Moore's ethics, legitimately or not, were held by his disciples to be consistent with homosexuality. Another leading figure at Cambridge, included on Russell's list of "contacts" for Lawrence, was the political scientist Goldsworthy Lowes Dickinson, who in 1915 was already planning a postwar league of nations. Dickinson's tender feelings were mainly directed toward young men; following Plato, he held that love between persons of the same sex was a higher, because more disinterested, relationship than marriage. He disliked having female students at his lectures, remarking, with what passed for wit in donnish circles, that he could never tell them apart because they all resembled cows.[80]

On Sunday Russell gave a breakfast party for Lawrence to follow up the acquaintance he had made with Keynes the night before. Keynes walked over from his rooms at King's without dressing, which gave an immediate shock to Lawrence's sense of propriety: "Lawrence had rather liked him before," Russell told Ottoline, "—but seeing him this morning at 11 in pyjamas, just awake, he felt him corrupt and unclean. Lawrence has quick sensitive impressions which I don't understand, tho' they would seem quite natural to you. They are marvellous."[81] Russell must have told Lawrence about Keynes's homosexuality, and also perhaps about his affair with Duncan Grant; it would seem that mere proximity to Keynes *en déshabille* made Lawrence acutely uncomfortable, since, Keynes has recalled, "he was morose from the outset and said very little, apart from indefinite expressions of irritable dissent." Nonetheless, the three men agreed to meet for dinner—where Lawrence, now that Keynes was dressed, was at least willing to talk:

> We had an interesting but rather dreadful evening [Russell reported]. Keynes was hard, intellectual, insincere—using intellect to hide the torment and discord in his soul. We pressed him hard about his purpose in life—he spoke as tho' he only wanted a succession of agreeable moments, which of course is not really true. Lawrence likes him but can't get on with him; I get on with him, but dislike him. Lawrence has the same feeling against sodomy as I have; you had nearly made me believe there is no great harm in it, but I have reverted; and all the examples I know confirm me in thinking it sterilizing.[82]

In his memoir of the occasion Keynes sums up these conversations by observing that "Cambridge rationalism and cynicism, then at their height, were, of course, repulsive to [Lawrence]."[83] When one adds to this Cambridge's prevailing homoeroticism, one sees that Lawrence had so little in common with even the more enlightened dons that his hope of enlisting their political support was bound to be disappointed.

Yet the visit had not been altogether a failure. Russell, far from sharing his colleagues' unresponsiveness to Lawrence, became much closer to him. He was himself moving toward a break with the university, as the younger fellows joined up and left the elderly jingoes in uncontested control: "These fussy bloodthirsty old men are so unutterably contemptible," he told Ottoline. ". . . my soul is full of black horror and impotent hate." Whatever Lawrence's failings as a thinker, he seemed to Russell to have a true prophetic fire, vastly more exciting than the desiccated intellectualism of the academy:

> Lawrence is gone, disgusted with Cambridge, but not with me I think. I felt that we got on *very* well with each other, and made real progress towards intimacy. His intuitive perceptiveness is *wonderful*—it leaves me gasping in admiration. . . .
>
> Lawrence is wonderfully lovable. The mainspring of his life is love—the universal mystical love—which inspires even his most vehement and pas-

sionate hate. It is odd that his *thinking* is coloured by self—he imagines men
more like him than they are. . . .

I love him more and more.[84]

Descent into Darkness

THE "universal mystical love" that Russell so admired in
Lawrence disappeared in March, as he began another descent
into the underworld like that of the winter months at Chesham.
For the next two years Lawrence would repeat the emotional cycle
that had started at his auspicious return to England the previous
summer. A period of elation and social involvement would alternate with one of unhappiness and withdrawal, but each swing of
the pendulum seemed to produce a further depletion of his re-
serves, so that his depressions became progressively deeper; his
health declined, he had fewer moments of simple cheerfulness,
and he quarreled more frequently and bitterly with his friends.
By summer 1917 this exhaustive process was complete, and he
then passed through the most barren period of his life, until he
was revived by moving to new surroundings in the 1920s.

The March 1915 depression was undoubtedly linked with his
chronic ill health. He and Frieda had both been sick with influenza before the Cambridge visit. In the previous months he had
worked "frightfully hard" on *The Rainbow,* his longest novel, and
during March he was still making extensive revisions on the typed
copy. At the beginning of April he was forced to stay in bed for
several days: "My old cold that I have had so long never really gets
better," he told Ottoline, "and occasionally comes full tilt back
again. It is a sort of cold in the stomach: it feels like a sore throat
in the middle of one's belly—very horrid and tiring and irritating."[85] When he got up, feeling "very limp and weed-like," he
sent his friend Dr. Eder a list of all his symptoms, hoping to be
cured once and for all. Eder sent him "various concoctions" that
gave some temporary relief, though there was no cure, of course,
for the tuberculosis that lay at the root of Lawrence's problems.

In addition to ill health and fatigue, the visit to Cambridge left Lawrence "very black and down." Not only had he failed to find political allies, he had sensed a positive evil in the place with "its smell of rottenness, marsh-stagnancy." Nor did he exempt Russell from his strictures; at Cambridge he had accused him of being a "fake" in claiming to do philosophy for the love of humanity, and soon after he extended the indictment to Russell's work against the war:

> Do you still speak at the W. D. C. of the nations kissing each other, when your soul prowls the frontier all the time most jealously, to defend what it has and to seize what it can. It makes me laugh when you admit it. But we are all like that. Only, let us seize and defend that which is worth having, and which we want.[86]

This criticism of Russell's motives would be renewed later, in more violent terms; but for now Lawrence was preoccupied with his own dismal plight:

> I am struggling in the dark—very deep in the dark—and cut off from everybody and everything. . . . sometimes I am afraid of the terrible things that are real, in the darkness, and of the entire unreality of these things I see. It becomes like a madness at last, to know one is all the time walking in a pale assembly of an unreal world—this house, this furniture, the sky and the earth—whilst oneself is all the while a piece of darkness pulsating in shocks, and the shocks and the darkness are real. The whole universe of darkness and dark passions . . . the subterranean black universe of the things which have not yet had being—has conquered me for now, and I can't escape.[87]

This dark world first seems a chaos of random passions; but as Lawrence describes it further we see that it contains his characteristic polarities of life and death, creation and dissolution. He now begins a period of reaction against his fellow men, in which he repeatedly discovers a tangle of evil impulses beneath an outer facade of amiability and altruism:

> It is no good now, thinking that to understand a man from his own point of view is to be happy about him. I can imagine the mind of a rat, as it slithers along in the dark, pointing its sharp nose. But I can never feel happy about it, I must always want to kill it. It contains a principle of evil. There *is* a principle of evil. Let us acknowledge it once and for all. I saw it so plainly in Keynes at Cambridge, it made me sick. I am sick with the knowledge of the prevalence of evil, as if it were some insidious disease.[88]

Keynes's features were indeed somewhat ratlike, apart from his other repellent traits. But Lawrence was disgusted with all his fellowmen: those who supported the war were possessed by the will to destroy, those who opposed it had the same will but refused to admit it. Worst of all were those hypocrites who clung to the remnants of Christian tradition:

> I have been reading Dostoievsky's *Idiot*. I don't like Dostoievsky. He is again like the rat, slithering along in hate, in the shadows, and, in order to belong to the light, professing love, all love. But his nose is sharp with hate, his running is shadowy and rat-like, he is a will fixed and gripped like a trap. He is not nice.[89]

Lawrence when young had considered Tolstoy far superior to Dostoevsky, but at Greatham he made a grudging reversal of the verdict. Despite his opposition to Dostoevsky, Lawrence could still recognize in the Russian an idiom and a concept of human nature that were much closer to his own practice than the civility of the traditional English novel; he may also have identified with him as a fellow consumptive, though he does not say so. After finishing *The Idiot* in early April he went on to Dostoevsky's *Letters:*

> What an amazing person he was—a pure introvert, a purely disintegrating will—there was not a grain of the passion of love within him—all the passion of hate, of evil. Yet a great man. It has become, I think, now, a supreme wickedness to set up a Christ worship as Dostoievsky did: it is the outcome of an evil will, disguising itself in terms of love.[90]

Lawrence includes in "Christ worship" both Dostoevsky's deference to the tsar and the orthodox church, and the "humanitarianism" of the progressives; insofar as both sides try to deny man's innate sensuality and aggression, both are liars.

When Russell came down to stay at Greatham again for two nights, at the beginning of April, Lawrence sent a cheerful account of the visit to Ottoline: "We have had a good time. . . . really been people living together. . . . I know [he] is with me, really, now." But, privately, Russell was foreseeing "awful fights" with him.[91] There were troubles brewing for Ottoline too: she had been sequestered for some time with ill health and depression, which aroused dark suspicions in Lawrence. "He thought if you went mad you would be fierce—" Russell told Ottoline, "I don't think so, I think you would be just as gentle as you are now."[92]

Lawrence was clearly winding up for an attack on the dark under-side of Ottoline's personality, while Russell apparently approved of his methods except in the case of this particular target:

> Lawrence hasn't at all made me want to bang you about [Ottoline]—quite the opposite. I think Wittgenstein did, but he had not the fund of gentleness and universal love that Lawrence has underneath. His view of human nature is very congenial to me, only I don't think *everybody* is a "Tyger, Tyger," as he does.[93]

Meanwhile Lawrence's own skirmish with madness was moving toward some resolution. On 8 April, after three days of illness, he told Ottoline he was tired of living at Greatham: it was damp, and there were too many casual visitors to the colony. He began to rewrite his philosophy, this time incorporating his inner up-heavals since the Cambridge visit:

> I have had a great struggle with the Powers of Darkness lately. I think I have just got the better of them again. Don't tell me there is no Devil; there is a Prince of Darkness. Sometimes I wish I could let go and be really wicked—kill and murder—but kill chiefly. I do want to kill. But I want to select whom I shall kill. Then I shall enjoy it. The war is no good. It is this black desire I have become conscious of. We cant so much about goodness—it is canting. Tell Russell he does the same—let him recognize the powerful malignant will in him. This is the very worst wickedness, that we refuse to acknowledge the pas-sionate evil that is in us. This makes us secret and rotten.[94]

The second version of Lawrence's philosophy was to be called "Morgenrot"*—the redness of dawn—and he worked at it sporad-ically over the next three months: "I will not tell them, the peo-ple, this time that they are angels in disguise," he told Kot. "Curse them, I will tell them they are dogs and swine, bloodsuckers."[95] As parts of it were completed he sent them also to Ottoline, Russell, and Forster, asking them not to dismiss it too quickly; Russell nonetheless complained that he couldn't "make head or tail" of it.[96] Unfortunately, the manuscript has not survived, so we have no specific knowledge of its contents. But clearly its main concern was Lawrence's discovery in March of the "principle of evil," which led him to reconsider both the viewpoint of the *Study of Thomas Hardy* and his revolutionary enthusiasm of February. The *Study* argued for a benevolent principle of growth and freedom in

---

* Presumably borrowed from Nietzsche's work of the same title.

nature; Lawrence's socialistic views were grounded on an analogous faith in the unconscious aspirations of humanity. His key metaphor was of vital force breaking through a dead shell of restraint; but, he now realized, would it not be more accurate to represent the conflict as between two equally strong and active forces? And should not these forces be given a moral rather than a vegetative nature—as good and evil, God and the Devil? H. N. Brailsford's book on Shelley gave him a formula that fit the case: "Shelley believed in the principle of evil, coeval with the principle of good. That is right."[97]

It is tempting to explain Lawrence's obsession with murder and evil as the response of an oversensitive mind to his personal misfortunes and the general bitterness of the war. But his conversion to this way of thinking was complete within a month of his visit to Cambridge, at a time when his situation was, on the surface at least, better than it had been at any time since the war began. He had pushed *The Rainbow* through to its triumphant conclusion, and could count on receiving the remaining two hundred pounds of his advance, perhaps more if the book succeeded. Relations with Ottoline and Russell were still harmonious, and he expected the war to be over by autumn. His reaction against the benevolent optimism he had proclaimed in February must be attributed to some drastic shift in his inner disposition, rather than to any adequate external cause—though the encounter with Keynes acted as a trigger. Over the next three years he would be confirmed in his misanthropy by many bitter shocks, but they served only to drive him further along a road that he had already chosen.

Ottoline, apparently disturbed by Lawrence's desire for a few therapeutic murders, urged on him her own conviction that "love is all." He agreed, but warned her that much rottenness had to be destroyed before love could prevail:

> If I have toothache I don't depend on hope nor faith nor love, but on surgery. And surgery is pure hate of the defect in the loved thing. And it is surgery we want, Cambridge wants, England wants, I want. There is in us what the common people call "proud flesh"—i.e., mortified flesh: which must be cut out; it cannot be kissed out, nor hoped out, nor removed by faith. It must be removed by surgery. And it is in us now, "proud flesh."
>
> I thought the war would surgeon us. Still it may. But this England at home is as yet entirely unaffected, entirely unaware of the mortification in its own body. . . .
>
> "If thine eye offend thee, pluck it out." It has all been said before, plainly.

It is all there, for every man to hear. But if no man wants to hear?—will cajolery or the toleration of love affect him? Curse him, let him die, and let us look to the young. That is all the faith and hope one can have—or even love.[98]

Implicitly, Lawrence was admitting that his political initiative for a "new life" in England was doomed to futility, if the country was so sick and so unwilling to submit to treatment. He would have to rethink the whole question of his involvement in public life, drawing the right lessons from his encounter with Cambridge. But also there seemed to be some lessons for his private life, that he could take action on without delay.

A Visit from David and Frankie

LAWRENCE had first met Edward Garnett's son David three years before in Bavaria: he was then an exuberantly physical young man, whom Lawrence found "lucky and adorable." They had seen each other often since then, though a visit to Chesham with Garnett's acquaintance Frankie Birrell had turned sour when Birrell irritated Lawrence by talking loudly and snobbishly to Frieda about their mutual friends in the German aristocracy. When the two young men accepted an invitation to Greatham, for 16–18 April, David had become a protegé of Birrell, who was three years older than himself. The son of a cabinet minister, Augustine Birrell, Frankie (unlike David) had gone to the "right" schools—Eton and King's College, Cambridge. As an undergraduate he had caught the eye of Lytton Strachey, who invited him to spend Christmas 1914 at his country house, The Lacket, and to bring David along. David's good looks and friendliness made a favorable impression even though he was not homosexual. Within a couple of weeks he was taken up by the Bloomsbury group, becoming a constant companion of Duncan Grant, Keynes, Clive and Vanessa Bell, and the rest. This was a heady social success for one who was still a rather shy and awkward graduate student, and David was more than a little starstruck by his talented new friends.

At Greatham, then, Lawrence was somberly declaring to Otto-line that England and Cambridge wanted "surgery" when pat on the next day arrived David Garnett, very much in the shadow of Birrell—who talked endlessly and superficially, was a Cambridge man (from the same college as Keynes), and obviously homosexual. This was more than enough to damn him in Lawrence's eyes, and his chumminess with Frieda added a further irritant. In fact, Birrell was not a mere social butterfly; he was generous, almost everyone found him charming, and later he became an outstanding worker with the Quaker mission in France for the relief of war victims. But his presence at Greatham only intensified Lawrence's current obsession. On the second evening of the visit Lawrence fell silent and showed signs that "something dreadful was going on inside him. He was in the throes of some dark religious crisis and seemed to shrink in size with the effort of summoning up all his powers, all his spiritual strength." Yet he did not force a confrontation with the one responsible for his pain, though he seemed pleased when Birrell's tongue swelled up to a grotesque size in the middle of the night—perhaps because it had been so overworked during the day.

Not until after the visitors left did Lawrence's rage boil over, in one of his famous "comminatory" letters to David:

> Never bring Birrell to see me any more. There is something nasty about him like black beetles. He is horrible and unclean. I feel I should go mad when I think of your set, Duncan Grant and Keynes and Birrell. It makes me dream of beetles. In Cambridge I had a similar dream. I had felt it slightly before in the Stracheys. But it came full upon me in Keynes and in Duncan Grant. And yesterday I knew it again in Birrell—you must leave these friends, these beetles. Birrell and Duncan Grant are done for forever. . . . The Oliviers and such girls are wrong. . . . You have always known the wrong people.

Despite his ingenuous manner, David had more resistance to such invective than Murry or Russell, whose deep inner uncertainties made them easily rattled. He decided that Lawrence was "mad and determined to interfere in [his] life," and that he would therefore not see him again.[99] Lawrence's intrusiveness, his high-strung and moralistic attitude to sex, ran counter to David's eupeptic and sensual disposition. As he summed it up later: "Lawrence wanted disciples, and I wasn't disciple material nor was anybody in Bloomsbury. He was always collecting new people, and his interest in you when he first knew you was very flattering. Then he started explaining you to yourself. But I thought he was wrong, though many people liked it."[100]

All these imprecations against Birrell and his circle were aftershocks from Lawrence's disastrous visit to Cambridge six weeks before. "I like David," Lawrence told Kot, "but Birrell I have come to detest. These horrible little frowsty people, men lovers of men, they give me such a sense of corruption, almost putrescence, that I dream of beetles. It is abominable."[101] With Ottoline he tried to be more circumspect, but he soon began harping on his obsession:

> I *will not* have people like this—I had rather be alone. They made me dream in the night of a beetle that bites like a scorpion. But I killed it—a very large beetle. I scotched it and it ran off—but I came upon it again and killed it. It is this horror of little swarming selves that I can't stand: Birrells, D. Grants, and Keyneses. . . .
> I like David Garnett—but there is something wrong with him. Is he also like Keynes and Grant. It is enough to drive one frantic. It makes me long for my Italy. Sometimes I think I can't stand this England any more—it is too wicked and perverse.[102]

Lawrence's dislike of Cambridge "rationalism and cynicism" was fair enough, but underlying it was panic and hysteria at any intimacy with homosexuals. He may indeed have unconsciously envied Birrell, since he himself had been physically attracted to David when they first vacationed together in Bavaria, with some overtones of the homoerotic friendship he had described in *The White Peacock* between Cyril Beardsall and George Saxton. Nonetheless, he felt a violent repugnance for the particular style of upper-class homosexuality he encountered at Cambridge and in Bloomsbury. His obsessive references to beetles provide a complex image for Lawrence's hatred of that milieu.

There is, first, the hard black shell of the beetle, which stands for an aridly intellectual mode of being that precludes any warm human contact between people; instead, there is only a mechanical self-stimulation. Secondly, beetles copulated by mounting from behind, which Lawrence found disgusting—as he explained a few days after Birrell left, apropos of some soldiers he saw: "Can I ever tell you how ugly they were. 'To insects—sensual lust.' I like sensual lust—but insectwise, no—it is obscene. I like men to be beasts—but insects—one insect mounted on another—oh God!

The soldiers at Worthing are like that—they remind me of lice or bugs."[103] Finally, Lawrence probably thought beetles to be appropriate symbols for anal intercourse because scarabs collect balls of dung to lay their eggs in, and feed from. He may also have known that the Egyptians believed scarabs to be all males, though still capable of reproduction; perhaps this is why the ultrafeminine Pussum, in *Women in Love,* has a "metaphysical antipathy" to black beetles.

The prevalence of homosexuality in the Bloomsbury circle caused Lawrence to deliberately slam the door on relationships that might have been both intrinsically rewarding and a support in his later troubles with the authorities. Yet he simultaneously fulminated against the "Bloomsbuggers" (as some called them), and pursued his own esoteric ideal of male comradeship with Murry and Russell (whom he asked to "swear a sort of allegiance" with him in March). This comradeship was ostensibly not sexual, but he still hoped that it would meet some of the emotional needs that, normally, only a wife or lover could satisfy. For another year he continued to thus carry water on both shoulders, until the failure of his demand on Murry for blood brotherhood forced him to be more explicit, and more realistic, about the kind of fulfillment he wanted from his own sex.

The encounters with Keynes and Birrell seem also to have provoked Lawrence to intensify his credo of heterosexual love. Early in April he began sending Ottoline installments of *The Rainbow* as they were typed by Viola Meynell; before forwarding these typescripts Lawrence revised them in longhand. On 23 April, five days after Garnett and Birrell left, he sent Ottoline a section that probably included the most important of these late revisions, the whole last section of chapter 8.[104] At the end of chapter 7 Anna Brangwen had lapsed into domesticity, renouncing "the adventure to the unknown." But then Lawrence decided to add a further episode, the sensual culmination of Will and Anna's marriage. Roused by an incomplete affair with a working-class girl, Will seeks a realm of sheer, impersonal sex, and Anna chooses to meet him on his own ground: ". . . they lived in the darkness and death of their own sensual activities. Sometimes he felt he was going mad with a sense of Absolute Beauty, perceived by him in her through his senses. . . . He wanted to wallow in her, bury himself in her flesh, cover himself over with her flesh." The experience parallels a poem written at Greatham, probably about the same time, "New Heaven and Earth." The poet speaks of an interlude of "maniacal horror" in which the boundaries between himself and every other thing in the universe are obliterated:

> I was the author and the result
> I was the God and the creation at once; . . .
> I was a lover, I kissed the woman I loved,
> and God of horror, I was kissing also myself.

He can only find relief by a spiritual death, after which he rises again "greedy . . . mad for the unknown. . . . starved from a life of devouring always myself." He stretches out his hands and finds himself "thrown upon the shore" of the unknown:

> I am covering myself with the sand.
> I am filling my mouth with the earth.
> I am burrowing my body into the soil.
> The unknown, the new world!

The new world is revealed to be the body of his wife, and the poem ends with a paean to "the mad, astounded rapture" of their new relationship. As so often in Lawrence, it is the strangeness, the "utter mystery" of their union that he most celebrates.

In *The Rainbow* Lawrence attributes a similar experience to Will and Anna, but he lays more emphasis on their willful breaking of sexual taboos:

> All the shameful, natural and unnatural acts of sensual voluptuousness which he and the woman partook of together, created together, they had their heavy beauty and their delight. Shame, what was it? It was part of extreme delight. . . .
> They accepted shame, and were one with it in their most unlicensed pleasures. It was incorporated. It was a bud that blossomed into beauty and heavy, fundamental gratification.

Will and Anna's exploration of the limits of sensuality is now generally believed to include anal intercourse, and Lawrence seems to have asserted this "last word" in sex between man and woman as a challenge to the homosexuality that had so disturbed him in Grant, Keynes, and Birrell. Yet Will and Anna's anarchic passion calls in question the very distinction between hetero- and homosexuality, between "natural and unnatural acts." The key to the question, for Lawrence at least, lies in his mystical belief that each sex should be utterly and intrinsically alien to the other; the only true perversity is the repetition of the "known reaction," which he believes to be unavoidable in homosexual intercourse. But his dogma obliges him to wrestle endlessly with the paradox that men and women come closest together when they are furthest apart.

Ottoline: The Tyranny of Will

IN MID-APRIL Lawrence still planned to move to Garsington with Frieda though he warned Ottoline that he was not likely to settle in easily: "If I had a house and home, I should become wicked. I hate any thought of possessions sticking on to me like barnacles, at once I feel destructive. And wherever I am, after a while I begin to ail me to go away."[105] On 20 April, however, he heard from Philip Morrell that the renovations would cost much more than the 200 pounds he had expected. It is possible that Ottoline and Philip were by now having second thoughts about the Lawrences as tenants and that Philip therefore deliberately exaggerated the expense, though the war had already driven up wages substantially. Lawrence, still chafing over Birrell's visit, told the Morrells to scrap the whole project:

> Not a brick nor a stone will I have laid on my account, at such prices. I would not live in such costly monastic buildings, not for a day: I should hate the place. . . . The thought of your being swindled to this extent makes me feel I would rather be a rabbit in a rabbit-hole, than hire a bricklayer for even half an hour. . . . Those vile greedy contractors, they set my blood boiling to such a degree, I can scarcely bear to write.[106]

His anger at the contractors was no doubt genuine enough, but it was also a handy excuse to break the agreement: "Thank heaven we shall get out of the Lady Ottoline cottage," he told Kot on the same day, "I cannot have such a place like a log on my ankle."[107]

Made irritable by nagging illness, and by Birrell's visit, Lawrence was working himself up to tell Ottoline a few home truths; and an occasion soon presented itself. Since December she had provided hospitality to Maria Nys, a sixteen-year-old Belgian refugee. Although her mother and three sisters were also living in

London, Maria became so passionately attached to Ottoline as to be an embarrassment and a nuisance; so Ottoline made her forthcoming move to Garsington an excuse to tell Maria she must find another home. On the night of 16 April Ottoline returned home to discover that Maria had just swallowed a large dose of mercuric chloride; a doctor was called in time to save her. When Lawrence heard the news, he pressed on Ottoline his current doctrine that we must "acknowledge the passionate evil that is in us":

> We were shocked about Maria: it really is rather horrible. I'm not sure whether you aren't really more wicked than I had at first thought you. I think you can't help torturing a bit.
>
> But I think it has [shown] something—as if you, with a strong, old-developed *will* had enveloped the girl, in this will, so that she lived under the dominance of your will: and then you want to put her away from you, eject her from your will. So that when she says it was because she couldn't bear being left, that she took the poison, it is a great deal true. . . .
>
> Why must you always use your *will* so much, why can't you let things be, without always grasping and trying to know and to dominate. I'm too much like this myself.[108]

Despite the placatory last sentence, this must have struck Ottoline as a gratuitous attack. She had been kind to Maria, as to many other needy people, and stood by her after the suicide attempt: Maria went to Garsington after all, where she met her future husband, Aldous Huxley. Her attachment to Ottoline was of her own making, and its blend of childish dependence and adolescent lesbian infatuation must have been most tiresome to its object. Ottoline's striking appearance and personality could have a hypnotic effect on weaker natures, but Maria was too small a fish for Ottoline to exult in her conquest. Nonetheless, Lawrence had touched a raw nerve by pointing to an imperiousness that many others discerned in her—David Garnett, for example:

> If her love of power, or longing for love (often the same thing in her) were not aroused, her generosity would have it all its own way. Those whom she merely *liked* were indebted to her for a hundred acts of kindness, sympathy and help. When, however, her passions became more deeply involved, it was another matter. Love can be tigerish and those whom Ottoline loved were lucky if, sooner or later, a tiger's claws did not rend them in pieces.[109]

Russell, however, encouraged Ottoline to shrug off the criticism: "Lawrence is absurd about your will. Of course you have a terrific will, but you don't use it tyrannously. . . . Lawrence himself has plenty of will—it is only that his theory doesn't recognize will, because, like most tyrants, he dislikes will in others. . . . and he doesn't realize the place of will in the world. He seems to think instinct alone sufficient."[110] No doubt he went out of his way to be soothing because he knew Ottoline was nervous and depressed, and that any reference to her will was likely to upset her further. Since 1913 she had been receiving regular treatments from the nerve specialist Dr. Roger Vittoz of Lausanne, who believed that neurotic symptoms could be eliminated by daily exercises to strengthen the will:*

> [The patient] should draw in a long breath, hold it for from two to four seconds, and before exhaling say to himself, "I will," while at the same time, perhaps, clenching his fists. . . . The effort of will must be applied, not only to the actions, but also to abstract ideas, feelings and sentiments. The patient should, therefore, be trained by this method to use his will power, by, for instance, saying to himself, "I *will* control myself," "I *will* be energetic," or "I *will* use my will," merely with the object of making him feel he is using his will.[111]

The effects of Ottoline's regimen were obvious to Lawrence's keen eye; in *Women in Love* Birkin makes a savage exposé of Hermione's nervous eccentricities, her complete lack of spontaneity or sensuality. From the beginning of their acquaintance Lawrence must have been storing up impressions of such defects in Ottoline. But after admitting he was scolding her, he tried to end on a conciliatory note: "Don't mind what I say. . . . Still we must form the nucleus of a new society, as we said at the very first. But you use your will so much, always your will. Our love to you."[112]

Frieda as "The Hun"

LAWRENCE had passed through the first weeks of his post-Cambridge bout of illness and depression without any serious external troubles to aggravate his mood. But from about the end of

---

* When T. S. Eliot suffered a nervous breakdown in 1921 he spent six weeks at Vittoz' sanitarium, on Ottoline's recommendation; *The Waste Land* begins with fragmentary recollections of his stay there.

April new threats to his peace of mind arose, most of them connected with Frieda.

The first ill omen however, appeared on the battle lines. Each side launched massive spring offensives, hoping for quick victory; they had not yet grasped the intrinsic advantage of defense in trench warfare, and it would take tens of thousands of casualties to show them that their war effort must be more highly organized, more intense, and more prolonged than they had ever imagined. The Germans, numerically inferior, soon began looking for short cuts to success. In January they used zeppelins to bomb civilian targets in Britain; the first raids had little effect, but one on Southend on 10 May was more damaging and the attacks progressed to London later in the year. In February they warned that British passenger ships might be subject to attack if they carried munitions, and the tragedy of the *Lusitania* would prove that the threat was not idle. Finally, on 22 April, the German offensive at Ypres was supported by the discharge of xylyl gas. The Geneva Conventions of 1899 and 1907 had banned the use of poison gas, but the Germans claimed it was not poisonous, merely incapacitating. Nonetheless, many who breathed it died. The Allies soon followed suit and far more deadly gases, such as phosgene, were introduced later—though the war was not made any shorter by their use. Worse horrors were yet to come, but in spring 1915 it must already have become evident to the shrewd observer that the war was going to be much longer and nastier than anyone expected when it began. Lawrence, however, was slow to realize this; he did not read newspapers or have much contact with soldiers, and the censorship was still able to cast a rosy hue on events at the Front. His real bitterness developed only when he began to suffer personally from the government's war measures, especially conscription.

Meanwhile, Lawrence had his very future as a writer to worry about. After completing the handwritten manuscript of *The Rainbow* on 2 March he was reluctant to submit the novel to Pinker's judgment. He held back for two months, but by late April Pinker told him the manuscript must go to Methuen soon if it were to be ready for autumn publication. Lawrence now had to face the prospect of a second rejection:

> I'm afraid there are parts of it Methuen won't want to publish. He must. I will take out sentences and phrases, but I won't take out paragraphs or pages. . . .

You see a novel, after all this period of coming into being, has a definite organic form, just as a man has when he is grown. And we don't ask a man to cut his nose off because the public don't like it: because he must have a nose, and his own nose, too.

Oh God, I hope I'm not going to have a miserable time over this book, now I've at last got it pretty much to its real being.[113]

A few days later came a blow that made Lawrence's financial future seem truly hopeless. When Weekley divorced Frieda on 28 May 1914 the costs of the action were charged against Lawrence as corespondent. Lawrence decided he would never pay, and got away with it for nearly a year. But on 29 April the jig was up: "Today a very unclean creature came and gave me a paper," he told Russell, "saying I must go on May 10th before the registrar and declare what debts are owing me."[114] Though the next step would be the seizure of Lawrence's assets, he still vowed to hold out: "I wouldn't pay them if I were a millionaire—I would rather go to prison. Messrs. Goldberg Newall and Co, beasts, bugs, leeches, shall not have a penny from me if I can help it." The costs amounted to one hundred forty-four pounds, which represented roughly a year's income for Lawrence. His plan for living at Garsington had collapsed just a few days before, depriving him of the prospect of a cheap and secure home; now it looked as if he would become a bankrupt into the bargain. His anger went far beyond Weekley and his lawyers:

I cannot tell you how this reinforces in me my utter hatred of the whole establishment—the whole constitution of England as it now stands. I wish I were a criminal instead of a bankrupt. But softly—softly. I will do my best to lay a mine under their foundations. . . . you can't imagine how it wears on one, having at every monent to resist this established world, and to know its unconscious hostility. For I am hostile, hostile, hostile to all that is, in our public and national life. I want to destroy it.

Russell passed on this declaration of one-man civil war to Ottoline: "It is very unfortunate that he should be driven to hate society more than he already did," Russell noted. "It will make it harder to bring him to a less hostile frame of mind. On the other hand, it will distract him from sex. I think political pre-occupations are good for him, tho' not likely to do any political good."[115]

Lawrence's instinctive response in such moods was to move. He took a day trip to the nearby seaside resort of Worthing, but this was scarcely far enough:

> I wish I were going to Tibet—or Kamschatka—or Tahiti—to the ultima, ultima, ultima Thule. I feel sometimes I shall go mad, because there is nowhere to go, no 'new world.' . . .
>
> I almost wish I could go to the war—not to shoot: I have vowed an eternal oath that I won't shoot in this war, not even if I am shot. I should like to be a bus conductor at the front—anything to escape this, that is.[116]

His friend Horne—from the walking tour in Westmoreland at the beginning of the war—had written to say he was going to drive an army bus in France. This may have been an escape, but it was hardly a glamorous one. Indeed, if the war ever had a romantic phase, it had now ended with the death on 23 April of Rupert Brooke (the day after the first use of poison gas on the Western Front.) Brooke was not a hero—he had only seen action for seven days, in October—but he had been made a figurehead by Dean Inge, who in an Easter sermon at St. Paul's Cathedral had read his sonnet: "If I should die, think only this of me . . ." His death only nineteen days later, on a hospital ship off Skyros, came so pat as to seal his fame; the tributes failed to mention that his fatal septicemia was caused by a gnat bite. Lawrence, too, was moved—even though, after Cambridge, one would have expected him to loathe Brooke and everything he stood for:

> The death of Rupert Brooke fills me more and more with the sense of the fatuity of it all. He was slain by bright Phoebus' shaft—it was in keeping with his general sunniness—it was the real climax of his pose. I first heard of him as a Greek god under a Japanese sunshade, reading poetry in his pyjamas, at Grantchester,—at Grantchester upon the lawns where the river goes. Bright Phoebus smote him down. It is all in the saga.
>
> O God, O God, it is all too much of a piece: it is like madness.[117]

Phoebus Apollo, the sungod, commonly struck down mortals who claimed to be his equal as singers (Brooke's death was attributed to sunstroke). Lawrence certainly was not one to be swept off his feet by Brooke's sentimental patriotism or his shallow poetic talent; but, poseur or not, he had his own radiance as the golden boy of his generation and class—a young man so good-looking, Frieda recalled, "he took your breath away."[118] Lawrence's sympathy for Brooke shows the protean quality of his imagination: intuitively he casts the two fellows of King's in opposite roles—Keynes ratlike and corrupt, Brooke a luminous Greek hero. And both in pajamas! Against Brooke's mythic death among the isles of Greece

Lawrence set the mechanical butchery of the Western Front; against Brooke's glamor the obscenity of the soldiers he had seen at Worthing:

> They will murder their officers one day. They are teeming insects. What massive creeping hell is let loose nowadays.
>
> It isn't my disordered imagination. There is a wag-tail sitting on the gatepost. I see how sweet and swift heaven is. But hell is slow and creeping and viscous and insect-teeming: as is this Europe now, this England.[119]

The sweetness of nature became almost the only solace for Lawrence as militarism laid its blight on the old England. On 6 May he took a twenty-mile walk from Greatham to Chichester with Eleanor Farjeon, a literary friend of Viola Meynell. Released from the swarms of visitors at Greatham, Lawrence was in an "angelic, child-like mood. . . . In one of the deep bottoms, where the whitebeams looked like trees in silver blossom, he cried, 'We must be spring-like!' and broke green branches and stuck them around our hats." Only at the end of the day did his darker self appear, when they descended from the open hills to a group of laborers' cottages: "Lawrence sunk his voice to say, 'I know the people who live in homes like that. I know them as I know my own skin. I know what they think and do. I know their lives.' His voice rose to a shrill pipe. 'I *hate* them!' "[120] Nonetheless, in a few minutes he was amiably chatting with some of them in the local pub.

The next day Lawrence and Frieda went to London for four days, mainly to settle their troublesome financial affairs. Lawrence had resigned himself to attesting his assets and engaged the legal services of Robert Garnett, David's uncle. His great fear was that Weekley's lawyers would claim their costs directly from Methuen, leaving him with almost nothing to live on. However, Pinker was able to avoid this, and Lawrence asked Garnett "to compound with the detestable Goldbergs. . . . to pay over a term of years."[121] Presumably he did so; but if Lawrence was making regular payments to Weekley's account it must have fed his rage over money in the penurious days to come.

Lawrence had not been in London for several weeks and he found the atmosphere oppressively warlike, the city "a hoary ponderous inferno." On 8 May, the day after he arrived, the papers were full of the sinking of the Cunard liner *Lusitania* just off the Irish coast. A massive British propaganda campaign spread the news around the world, presenting it as a mindless atrocity and trying to draw America into the war, since 140 U. S. citizens had died. The Germans claimed that the liner was carrying munitions—modern research has shown that she almost certainly was—so that she sank in eighteen minutes after being hit by only one small torpedo (a smaller liner, the *Olympic,* once took twelve torpedoes without sinking).[122] The passengers, of course, had not known of this added peril. Many of the twelve hundred who drowned were children, and the papers carried pictures of their corpses washed up on the beaches; on the night of 12 May riots broke out in the East End of London, shops thought to be German-owned were smashed and looted, their occupants beaten. Despite his opposition to the war, Lawrence felt himself being sucked into the maelstrom:

> It is not a question of me, it is the world of men. The world of men is dreaming, it has gone mad in its sleep, and a snake is strangling it, but it can't wake up.
>
> When I read of the *Lusitania,* and of the riots in London, I know it is so. . . .
>
> I cannot bear it much longer, to let the madness get stronger and stronger possession. Soon we in England shall go fully mad, with hate. I too hate the Germans so much, I could kill every one of them. Why should they goad us to this frenzy of hatred, why should we be tortured to bloody madness, when we are only grieved in our souls, and heavy? . . . I am mad with rage myself. I would like to kill a million Germans—two million.[123]

Lawrence was probably referring to the German propaganda that justified the sinking, such as the famous medal showing a skeleton selling tickets with the inscription "Profits before Lives." He had come far since his thoughtless comment at the beginning of the war, that Germany was "a young and adorable country . . . with the faults of adolescence."[124]

The passions of war also caused tension between Lawrence and Frieda, who was not one to hide her nationality under a bushel even though she ostensibly opposed the war. In response to the *Lusitania* sinking the British government on 14 May announced stricter measures against enemy aliens. Nineteen thousand men of military age had already been interned; now all the rest would be too, while women, children, and overage men would be deported to their home countries. Frieda was technically safe as a naturalized British subject, but at various times during the war people in her category were threatened with similar draconian measures. A question in Parliament later in the year revealed that she might not be considered a British subject in all respects: Sir John Simon, the home secretary, stated that "women of hostile origin married to British subjects come within the scope of Regulation 14b of the Defence of the Realm Regulations, and are subject to the general supervision which is kept over suspected persons of hostile origin."[125] Apart from the fear of her being interned or deported, Lawrence had also to cope with the rows she regularly managed to provoke with English people of patriotic sentiment.

These frictions, and others of longer standing, made the Lawrences decide to look for rooms in London while retaining the cottage at Greatham. "She spends her time thinking herself a wronged, injured and aggrieved person," Lawrence told Kot, "because of the children, and because she is a German. I am angry and bored. I wish she would have her rooms in Hampstead and leave me alone."[126] Lawrence had exalted his bond to Frieda in reaction against Birrell and Keynes, but now the pendulum was swinging the other way. Though Frieda had got on reasonably well with their friends in the Chesham circle, except for Kot, Ottoline and her group were a more formidable proposition. They were fascinated by Lawrence's charm and literary brilliance, but found Frieda merely gushing and intrusive. When E. M. Forster proclaimed he would "have no dealings with a firm" Frieda deluged him with her long-standing grievances on that score:

> As to the firm you *did* hit a little sore point with me—Poor author's wife, who does her little best and everybody wishes her to Jericho—Poor second fiddle, the surprise at her existence! She goes on playing her little accompaniment so bravely! Tut-Tut, tra-la-la! .... Yours sincerely die zweite Flöte

About the same time she wrote to Kot, who had criticized her for being shrewish to Lawrence: ". . . you see I am also his wife on this earth, the wife to the *man* as distinguished from the *artist;* to that latter I would always submit but, you see, some things I just *know* and he doesn't. . . . You think I do not count besides Lawrence, but I take myself, my ideals and life quite as seriously as he does his. . . . I feel everybody against me, but then I can stand up to it, thank God."[127]

If their friends idolized Lawrence and neglected her, Frieda had no qualms about demanding her own share of the limelight. The heart of the problem lay in Lawrence's attitude. He claimed that Frieda's grand, impersonal quality challenged his creative powers; so if people admired his work, why did they withhold credit from the woman who was his muse? But he was unwilling to recognize that Frieda's special value to him did not exist for people of different temperament. To outsiders he seemed the mere emotional slave of a woman who provoked in him passions disproportionate to her real stature; but of course this had always been his way, with his mother and Jessie Chambers playing their parts before Frieda.

Even if Lawrence had wanted to conduct friendships separately from Frieda, she would not have tolerated it. After Russell's second visit to Greatham she accused him in a letter of being narrow in his social outlook and "against women." When Russell did not reply, Lawrence asked Ottoline to intervene: "Tell Russell to write to Frieda, or else she feels he is trying to insult her. Everything is perfectly all right and she likes him very much. But I hope to God he's not assuming the Olympic, the high horse."[128] Of course everything was not all right, nor was Lawrence's initiative likely to make it so. Frieda also wrote to Ottoline, appealing to female solidarity:

> He should be grateful that I apply my wits to understand him—But he is conceited and as long as he approaches women in his irreverent, superior way *he* will be dissatisfied and I am glad—One does *not* fall in love like one buys a pound of tea—He is quite coarse in his emotions, he might learn from almost any woman there—and he knows it—[129]

Eventually Russell did his duty with a "very nice letter" and Frieda, who rarely bore a grudge for long, relented. So an uneasy peace was restored; but no exchange of civilities could remove the underlying resentments between those concerned, and they were soon to flare up again more violently.

Another contretemps of Frieda's may have had more serious long-term consequences. One afternoon while Lawrence was away—probably on his visit to Cambridge—Frieda was visited by Ford Madox Ford (then named Hueffer), his mistress Violet Hunt, and Mrs. H. G. Wells. Frieda gave them tea, there was a row, and they left. But not even this skeleton of fact is agreed on by all concerned, and their other memories of the affair are radically at variance. Ford had of course launched Lawrence's career in 1909 when he published his story "Odour of Chrysanthemums" in the *English Review* and proclaimed him a genius. But two years later he disliked *The Trespasser,* Lawrence's second novel, so he handed over his protegé to the care of Edward Garnett. By Ford's account, his desire to be Lawrence's advocate revived in 1915: "The last time I saw [Lawrence] was during the War when, of course, he was a pro-German and was supposed to be a good deal persecuted. That is to say, Authority—in the shape of the Minister of Information—was afraid he was being persecuted and I was sent down to see what could be done for him."[130] This was a curious assertion for Ford to make. The Lawrences had been questioned by police earlier, but at Greatham they had not had any trouble—perhaps because they lived with the irreproachable Meynells—and even if they had, why should the "Minister of Information" be responsible for doing something about it?

A more likely explanation for Ford's mission lies in his bland assertion that Lawrence was "pro-German"; one may surmise that "Authority" wanted to keep an eye on him, and sent Ford to Greatham to spy out the land. If Ford really wanted to give Lawrence some official backing, why arrive unannounced, as if he were "just passing by"—and then miss seeing him altogether?* There was no minister of information in 1915, but Ford was working for an old golfing crony, C. F. G. Masterman, a former cabinet minister who now directed the secret propaganda bureau known as Wellington House.[131] Masterman commissioned two propaganda books from him, and may well have employed him in clandestine activities. Ford was eager to prove his loyalty to Britain because he had already come under suspicion himself, being of German origin. At the beginning of January the chief constable of West Sussex had tried to expel him from his home on the coast at Selsey. The constable had a grudge against Ford, whom he referred to privately as a "German journalist," and his spiteful action was quickly revoked—"doubtless at Masterman's request."[132] It is barely possible that Masterman had got wind of similar measures that the constable was planning against the Lawrences, and wanted to forestall them. But it is far more likely that Ford's mission was part of the routine surveillance of suspected persons. Frieda's family, with whom she communicated regularly via Swit-

---

* Ford claims that Lawrence *was* there, but the weight of the evidence is to the contrary.

zerland, had close ties with the German High Command. On Lawrence's side there were his links with Philip Morrell, one of the few M. P.'s sympathetic to pacifist causes, and with the already notorious Bertrand Russell; his intimacy with Lady Cynthia Asquith, the prime minister's daughter-in-law, must have helped season the plot. It is possible that Lawrence's mail was being intercepted and, if so, letters like the one to Mary Cannan on 24 February—two weeks before Ford's visit—would make lively reading. Lawrence told her "We must form a revolutionary party. I have talked about it with various people—also Bertrand Russell"; he ended with "Auf Wiedersehen"![133]

All this is of course quite speculative, since the security files relevant to the Lawrences have been destroyed.* In any case, what happened at Greatham on Ford's arrival was worthy of a Graham Greene spy farce. Frieda recalls that she greeted Ford by asking him "Wir sind auch Deutsch?"—Are you a German too?"—which "made him squirm and he hummed and hawed."[134] This has the ring of truth, for the question was wonderfully apt to embarrass both Ford and Violet Hunt. Five years previously Ford had been desperate to divorce his wife and marry Violet. He was a British subject by birth, but his father was German; so he concocted a scheme to acquire German citizenship and then get a German divorce. He and Violet moved to Germany and wrote jointly a book called *The Desirable Alien* about their wish to make it their homeland. Ford called Germany his "beloved country," while Violet rhapsodized: "Some persons are, of course, born Germans; some achieve citizenship of that great and good nation. Others, again, [like herself] have the honour thrust upon them."[135] But the scheme collapsed; Ford got no German divorce and by 1915, far from being eager to marry Violet, he wanted to get rid of her. He was soon to prove his patriotism by joining the British army; the last thing he wanted to be reminded of was his old infatuation with the idea of becoming German, and even to speak German where one might be overheard was dangerous.

---

* However, David Garnett told me that he knew a woman during the war whose job it was to read letters, then reseal them and send them on. I have found no firm evidence that Lawrence's mail was thus tampered with, though a number of letters from Gertler to Koteliansky during the war mysteriously disappeared en route; they were sent from Garsington, a well-known center of pacifist activities, and Gertler might have been considered a suspicious alien since his family came from Austrian Poland (Koteliansky Papers, British Museum).

In January 1915 Ford had published *Antwerp,* an enormously popular poem about the sufferings of the Belgians under German occupation. Violet Hunt claimed that Frieda's contribution, when the conversation turned to this subject, was "Dirty Belgians! Who cares for them!," and that a bitter argument ensued from which Ford retreated in dismay—an action, Mizener remarks, "too characteristic of him not to be true." Frieda has denied jeering at the Belgians, claiming she "never felt like that."[136] Violet, by all accounts, was a woman of remarkable irrationality and malice; she may well have exaggerated Frieda's sentiments, partly out of dislike and partly from a desire to reinforce the suspect patriotism of herself and Ford. But it would have been typical of Frieda to be insensitive, at least, to the Belgians' plight, and Maria Nys certainly disliked her intensely at the time (though not after the war). Frieda cared about the loss in the war of people she knew, or who were extraordinary in some way, but not much about the rest; in 1916 she urged Cynthia Asquith to keep her husband out of the trenches, because "it does *not* matter whether hundreds of dull young men die early instead of going into a dull old age, but the few that matter ought to be preserved." When she heard of Ottoline's sympathy for the Irish rebels, after the failure of the Easter Rising, she sneered: "Oh, those stunts humanity and kindness; they are really for the people whose inside is frozen!"[137] In any case, it is unquestioned that Frieda and Violet quarrelled, and that Frieda disliked and despised her visitors. By Violet's account the matter ended there, though one would expect Masterman to be told of the incident, and it may have counted as a black mark against the Lawrences later in the war.

Early Summer: Lawrence in Retreat

THE LATTER PART of May, June, and early July were mainly a fallow period for Lawrence, though one from which he was to emerge, as usual, with renewed energy and creative plans. Following his struggle in March with "the powers of darkness" he worked sporadically at a new version of his philosophy, and decided that he would have to leave Greatham soon; his inner turmoil gradually receded. During this quieter time Lawrence occupied himself with two practical tasks; the tutoring of ten-year-old Mary Saleeby, a niece of Viola Meynell, and the correction of the manuscript and proofs of *The Rainbow*.

Mary's mother, Monica Saleeby, was the eldest daughter of Wilfred and Alice Meynell; she lived at Greatham, having separated from her husband some years before. At the start of May she suffered a nervous breakdown: ". . . just flops in bed," Frieda reported, ". . . no interest at all in anything, it's the spring, I suppose and nothing for her to do—and no man."[138] Her daughter was a "rough-and-tumble ragamuffin little rebel" who had had practically no schooling. In the crisis, Lawrence volunteered to "civilize and educate" her so that she could be sent to boarding school; he gave her lessons every morning for three and a half hours, which she enjoyed very much, especially the songs he taught her. He began around 14 May and planned originally to continue for a month, in recompense for the loan of Viola's cottage. As it happened, the lessons lasted nearly two and a half months since it took the Lawrences that long to prepare their next move. Eleanor Farjeon remembers the value of Lawrence's classes to Mary, who went on to a successful career as a doctor:

> He must have been a genius as a teacher, not necessarily kind or patient (he was neither in his relationships), but making children vitally interested in the subject, and in themselves. Wilfred Meynell was pathetically grateful to him, and expressed this one day when he and I and Lawrence were together. When Wilfred left us, Lawrence exploded—"I don't want gratitude! I'm not taking Mary on because I *like* it! *But somebody has got to.*"[139]

At the time Lawrence began teaching Mary Saleeby he visited Lady Cynthia Asquith at Brighton and prescribed for an even more difficult pupil. The abnormality of her four-year-old son, John, was to cause Lady Cynthia endless misery and expense; today he would probably be diagnosed as autistic, but at that time he was a complete puzzle to the specialists. "The Lawrences were riveted by the freakishness of John," she wrote in her diary, "about whom they showed extraordinary interest and sympathy."[140] At her request, Lawrence analyzed John, though he "rather resented" doing so and did not spare her feelings:

I don't think John is very extraordinary, I think, if we could consider it intrinsically, he has a sensitive, happy soul. But every soul is born into an existing world. The world is not made fresh for every new soul, as the shell for every egg. And long before John was ever born or conceived, your soul knew that, within the hard form of existing conditions, of the existing 'world,' it was like a thing born to remain for ever in prison. Your own soul knew, before ever John was possible, that it was itself bound in like a tree that grows under a low roof and can never break through, and which must be deformed, unfulfilled. Herbert Asquith must have known the same thing, in his soul.

Lady Cynthia, Lawrence continued, believed in God or "the Great Will," but not in her own capacity for fulfillment; she was thus "an unbeliever affirming belief. . . . *much more insidious* than atheism." John, born into the unbelief of his parents, was a divided soul from the start:

> he knows that you are Unbelief, and he reacts from your affirmation of belief always with hostility. . . .
> Don't try to make him love you, or obey you—don't do it. The love that he would have for you would be a much greater love than he would ever have for his nurse. . . . But you can never fight for this love. That you fight is only a sign that you are wanting in yourself. The child knows that.[141]

In effect, Lawrence was advising Lady Cynthia she could not be a good mother to her son until she had changed her own spiritual condition. She must "learn to believe in God": not, that is, to become conventionally religious but to join in bringing the whole of England into unanimity of faith, "Prime Ministers and Capitalists and artisans all working in pure effort towards God." This was the kind of language Lawrence had been using three months earlier, when he had been most absolute and optimistic in his vision of a new England. He was now in a more chastened mood, but his old aspirations revived with Lady Cynthia: in part because he was usually most lyrical and positive when under the spell of her charm, in part because her closeness to the center of power sustained his hope that through her something might still be achieved in the political realm.

Lawrence's dissection of Lady Cynthia's deficiencies as a mother may seem gratuitously cruel, and he may have blamed her unfairly for John's condition. But he was still trying to shock her into leaving her empty life as a society woman in order to fulfill a deeper, more authentic side of her nature. Years afterward, when it had become clear that she would not change, he no longer pressed her with advice but instead used her as a "case" in his stories. In "Glad Ghosts" we see much of Lady Cynthia in Carlotta Fell, daughter of a peer, who dabbles in art but "belonged finally, fatally, to her own class. . . . the coronet was wedged into her brow, like a ring of iron grown into a tree." And in "The Rocking-Horse Winner" there is the neurotic mother of a deranged son: "She had bonny children, yet she felt they had been thrust upon her, and she could not love them. They looked at her coldly, as if they were finding fault with her. And hurriedly she felt she must cover up some fault in herself. Yet what it was she must cover up she never knew."

Lawrence's other occupation at this time was the preparation of *The Rainbow* for the press. It took Viola Meynell and an assistant a full three months to complete the typed copy after Lawrence finished the manuscript on 2 March; during all this time he was making revisions and sending the final text to Ottoline. She found Lawrence's new concerns hard to take, after her enthusiasm for *Sons and Lovers* and *The Prussian Officer*:

> It jars on me a good deal. It is too *intensely* sexual and I don't like it—but I feel it is well done and good Psychology: tho *quite* alien to one.
> It has fine writing in it too—tho Not the writing of an *Educated* man I think. But one feels he *is* great—and has probably a great future—if he could see the world more. . . . I don't think his Female Psychology is really good—especially in very young cases. It is always his wife.[142]

By the time Lawrence sent Pinker the final batch of revised typescript, on 31 May, he must have realized that others besides Ottoline were likely to find an excess of sex in it. Nonetheless, he threw in a further provocation to John Bull—a dedication to Else von Richthofen Jaffe, Frieda's elder sister:

> I want on the fly-leaf, in German characters, the inscription "Zu Else"—i.e.,
>
> ZU ELSE
>
> Put that in for me, will you? It is just "To Else." But it must be in Gothic letters.
> We shall have peace by the time this book is published.[143]

The dedication was included, though Lawrence did not get his Gothic letters, nor did the novel in any sense arrive peacefully. Pinker achieved a nimble feat of negotiation by inducing Methuen to rush the novel into type, in time for autumn publication, with the promise that Lawrence would do whatever was needed to make it "decent." Lawrence had indeed agreed, on 23 April, to take out objectionable sentences and phrases—but no more. As he started to correct page proofs in early July, Pinker sent him concurrently proof slips (presumably of earlier parts) and pages from the typescript with passages marked for changes or deletions. Lawrence adhered to the agreement as he understood it, though Pinker had obviously promised Methuen more than Lawrence would deliver:

> I have cut out, as I said I would, all the *phrases* objected to. The passages and paragraphs marked I cannot alter. There is nothing offensive in them, beyond the very substance they contain, and that is no more offensive than that of all the rest of the novel. The libraries won't object to the book any less, or approve of it any more, if these passages are cut out. . . . Tell Methuen, he need not be afraid. If the novel doesn't pay him back this year, it will before very long.[144]

A collation of the corrected typescript of *The Rainbow* with the first edition shows that Lawrence ignored the spirit of Methuen's request for changes, and only grudgingly complied with the letter. Most of the chapter "Shame" must have shocked Methuen, but it was printed unchanged; in all, Lawrence made only a few minor revisions. "They stood enfolded in the unmitigated kiss," for example, was changed in the printed text to "They stood enjoying the unmitigated kiss"; "His body was warm and fulfilled, his veins drenched with satisfaction" became "quiet and fulfilled, his veins complete with satisfaction"; "a man who would give you a really reckless time" became "a man who could really let go."[145] Methuen now faced a dilemma: the novel had not been expurgated as they wished, but in June they had paid Lawrence a further 150 pounds on his advance—making 250 pounds in all— and they had gone to the expense of setting the book in type. Rather than contest the issue further they decided to let publication go ahead, though when the book ran into trouble they were quick to disavow it, and even to claim that they had not really known what it was like.

Lawrence's mood in these months of early summer was turning more toward isolation and fear, after his aggressive outbursts in April. He enjoyed working in the garden at Rackham Cottage, the most secluded one on the estate, where Percy Lucas lived with his wife, Madeline Meynell; there Lawrence was "quite happy, with the plants."[146] He also went to Bognor for the day, where he saw on the pier a young soldier whose leg had been amputated, "strangely self-conscious, and slightly ostentatious: but confused. As yet, he does not realise anything, he is still in shock." Lawrence seemed to see in him an image of his own condition, reduced almost to a shade by his nervous crisis and gazing out, still dazed, at the sea:

> a white, vague, powerful sea, with long waves falling heavily, with a crash of frosty white out of the pearly whiteness of the day, of the wide sea. . . . I cannot tell you why, but I am afraid. I am afraid of the ghosts of the dead. They seem to come marching home in legions over the white, silent sea, breaking in on us with a roar and a white iciness. . . .
>
> So they are making a Coalition government. I cannot tell you how icy cold my heart is with fear. It is as if we were all going to die. Did I not tell you my revolution would come? It will come, God help us. The ghosts will bring it. Why does one feel so coldly afraid? Why does even the coalition of the Government fill me with terror? Some say it is for peace negotiations. It may be, because we are all afraid. But it is most probably for conscription. The touch of death is very cold and horrible on us all. . . . It is the whiteness of the ghost legions that is so awful.[147]

The Coalition was forced on Asquith by popular dissatisfaction with the sinking of the *Lusitania* and the failure—blamed on lack of munitions—of the spring offensives in Flanders and the Dardanelles. The new Cabinet included as minister of munitions David Lloyd George, Asquith's most dangerous rival. Lawrence was right in fearing that the Coalition would bring in conscription, for they were determined to prosecute the war more ruthlessly. Though Asquith remained in power, his gentlemanly scruples did little to restrain the inexorable hardening of war policy, and he would in due course be discarded as not fierce enough to meet the crisis. All this Lawrence foresaw.

In his spectral mood Lawrence lacked will to continue his struggles with Frieda, for the moment at least, so he agreed that she should go off to her own rooms in London. "I simply must be by myself sometimes," she told Ottoline near the end of May. "L. is very wearing and also I will see the children on their way to school, that they dont get used to *not* seeing me." To this Lawrence appended his own sardonic commentary:

Isn't it a funny thing, if a woman has got her children, she doesn't care about them, and if she has a man, she doesn't care about him, she only wants her children. There is something in the talk about female perversity. Frieda only cares about her children now. It is as if women—or she—persisted in being unfortunate and hopelessly unsatisfied: if a man wants much, she becomes violently a mother and a man-hater, if her children want much, she becomes a violent disciple of "love" as against domesticity or maternity. What a miserable creature![148]

A few days later Lawrence told Forster that Frieda was flathunting in London, "unless a bomb has dropped on her—killed by her own countrymen—it is the kind of fate she is cut out for." Tired of all this unworthy squabbling, he was even tempted to agree with Ottoline's solution: "One tries hard to stick to one's ideal of one man—one woman, in love, but probably you are right, and one should go to different persons to get companionship for the different sides of one's nature."[149] His desire to put more space between himself and Frieda was a tentative first step in this direction.

Garsington: The Nucleus of a New Belief?

WHILE FRIEDA was looking for her rooms, Lawrence improved the occasion by sending off a volley of letters to friends to whom she had been a fly in the ointment: Ottoline, E. M. Forster, and Russell. He told Forster that everyone in the group was isolated; this was largely a projection of his own emotional state, though Russell had some reason to agree with him. After the Cambridge visit their friendship had cooled somewhat, but when Russell ran into difficulties with his college Lawrence began hoping for a radical change in his friend's way of life. By February 1915 Russell's eminence as a logician had become so unquestioned that the Council of Trinity voted to appoint him a fellow when the term of his lectureship expired in October. During the next three months, however, feelings about the war became more bitter, and Russell's well-known pacifism more obnoxious to the clerical and conservative majority of the Council. In May he applied to take leave of absence for the first two terms of his fellowship; the Council met on the twenty-first and voted to make his appointment conditional on his being "engaged in the systematic study of Philosophy and Mathematics"—i.e., not engaged in work against the war.[150]

A week later Russell himself avoided a confrontation by renouncing his claim to a fellowship, asking only that his modest lectureship be renewed for another five years and that his leave be granted. The Council agreed, but they had shown that they considered him a marked man. This Lawrence welcomed: "If they hound you out of Trinity, so much the better: I am glad. Entire separation, that is what must happen to one: not even the nominal shelter left, not even the mere fact of inclusion in the host. One must be entirely cast forth." Social transformation, he now felt, must begin with a withdrawal of the elect into the desert; like the prophets of all ages, they must have experience of the primal powers before beginning their mission:

> As for political revolution, that too must come. But now, only the darkness thrusts more and more between us all, like a sword, cutting us off entirely each from the other. . . . Leave your Cambridge then: that is very good. And let us die from this life, and this year of life, and rise up when the winter is drawing over, after the time in the tomb. But we are never dead. When everything else is gone, and there is no touch nor sense of each other left, there is always the sense of God, of the Absolute. Our sense of the Absolute is the only sense left to us.

This sole reliance on the Absolute, or "pure truth," becomes one of Lawrence's insistent themes at this time. It partly accounts for his rejection of the social world, where any truth loses its sharpness of outline like a coin that passes from hand to hand. But Lawrence's hope was that a few kindred spirits might separately grasp the Absolute, then unite in a common faith for social action. Russell, he believed, would be one of them: "We are one in allegiance, really, you and I. We have one faith, we must unite in one fight."[151]

Russell, beleaguered at Trinity, was receptive to the message. "I *feel* he is right," he told Ottoline, "that I should have 10 times the energy if I were done with respectability. But perhaps not. . . . The world grows more and more black and furious. We are nowhere near the worst yet. But a new order *must* emerge from all this." He agreed to visit Greatham on 19 June and Lawrence, encouraged, pressed him harder:

> I shall be glad when you have strangled the invincible respectability that dogs your steps. What does it mean, really—*Integer vitae Scelerisque purus?* But before what tribunal? I refuse to be judged by them. . . . They are not my peers. Where are my peers? I acknowledge no more than five or six—not so many—in the world. But one must take care of the pack. . . .
>
> And whoever dies, let us not die. Let us kill this hydra, this pack, before we die.[152]

Lawrence's advice was impressively drastic, but not very sensitive to Russell's actual situation. For him, "the pack" was not a gang of mindless jingoes but the fellows of Trinity, a distinguished body of intellectuals. The Council was aging and conservative but among the fellows as a whole nearly half had some sympathy with Russell's position. Four were conscientious objectors and thirteen members of the U. D. C. In the popular mind Cambridge, unlike Oxford, was considered a center of opposition to the war; outside Trinity there was a substantial peace movement, led by Goldsworthy Lowes Dickinson and C. K. Ogden, editor of *The Cambridge Magazine.* It was not, therefore, a simple decision for Russell to sever his ties with the university. Eventually the decision would be made for him, when he was dismissed from Trinity; until then he compromised by taking leave to work full time against the war, while maintaining his rooms in college and his intellectual connections. Lawrence, of course, wanted him to go further: "Bertie Russell is being separated out from the pack," he wrote Ottoline, "I am very glad. Soon he will be an outlaw. I am very glad. Then we are brothers."[153]

No believer in half measures, Lawrence wanted Russell to be separated from the antiwar movement also. Russell had begun to write for the *Labour Leader,* the I.L.P. weekly that now also became the chief public voice of the U. D. C. The two organizations, one based on industrial workers and the other on liberal intellectuals, were forming a coalition against the war. When Russell attacked the press baron Lord Northcliffe, a formidable leader of the jingoes, Lawrence took alarm:

> I think Lord Northcliffe wants sinking to the bottom, but you do say rash things, and give yourself away. Let me beg you not to get into trouble now, at this juncture. . . . We must go much deeper and beyond Lord Northcliffe. Let

us wait a little while, till we can assemble the nucleus of a new belief, get a new centre of attack, not using Labour Leaders and so on.[154]

Lawrence included in this letter, of 8 June, the first quarter of his new philosophy. He had begun it two months before, while under the influence of Dostoevsky and his own struggle with the "powers of darkness," and was to continue working on it for another month until he abandoned it when half done. He hoped to publish it as a book, and asked Ottoline, Forster, and Russell to suggest revisions. Since the work has been lost, we know of it mainly from their comments and from Lawrence's comments in July on a lecture syllabus prepared by Russell. Russell at first found it unsympathetic and dreaded talking to Lawrence about it:

> It is rather uneducated stuff—I feel as you [Ottoline] would if I wrote about pictures. Yet I believe there is a great deal in it—only the form is bad, and he doesn't know how to say only what is to the purpose. He will be angry, and fight like a devil. I think the imagination out of which it springs is good— rather Blake-ish.

Later, having discussed the philosophy with Lawrence, he was more enthusiastic. "At first, the absence of movement seemed to me a defect," he told Ottoline," and my intellectual taste was offended now and then. . . . [nonetheless] Lawrence is splendid. I like his philosophy very much now that I have read more."[155]

Lawrence and Russell agreed to discuss further action at Garsington between 12 and 16 June. Ottoline had been in the house for nearly a month, painting and moving furniture, but the Lawrences (with Gilbert Cannan) were her first guests—in honor of her forty-second birthday, 16 June. Lawrence did not just expound his philosophy; he also took a hand in the decorating and helped entertain Ottoline's nine-year-old daughter, Julian, who was now reunited with her mother after several years of living in the country with an aunt. Her memories of his visit remained vivid:

> Lawrence helped us to decorate our sitting-room, the Red Room. With an overall on he used to mount the steps with an egg-cup of gold paint in his hand and trace gold lines on each red panel. . . . [his] lines were far straighter and quicker than ours. . . .
>
> In the evenings he read poetry aloud to us, mostly Swinburne. Or he'd tell us stories of his early life in Nottinghamshire dialect. (He used to speak this to my mother occasionally.) One afternoon he organized a play and made everyone act. He was Othello, in a straw hat and long magenta Arab robe.[156]

This side of Lawrence always endeared him to his friends, but Ottoline found Frieda an unbearable nuisance:

> Frieda sat on the table in the middle of the room, swinging her legs and laughing and mocking at us, giving advice as to what curtains she would have. She has a terrible irritant quality, and enjoys tormenting, and she liked to taunt me because I was taking trouble to make the house nice. . . . She was jealous that we all liked and admired Lawrence, or Lorenzo as she calls him, and that we did not consider her as important a person as he is. She even said in a loud, challenging voice, "I am just as remarkable and important as Lorenzo". . . . She has educated herself on Nietzsche; she appears to be a woman that Strindberg might have married and hated, and is what is called a "clever fool."[157]

At the beginning of the month Lawrence had told Ottoline of Frieda's desire to live by herself. Three days later, when she returned to Greatham from London, he wrote again to say they would take the flat together—explaining, rather lamely, that he needed to be in London for his work. But the wounds of the projected separation were reopened when Frieda saw Lawrence lionized by Ottoline and herself slighted. The night before they were to leave she quarrelled bitterly with Lawrence and in the morning she set off angrily for London alone. "I shall always see that unhappy, distraught, pathetic figure standing in the hall," Ottoline wrote, "hesitating whether he should remain here or whether he should follow her to London. Philip strongly urged him to assert himself and leave her. Of course he didn't. . . . I retired from the controversy for I felt certain that he was too bound up with her ever to leave her." Ottoline added a malicious but prescient analysis of Lawrence's political aspirations:

> He is by tradition and instinct faithful to a wife, and far too timid and sensitive to face life alone, for although he has the flaming ideas of a propagandist he has neither knowledge of the world nor the calm assurance that carries conviction. He soon becomes disappointed, angry, fierce and intolerant at not being attended to, and after a frenzy of angry barks he turns with drooping tail and seeks refuge in Frieda, his "dark abode."[158]

Back at Greatham, Frieda complained to Cynthia Asquith that "Lady Ottoline, etc., were horrid to her, treating her as an appendage and explaining her husband to her as being dropped straight from the sky."[159] It is significant that Frieda never quarrelled with Lady Cynthia, even though she was an object of fascination, perhaps even infatuation, to Lawrence. Lady Cynthia was helpful but not possessive, and as a society beauty she knew how to keep admirers at just the right distance.

In spite of her dudgeon, Frieda sent Ottoline a conciliatory letter of thanks for the visit; she may have been pressured by Lawrence to do so, but it was typical of her to continue doggedly trying to remain friends with people who plainly disliked her:

> When we came to you last time we were very antagonistic he and I and I was not at all happy—I thought you idealized him and you had a sort of unholy soulfulness between you that seems to me quite contrary to all good life—Say, I was jealous, I may have been—but it was not only that—I know you are big and generous at the bottom and I want us to be friends . . . You can help us a lot if you want to—But if you leave me out then there can be no good anywhere it seems to me—But perhaps L. will come to you alone next time—We all want love and the good things to be, don't we?[160]

Ottoline, meanwhile, had suggested to Russell a different solution to the problem: "She is a mad Egotist. I wish she could die or go off with another man who would beat her!"[161] Russell went down to Greatham on 20 June to discuss politics with Lawrence, and sent Ottoline a report that was guaranteed to keep the pot boiling:

> I am glad I went, it was really not trying. I mind her much more when you are about. Lawrence wrote you a long letter yesterday, but she possessed herself of it and tore it up. Then he wrote another, which I hope will reach you. He was *very* angry. She appeared on the little walk by the flower bed, jeering—He said "Come off that, lass, or I'll hit thee in the mouth. You've gone too far this time."
>
> He has a very profound and wise admiration for you. He keeps saying you are a priestess, a Cassandra, and that your tragedy is to have never found the God Apollo. He is quite right. He *feels* all your quality as no one else seems to. It makes me love him.
>
> I don't think, tho', that he knows that kindness is as deep as anything in you.[162]

Indeed, in his letter to Ottoline—which reached her intact—Lawrence insisted she must preside over the group that was to plan, at Garsington, England's spiritual renewal: "You must be the centre-pin that holds us together, and the needle which keeps our direction constant, always towards the Eternal thing." Other possible recruits were Cannan, perhaps Gordon Campbell, and the Murrys: "Murry has a genuine side to his nature: so has Mrs. Murry. Don't mistrust them. They are valuable, I know." Frieda, he promised, would "come round soon. It is the same thing with her as with all the Germans—all the world—she hates the Infinite—my immortality. But she will come round."[163] These proposals were not entirely welcome to Ottoline, whose affection for Lawrence did not extend to many of his friends, not to mention his wife. For the next five months they continued to correspond, but could not agree on terms for a meeting; when Lawrence finally came to Garsington again, he came alone.

But Frieda did not seriously disturb Lawrence's developing friendship with Russell. After his visit to Greatham on 20 June both men sent optimistic reports to Ottoline:

> We think to have a lecture hall in London in the autumn, [Lawrence wrote] and give lectures: he on Ethics, I on Immortality: also to have meetings, to establish a little society or body around a *religious belief, which leads to action*. We must centre in the knowledge of the Infinite, of God. . . . [Russell] is coming to have a real, actual, logical belief in Eternity, and upon this he can work: a belief in the absolute, an existence in the Infinite. It is very good and I am very glad.[164]

Russell was equally enthusiastic about their collaboration: Lawrence would provide the spirit, he the mind, so that they could deal both with the world as it was, and as it might be: "I could make a splendid course on political ideas: morality, the state, property, marriage, war, taking them to their roots in human nature, and showing how each is a prison for the infinite in us. And leading on to the hope of a happier world."[165] Having shelved his academic responsibilities, Russell was ready to undertake a popular work on the world crisis, and to play a larger role on the political scene. In a couple of weeks he wrote a long outline of his proposed lectures, under the title "Philosophy of Social Reconstruction," and sent it off to Greatham. By 8 July his manuscript was returned; Lawrence had torn it to shreds like a schoolmaster berating some especially dim pupil.

In his covering letter Lawrence had summed up his objections as: ". . . this which you say is all social criticism: it isn't social reconstruction."[166] Russell's outline attacked the state for interfering with individual happiness, above all by making war, whereas Lawrence argued that if the state represented "Unanimity of Purpose"—some great common belief—then its citizens would be happy. Russell was thinking within the tradition of liberal utilitarianism; Lawrence, like Carlyle and William Morris in their different ways, wanted to resurrect the ideal of an organic society. The result is a dialogue whose interest lies in the utter opposition of its two voices, like Blake's annotations on *The Works of Sir Joshua Reynolds*. Some examples:

Russell: *One great source [of social disintegration]: prevention of children; turns thought to momentary sensation, isolates [the sexual] act.*

Lawrence: Prevention of children is only a result of disintegration—We prevent children because we want individual power (money). The act is isolated in us beforehand. The prevention is only a following out of what *is*. Don't dwell on children so much.

Russell: *Another source: living in towns, away from earth.*

Lawrence: We live in towns from choice, when we subscribe to our great civilized form. The nostalgia for the country is not *so* important. What is important is that our towns are *false* towns—every street a blow, every corner a stab.

Russell: *Strength in the State is like discipline on a pirate ship. The State is in its very essence an evil thing, by its exclusions and by the fact that it is a combination of men for murder and robbery.*

Lawrence: The State is the expression of a great metaphysical conception: the conception of God the Creator, who created the earth according to certain Laws, which, if obeyed, would give happiness. . . . The State *must* represent the deepest philosophical or religious belief.

Russell: *We can not have an absolute principle against force, but we must look out for ways of minimizing its employment.*

Lawrence: Let the law be established on the sense of truth, and then you can use force. Because the truth is greater than any one of us.

Russell: *Why should a man be moral? Because action against the desires of others makes him disliked, which is disagreeable to him.*

Lawrence: No! No! No! No! No! Why do you use "moral" when you only mean "well-behaved"?

Russell: *Successful monogamy depends upon the successful substitution of habit for emotion in the course of years. A character which does not readily form habits, or does not find habits an adequate safeguard against emotion, is not suited to monogamy.*

Lawrence: No! The desire for monogamy is profound in us. But the most difficult thing in the world is to find a mate. It is still true, that a man and wife are one flesh. A man alone is only fragmentary—also a woman. *Completeness is in marriage.* But State-marriage is a *lie*.

Russell: *To prevent wars, men must not be balked in their instincts, since this leads to cruelty; they must have opportunities of showing manhood and running risks.*

Lawrence: This . . . is good.

Russell: *No need of hate or conflict: only the failure of inward joy brings them about.*

Lawrence: There will always be hate and conflict. It is a principle of growth: every bud must burst its cover, and the cover doesn't want to be burst. But let our hatred and conflict be *really* part of our vital growth, the outcome of our *growing*, not of our desire for sensation.[167]

(116)

"As yet [Russell] stands too much on the shore of this existing world," Lawrence told Ottoline. "He must get into a boat and preach from out of the waters of eternity, if he is going to do any good. But I hope he isn't angry with me."[168] Russell was more disturbed than angry. Intellectually he felt sure of his ground against Lawrence, but emotionally he was still under his spell: "I am depressed, partly by Lawrence's criticisms. I feel a worm, a useless creature. Sometimes I enumerate my capacities, and wonder why I am not more use in the world. I suppose scepticism is my real trouble."[169]

If it was any consolation to Russell, Lawrence had just "broken down" in the middle of his own philosophy—though not because of any crisis of nerve, rather because new ideas were germinating and he wanted to start again from the beginning. He had to come to London for a weekend to help Frieda prepare the move to their new flat on Hampstead Heath, so it was agreed that he and Russell would spend a day together, 10 July, and try to thrash out their differences over the lecture syllabus. Russell was gloomy, but he was shocked to find Lawrence's friends even more negative than himself: "He took me to see a Russian Jew, Kotiliansky, and Murry and Mrs. Murry—they were all sitting together in a bare office . . . with the windows shut, smoking Russian cigarettes without a moment's intermission, idle and cynical. I thought Murry *beastly* and the whole atmosphere of the three dead and putrefying." Then, after an equally depressing trip to the zoo, Russell—no doubt still smarting from the treatment Lawrence had given his syllabus—tried to tear down some of his friend's more grandiose beliefs:

> He says "facts" are quite unimportant, only "truths" matter. London is a "fact" not a "truth." But he wants London pulled down. I tried to make him see that that would be absurd if London were unimportant, but he kept reiterating that London doesn't really exist, and that he could easily make people see it doesn't, and then they would pull it down. He was so confident of his powers of persuasion that I challenged him to come to Trafalgar Square at once and begin preaching. That brought him to earth and he began to shuffle. . . . When one gets a glimmer of the facts into his head, as I did at last, he gets discouraged, and says he will go to the South Sea Islands, and bask in the sun with 6 native wives. He is tough work.

Russell felt Lawrence was "very like Shelley—just as fine, but with a similar impatience of fact. The revolution he hopes for is just like Shelley's prophecy of banded anarchs fleeing while the people celebrate a feast of love."[170] Yet Lawrence seemed to have no idea of how far apart he and Russell really were; he was still assuring Ottoline that he had quarreled with Russell's lectures but not with him—on the contrary, "We have almost sworn *Blutbruderschaft*. We will set out together, he and I."[171] In any case, the terms of their quarrel had suddenly become obsolete, for at their London meeting Russell had lent Lawrence a book that struck him like a mental lightning bolt. The volume bore the innocuous title of *Early Greek Philosophy*, by John Burnet, an Edinburgh professor.

A Caesar for England?

BURNET'S BOOK was an anthology of the pre-Socratic philosophers. One of them, above all, spoke directly to Lawrence: the dark and contemptuous Heraclitus, a shadowy figure of the fifth century B.C. Lawrence had recently recommended to Russell the example of Christ preaching the parable of the sower from a boat in the lake; now, after three days of reading Burnet, he felt that England needed stronger medicine than prophets and parables:

> I have been wrong, much too Christian, in my philosophy. These early Greeks have clarified my soul. I must drop all about God.
> You must drop all your democracy. You must not believe in 'the people'. One class is no better than another. It must be a case of Wisdom, or Truth. Let the working classes *be* working classes. That is the truth. There must be an aristocracy of people who have wisdom, and there must be a Ruler: a Kaiser: no Presidents and democracies. I shall write out Herakleitos, on tablets of bronze.
> 'And it is law, too, to obey the Council of one.' . . .
> I am rid of all my Christian religiosity. It was only a muddiness.[172]

In his philosophy, Lawrence had relied up to now on such Judaeo-Christian dualisms as Love and Law, Body and Spirit, God and the Devil. Heraclitus' cosmology was similar in structure—Hegel revered him as the inventor of the dialectic—but Pagan and elemental in its concepts. He argued that a constant intermingling of opposites constitutes the world; it followed that to distinguish between, for example, good and evil was meaningless, and that to deplore violence and war was to deny life itself:

> Homer was wrong in saying: "Would that strife might perish from among gods and men!" He did not see that he was praying for the destruction of the universe; for, if his prayer was heard, all things would pass away. . . .
> We must know that war is common to all and strife is justice, and that all things come into being and pass away through strife.[173]

In politics, Heraclitus opposed democracy because he disbelieved absolutely in the wisdom or virtue of the average man. The few who were wise had the right to govern the foolish crowd; by the general law of struggle, the superior man might aggrandize himself as much as he could over his inferiors. In his letter of 14 July Lawrence told Russell that England was "a beaten nation" unless something unexpected came to the rescue; he implied that Germany was winning because it had a kaiser, and that England needed a similar supreme leader. Certainly the Germans had checked the Allied offensives and driven the Russians back hundreds of miles, though it does not seem to have struck Lawrence as a flaw in his theory that the Russians were led by a kaiser—i.e. a "caesar" (tsar)—too.

But the front that most concerned Lawrence was apparently the Home Front, as he explained to Russell a day later:

> What we must hasten to prevent is this young democratic party from getting into power. The idea of giving power to the hands of the working class is *wrong*. The working man must elect the immediate government, of his work, of his district, not the ultimate government of the nation. There must be a body of chosen patricians. . . .
> Can't you see the whole state is collapsing. Look at the Welsh strike. This war is going to develop into the last great war between labour and capital. It will be a ghastly chaos of destruction, if it is left to Labour to be constructive. The fight must immediately be given a higher aim than the triumph of Labour, or we shall have another French Revolution. The deadly Hydra now is the hydra of Equality. Liberty, Equality and Fraternity is the three-fanged serpent. You must have a government based upon good, better and best.[174]

By the "young democratic party" Lawrence seems to mean the Labour Party, whose representation in Parliament had risen from two in 1900 to forty-two in December 1910 (by 1924 they were to form their first government). When Asquith announced his Coalition Cabinet on 26 May 1915 it included Arthur Henderson, the first Labour minister. This was an admission that England's traditional ruling classes needed the cooperation of the trade unions. The "munitions crisis" of spring 1915 had shown that in a war of attrition the side that could produce the most war material was likely to win; industrial workers must therefore be mobilized as systematically as those on the actual fighting line. Labour's bargaining position was naturally improved, and the Welsh strike that so disturbed Lawrence reflected the new balance of power.

The South Wales miners wanted a contract separate from a national agreement on miners' wages; when the owners refused, a strike was called. Invoking the recently passed Munitions of War Act, the government forbade the strike and threatened retaliation against the miners if they disobeyed. Nothing daunted, they struck on the appointed date, 14 July—the day Lawrence told Russell he must "drop all [his] democracy." Five days later Lloyd George and Arthur Henderson were obliged to go to Cardiff and concede all the miners' demands. Lawrence's advocacy of personal rule and a corporate state was thus provoked, in part, by the miners' successful flouting of the law. As a child he had observed the conflict between the defiant, holiday spirit of striking miners, and the disapproval of their wives, who had to keep the household running with less money and therefore worked harder than ever. The male principle, for Lawrence, was rebellious, sensuous, and anarchic; the female constructive, sustaining culture and the social order. He favored different sides of this opposition at different times in his life; but in July 1915 the miners' unruly self-assertion threatened his vision of a hierarchical new society:

> A new constructive idea of a new state is needed *immediately*. Criticism is *unnecessary*. It is behind the times. You *must* work out the idea of a new state, not go on criticising this old one. . . . the idea is, that every man shall vote according to his understanding, and that the highest understanding must dictate for the lower understandings. And the desire is to have a perfect government perfectly related in all its parts, the highest aim of the government is the highest good of the *soul*, of the individual, the fulfilment in the Infinite, in the Absolute.[175]

The governing principle in Lawrence's ideal state—as in Plato's—is that each group or class should control only what it knows from direct experience. Since women have a different experience from men, it follows that they should have their own political structure: ". . . as the men elect and govern the industrial side of life, so the women must elect and govern the domestic side. And there must be a rising rank of women governors, as of men, culminating in a woman Dictator, of equal authority with the supreme Man."[176] So Lawrence settled the suffrage issue. This functional division of the sexes has of course been typical of rightist regimes in our century; the closest analogue to Lawrence's scheme in real life would be the regime of Juan and Eva Peron in Argentina.

We do not have Russell's reply to these proposals, but no doubt he raised the standard liberal-democratic objections. Lawrence's response was that he didn't want "tyrants," but neither did he believe in "democratic control"—a reference to Russell's work for the U. D. C. The popular will, Lawrence felt, was becoming more and more bloodthirsty and could only be checked by an elite devoted to absolute Truth: ". . . the [state] must culminate in one real head, as every organic thing must—no foolish republics with foolish presidents, but an elected King, something like Julius Caesar."[177] Russell of course pointed out the logical flaw in this argument: how could a foolish populace be expected to "culminate" in a wise ruler? would they not acclaim someone much worse than Asquith or Lloyd George, like the jingo Horatio Bottomley who threatened to become the "man on horseback" of English politics? Lawrence's response simply begged the question: "As for . . . Bottomley, a nation in a false system acting in a false spirit will quite rightly choose him. But a nation striving for the truth and the establishment of truth and right will forget him in a second."[178]

One can account for Lawrence's sudden enthusiasm for dictatorship in various ways: the influence of Heraclitus, the impact of outside political events, and so forth. But all such explanations seem inadequate to the radical shift in his ideas. His conversion to belief in "a kaiser" was just one of a series of intellectual somersaults he had made since he and Frieda were confined to England in August 1914, and only by forcing the facts can we fit these changes into a coherent pattern of intellectual or emotional development. They are, rather, a gratuitous sequence of obsessions— now with evil, now with homosexuality; in February with an ideal socialism, in July with the need for autocracy. What *is* coherent about these beliefs, though, is the style in which they are proclaimed: Lawrence's passionate single-mindedness and his consignment of his previous ideas to oblivion does not vary, nor does his habit of inserting new terms into his basic system of binary opposites. One cannot miss the analogy between this pattern of behavior and that of the chronic invalid—which Lawrence was—who restlessly seeks relief by some new treatment or new scene. A person thus afflicted cannot accept that there may be *no* remedy for his illness, for to give up the search for a cure is to acquiesce in his own death. The pattern of Katherine Mansfield's last years, after she became tubercular, was similar to Lawrence's—though she placed her faith in different solutions.

Departure from Greatham

FOR THEIR last month at Greatham the Lawrences were even more restless than usual, partly because of their uncertainty about what they would do in London and partly because more people were coming to stay at Greatham and the position of their cottage, a few paces from two others, gave them practically no privacy. Frieda often went up to Hampstead to visit Dollie Radford, a cheerful and hospitable middle-aged poetess. Lawrence came for two weekends, helping Frieda to furnish their new house and discussing the projected lectures with Russell. He also engaged in some elaborate beating around the bush with Ottoline about a visit to Garsington. After the visit in June, Frieda had suggested that Lawrence might come by himself next time; when Ottoline duly invited him for early July he excused himself by saying he must continue with his tutoring of Mary Saleeby. To be put off in favor of a ten-year-old was scarcely flattering, and Lawrence sharpened the snub by telling Ottoline not to reserve the gardener's rooms for himself and Frieda, but to let the Cannans have them if they wished. This was the coup de grâce to the plans for the Lawrences to have regular quarters at Garsington. Still, Lawrence said he would like to stay at the main house for part of

August, adding pointedly that Frieda might not come. A week later he wrote that he would come on 31 July to "discuss propaganda" with Ottoline, the Cannans, and Russell. But he said Frieda would accompany him, to which Ottoline replied that there wasn't room for her; Frieda was furious, the visit was canceled, and Lawrence could not meet with Ottoline until one of them backed down.[179]

Lawrence recognized that his plans for a new community at Garsington had reached an impasse; but, rather evasively, he blamed it on Russell's disagreement with him over England's need for a Caesar:

> Are we never going to unite [he complained to Ottoline] in one idea and one purpose? Is it to be a case of each one of us having his own personal and private fling? That is nothing. . . . individuals do not *vitally* concern me any more. Only a purpose vitally concerns me, not individuals. . . . I want very much to come to Garsington if we are going to be a little group filled with one spirit and striving for one end. But if we are going to be a little set of individuals each one concerned with himself and his own personal fling at the world, I can't bear it.[180]

In fact, Lawrence was becoming *more* individual rather than less, as he began the new "Heraclitan" version of his philosophy. "I am so sure of what I know, and what is true, now," he told Ottoline, "that I am sure I am stronger, in the truth, in the knowledge I have, than all the world outside that knowledge."[181] This was a declaration of solipsism that was bound to alienate him from his intimates to the degree that they failed to share his beliefs. If he wanted to merge his individuality with others, they would first have to agree on a common purpose; instead, Lawrence took his current beliefs as dogma and demanded submission from those around him. Frieda, Ottoline, and Russell—to extend the circle no further—were plainly unwilling to do so.

Though Lawrence hated the war he longed to take part in some collective enterprise that might be equally engrossing, equally purgative of selfish concerns, yet constructive rather than destructive. Even Russell suffered great loneliness during the war through being cut off from the mass emotions of his country; Lawrence's plight was similar, and even more acute. As the war fever spread he felt more isolated, more desperately in need of some countervailing faith in which he could unite with his friends.

The natural alternative was organized pacifism, for which Garsington was to provide the most important center and refuge. But this movement was based on the belief that civilized values were endangered by the "primitive" passions of war; Lawrence, almost alone among the war's opponents, could not agree.

Lawrence's deep disagreement with pacifism can be seen in his attitudes to two men he knew who went to the war: Perceval Lucas and Herbert Asquith. Asquith, an officer in the artillery, visited Greatham on 19 June with his wife, Lady Cynthia; they arrived in a car borrowed from the motorpool at 10, Downing Street! Lawrence told Ottoline of his visitors:

> He is home slightly wounded—three teeth knocked out. But he is well. Only all his soul is left at the war. The war is the only reality to him. All this here is unreal, this England: only the trenches are Life to him. Cynthia is very unhappy—he is not even aware of her existence. He is spell-bound by the fighting line. He ought to die. It all seemed horrid, like hypnotism.[182]

Lawrence saw the war as a destructive rival to what should be man's great adventure: his relation to woman. When Pinker asked him to write a story for the *Strand Magazine* he began it almost at once, in the first week of June, and found his subject ready to hand in the marriage of Percy Lucas and Madeline, a daughter of the elder Meynells.[183] The first part of the story, the married life of Winifred and Evelyn, was Lawrence's interpretation of what he had seen of the Lucases (who lived at Greatham); the second, Evelyn's experience at the front, was mostly pure invention mixed with some details of soldiering picked up from Herbert Asquith. The marriage begins in sheer physical passion, then turns into a conflict between Winifred's crude, ethical nature and Evelyn's dilettantish inertia. He cares only to work around their cottage and refuses to find a job, so that they must live off Winifred's father; already bitter, Winifred blames Evelyn when their eldest daughter is crippled in an accident: "Her soul was fierce as iron against him, thrusting him away, always away. And his heart was hard as iron against her in resistance. . . . She hated his passivity as if it were something evil."[184]

Lawrence attributes the more active role in destroying the marriage to Winifred, whose strict moral sense—she is a north of England Quaker—goads her on to attack her negative husband. In the second part, however, the roles are reversed; when war is declared Evelyn at last discovers a purpose, and an escape from Winifred's ethical imperatives: "She tried to tell him he was one of the saviours of mankind. He listened to these things; they were very gratifying to his self-esteem. But he knew it was all cant. He was out to kill and destroy; he did not even want to be an angel of salvation. Some chaps might feel that way. He couldn't; that was all."

The story ends with the fulfillment of Evelyn's desires in France. He is posted to cover a retreat and is wounded by a German shell. As he lies by himself, he coldly considers his fate: "The outcome should be a pure, eternal, logical judgment: whether he should live or die. . . . He was now no longer a man, but a disembodied, clear abstraction." His decision, of course, is for death; his wife and children cannot hold him back, for spiritually he has already passed over to the other side. When a group of Germans appear he cold-bloodedly kills three of them with his revolver, and is himself killed by the fourth—who is so appalled by the "almost ghoulish, slight smile" on Evelyn's face that he mutilates it with a knife and runs mad.

In its original version of June 1915 "England, my England" was a powerful but thesis-ridden story; Lawrence was all too eager to grind his axe—that the mildest and most civilized of Englishmen bore within himself enough destructive frenzy to give even a German cavalryman nightmares. When he rewrote the story for book publication in December 1921, he dropped the hero's awakening into destructiveness: Evelyn goes to war, passively, because his wife and father-in-law push him into it, and dies because he can no longer bear to live. His shooting of the Germans at the end was eliminated also in the second version, so that he is merely discarded instead of fulfilled.

When "England, my England" was published in the *English Review* for October 1915 it must have been deeply resented by the Meynells. The story, with its distinctly unpatriotic tone, may also have added to the ill repute of *The Rainbow*, which was banned a month later. The following summer brought the final twist of fate, when Percy Lucas was fatally wounded in the battle of the Somme. On hearing the news from Catherine Carswell, Lawrence expressed remorse—rare for him—at the way he had repaid the Meynells' hospitality; yet in the end he held to his creed that literature's essential function was to present the truth about life, however painful:

> It upsets me very much to hear of Percy Lucas. I did not know he was dead. I wish that story at the bottom of the sea, before ever it had been printed. Yet it seems to me, man must find a new expression, give a new value to life, or his women will reject him, and he must die. I liked Madeleine Lucas the best of the Meynells really. She was the one who was capable of honest love: she and Monica. Lucas was, somehow, a spiritual coward. But who isn't? I ought never, never to have gone to live at Greatham. Perhaps Madeleine won't be hurt by that wretched story—that is all that matters. If it was a true story, it shouldn't really damage. . . .
>
> [P.S.] No, I don't wish I had never written that story. It should do good, at the long run.*

It was a conspicuous trait in Lawrence that he hated to be under an obligation to anyone; those who had been his benefactors were also those most likely to find themselves pilloried in his fiction, as if he wanted to be revenged on them for the discomfort they had caused him. Yet his letter of thanks to Viola Meynell was perhaps sincere enough, within its own terms: "I am *very glad* you lent [the cottage] to us. It has a special atmosphere, and I feel as if I had been born afresh there, got a new, sure, separate soul: as a monk in a monastery, or St John in the wilderness. Now we must go back into the world to fight."[185]

Before moving to London the Lawrences went to spend five days at Littlehampton with Dollie Radford; after the strain of six months at close quarters with the Meynells, and the other mental crises of Greatham, Lawrence sought comfort from the alien sea—"to be blown and washed and to forget."[186] At the same time, the brief holiday was an interlude in which he could take stock of his country's crisis and of the part he had played, and would play in it. Writing to Cynthia Asquith, he gave her the warning he had embodied in "England, my England": "Of course your husband will go to war and love it much better than you, if you want him to make money. It doesn't matter whether you *need* money or not. You *do* need it. But the fact that you would ask him

---

* Lacy 1103, 16 July 1916; most of the passage quoted is omitted in CL. Lawrence was probably also thinking of Percy Lucas in a sneering remark to Cynthia Asquith: "The young authoritarian, the young man who turns Roman Catholic in order to put himself under the authority of the Church, in order to enjoy the aesthetic quality of obedience, he is such a swine with cringing hind-quarters, that I am delighted, I dance with joy when I see him rushing down the Gadarene slope of the war." (CL 360).

to work, put his soul into getting it, makes him love better war and pure destruction." Yet the only *lasting* answer to this dilemma, Lawrence felt, was to change the very basis of English life by destroying "the blind spirit of possession." His mood reverted to that of earlier in the year when he had been completing *The Rainbow,* as he mused on the contrast between the ugly little resort town and the stretch of open coastline that lay just to the west of it:

> ... the flat unfinished world running with foam and noise and silvery light, and a few gulls swinging like a half-born thought. It is a great thing to realise that the original world is still there—perfectly clean and pure, many white advancing foams, and only the gulls swinging between the sky and the shore; and in the wind the yellow sea poppies fluttering very hard, like yellow gleams in the wind, and the windy flourish of the seed-horns.
>
> It is this mass of unclean world that we have superimposed on the clean world that we cannot bear. When I looked back, out of the clearness of the open evening, at this Littlehampton dark and amorphous like a bad eruption on the edge of the land, I was so sick I felt I could not come back: all these little amorphous houses like an eruption, a disease on the clean earth; and all of them full of such a diseased spirit, every landlady harping on her money, her furniture, every visitor harping on his latitude of escape from money and furniture. The whole thing like an active disease, fighting out the health. . . . One can no longer live with people: it is too hideous and nauseating. Owners and owned, they are like the two sides of a ghastly disease. One feels a sort of madness come over one, as if the world had become hell. But it is only superimposed: it is only a temporary disease. It can be cleaned away.[187]

If this chartered and unclean world of cities were to be cleansed, it would have to be attacked at the root; so Lawrence came, for the first and last time in his life, to make his home in London. From Littlehampton he and Frieda went to Greatham to pick up their few belongings. They would never set foot there again. They arrived in London on 4 August, the first anniversary of England's entry into the war.

CHAPTER IV

HAMPSTEAD

ONE, BYRON VILLAS was the lower half of a small semide-tached house in the Vale of Health, a quiet corner of Hampstead Heath. Like most places the Lawrences lived in it was nondescript as a dwelling but redeemed by the natural setting—in this case the eight hundred acres of park and woodland that completely surrounded it. The rent was 3 pounds a month, which it seemed they could easily afford now that Lawrence had received his £132.10 from Methuen. They canvassed their friends for furnishings and searched the secondhand stalls of the Caledonian market; when Cynthia Asquith came to visit she found their rooms "delightful." Hampstead was also an ideal quarter in which to mingle with artists and intellectuals, the most likely recruits for Lawrence's political enterprises. Still, he never liked cities or felt at home in them, and he would leave Byron Villas without regret when the time came to move on.

The move to London soon gave Frieda a reward. While staying with Dollie Radford in the preceding weeks she had made several attempts to see her two daughters on their way to school. They were told to run away if she appeared, but such scenes were apparently too grotesque for even Ernest Weekley's vindictiveness. He agreed that Frieda might see the children in his lawyer's office for half an hour on her thirty-sixth birthday, 11 August. The children were tense and Frieda in tears; but at least her right to see them had been recognized, after three years of exclusion. Fortunately, the children became a less bitter issue between Lawrence and Frieda after this meeting. Even so, Frieda had to wait over a year for the next meeting; others followed, but essentially her ties with the children were broken until they reached their majority and could go where they wished.

Lawrence's Quarrel with Liberalism

LAWRENCE spent his first month at Hampstead on modest tasks: correcting the remaining proofs of *The Rainbow,* revising some prewar travel sketches, and putting the flat in order. He also was reassessing his alliance with Ottoline and Russell. The plan for joint lectures was in limbo, thanks to his criticisms of Russell's syllabus; indeed, Lawrence was tempted to abandon them altogether. "I feel like knocking my head against the wall," he complained to Cynthia Asquith, "or of running off to some unformed South American place where there is no thought of civilised effort." His vision of an England reborn still seemed splendid to him, but what had the Englishmen he knew done to show that they deserved it?

> I am so sick of people: they preserve an evil, bad, separating spirit under the warm cloak of good words. . . . What does Russell really want? He wants to keep his own established ego, his finite and ready-defined self intact, free from contact and connection. He wants to be ultimately a free agent. This is what they all want, ultimately—that is what is at the back of all international peace-forever and democratic control talks: they want an outward system of nullity, which they call peace and goodwill, so that in their own souls they can be independent little gods, referred nowhere and to nothing, little mortal Absolutes, secure from question. That is at the back of all Liberalism, Fabianism and democracy. It stinks. It is the will of the louse. And the Conservative either wants to bully or to be bullied.[1]

Bourgeois democracy and reformism, Lawrence argues, have created a society in which each person strives to create a highly developed, autonomous, inner self, then competes with all the others in the open market of personalities; private life is thus drawn into the economic competition that forces each individual to exploit his capacities in order to be financially secure. The welfare state—"Fabianism" in Lawrence's terms—moderates this competition and allays the worst misfortunes of those who fail in it, but does not challenge the basic individualism of the system. A true community is built from a multitude of close human contacts, but the present order of society only raises ever higher the walls that separate one from another. Immured in the prison of self, the modern European rots inwardly until he will do anything to escape: so, a hundred years of bourgeois peace and security erupt into the most destructive war ever known. If Lawrence heard of it, he would have been grimly satisfied by an episode in September when the Asquiths were staying with friends:

> "[Herbert] came in looking rather queer and said he had broken a vase. He had smashed an inoffensive vase in Edward's room, because it 'wasn't pretty'—I remembered Lawrence's statement that Beb's destructive spirit had been aroused, and that he couldn't bear 'to see a house with its roof on' and I felt alarmed. I believe the desire to smash is a recognised symptom of nervous strain from Artillery work."[2]

If modern Liberalism led to disintegration nonetheless Lawrence had little sympathy with its traditional opponents: the Conservative party and those who called for a religious revival. Both, he felt, wanted only to restore the old coercive hierarchies. What, then, was his solution? The kernel of it—and he was moving toward a similar formula for personal relations—was the desire, not for authoritarianism, but for authority. Mankind, he argues, has a potential for "unanimity in truth"; if this be recognized then the state can be reshaped, without coercion, into an organic form that will be both collectively and individually satisfying:

> Let us have done with this foolish form of government, and this idea of democratic control. Let us submit to the knowledge that there are aristocrats and plebeians born, not made. Some amongst us are born fit to govern, and some are born only fit to be governed. . . . But it is not a question of tradition or heritage. . . .
> It is a question of the spirit. *Why* are we a nation? We are a nation which must be built up according to a living idea, a great architecture of living people, which shall express the greatest truth of which we are capable. There must be King and Queen, and Lords and Ladies, and Burghers and Burgesses, and Servants: but not King George and Queen Mary, not Lord Kitchener or Earl Grey (or Mr. Asquith) or Lloyd George. . . .
> We must rid ourselves of this ponderous incubus of falsehood, this massive London, with its streets of nullity: we must, with one accord and in purity of spirit, pull it down and build up a beautiful thing.[3]

One may find various parallels to Lawrence's theory in Plato's ideal republic, in actual tribal societies, or in certain third-world regimes. But Lawrence's political views have inevitably been associated with nazism, by Bertrand Russell and, most insistently, by

Emile Delavenay. Hitler was four years younger than Lawrence; in 1915 he was a private in the Austrian army. The two men had some similarity of background and even of temperament, and both were indebted to the antidemocratic ideologies current around the turn of the century. But Lawrence never joined any right-wing political organization, though in the 1920s he could easily have associated himself with Italian or German fascism, since he spent long periods in both countries.

He ignored Hitler, and jeered at Mussolini as a cardboard hero. Nonetheless, his sympathies were clearly with the right on such issues as education or sexual roles; but his ideas were so individual and eccentric that one cannot fairly say more without descending to minute particulars, and tracing the many fluctuations of his political beliefs over the years.

These fluctuations were at their most extreme in 1915, when by the time the year was half over he had moved from a messianic belief in socialism to the most complete contempt for popular sovereignty and advocacy of a corporate state. In tracing his development, one must allow for his extreme naiveté about both the English political tradition and current affairs. From his university years he knew such social thinkers as Carlyle, Hegel, Nietzsche, Locke, and Ruskin; when he became interested in politics in 1915 he did not think it necessary to expand his knowledge by systematic study. He read only one political book that year, H. N. Brailsford's *Shelley, Godwin, and their Circle* (in late March). The concrete political proposals in Russell's lecture syllabus disgusted him; though Russell had run for Parliament and was the grandson of a prime minister, Lawrence did not care to be guided by his friend's knowledge of the elementary realities of British politics. His own analysis was, simply, that in the political realm things were "all wrong"—and therefore should altogether and at once be set right. Since conventional means of political change could not effect such a transformation, this was, for Lawrence, sufficient cause to dismiss them altogether.

Lawrence's political ambitions, then, depended entirely on his powers of persuasion: he assumed a prophetic stance and scorned the mundane tasks of political organization. In our century revolutionary changes have indeed been initiated by men of superlative oratorical talent or spiritual authority, such as Hitler, Mussolini, Trotsky, and Gandhi. But these men also created political organizations that would implement their visions in detail;

Lawrence never even began this task, and if he had tried he would certainly have been too naive and willful to succeed at it. Making grandiose plans with his friends, and arguing with them, had been his only political action up to this time, and when this proved ineffectual he angrily blamed the friends:

> I've got a real bitterness in my soul, just now, as if Russell and Lady Otto-line were traitors—they are traitors. They betray the real truth. . . . they say I, D. H. L., am wonderful, I am an exceedingly valuable personality, and that the things I say are extravaganzas, illusions. They say I cannot think.
>
> All that is dynamic in the world, they convert to a sensation, to the gratifica-tion of what is static. They are static, static, static, they come, they say to me, 'You are wonderful, you are dynamic,' then they filch my life for a sensation unto themselves, all my effort, which is my life, they betray, they are like Judas: they turn it all to their own static selves, convert it into the static nullity. The result is for them a gratifying sensation, a tickling, and for me a real bleeding.[4]

There may have been some truth in Lawrence's suspicion that his friends were aristocratic sensationalists who lived parasitically off his vitality. But it is curious that he should make his complaints to Cynthia Asquith, for they were much more chargeable to her. Ottoline and Russell were living lives of their own, however trou-bled by neurotic conflicts. They admired Lawrence's personal gifts and relished his company, but could not fully endorse his po-litical views; to continue relations with him on this basis may con-ceivably have been exploitive or hypocritical but it was not treach-erous, since they never committed themselves to becoming his philosophical disciples. They upset him, to be sure, by their skep-ticism about his schemes for ending the war and transforming En-gland, but Lawrence himself admitted ten years later that they were right: "In a great issue like the war, there was nothing to be 'done' . . . There is still nothing to be 'done.' Probably not for many, many years will men start to 'do' something. And even then, only after they have changed gradually, and deeply."[5]

Meanwhile, Lawrence had at last realized that collaboration with Russell was unlikely, so that if he still wanted to "lift up [his] voice in the autumn" he would have to find a different way of making it heard:

> Everything is so awful and static, so large and ponderous, like the physical mass of London lying on the plain of south England. And one must shift that mass: it is the mountain that faith must move. I do believe there are people

who wait for the spirit of truth. But I think one can't find them personally. I had hoped and tried to get a little nucleus of living people together. But I think it is no good. One must start direct with the open public, without associates. But how to begin, and when, I don't know yet.[6]

Though Lawrence wanted his new philosophy to be Greek rather than Christian his style of proclaiming it was as Christian as ever. At first he had expressed his vision in political terms, but from August on he began to move beyond politics as a means of changing the world, and to speak directly on his deeper, metaphysical concerns. His right-wing views remained, but he did not try to apply them until he wrote "Education of the People" in late 1918. Moreover, he was becoming less vitally concerned with the condition of England; within a few months he would be convinced that his destiny lay elsewhere. Only his inability to leave would keep him unwillingly bound to his native land for the duration of the war.

Twilight in Italy

LAWRENCE seems to have begun *Twilight in Italy* simply because he wanted to follow the publication of *The Rainbow* with another book as soon as possible; but the task of writing it contributed to the longing to escape England that possessed him by the end of October. The materials for the book were already at hand: during his first years abroad with Frieda he had written sketches of life in the Rhineland, Austria, and Italy, some of which were published in England during 1912–13. In July 1915 Duckworth suggested that Lawrence might collect them into a book; they had promoted *The Prussian Officer* as having a war interest, and hoped to do the same with his travel sketches. Lawrence approved of the scheme, he told Pinker on 29 July: "I always feel a sort of gratitude to Duckworth. I believe my sketches may easily prove good selling stuff, better than a novel."[7] He had already completed a revision of "Christs in the Tirol," making it more than twice as long, and was ready to go on with the remaining sketches. However, the first two he had written, "German Impressions," were not included in the book—probably because they showed German people as simple and normal, not a salable point of view in 1915.

It was agreed that the book would be published the following spring as "Italian Studies," and Lawrence finished revising it in October. His changes made the final text something of a patchwork. The original sketches were fine examples of what Russell called Lawrence's "quick, sensitive impressions," written in the exhilaration of this first months on the Continent with Frieda. But when he revised the sketches two years later he was far from the natural beauty of Lake Garda, and preoccupied by his political quarrel with Russell. He made two sorts of changes. One was the expanding and deepening of an original impression in order to point a moral:

> And by the track where the pack-horses go, in the cold gloom, hangs the large, pale Christ. He has fallen forward, just dead, and the weight of his full-grown, mature body is on the nails of the hands. So he drops, as if his hands would tear away, and he would fall to earth. The face is strangely brutal, and is set with an ache of weariness and pain and bitterness, and his rather ugly, passionate mouth is shut with bitter despair. After all, he had wanted to live and to enjoy his manhood. But fools had ruined his body, and thrown his life away, when he wanted it. No one had helped. His youth and health and vigour, all his life, and himself, were just thrown away as waste. He had died in bitterness [1913]

> And just below the path, where the pack-horses go climbing to the remote, in-folded villages, in the cold gloom of the pass hangs the large, pale Christ. He is larger than life-size. He has fallen forward, just dead, and the weight of the full-grown, mature body hangs on the nails of the hands. So the dead, heavy body drops forward, sags, as if it would tear away and fall under its own weight.
> It is the end. The face is barren with a dead expression of weariness, and brutalized with pain and bitterness. The rather ugly, passionate mouth is set for ever in the disillusionment of death. Death is the complete disillusionment, set like a seal over the whole body and being, over the suffering and weariness and the bodily passion. [1915][8]

The second version is less vital than the original, more generalized, and heavy with overemphatic repetition. In the earlier version the prose reflects the tension between life and death; we see the young man who wanted to live caught at the instant of being "ruined by fools" and dropping toward the ground. In the second version this conflict has been resolved; the mood is one of "complete disillusionment" and Christ "sags" as if acquiescing in his own defeat. What was originally a moment of vision has become a moralized picture.

Lawrence also added to the earlier sections of *Twilight in Italy* long meditations on national character and the future of industrial society. Emile Delavenay has accused him of becoming, in these passages, "an irresponsible propagandist advancing, under cover of studies 'about the nations,' the very arguments of the Kaiser's Germany."[9] If this is so, it is curious that Lawrence excluded from the book whole sections that showed the Germans in an agreeable light. Certainly he makes the book a sounding board for his "philosophy," but he is already moving beyond political issues toward the esoteric cosmology of "The Crown." He refers only obliquely to the war, in his opening description of the "imperial road" south from Bavaria where, in the Middle Ages, the great processions of the Holy Roman emperors went back and forth to Italy. "And how much has that old imperial vanity clung to the German soul," Lawrence muses, ". . . Maybe a certain Grossenwahn [delusion of grandeur] is inherent in the German nature. If only nations would realize that they have certain national characteristics, if only they could understand and agree to each other's particular nature, how much simpler it would all be." This is no doubt an ingenuous remark for 1915, though Lawrence certainly does not identify with Germany's imperial pretensions; he suggests, perhaps, that if the other nations were more secure in their own identities they might have avoided war by humoring German vanity instead of provoking it.

Lawrence feels that each nation's character should be organically based on its landscape and history. He believes in national or local types, but he does not make the racist claim that there is a hierarchy of types, or that they should be kept separate from each other; on the contrary, he is fascinated by their mingling—as in the marriage of Paolo and Maria: "He was strangely like the pictures of peasants in the northern Italian pictures, with the same curious nobility, the same aristocratic, eternal look of motionlessness. . . . His head was hard and fine, the bone finely constructed . . . Maria Fiori was different. She was from the plain. . . . She reminded me again of oxen, broad-boned and massive in physique, dark-skinned, slow in her soul. . . . Paolo and she were the opposite sides of the universe, the light and the dark" (p. 91).

Another important difference between Lawrence and the fascists lies in his attitude to industry, and to modernism generally. In Italy he and Frieda had sought out isolated villages, in Germany he had responded to the peasants of Bavaria and ignored entirely the progressive industrial north. For him, the peasant is autochthonous and the true individual, whereas men who work in factories or offices have no definite personality. Insofar as *Twilight in Italy* is a political book it preaches a reactionary agrarianism; Lawrence mourns a peasant culture that is being shattered by outside competition and emigration. Against this world on the wane there stands the ultramodernism of Marinetti and his Futurists, celebrating "the nocturnal vibrations of arsenals and workshops beneath their violent electric moons. . . . broad-chested locomotives prancing on the rails, like huge steel horses bridled with long tubes." Lawrence was intrigued by their rhetoric but thought they were taking a wrong turn: "I agree with them about the weary sickness of pedantry and tradition and inertness, but I don't agree with them as to the cure and the escape. They will progress down the purely male or intellectual or scientific line. . . . 'Italy is like a great Dreadnought surrounded by her torpedo boats.' That is it exactly—a great mechanism."[10]

Lawrence did not make any moral distinction between German expansionism, based on the cult of progress and the machine, and British imperialism, which had pioneered that line for the whole world. Yet he still hoped that industrialism might prove to be only an evolutionary stage on the way to some better system:

> I sat on the roof of the lemon-house, with the lake below and the snowy mountain opposite, and looked at the ruins on the old, olive-fuming shores, at all the peace of the ancient world still covered in sunshine, and the past seemed to me so lovely that one must look towards it, backwards, only backwards, where there is peace and beauty and no more dissonance.
>
> I thought of England, the great mass of London, and the black, fuming, laborious Midlands and north-country. It seemed horrible. And yet, it was better than the padrone, this old, monkey-like cunning of fatality. It is better to go forward into error than to stay fixed inextricably in the past.
>
> Yet what should become of the world? . . . England was conquering the world with her machines and her horrible destruction of natural life. . . .
>
> And yet, was she not herself finished in this work? She had had enough. She had conquered the natural life to the end: she was replete with the conquest of the outer world, satisfied with the destruction of the Self. She would cease, she would turn round; or else expire.
>
> If she still lived, she would begin to build her knowledge into a great structure of truth (pp. 60–61).

England's future, then, was to be Death, or Transfiguration. At the beginning of September Lawrence decided that he must make his attempt, publicly, to influence the result.

Launching *The Signature*

LAWRENCE'S relations with Ottoline and Russell were now so strained that he could not ask them for help with the day-to-day tasks of starting a magazine. The obvious people to fall back on were Jack and Katherine, who were still the Lawrences' closest friends and had run the little magazine *Rhythm* before the war. The two couples had seen each other only intermittently for some months. After Katherine returned from her escapade with Carco she had come down to Greatham for a pleasant visit with Kot, on 13–14 March. Later she had gone back to Paris twice; she needed an "inflow of rich, sensational life" to help her with her writing, though the affair with Carco was not renewed. In March Jack obtained rooms for them in London, a relief after the hardships of their cottage in Bucks; but he was at a low ebb for some months. Katherine's absences and her preoccupation with her work left him lonely, and he was finding it difficult to make a living by writing.

When Lawrence proposed the new magazine and offered the means to finance it—from the advance on *The Rainbow*—Jack agreed to join in. He and Katherine even moved from Notting Hill to 5, Acacia Road, St. John's Wood, in order to be, as he put it, "near, and not too near" to Hampstead. As usual, Katherine was skeptical of Lawrence's schemes, and Jack in a muddle. "He says the whole thing is personal," Lawrence told Cynthia Asquith, "that between him and me it is a case of Lawrence and Murry, not of any union in an *idea*. He thinks the introduction of any idea, particularly of any political idea, highly dangerous and deplorable."[11] Jack's main livelihood came from reviewing French books for the *Times Literary Supplement;* if he provoked the authorities he might be denied entry to France, a serious handicap to his work. In the middle of August this danger was emphasized by a police raid on the National Labour Press, printers of the *Labour Leader* for the U. D. C. The police seized sample copies and prohibited the printing of further issues; though the ban was soon lifted the episode was a clear warning to those who wanted to oppose British war policy in print. Lawrence himself had no desire to become a martyr; when he asked Lady Cynthia for help with the new venture he told her not to be alarmed by it: ". . . my contribution is purely philosophic and metaphysical, and on these grounds sociological." He even asked her to solicit a subscription from Arthur Balfour, the former Conservative prime minister who was now first lord of the Admiralty.[12]

For Katherine the magazine was simply a place to publish her stories, which up to now had been neither lucrative nor widely popular. To formalize the divisions in its editorial team they adopted the title proposed by Jack, *The Signature,* as "an indication that we took no responsibility for one another's creeds." The magazine would be printed cheaply by "a little Jew in the East End" and sold by subscription at two shillings six pence for six issues, appearing biweekly; Lawrence calculated that it would be self-supporting if they could get 250 subscribers.[13] The faithful Kot found the printer and served as business manager. Once the project was under way Lawrence invited Russell to join:

> I shall be the preacher, Murry will be the revealer of the individual soul with respect to the big questions, particularly he will give an account of the real freedom of the individual soul, as he conceives it; Katherine will do satirical sketches. You will do something serious, I hope, and Gilbert [Cannan] can flounder prehistorically.[14]

Russell and Cannan would have been valuable recruits. One was by now a famous opponent of the war, the other a best-selling popular novelist; compared to them, Jack and Katherine were almost unknown. *The Signature* would not have sparked a revolution in any case, but it might have achieved a modest success. Cannan, however, never contributed, while Russell's first contribution so enraged Lawrence that they ceased to be on speaking terms. The burden of making the magazine known thus fell on Lawrence; that is, on the appeal his "philosophy" might have for a general audience.

The Signature was only part of Lawrence's attempt to spread his word; he also rented two small rooms at 12 Fisher Street as an office and meeting place. "Perhaps by Christmas we shall have some little footing," he told Lady Cynthia, "and I can be reconciled to all my friends—Frieda still abhors the Ottoline, and will have no relation at all with her—and we can unite in a bigger effort, a bigger paper, and Russell give his Lectures, and we can have good Club Meetings. Perhaps—God knows. And perhaps, everything will fizzle out."[15] Lawrence felt that he must create a movement through personal contact or not at all, for despite his years as a teacher he disliked speaking in public. But he had lost many friends over the past year, as he ruefully admitted, so in the month before *The Signature* appeared he worked hard at making new acquaintances and sending diplomatic overtures to old ones that had become estranged.

One of the first people he approached was E. M. Forster. With his usual politeness Forster accepted an invitation to tea, examined the painted boxes the Lawrences were selling as a sideline, and introduced to them his friend H. O. Meredith, a Cambridge economist to whom he had dedicated *A Room With a View* in 1908. Forster himself was not going to be roped into working on *The Signature* but Meredith was a possible recruit. However, when he came to see Lawrence even that evangelist of impulse found that he had met his match:

> [Meredith] led off by saying "I'm tired of language, both written and spoken." Of course, after that, what was to be done. I asked him to turn cart wheels in the passage, or to gambol and bark like a dog on the rug. But he didn't rise to the occasion.
>
> Then suddenly he appeared at eleven at night, the same night, for no reason whatever, and we talked till one oclock. He says he's going mad. I say it's very undistinguished, because most folks are. We have a fireworky sort of conversation.
>
> There's no earthly reason why he *should* go mad, except the important one, that he wants to.[16]

Lawrence liked his odd visitor, despite his obvious uselessness to *The Signature;* he apparently did not recognize in Meredith the original of Stephen Wonham, the splendidly uncouth child of nature in Forster's *The Longest Journey.*

There were other new acquaintances, such as H. J. Massingham, son of H. W. Massingham, the prominent liberal editor of *The Nation.* But Lawrence wanted most to rally his old friends, even from Eastwood days. He urged Willie and Sallie Hopkin to visit, and asked them to recommend *The Signature* to his former loves, Jessie Chambers and Alice Dax:

> Ask Sallie to write to Mrs. Dax—I would rather not open a correspondence with her again, after so long a silence; though I like her, and always shall feel her an integral part of my life; but that is in the past, and the future is separate. Yet I want her to have this paper, which will contain my essential beliefs, the ideas I struggle with.[17]

Lawrence also asked Hopkin to send a leaflet to the sexologist and simple-lifer Edward Carpenter: ". . . he is not in my line. But he may give the paper to some young creature" (a sardonic reference to Carpenter's entourage of homosexual young men).[18]

Finally there was Ottoline, whom Lawrence now had not seen for three months because of the deadlock over Frieda; but he swallowed his pride and asked her help too:

> One can't help the silences that intervene nowadays, it must be so. But I think they are times when new things are born, and like winter, when trees are rid of their old leaves, to start again. . . .
>
> I always want us to be friends, real friends in the deep, honourable, permanent sense. But it is very difficult for me to be clear and true to my deepest self. We must allow first of all for the extreme lapses in ourselves. But the little hard buds of a new world are not destroyed. I do believe in our permanent friendship, something not temporal. . . .
>
> Our coming to see you depends on us all three, you and me and Frieda. When we all want it, to make the new thing, the new world that is to be, then we will come.[19]

This seems to have brought a friendly reply, since five days later Lawrence sent Ottoline some *Signature* leaflets to distribute. Meanwhile he had reached his thirtieth birthday, on the eleventh, but as usual he was not drawing his friends' attention to it.

The fence-mending policy soon bore another fruit, when Russell promptly replied to Lawrence's invitation of 5 September by submitting an article, later published as "The Danger to Civilization." He argued that the war should be ended by negotiation as soon as possible, since it was endangering Europe's historic "effort after mental advancement," and if it went on much longer, "the moral level everywhere will be lowered by familiarity with horrors, leading, in most men, to an easy acquiescence. . . . The collective life of Europe, which has carried it on since the Renaissance in the most wonderful upward movement known to history, will have received a wound which may well prove mortal." Such a view of history was not welcome to Lawrence, for he considered the war a natural consequence of the progress of modern civilization rather than a disastrous interruption of it. But what really infuriated him was Russell's usual plea for emotional restraint: ". . . it is of the last importance to control hatred, to realise that almost all that is detestable in the enemy is the result of war. . . . and will cease with the conclusion of peace."[20]

Lawrence, knowing Russell as he did, saw in all these fine sentiments no more than a "plausible lie":

> Your basic desire is the maximum of desire of war, you are really the super-war-spirit. What you want is to jab and strike, like the soldier with the bayonet, only you are sublimated into words. . . . it isn't in the least true that you, your basic self, want ultimate peace. You are satisfying in an indirect, false way your lust to jab and strike. Either satisfy it in a direct and honourable way, saying, "I hate you all, liars and swine, and am out to set upon you," or stick to mathematics, where you can be true—But to come as the angel of peace—no, I prefer Tirpitz a thousand times in that role.

Tirpitz was a German admiral who argued for unlimited submarine warfare against Allied shipping; he was thus a logical person to blame for the *Lusitania* sinking, which had made Lawrence "mad with rage" and eager to kill "a million Germans—two millions." But Russell's claim to be immune to such violent passions made him equally angry:

> You are simply *full* of repressed desires, which have become savage and anti-social. And they come out in this sheep's clothing of peace propaganda. As a woman said to me, who had been to one of your meetings: 'It seemed so strange, with his face looking so evil, to be talking about peace and love. He can't have *meant* what he said.'
> I believe in your inherent power for realising the truth. But I don't believe in your will, not for a second. Your will is false and cruel. You are too full of devilish repressions to be anything but lustful and cruel. I would rather have the German soldiers with rapine and cruelty, than you with your words of goodness. It is the falsity I can't bear. I wouldn't care if you were six times a murderer, so long as you said to yourself, 'I am this.' The enemy of all mankind, you are, full of the lust of enmity. It is *not* the hatred of falsehood which inspires you. It is the hatred of people, of flesh and blood. It is a perverted, mental blood-lust. Why don't you own it. Let us become strangers again, I think it is better.[21]

In his memoirs, written some forty years after the event, Russell describes the "devastating effect" this letter had on him:

> I was inclined to believe that he had some insight denied to me, and when he said that my pacifism was rooted in blood-lust I supposed he must be right. For twenty-four hours I thought that I was not fit to live and contemplated suicide. But at the end of that time, a healthier reaction set in, and I decided to have done with such morbidness.

Russell's contemporary correspondence with Ottoline gives a different impression. About the time of Lawrence's attack they apparently stopped their physical intimacy, by her wish rather than his; she was going through a nervous crisis that made her insensitive to his troubles and hurt him deeply. Her painful self-consciousness resembled his own, Russell explained, but for this very reason it was hard for them to help each other:

> I have become like you, by a different road. Last Thursday evening, in my despair, I realized that I shall never again be in close touch with any one. That was the substance of my despair. When I got back to my rooms Thursday night, I reached a pitch of despair that I have never reached before. At last I resolved to commit suicide in the spring, after my lectures. That kept me happy till morning.[22]

If Russell had been truly convinced that his pacifism was "rooted in blood-lust" he should logically have killed himself at once, rather than waiting to give the very lectures against the war that Lawrence had so savagely denounced. It is likely, then, that he was most upset by Lawrence's criticisms of his inhibited personality. Russell had always suffered from extreme shyness and loneliness, whereas Lawrence's childhood in a turbulent and close-knit family had been at the opposite extreme. He fascinated Russell by his effortless capacity to be intimate with all kinds of people, and to find the key to their deepest emotions; yet his insights frightened Russell by questioning his sense of his own identity. The letter denouncing Russell's pacifism brought this ambivalence to crisis: he had either to submit entirely to Lawrence's power, or else to react violently away from him.

Lawrence's role in the affair was also an ambivalent one. He was "glad" he had attacked Russell, he told Ottoline, "because it had to be said some time. But also I am very sorry, and feel like going into a corner to cry, as I used to do when I was a child." [23] His confusion showed how much he was projecting his own mixed feelings about the war on to Russell. This trait was a perennial cause of trouble in Lawrence's relationships, though, unlike the full-fledged psychotic, he was not unconscious of his own responsibility for the problem. After lecturing Ottoline on her over-developed will, for example, he had admitted "I'm too much like this myself." He made a similar avowal to Russell, though not until two months after the original attack: "After all, my quarreling with you was largely a quarreling with something in *myself*, something I was struggling away from in myself." The savage misanthropy that he accused Russell of secretly harboring was in fact coming to dominate his own emotions; a year later he even applied to his own case the phrase he had hurled at Russell: "I am no longer an Englishman, I am the enemy of mankind." [24] Nonetheless, he had not chosen his target at random: he sensed the nature of Russell's crisis—that he felt himself an outcast from mankind, if not its enemy—and inserted the knife in a breast already prepared to receive it.

Russell and Ottoline were now effectively eliminated as supporters of *The Signature,* but such setbacks did not weaken Lawrence's intense commitment to the project. By the beginning of October, before even the first issue had appeared, he had completed his own contribution, sufficient for six numbers when run in installments. This was "The Crown," the latest version of his philosophy and now rewritten in accordance with his shift from Christianity toward the "early Greeks." When it came to be reprinted in 1925 he had repented of his enthusiasm, and disingenuously laid the responsibility for *The Signature* on Jack:

> The Crown was written in 1915, when the war was already twelve months old, and had gone pretty deep. John Middleton Murry said to me: "Let us do something." . . . To me the venture meant nothing real: a little escapade. I can't believe in "doing things" like that. . . . I knew then, and I know now, it is no use trying to do anything—I speak only for myself—publicly. [25]

At the time though, he had valued "The Crown" more highly than even his two simultaneous publications, *The Rainbow* and "England, my England." Two months after his arrival in London, therefore, he had got ready the message that he had come there to deliver; now he had only to await London's verdict.

The Rainbow and "The Crown"

THE RAINBOW was published on 30 September. Next day an unsigned review appeared in the *Standard;* it was generally favorable, but gave an ominous hint of what lay ahead: *"The Rainbow* may cause offence and be condemned, for it takes more liberties than English novelists for many years past have claimed." [26] From then on the hunt was up, with Robert Lynd's review in the *Daily News* of 5 October setting the pace. "Mr. Lawrence's reputation must suffer from the publication of such a book as this," he began, with an affected sobriety that was soon cast aside:

> A critic once compared Ibsen in his realistic art to a surgeon. If the author of the present book is like any kind of surgeon, it is a veterinary surgeon. His men and women are cattle who chronically suffer from the staggers. They have both the mental staggers and the moral staggers. If men and women are just this and nothing more, then the imaginative literature of the world is false from Homer down. . . .
>
> Here and there is a little break of beauty, but for the most part the book is windy, tedious, and even in its excitements nauseating. . . . It seems to me largely a monotonous wilderness of phallicism. It is the sort of book which many an artistic schoolboy desires to write, but, on growing to maturity, he refrains. [27]

When Lawrence showed the review to Jack and Katherine their response must have brought home to him how rough a passage *The Rainbow* was likely to encounter:

> Lawrence scented the danger, and sat mute in a chair while we read it. But we had nothing to say. We neither of us liked *The Rainbow* and Katherine quite definitely hated parts of it—in particular the scene where Anna, pregnant, dances naked before the mirror. That, Katherine said to me, was 'female'— her most damning adjective.. . . But whereas Katherine in a sense understood the book and hated it positively, I could not understand it at all. I disliked it on instinct. There was a warm, close, heavy promiscuity of flesh about it which repelled me, and I could not understand the compulsion which was upon Lawrence to write in that fashion and of those themes; neither could I understand his surprise and dismay that the critics were out for his blood. As far as mere feeling went, I felt with them. I happened to be friends with Lawrence, and Robert Lynd didn't: that was about the only difference. [28]

The Murrys blamed everything they disliked about the book on the unhealthy influence of Frieda. Cynthia Asquith did not share their prejudice, yet she too was dismayed by the physicality of the novel's world: "A strange, bewildering, disturbing book. It is full of his obsessions about sex conflict (all the lovers hate one another) and the 'amorphousness' of actual life. Excellent bits of writing, but still too much over-emphasis and brutality. One cannot count how often and how gratuitously he employs the word 'belly' "[29]

Meanwhile the first issue of *The Signature* on 4 October created bafflement rather than outright anger. Though Lawrence had castigated Russell for being a wolf in sheep's clothing, he had himself disguised his opposition to the war behind a veil of esoteric symbolism. Even so, Cynthia Asquith got a sufficient inkling that she worried about her own complicity in publicizing the magazine:

> I *am* amused at the sort of stuff I have been circulating. They take such an exalted view about the war—calling it blasphemy, etc.—that I'm not at all sure that technically it doesn't amount to treason. Certainly it might be said to be discouraging to recruiting. Poor fools, it's not a good moment in which to hope to found a new religion!

Lawrence could offer only a logic-chopping defense of his term, and went on to warn Lady Cynthia that *"The Signature* will get *worse,* not better, from the standpoint of comfortlessness with regard to the war, etc. So please, if you think we had better *not* send it to any of your responsible addresses, let me know."[30] It is not likely, however, that the authorities would have moved against *The Signature* if it had survived; it did not speak for an organized opposition and even in 1915 it would have been hard to prove that Lawrence's dark sayings constituted an offence under DORA.

Those who already admired Lawrence as a promising young English writer must have been perplexed by "The Crown." His two previous books, *Sons and Lovers* and *The Prussian Officer,* gave no clue to its language or symbolism, and even *The Rainbow* belonged essentially to an earlier phase of his intellectual development. "The Crown" derived from two predecessors, *Study of Thomas Hardy* and "Le Gai Savaire," whose very existence was unknown to the general reading public. It is a more unified work than the *Study,* but also more abstract and elliptical. "The old stable *ego*" has now disappeared altogether: "Our individuality, our personality," Lawrence writes, "is no more than an accidental cohesion in the flux of time. The cohesion will break down and utterly cease to be. The atoms will return into the flux of the universe."[31] Lawrence's earlier books had shown his genius for observation, but now he is weary of man's social forms and even of the shapes and textures of the external world. Like Melville's Ahab he asserts that "all visible objects, man, are but as pasteboard masks," and aspires only to "strike through the mask."

Behind the mask lies the eternal contention of opposing forces, as in the *Study,* but they now have different names. After his reading of Heraclitus Lawrence no longer assigns a central role to Christ and Jahweh; the primal opposites are now Flesh against Spirit, Darkness against Light. Each pair is embodied in an animal, Flesh and Darkness in the Lion, Spirit and Light in the Unicorn. The "wrath and splendour" of the Lion contends for the Crown against the "virtue and virginity" of the Unicorn; yet neither should expect victory:

> Is not the unicorn necessary to the very existence of the lion, is not each opposite kept in stable equilibrium by the opposition of the other?
>
> This is a terrible position: to have for a *raison d'être* a purpose which, if once fulfilled, would of necessity entail the cessation from existence of both opponents.[32]

The Crown hovers above the contestants but neither can take possession of it, since it is the consummation of their struggle—the symbol of the eternal truth beyond the temporal ebb and flow of their context. Drawing on Heraclitus' philosophy of flux, Lawrence argues that stability can exist even in the perpetual conflict of cosmic forces:

> Unless the sun were enveloped in the body of darkness, would a cast shadow run with me as I walk? Unless the night lay within the embrace of light, would the fish gleam phosphorescent in the sea, would the light break out of the black coals of the hearth, would the electricity gleam out of itself, suddenly declaring an opposite being?
>
> Love and hate, light and darkness, these are the temporary conquest of the one infinite by the other. In love, the Christian love, the End asserts itself supreme: in hate, in wrath like the lions, the Beginning reestablishes itself unique. But when the opposition is complete on either side, then there is perfection.[33]

In the present era of history the Lion prevails, in the forces of monotheism and dictatorship:

> The One God of Power and Might and Glory, this is David who slays Goliath and dances naked before the Ark, this is Agamemnon who sacrifices Iphigeneia and departs for the glory of killing, the splendour of the Trojan war; it is the later ecstasy of naked Dionysos, it is bread and circuses of Rome, it is Napoleon, with his conquests, his "vite, une femme," his ermine and self-display.[34]

In 1925, when Lawrence was approaching his final disillusionment with the idea of "leaders and followers," he carried his critique of the Lion through to its logical conclusion: "Take care of asserting any absolute, either of power or love, of empire or democracy. The moment power *triumphs,* it becomes spurious with sheer egoism, like Caesar and Napoleon. And the moment democracy triumphs, it too becomes hideous with egoism, like Russia now."[35] The original version, however, launches into a mystical apotheosis of another race who surpass both Lion and Unicorn—the Tigers:

> They are supreme, perfect, supremely beautiful, the pure revelation of one eternity, pure, terrible in its awful concentricity, its awful swoon into conclusiveness that is never even then conclusive, never free, never absolute, always tense with fierce obliviousness. They are perfect in their singleness, but they are trembling, they are brindled shadows wavering back into the utter darkness. Their eyes are concentrated upon oblivion. Soon the last light will go out of their night, and they will be back in the dark source, gone.[36]

The Tigers represent for Lawrence a way of perfection: they incorporate the flux of opposites (symbolized by their stripes)) but also transcend it. Within the political realm their authority is so complete as to be above challenge, but they also, being perfect, belong more to eternity than to the ordinary sublunar world.

One way to transcend the equilibrium of Lion and Unicorn is therefore to rise above it like the Tigers; but there is another way, a movement *downward* into the "flux of corruption." Not surprisingly, this process seems to make a stronger claim on Lawrence's imagination. He subdivides it into healthy and morbid forms. "The spirit of destruction is divine, when it breaks the ego and opens the soul to the wide heavens. In corruption there is divinity."[37] Against this there is the incomplete corruption of those who try to salvage the established social form: "The most unselfish, the most humanitarian of us all, he is the hollowest and fullest of rottenness."[38] Lawrence obviously had in mind Fabianism, which he denounced as "the will of the louse"—a creature that "in its little glassy envelope, brings everything into the corrupting pot of its little belly."[39]

Lawrence hates reformers because they batten on the faults and injustices of their fellowmen, instead of emulating the ruthlessness of nature toward the weak and the unfit:

> It is absurd to talk about all men being immortal, all having souls. Very few men have being at all. . . . Most men are just transitory natural phenomena. Whether they live or die does not matter. . . .
> They are all just fat lies, these people, these many people, these mortals. They are innumerable cabbages in the regulated cabbage plot. . . .
> The cabbage is a nice fat lie. That is why we eat it. It is the business of the truthful to eat up the lies.[40]

Such contempt for the general run of humanity goes beyond any conventional political stance, even the most reactionary; though Lawrence is a Social Darwinist of sorts he scorns the businessman as well as the socialist, and considers economic competition quite irrelevant to the true business of life. Because he lived frugally and independently of any institution, he believed he owed society nothing; and he wished that society would return the favor by leaving him strictly alone.

The great network of mutual interdependence woven by modern capitalism was to him no more than an enormous heaping of chains upon man's vital spontaneity; it meant the transformation of the eagle into the vulture, the lion into the hyena. The war was the appalling consequence of this morbid growth of social obligation, yet even more appalling was that people expected to live in the same manner after it was over; for Lawrence saw the conflict between Germans and Allies as merely sterile and static, pitting the vulture against the dog. In his conclusion, he defined a purpose for life which was entirely different from any official war aims:

> In truth, we proceed to die because the whole frame of our life is a falsity, and we know that, if we die sufficiently, the whole frame and form and edifice will collapse upon itself. But it were much better to pull it down and have a great clear space, than to have it collapse on top of us. . . .
> Our universe is not much more than a mannerism with us now. If we break

through, we shall find, that man is not man, as he seems to be, nor woman woman. The present seeming is a ridiculous travesty. And even the sun is not the sun as it appears to be. It is something tingling with magnificence.

And then starts the one glorious activity of man: the getting himself into a new relationship with a new heaven and a new earth.[41]

"Everything Comes to an End"

BUT NO ONE read Lawrence's fervid peroration or his diatribe on the vulture and the dog, for *The Signature* died before the second half of "The Crown" could be printed. Three days after the first issue appeared the venture was already doomed when Jack and Katherine, the only other contributors, withdrew. In the previous weeks Katherine's beloved younger brother, Leslie, had been a regular visitor at Acacia Road; he went out to France in late September and was killed on 7 October, before even reaching the trenches, by a grenade that exploded in his hand. He was twenty-one. Katherine's nerves were shattered by the tragedy;* she could not bear to stay in the house where they had been happy together, and the following month she left with Jack for the south of France. She felt that her life was over, and that she could never be Jack's lover again because her deepest love was given to her dead brother. "Why don't I commit suicide?" she wrote in her *Journal,* "Because I feel I have a duty to perform to the lovely time when we were both alive. I want to write about it, and he wanted me to." Jack felt himself so rejected by Katherine that he returned to England for three weeks in December, but her unhappiness at the separation caused him to go back to Bandol for another three months. Lawrence was thus denied the Murrys' support and comradeship for six months, which turned out to be among the most painful periods of his life.

* Lady Glenavy recalls (Gossip, 82): "I took up the photograph [of Katherine's brother] to look at it and asked if she had heard from him since his leave. I noticed that she was looking at me in a queer, wild, hard way; then she said, 'Blown to bits.' I was stunned. I asked when she had heard the news. She mentioned a date a few days previously. I remembered that she and Murry and Kot had come round to us that evening, and that Kot and Murry had been very silent but Katherine had seemed exceptionally talkative and gay. . . . Evidently she had told Kot and Murry not to mention her brother's death to us."

Scarcely had this blow sunk in when a similar tragedy befell another of Lawrence's circle. Lady Cynthia Asquith had failed to share his rage against the war: "I felt really sorry for him," she noted, "it is a genuine *supplice* for him."[42] She, meanwhile, was thrilled by the zeppelin raids on London and continued to enjoy her usual round of social activities. The war itself, however, was getting steadily more cruel. On 11 October the Germans shot Edith Cavell, an English nurse who had helped Allied officers to escape from Belgium and Holland; they ignored worldwide pleas for clemency. By then the French and British autumn offensive, designed to end the war by Christmas, was already faltering. The Allies made an unprecedented concentration of over a thousand heavy guns, and used gas extensively, hoping to break through on a narrow front; the German countertactic was the recently developed "defence in depth," which limited the Allied advance to a few miles at a high cost in casualties. One of those who fell in the futile battles of October was Yvo Charteris, Lady Cynthia's younger brother. Only nineteen, he had gone directly from Eton into the army and was killed three weeks after arriving at the Front.

Lady Cynthia was told on 19 October, and felt for the first time since it began "the full mad horror of the war." Though Lawrence had never met Yvo his death, following so closely on that of Leslie Beauchamp, precipitated a decision that he had probably been weighing for some time, to leave England forever:

> What can one say about your brother's death except that it *should not be*. How long will the nations continue to empty the future—it is your own phrase—think what it means—I am sick in my soul, sick to death. But not angry any more, only unfathomably miserable about it all. I think I shall go away to America if they will let me. . . . Perhaps you will say it is cowardice: but how shall one submit to such ultimate wrong as this which we commit now, England—and the other nations? If thine eye offend thee, pluck it out. And I am English, and my Englishness is my very vision. But now I must go away, if my soul is sightless for ever. Let it then be blind, rather than commit the vast wickedness of acquiescence.

On the same day, 21 October, he told Kot that he would vacate the *Signature* office in a week and sell off the furniture: "Everything comes to an end."[43] When the first issue appeared only about sixty people had subscribed, and the number rose gradually to less than a hundred; this meant that the magazine was costing

Lawrence two or three pounds a week, which he could not afford for long. Still, he might have raised the money if there had been any sign that his message was being heard. As it was, the Monday-night meetings had attracted only a handful of people; none of his friends had liked "The Crown"; and his hope of influencing British political life had to be written off as the sheerest fantasy. That all these results could have been foreseen by anyone with a grain of political common sense did not make Lawrence's disappointment any less bitter.

His political views had now been reduced to a single article, which he seems to have revealed only to Lady Cynthia: that England should surrender, "give the Germans England and the whole empire, if they want it, so we may save the hope of a resurrection from the dead."[44] In his personal life also he hoped to make a separate peace; at her first meeting with him after Yvo's death Lady Cynthia noted "he is much calmer and less tortured. . . . He has decided to what he calls 'lapse.' . . . I think he really dreads being recruited . . . but of course he is much too consumptive."[45] Though she sympathized with his plight, not even her bereavement had brought her to agree with him about the war; still, in a closely argued letter, he tried again to convince her:

> You say that the war does not prevent personal life from going on, that the individual can still love and be complete. It isn't true. The one quality of love is that it universalises the individual. If I love, then I am extended over all people, but particularly over my own nation. It is an extending in concentric waves over all people. This is the process of love. . . . And how can this be, in war, when the spirit is against love?

If the only way to end the war is to yield to Prussian rule, so be it; this would be an "external evil" only, whereas "the disintegrating process of the war has become an internal evil, so vast as to be almost unthinkable." Lawrence supports his claim with the analogy of a fractious child—perhaps like Lady Cynthia's autistic son:

> . . . senile Europe, with her conventions and arbitrary rules of conduct and life and very being, has provoked Germany into a purely destructive mood. If a mother does this to a child—and it often happens—is she to go on until the child is killed or broken, so that the mother have her way? Is she not rather, at a certain point, to yield to the paroxysm of the child, which passes away *swiftly* when the opposition is removed? And if Prussia for a time imposes her rule on us, let us bear it, as a mother temporarily bears the ugly tyranny of the child, trusting to the ultimate good. The good will not be long in coming, all

over Europe, if we can but trust it within ourselves. (This is not yielding to the child—this is knowing beyond the child's knowledge.) [46]

Lawrence enclosed with this letter a poem he had written, "The Turning Back." [47] He describes the "ghosts of the slain" who restlessly throng about our hearts, demanding that they be allowed to "sleep at last in immemorial love." The poem ends with a simple plea that, for their sake, we should yield to the enemy. The only hope for this policy of surrender, Lawrence told Lady Cynthia, lay with the women of England, for no man would listen to him. But, inevitably, she would not listen either. She told him that his feet were not on the ground, to which he could only retort, in one of his rare snubs to her, "Believe me, my feet are more sure upon the earth than you will allow—given that the earth is a living body, not a dead fact." [48] Since we can never know what might have been, it is futile to argue whether Lawrence was "right"; but certainly if the Allies had yielded in late 1915 the roughly eight million soldiers killed in the remainder of the war would have been spared. A peace on terms similar to those following the German victory of 1870 would have been obnoxious to France and Britain, but would probably have avoided the horrors of nazism, Stalinism, and the Second World War. None of this mattered, anyway, because neither side was willing to surrender so long as they thought they had even a small chance of winning. If Lawrence had pressed his case publicly he would have been sent to jail, which would have killed him. At this point, fortunately, he was sensible enough to abandon his political dreams and pursue his destiny as a private citizen. The state, however, was about to make a violent intrusion on him in that realm also.

Prosecution of *The Rainbow*

BY THE TIME the second issue of *The Signature* appeared, on 18 October, Lawrence was already turning away from politics. He was also inclined to patch up old quarrels, so when Ottoline wrote to praise *The Rainbow* he suggested meeting when she next came to London: "Frieda and I will come together, and we will all be friends. This has been a crisis which for me is beginning to pass away, now." [49] The outcome of this exchange was a friendly appearance at Byron Villas by Ottoline, and an agreement by Lawrence to visit Garsington early in November—by which time the crisis had returned with a vengeance.

It began on 22 October, the day after Lawrence had determined to wind up *The Signature* and leave England. James Douglas reviewed *The Rainbow* for *The Star* in terms that amounted to raising a hue and cry. It was yellow journalism at its most Pecksniffian and unscrupulous:

> There is no doubt that a book of this kind has no right to exist. It is a deliberate denial of the soul that leavens matter. These people are not human beings. They are creatures who are immeasurably lower than the lowest animal in the Zoo. . . .
>
> Genius is a trust, a sacred trust. . . . The artist is not his own law-giver. . . . Art is a public thing. It is a dweller in the clean homes and swept streets of life. It must conform to the ordered laws that govern human society. If it refuse to do so, it must pay the penalty. The sanitary inspector of literature must notify it and call for its isolation.

Douglas even claimed that *The Rainbow* degraded Britain's war effort—an absurd argument, but one that may have carried some weight in the general mood of disappointment over the failure of the autumn offensive:

> The wind of war is sweeping over our life, and it is demolishing many of the noisome pestilences of peace . . . I know it will be said that literature must live at all costs and at any expense of spirit in any waste of shame. Frankly, I do not see the necessity. Life is infinitely more precious than literature. It has got to go on climbing up and up, and if literature strives to drag it down to the nethermost deeps, then literature must be hacked off the limbs of life.

It was a curious paradox that as the drama of the Western Front became more savage and irrational journalists like Douglas were all the more vigilant in defence of civilized morality and the dignity of man—but also more insistent that the war be carried on to the bitter end.

Douglas gave a grudging acknowledgment of Lawrence's talent, then ended with some instruction on how to write novels:

If Mr. Lawrence desires to save his genius from destruction, let me tell him how to do it. He must discover or rediscover the oldest truth in the world—that man is a moral being with a conscience and an aim, with responsibility to himself and to others. If that truth be not true, then life is a tale told by an idiot, full of sound and fury, and signifying nothing. The young men who are dying for liberty are moral beings. They are the living repudiation of such impious denials of life as *The Rainbow*. The life they lay down is a lofty thing. It is not the thing that creeps and crawls in this novel.[50]

Soon after Douglas's review another influential journalist, Clement Shorter, attacked *The Rainbow* in his magazine *The Sphere*. He was more appreciative of the novel's quality than Douglas had been, yet felt it was vitiated by the author's "orgie of sexiness." "Mr. Lawrence has ceased to be an artist," Shorter concluded, "and I can find no justification whatever for the perpetration of such a book." The most damaging passage in the review, however, was addressed to the publisher:

I can only suppose that Mr. Methuen and his two partners for some reason failed to read this book in manuscript and published it upon the strength of the previously well-deserved reputation of the author. Let them turn to the chapter entitled "Shame," and unless they hold the view that Lesbianism is a fit subject for family fiction I imagine that they will regret this venture.[51]

Lawrence still hoped to ride out the storm until he and Frieda could leave for America. But bad news was also arriving from that side of the Atlantic: the firm of Doran refused to publish *The Rainbow* unless extensive changes were made. Lawrence decided not to publish at all on such terms, but then a timely offer came from B. W. Huebsch to take over the book from Doran and make only minor changes. This Lawrence accepted. The hostile reception of *The Rainbow* was making him wonder about his future as a professional writer. During October he had written a short story about Cynthia and Herbert Asquith, "The Thimble," and he now sent this off to Pinker to assess its commercial possibilities. His next stories, he assured him, would be "even more suitable for the family"[52]—an ironic reference to Shorter's review of *The Rainbow*. But the notoriety of the novel scotched these hopes; "The Thimble" was not placed with any English magazine, and after the suppression of *The Rainbow* only one story by Lawrence was published in England until the end of the war.

Although police action against *The Rainbow* may have been considered earlier, it was most likely set in motion by the attacks of Douglas and Shorter on 22 and 23 October. On 3 November a Scotland Yard detective served a warrant on Methuen & Co. requiring it to hand over all copies of the novel in stock, which it did without contest. The police acted under the Obscene Prints Act of 1857, which empowered them to make such raids "If upon complaint there is any reason to believe that any obscene books, etc., are kept in any house . . . for the purpose of sale or distribution." A magistrate could then decide if the materials were obscene, and order them destroyed. The original purpose of the Act was to prevent the open sale of pornography in London; it "was regarded as a mere police measure," and was largely ignored by the literary men of the time.[53] The magistrate could have books destroyed entirely at his own discretion, and without reference to their authors—probably because most erotic works appeared pseudonymously.

A Home Office minute of 1930, brought to light by Emile Delavenay, notes that proceedings against *The Rainbow* "were practically initiated by the late Sir Charles Mathews," who was the director of public prosecutions.[54] Mathews' chief was the attorney general, F. E. Smith, who would presumably have approved his deputy's action in advance. Delavenay has further shown that a security file existed for Frieda, but his suggestion that prosecution of *The Rainbow* was a political maneuver designed to discredit Lawrence as an opponent of the war is unsupported by firm evidence. Lawrence was a minor, isolated figure in the antiwar movement, and the repeated journalistic attacks against *The Rainbow* were quite enough in themselves to move Mathews to action. In particular, the lesbian scenes had shocked several reviewers and J. C. Squire, literary editor of the *New Statesman,* was told by an unidentified person "that the book had . . . been suppressed because it mentioned sapphism."[55] It may have been counted against Lawrence that he opposed the war and had a German wife, but, as we have seen, the Obscene Prints Act treated the author as legally a nonperson. Two days after Methuen had given their stock of *The Rainbow* to the police, Lawrence still knew nothing about it; he mistrusted the firm from the start, and preferred to communicate with them through Pinker rather than directly. Earlier in the year he had called himself a "safe speculation for a publisher"; to Methuen he was precisely that. Now that the speculation was proving both unsafe and unprofitable, they were eager to cut their losses.

On 5 November Lawrence received passports for himself and Frieda from the Foreign Office; he had some difficulty in getting them but the intervention of Lady Cynthia seems to have secured their release. "I feel awfully queer and trembling in my spirit," he told Ottoline, "because I am going away from the land and the nation I have belonged to: departing, emigrating, changing the land of my soul as well as my mere domicile. It is rather terrible, a form of death. But I feel as if it were my fate, I must to live." Later in the day he heard from the novelist W. L. George about the seizure of *The Rainbow,* but at first he refused to admit the force of the blow. The next day, when he received a letter of confirmation from Pinker, he said only "I am not very much moved: am beyond that by now. I only curse them all, body and soul, root, branch and leaf, to eternal damnation."[56] The news did not deter him from attending a party the same night at the studio of a new acquaintance, Dorothy Brett.

Brett (as everyone called her) was a young painter who had been a fellow student of Gertler's at the Slade, and it was through him that she met the Lawrences. She and Gertler were an odd couple: he a Jew from the East End who spoke with an accent and looked like a curly-haired cherub; Brett the daughter of the wealthy Viscount Esher, and almost a parody of the aristocratic young Engliswoman—slender, with "nice brown hair and . . . slightly opened rabbit-mouth and . . . baffled, uncertain rabbit-eyes."[57] She was severely deaf, which made her shy and hypersensitive, but her handicap sharpened her shrewd and often malicious observation of the social life around her. When Gertler brought her to Byron Villas she soon found common ground with Lawrence in jeering at their mutual friend Ottoline; they "pull[ed] her feathers out in handfuls" until, feeling a grain of remorse, Lawrence agreed to "leave her just one draggled feather in her tail, the poor plucked hen!"[58] So began a lifelong devotion to Lawrence in which Brett submerged her own career, to a degree that came to irritate Lawrence and infuriate Frieda. After Murry she was next in the series of disciples, faithful and unfaithful, who would follow Lawrence from now on.

Brett had offered to give a farewell party for the Lawrences since they expected to leave for America toward the end of the month. Despite the bad news about *The Rainbow* the party started well with dinner and charades, Lawrence's favorite entertainment. The other guests were mostly close friends: Jack and Katherine (about to leave for France), Kot, Gertler, Carrington, and Estelle Rice, an artist friend of Katherine's from the days of *Rhythm*. But during the charades the studio was invaded by a rowdy crew of gate-crashers, much to the distress of Brett who did not want to share her lion with outsiders. Instead she was driven to playing the pianola and observing the various effects of liquor on her friends: Katherine the amorous drunk, Kot the singing drunk, Gertler the quarrelsome drunk, and Jack the falling-down drunk. Lawrence, in lifelong reaction against his drunken father, was as usual not drunk at all. In the midst of these revels a lanky, bearded young man, also uninvited, entered and cast a cold eye on the proceedings; he was an aspiring writer, but although he was five years older than Lawrence he had published only one book, a popularized history of French literature.[59] Within three years he would become as notorious an iconoclast as Lawrence was now, but his iconoclasm was nicely calculated to bring him fortune rather than retribution. Being homosexual, he knew how dangerous it was to provoke the mob in the way Lawrence insisted on doing. His behavior at Brett's showed this characteristic wariness:

> I examined [the Lawrences] carefully and closely for several hours, though I didn't venture to have myself introduced. I was surprised to find that I liked her looks very much—she actually seemed (there's no other word for it) a lady: as for him I've rarely seen anyone so pathetic, miserable, ill, and obviously devoured by internal distresses. He behaved to everyone with the greatest cordiality, but I noticed for a second a look of intense disgust and hatred flash into his face . . . caused by—ah!—whom?[60]

This exact observer was Lytton Strachey, reporting the event to David Garnett; his surprise at finding Frieda so personable was no doubt due to his friend Ottoline having described her as a monster of vulgarity. The object of Lawrence's disgust cannot be known, though he can scarcely have felt much empathy with the young and cheerful crowd—led by Iris Tree, the eighteen-year-old daughter of the famous actor Beerbohm Tree—when his own prospects had just been so definitively crushed. Strachey's awareness of Lawrence's plight remained a detached vote of sympathy;

he knew about Lawrence's dislike for homosexuals and for the Cambridge intellectual set, and chose not to be affronted with these prejudices. The two men, who did so much to discomfort and discredit the respectable opinions of their time, never met again; thereby missing the opportunity of discomforting each other.

The day after Brett's party, Lawrence took up the seizure of *The Rainbow*. When Methuen rejected *The Wedding Ring* in August 1914 he had withdrawn to the obscurity of Chesham and immersed himself in the profundities of the *Study of Thomas Hardy*. Now he had a home in London and influential friends, yet the situation seemed even more critical, an escape route harder to find. His letters of 6 November mention three solutions, none very hopeful. To Pinker he suggested that he would stop writing for England and "try to change [his] public." For someone with so distinctive a style the idea of camouflaging his natural bent in order to achieve commercial success was hardly practical. Then, there was the chance that he could "move a body of people" to get the police action reversed; this was certainly worth a try, though the chances of success were small. Finally, he and Frieda could simply carry through their plan to flee to America. For this they could at least count on the help of a few generous friends such as Eddie Marsh, even though he had disliked *The Rainbow*. "I am so sick, in body and soul," Lawrence told him, "that if I don't go away I shall die . . . if I can get a little money now, so that my wife and I can go away, I will work at anything over there."[61] It was Marsh's fate to be asked for help to his face and laughed at behind his back, like a figure from some Wodehouse novel with monocle and piping voice. But again he rose to the emergency with a loan of twenty pounds from his modest capital. Still, having passports and money was only the first step; Lawrence would also need official permission to leave, and this was more than just a formality.

Meanwhile Methuen were handling their author's case with signal hypocrisy and meanness of spirit; they even tried to sabotage Lawrence by telling Pinker they hoped he would do nothing to oppose the police action. On 11 November, eight days after the seizure, the detective returned with a summons to Methuen to appear two days later at the magistrate's court and show cause why the books should not be destroyed. Methuen later explained to the Society of Authors why they responded as they did:

We understood from Inspector Draper that this was merely a formal matter to obtain our formal consent on the destruction of the book; the impression we received was that it would not be heard in a public court, and we did not therefore obtain legal assistance or arrange to be legally represented.

We asked Inspector Draper if the author could have a voice in the destruction of the books, and understood him to say that the action of the Police Court was taken against us and the author had no right to appear in the matter.

We were very much surprised on Saturday, the 13th, to find on attending at the Police Court, that the case was to be heard in open court.

Methuen had been tricked by the police into a public humiliation. When their representative appeared on 13 November, unassisted by legal counsel and expecting at worst a mild rap on the knuckles, he was treated to a stern lecture by the police solicitor, Mr. Muskett, in front of the assembled newspaper reporters. *The Rainbow* was a "disgusting, detestable, and pernicious work," he thundered, "a mass of obscenity of thought, idea, and action, wrapped up in language which in some quarters might be considered artistic and intellectual. It was difficult to understand how Messrs. Methuen could have lent their great name to the publication of this bawdy volume." Muskett backed up his views with quotations from Clement Shorter's review. The magistrate, Sir John Dickinson, added his quota of indignation, describing the book as "utter filth" and observing "he was very glad to hear that the libraries refused to circulate it."[62] This boycott would in any case have made the novel a financial failure. Methuen's first printing was 2,500 of which they still had a thousand on hand when the police came; the royalties on the copies sold would not have covered Lawrence's advance, so he could expect no further income from the book. The magistrate concluded by ordering Methuen to pay ten guineas costs and the seized copies to be destroyed. A legend was passed down in the Methuen office that the books were burned by the public hangman outside the Royal Exchange. Sir Algernon Methuen, having barely salvaged his good name by repudiating his author, was made a baronet the following year at the recommendation of Prime Minister Asquith.

On Monday, 8 November Lawrence went up to Garsington alone; he had won a point by getting Ottoline to invite both of them, but now that honor was satisfied Frieda sent her a friendly note saying it was "good for L. and me to be apart if it's only a few days."[63] Lawrence spent four quiet days with Ottoline: only Philip and Julian were there, and without Frieda's disturbing presence he was able to restore the warmth and companionship of the early days of his friendship with Ottoline. But his mood was elegiac, as if the beauty and culture of Garsington only emphasized the predominant hostility of England to him and all his works:

> When I drive across this country, with autumn falling and rustling to pieces, I am so sad, for my country, for this great wave of civilisation, 2000 years, which is now collapsing, that it is hard to live. So much beauty and pathos of old things passing away and no new things coming: this house of the Ottoline's—it is England—my God, it breaks my soul—their England, these shafted windows, the elm-trees, the blue distance—the past, the great past, crumbling down, breaking down, not under the force of the coming birds, but under the weight of many exhausted lovely yellow leaves, that drift over the lawn, and over the pond, like the soldiers, passing away, into winter and the darkness of winter—no, I can't bear it. . . .
>
> I want to go to America, to Florida, as soon as I can: as soon as I have enough money to cross with Frieda. My life is ended here. I must go as a seed that falls into new ground. But this, this England, these elm-trees, the grey wind with yellow leaves—it is so awful, the being gone from it altogether, one must be blind henceforth. But better leave a quick of hope in the soul, than all the beauty that fills the eyes. . . . I don't think we shall be here very much longer. My life now is one repeated, tortured, *Vale! Vale! Vale!*
>
> Please burn this over-loose letter.[64]

In this cry of anguish, sent to Cynthia Asquith from Garsington, Lawrence again laments the loss of England as equivalent to loss of his very sight. Yet in the past two years he had become a much less visual writer, as what lay beneath the surface came to seem more important to him than what was present to the eye. Indeed, before November ended he would tell Lady Cynthia that for her to withdraw from English society would not be a mutilation, but a means of self-discovery: ". . . the conscious life—which you adhere to—is no more than a masquerade of death: there is a living unconscious life. If only we would shut our eyes; if only we were all struck blind, and things vanished from our sight, we should marvel that we had fought and lived for shallow, visionary, peripheral nothingness. We should find reality in the darkness."[65]

This was both a personal consolation and an artistic program for the future. But that dark reality was hard to speak of, and the reception of *The Rainbow* showed that few readers would sympathize with Lawrence's quest. Meanwhile he was possessed by a "horrible feeling of hopelessness": "I wonder," he asked Eddie Marsh, "if ever I shall have strength to drag my feet over the next length of journey?"[66] Nonetheless, once he returned from Garsington Lawrence tried to organize a campaign against the ban on *The Rainbow,* though in retrospect we can see that Methuen's defection meant that the battle was already lost after the court hearing of 13 November. Even if the book could not be sold freely there remained the prospect of a private edition, and it would be several months before Lawrence gave up the cause of his novel altogether. His first initiative was to ask Cynthia Asquith to canvass her influential friends—including, he implied, her father-in-law the prime minister. Asquith was of course much too shrewd a politician to ally himself with Lawrence; his home secretary supported the police action and there is no evidence that anyone in the Cabinet opposed him.* Lady Cynthia was ostensibly sympathetic to Lawrence's outrage, but seems privately to have considered the whole affair as little more than a joke. On receiving his appeal for help she noted in her journal: "Some reader had appealed to a magistrate and got him to ban [*The Rainbow*]. Fancy taking the trouble! There is something very funny about my having godmothered the one suppressed book." Her father, the Earl of Wemyss, was similarly lacking in reverence: "Papa reading *The Rainbow* all day with many protestations of disgust. He has offered me five pounds for it as he thinks it would be a good investment."[67]

There remained three other, more feasible plans. One was for Ottoline to rally the forces of Bloomsbury to defend the novel; the second was to mount a legal challenge against the magistrate's order, either with the support of the Society of Authors or independently; the last was to get Pinker to organize a campaign by leading writers in Lawrence's favor, starting with such clients of his as Henry James, Arnold Bennett, and H. G. Wells.

Although most of the key figures in the Bloomsbury Group were by now quite wary of Lawrence, they recognized a common enemy in police censorship. They were too well acquainted with

---

*On 18 October (two weeks before the seizure) Lady Cynthia had dined at Downing Street with the prime minister and other family members. "I was much chaffed about D. H. Lawrence," she recorded (AD 89), "Apparently *The Rainbow* is causing an explosion on account of its 'belly', etc., motif. His incidental 'foulness' is a great pity, because he will be read flippantly for that only—the last thing he would wish."

British philistinism to tackle it head on, preferring to pull as many wires as they could privately and leave it to Philip Morrell, the most respectable of their number, to make the only public gesture of support. Despite his alienation from Lawrence, David Garnett wrote a furious letter about the case to Augustine Birrell, Frankie's father and a Cabinet minister. Birrell was himself a man of letters, but he fobbed off Garnett with his opinion that *The Rainbow* was a very bad novel. Clive Bell was equally indignant and undertook to rally support for Lawrence, whom he had not previously met. With Lytton Strachey he went to see J. C. Squire, a leading literary arbiter of the time, and asked him to protest the suppression in the *New Statesman*. But the "little worm . . . quite failed to see the point," Strachey reported to Garnett. "He thought that as in his opinion the book wasn't a good one it was difficult for him to complain about its suppression."[68] Finally Squire did write a piece, but it was so lukewarm and obfuscatory as to infuriate Lawrence's supporters. He criticized Douglas and Shorter as overzealous, and said that he doubted that "censorship in this case was desirable," but he also pronounced *The Rainbow* "a bad novel" that contained "opinions unpalatable to me and tendencies that I personally believe to be unhealthy."[69] Drawing attention to his own patriotism, he noted that the book "broods gloomily over the physical reactions of sex in a way so persistent that one wonders whether the author is under the spell of German psychologists." Squire concluded with the comforting observation that "we ought to thank our stars that the censorship in this country is not worse than it is." Egregious as his "defence" of Lawrence was, it was typical of conventional literary opinion: hardly any established critics opposed censorship on principle, and none of them liked *The Rainbow* enough to care deeply about its right to be read.

Philip Morrell's attempts to rouse the concern of the House of Commons met with similar indifference. His written question to the home secretary, for answer on 1 December, asked why the book had been seized "without any notice being given to the author . . . whose prospects and reputation were gravely affected by these proceedings; whether he is aware that no direct evidence was given by the prosecution in support of the charge, but that the counsel employed by the police . . . confined himself to reading the unfavorable comments of two journalists . . . ; and whether he will see that no further proceedings of this kind are taken by the police in respect of any work produced by an author of good standing and reputation."[70] To this broadside Sir John Simon blandly replied that "The police acted in accordance with the law, and I cannot give any instructions of the nature suggested." Since he had no supporters in the House, Morrell had to let the matter drop.

The Society of Authors at first held out enough hope to Lawrence that he put off his planned departure for America. But all he finally got for his subscription fee was a notification that the society had consulted its solicitors and decided "in the present circumstances they could not take any useful action on the general principles involved."[71] Catherine Carswell's husband, a lawyer, was still eager to fight the case without charge; but by December Lawrence was more in the mood for flight than fight.

Pinker had little more success in rallying his big guns to support Lawrence. Neither H. G. Wells nor Henry James seems to have liked *The Rainbow,* though we only know their views indirectly. Lawrence did not mind James's criticism since "he was always on a different line—subtle conventional design was his aim," but he thought that Wells was bound to see *The Rainbow* with the "yellow eye" of a rival. "He admires me really, at the bottom," Lawrence contended, "—too much perhaps."[72] Whether from an excess of admiration or not, Wells was no help. Arnold Bennett was even closer to Lawrence in his social origins and subject matter; his sure sense of the literary marketplace inclined him to be contemptuous of writers who lacked his shrewdness, but at least he was generous with the wealth his common touch had brought him. He did more for Lawrence in this crisis than any other established author: through Pinker he made him an anonymous gift of forty pounds—which was more than a year's rent on the Byron Villas flat—and he wrote a newspaper article defending *The Rainbow.* Though Lawrence dismissed Bennett as "an old imitator,"[73] he was appreciative of the gesture. But a gesture was all it was; and with it public opposition to the seizure fizzled out.

In mid-December Lawrence's spirits rose when he received a copy of the American edition of *The Rainbow,* published by B. W. Huebsch. The book, he found, only lacked about two pages altogether of the Methuen text. He was pleased that the novel would at least be available on the other side of the Atlantic, and tried for a while to issue another English edition using sheets supplied by Huebsch; G. H. Thring, the secretary of the Society of Authors, had given him to understand that a new issue could not be automatically suppressed—there would have to be another complaint to a magistrate, and another hearing. It was some time before he learned that Huebsch had not dared to actually put the novel on sale in America for fear of the powerful New York Society for the Suppression of Vice.[74] Not until after the war did he cautiously release copies, so Lawrence received no royalties for several years. The expurgated American text was republished in England in 1926, but the original Methuen text remained unavailable until nineteen years after Lawrence's death when it was used for the Penguin edition. In effect the police seizure had brought Lawrence's career as a novelist to a halt. He had published four novels in five years, each on better financial terms than the one before; but now he would have to wait five years before he could publish another.

An American Rananim?

WHILE FIGHTING the battle of *The Rainbow,* Lawrence had little inclination to write: after completing "The Thimble" on 29 October he wrote almost nothing until January 1916.[75] Once again he was casting around for new worlds and a new mode of being. The failure of *The Signature* had shown him that he could not influence English politics, and the suppression of *The Rainbow* that the state was actively hostile to him. His dream of an ideal authoritarian rule had therefore to be abandoned, and by the natural oscillation of his temperament he turned back to schemes for an ideal private life. Once again he revived the idea of Rananim.

Lawrence had decided to move to America on 21 October, the day he conceded that *The Signature* was done for. At first he planned to go to New York and Chicago, if only because he already had contacts there. When his doctor warned him against spending the winter in New York, he thought of Spain instead.

Then Dollie Radford told him of a cottage on the west coast of Florida, belonging to a friend, where the Lawrences might live rent-free. Lawrence at once began to expatiate on the delights of life among the palm trees and to people his estate in imagination with as many of his London friends as could be persuaded to pull up stakes and join him.

The new colonists, however, were to be a different group from the Chesham circle around whom Lawrence had planned the original Rananim. He still had faith in Jack and Katherine, but the Campbells and the Cannans he now dismissed as being on "the other side of the grave, the old, far side . . . We must not look back." [76] Gertler was still enmeshed in his painful love affair with Dora Carrington, and achieving some success as a painter; Kot had no money and was settling into a retired existence at 5, Acacia Road, where he had moved when the Murrys left for France. Fresh blood was therefore needed, for which Lawrence looked to a "new, young generation." [77] They were all too young to have much public reputation, and still sufficiently rootless and uncertain that Lawrence could readily become a powerful influence on their lives. The group included Dorothy Brett, who was twenty-four in 1915; Dikran Kouyoumdjian, twenty; Dorothy Warren, nineteen; Robert Nichols, twenty-two; and Aldous Huxley, twenty-one. They were a group from Lawrence's perspective rather than their own, since not all of them even knew each other. The key member of this circle was Philip Heseltine, who was twenty-two.

Heseltine's father died when he was two; he grew up unduly influenced by his mother, and gave early signs of emotional backwardness and instability. At Oxford he immersed himself in the study of the advanced sexual theorists of the day, such as Havelock Ellis, Edward Carpenter, Whitman, Nietzsche, Otto Weininger, and the psychoanalysts. He hated the idea of a conventional middle-class career and when war broke out he escaped from Oxford to London, where he hoped to become a professional musician. During the year before he met Lawrence he had been floundering in a postadolescent crisis, with no clear end in sight since he was medically unfit for military service. He was already suffering from a personality split, which he later formalized by taking a new name, "Peter Warlock." There was the manic Heseltine who liked to ride through villages on his motorbike at sixty miles an hour, stark naked; and the depressive Heseltine who felt he was "rolling downhill with increasing rapidity into a black, shiny cess-pool of stagnation." In addition, there was Heseltine the infa-tuated admirer of Lawrence: "a marvellous man—perhaps the one great literary genius of his generation, at any rate in En-gland."

Their meeting, on 16 November, created a volatile emotional compound. Invited to pioneer in Florida with his idol, Heseltine immediately accepted: "Casting all cautious fears to the winds I am going away, to the uttermost parts of the earth, to *live*," he told his friend Delius, the composer. Lawrence, for his part, was worn down by a year in which his messianic hopes had been frustrated by, as he felt, the pusillanimity of his friends. Now he had found someone who *really* believed in him, who admired his work with-out niggling reservations, who was willing to leave England at a week's notice. He was in no mood, therefore, to be niggling him-self about his new friend's character, or to worry that Heseltine's moods might fluctuate as violently as his own. Yet this was Hesel-tine's most prominent trait, as he himself admitted: "I am in a state of flux—my mind is a whirlpool of alternating excitement and depression."[78]

Clearly, Lawrence's friendship with Heseltine was not likely to be steady or lasting; nonetheless, he made it a touchstone of what was needed to make a success of the Florida colony. He told Kath-erine he was out of sympathy with Jack and with her friend Fred-erick Goodyear, both of whom, he complained, were "on the same Oxford introspective line. . . . I'm sick to death of people who are wrapped up in their own inner lives, inner selves." From now on, he wanted his relations with people to be on a different basis:

> One thing I know, I am tired of this insistence on the *personal* element; per-sonal truth, personal reality. It is very stale and profitless. I want some new non-personal activity, which is at the same time, a genuine vital activity. And I want relations . . . based upon some unanimous accord in truth or belief, and a harmony of *purpose,* rather than of personality . . . we must grow from our deepest underground roots, out of the *unconsciousness,* not from the conscious concepts which we falsely call ourselves.[79]

Till now Lawrence had mainly explored the unconscious links be-tween lovers, but he was beginning to imagine groups of friends, or even a whole society bound together by similar subterranean forces. The strain of life with Frieda also inclined him to demand more intimacy and support from other people, now that an "inevitable friction" had become part of his marriage. Young admirers like Heseltine could offer Lawrence the unqualified devotion he needed, yet as he asked more of his intimates he made himself more vulnerable to shock and disappointment if they should turn away from him.

On the same day he met Heseltine, Lawrence made a false step in his recruiting drive for Florida that showed how erratic his judgment of others had become. He sent Cynthia Asquith a "parting letter" in which he asked her, first, to go and stay with Ottoline; this must already have seemed an odd request since they had so often ridiculed Ottoline together. Then he warned her, ". . . you must get the *intrinsic* reality clear within your soul. . . . [and] keep the ultimate choice of your destiny." What this meant, in practice, was that she should consider moving to Florida with her children in order to save them for the future: ". . . you must not let them be drawn into this slow flux of destruction and nihilism, *unless they belong to it.* If John becomes wicked within the flux, then take him away into a new life; never mind how much it costs. . . . I shall try to start a new school . . . there." Lawrence was implying that John's abnormality could be cured if he were removed from wartime England and that he might be willing to take responsibility for the boy himself. There was also Lady Cynthia's husband to consider, but Lawrence had evidently written him off: "[he] should have left this decomposing life. . . . Perhaps now he is beaten. Perhaps now the true living is defeated in him. But it is not yet defeated in you."[80] The letter was a dubious proposal to someone of Lady Cynthia's character and social position, and Lawrence seems to have realized this because he saw her the day after sending it but made no mention of its content. Later in the day she went down to the country and got the letter, which she described in her diary as "amazing." The timing also was unfortunate in that her husband had just suffered a nervous breakdown from shell-shock; this may have confirmed Lawrence's suggestion that he was "beaten," but it was hardly the opportune moment to say so to his wife. Her response to Lawrence's letter has not been recorded, but since he did not mention the subject again he probably understood how much he had offended her sense of propriety.*

---

* Nonetheless, he used the Asquiths' marriage as a principal source for the Chatterleys in *Lady Chatterley's Lover.* In both cases they married when the bride was twenty-three, the

Lawrence found another prospect in Robert Nichols, a friend of Philip Heseltine's who was recovering from shell-shock; after visiting him in hospital, Lawrence waxed ecstatic about his unpublished poems. He invited Nichols to Florida, naturally, as soon as he could travel; but Nichols did not share Lawrence's euphoria, which he attributed to a "bad patch" of tuberculosis compounded by a "nervous condition." [81] Lawrence undertook to get his poems published, and also to match either him or Heseltine with a young lady of his acquaintance, probably Dorothy Warren. He invited his two young friends singly to Byron Villas to meet her, but nothing came of it except a lasting grudge by Nichols against Lawrence for trying such a maneuver. Dorothy Warren—if she was the one concerned—was the nineteen-year-old niece of Philip Morrell. Dorothy was a beautiful and eligible young lady, and it would not have satisfied either the world's or Lawrence's sense of propriety if she had gone off to Florida to live unattached in a utopian colony. Lawrence may have acted foolishly in trying to pair her off so that she could decently join his westward exodus, yet they remained friends. Thirteen years later she arranged, at her gallery in London, the famous exhibit of Lawrence's paintings which was raided by the police.

So Nichols turned out to be a nonstarter, but another of Heseltine's friends, Dikran Kouyoumdjian, was more at Lawrence's disposal. He was Armenian, and English society was not likely to let him forget it, though he had been raised in England since the age of three; later he changed his name to Michael Arlen and acquired enough protective coloration to write wildly successful novels about high society. On first acquaintance Lawrence liked his "sound decency. . . . He is not a bit rotten, which most young cultivated Englishmen are." [82] He admitted, though, that Kouyoumdjian seemed "a bit blatant and pushy," and by the time he came to lampoon him in *Lady Chatterley's Lover* under the name of Michaelis this had escalated to calling him "the last word in what was caddish and bounderish."

---

groom twenty-nine; Connie, like Lady Cynthia, is of Scots ancestry; Clifford, like Herbert Asquith, has an older brother who is killed in 1916, is shattered by a war wound, and dabbles in literature. The novel is the culmination of Lawrence's perennial fantasies of carrying off an imagined English aristocrat rather than a real German one; having chosen the path of exogamy and exile, he nonetheless hankered after an ideal reconciliation with English womanhood and thus, indirectly, with England itself.

Finally there was a young Oxford undergraduate whom Lawrence met through Ottoline and who would become one of his most loyal friends: Aldous Huxley. Lawrence invited him to tea at Byron Villas on 17 December and, naturally, invited him to come to Florida. Huxley would gain fame in the 1920s as a satirist of enthusiasms, though in his own life he espoused a long series of them; his response on this occasion was characteristically divided:

> this good man, who impresses me as a good man more than most, proposes . . . to go to the deserts of Florida with one Armenian, one German wife and, problematically, one young woman called Dorothy Warren . . . to await a sort of Pentecostal inspiration of new life, which, whether it will come is another question. But Lawrence is a great man, and as he finds the world too destructive for his taste, he must, I suppose be allowed to get out of it. . . . There is something almost alarming about his sincerity and seriousness—something that makes one feel oneself to be the most shameful dilettante, persifleur, waster and all the rest. Not but what I think he's wrong. . . . If, as seems probable, I go and visit my Texan brother next year, I shall certainly join his colony for a bit. I think it might be very good to lead the monastic life for a little.[83]

Huxley, with his near blindness and uncertain health, would scarcely have made a very capable pioneer in the orange groves of Florida; in any case, he had to finish his studies at Oxford and then make a living—unlike Heseltine, who had a private income. His admiration for Lawrence therefore did not develop into a close friendship until 1926, by which time he was no longer "disciple material"—being married, a father, and an established author.

In his enthusiasm for Florida Lawrence even suggested to Ottoline that she should join his exodus; there was no chance of her accepting, but with her usual generosity she organized a whip-round on his behalf—starting with Russell:

> I want to try and get some money for him to go away with as he hasn't enough to go. I think he would die if he remained. I think he was very much affection for you but at present the disappointment about Life here—and hope—is too keen and bitter not to make him think that we are all so uneffectual. Do you understand. It is *awfully* sad.

Six days later Ottoline thanked Russell for his check—"it is awfully good of you to give *so much*";[84] and two days afterward Lawrence told Pinker that Ottoline had given him thirty pounds to go to America. She also wrote to Eddie Marsh for a contribution to Lawrence, but Lawrence had already approached Marsh directly and extracted a loan of twenty pounds. To cap her fund-raising campaign, Ottoline succeeded in getting five pounds from Bernard Shaw, who was not known as a soft touch: "I suppose I cannot refuse," he replied, "but as the love of money grows on me you cannot imagine what a pang it costs me."[85]

Ottoline came to Byron Villas again for lunch on 19 November, where Lawrence sang the praises of Florida and of the young men who would go there with him; it was agreed that he would come to Garsington soon with them and Frieda. Russell came to tea on the same day; the first time he and Lawrence had met since July. "I liked Bertie very much on Friday," Lawrence reported to Otto-line, "really the simple man was there for once, almost childish. And then at the end he reproached me for my letter to him, as if I had wantonly hurt him. That was not manly of him. Sometimes he begs indulgence like a child. And after all he was more simple and real on Friday than I have ever known him. So my letter must have been productive in him, liberating something."[86]

Before long, naturally, Lawrence posed the inevitable question: "Won't you come to Florida too? Do! It is hopeless to stay in England. Do you come and be president of us."[87] But Russell had become as wary of Lawrence's affection and enthusiasm as of his hostility; furthermore, he had found new people to be fascinated by, in the persons of his former student Tom Eliot and his new wife, Vivien. "She is really very fond of him," he told Ottoline, "but has impulses of cruelty to him from time to time. It is a Dostojevsky type of cruelty, not a straightforward everyday kind. . . . She is a person who lives on a knife-edge, and will end as a criminal or a saint—I don't know which yet. She has a perfect capacity for both."[88] Vivien was to end as neither, but rather as a mental patient; still, she was a beautiful and mercurial young woman, which made the troubled waters of the Eliot ménage more intriguing to Russell than the predictable quarrels of the Lawrences. From now on Lawrence's gestures of friendship toward him were to be received somewhat coolly, until their final alienation a few months later.

The Lawrences' visit to Garsington was set for 29 November. While he was there Lawrence composed a rhapsodic description of the old house, which he saw as a symbol of everything doomed by the war; it was fitting that he did so, for he was never to set foot there again. The old triangular pattern of tension between himself, Ottoline, and Frieda again asserted itself: "We had some fine hours, all of us together, didn't we?" Lawrence asked, rather hollowly, in his thank-you note; but, he admitted, "there comes the inevitable friction. Frieda hates me because she says I am a *favorite*, which is ignominious (she says), also she says I am a traitor to her. But let it be—it is a bore."[89] Ottoline, meanwhile, was telling Russell that the Lawrences "had a quarrel over Nietzsche at dinner—she is a *devil!* I wish she wasn't allowed to be at large." She had misgivings about Lawrence's move to America, but felt that Frieda "would ruin any personal work here in England. If only we could put her in a sack and drown her."[90] The fuse was now burning toward a final explosion and Lawrence's caricature of Ottoline in *Women in Love.* They continued to correspond, but Lawrence and Ottoline would never meet again, Frieda and Ottoline not until after Lawrence's death.

A further irritant was Ottoline's dislike of the three young men whom Lawrence had persuaded her to invite too: Heseltine, Kouyoumdjian, and an Indian friend of Heseltine's named Sarawadi:

> What strange creatures Lawrence and Frieda attract to themselves. He is enthusiastic about both Heseltine and Kouyoumdjian, but I don't feel attracted to them, indeed quite the reverse. Heseltine is tall and blonde, soft and so degenerate that he seems somehow corrupt. Kouyoumdjian is a fat dark-blooded tight-skinned Armenian Jew, and though Lawrence believes that he will be a great writer, I find it hard to believe. Obviously he has a certain vulgar sexual force, but he is very coarse-grained and conceited.[91]

Kouyoumdjian was not in fact Jewish, though Ottoline took it for granted that he was. He and Heseltine came to Garsington again two weeks later, without the Lawrences. Heseltine had a notable talent for making complications, both in his own life and in other people's; during these two visits he managed to stoke up Ottoline's feud with Frieda and to start an unfortunate love affair with Juliette Baillot, a young Swiss who lived at Garsington as governess to Julian. But these entanglements did not bear their harvest of trouble until after the New Year.

Lawrence had devoted almost as much energy to the Florida scheme as he had to *The Signature,* but a week after his last visit to Garsington he suddenly threw the project into limbo. "I shall not go to America," he announced to Ottoline, "until a stronger force from there pulls me across the sea. It is not a case of my will."[92] In fact, he had been unable to face a direct clash between his will and that of the state, now mobilizing for total war.

British war policy in the first half of 1915 had focused on the shortage of munitions; in the rest of the year the issue became the shortage of men. On 11 October Lord Derby, a peer best known for his racehorses, was appointed director-general of recruiting; he produced the "Derby Scheme," aptly described by Arthur Marwick as "one of those shot-gun weddings between the fair maid of Liberal idealism and the ogre of Tory militarism."[93] All men of military age were required to "attest" their willingness to serve when called, but no married men would be taken until all the unmarried ones had been called up, and there would be exemptions for men doing essential work. The scheme included bars to the emigration of men of military age; in a much-publicized incident of 6 November six hundred Irishmen were refused permission to embark for the United States, and the Cunard Line announced it would accept no further bookings by men fit for service. Lawrence would therefore have to attest before he could leave— though this was only a formality since he would surely be rejected for military service because of his weak health. "It makes me angry," he told Lady Cynthia, "to go and say: 'I will serve my king and country' when, in the way of war, I won't. It makes me angry also to be stripped naked before two recruiting sergeants, and examined. But I would rather have all these things than stop here."[94]

The deadline to attest was 11 December, a day of patriotic fervor:

> Everywhere recruiting sergeants were busy in the streets button-holing young men with the query: "This is your last chance. Are you coming or will you wait till you are fetched?" . . .
> "House full" went up at Battersea Town Hall shortly before 11 p.m. . . . "This," said a sergeant, "has been the biggest thing we've done in a day yet. It has been one continuous swarm. Very good class men too! One simply wonders where they are coming from after a year of war. Seems to me the Derby scheme is smoking them out of their nests."[95]

Lawrence joined the crowd at Battersea Town Hall and stood in line for two hours. On the next day he told Ottoline the outcome:

> I felt, though I *hated* the situation almost to *madness*, so vile and false and degrading, such an utter travesty of action on my part, waiting even to be attested that I might be rejected, still I felt, when suddenly I broke out of the

queue, in face of the table where one's name was to be written, and went across the hall away from all the underworld of this spectral submission, and climbed a bus, and after a while saw the fugitive sunshine across the river on the spectral sunlit towers at Westminster, that I had triumphed, like Satan flying over the world and knowing he had won at last, though he had not come into even a fragment of his own. . . . In the long run I have the victory; for all those men in the queue, for those spectral, hazy, sunny towers hovering beyond the river, for the world that is to be.

Lawrence's exhilaration was caused both by having defied the state, and by a resurgent solidarity with his countrymen; waiting in the queue he felt "the *men* were very decent, and that the slumbering lion was going to wake up in them: not against the Germans either, but against the great lie of this life."[96] If the New Jerusalem was coming to Britain, why go to America? So he canceled his and Frieda's reservations, even though they were for a ship auspiciously called the *Crown de Leon*—the first chapter of "The Crown" had been titled "The Lion and the Unicorn Were Fighting for the Crown." His impulse to await a better day at home had fateful consequences. The political atmosphere in England would become worse, not better; conscription was on its way—only half of those eligible under the Derby scheme attested—and in six months Lawrence would be forced to submit to the humiliating military examination he thought he had escaped. He and Frieda had also missed their last practical chance of leaving, and were now committed to England for the duration. It was, he admitted after the war was over, "a great mistake."[97]

The Next Step

THE *Crown de Leon* was sailing from Glasgow, so Lawrence had planned to spend a few days with his sister Ada Clarke at Ripley on the way north. Now he and Frieda decided to make it a Christmas visit and in the meantime seek a new home, since they and given up the lease of 1, Byron Villas. After refusing to attest he had caught a severe cold, which made him think twice about having to face another English winter. "I *do* want to go to Florida," he told Ottoline, only three days after he had told her of his triumph at leaving the queue at Battersea, "—when I get sick like this I know I ought to have gone before."[98] Dollie Radford had offered to lend them her cottage in Berkshire, but when her friend J. D. Beresford suggested his house in Cornwall they quickly accepted, probably because it was farther from London. The Beresford house was on the Atlantic coast at Porthcothan, where Jack and Katherine had spent a happy holiday in September 1914; it was only available for two months, but that did not bother Lawrence. "Again I am *Vogelfrei,* thank God," he told Cynthia Asquith, ". . . no house nor possessions—thank Heaven again."[99]

As winter began, Lawrence hesitated between continuing his struggle with English society or seeking a new life in America. His refusal to attest and the illness that followed showed that for the moment he could only "lapse," drift with the current of events until he had a clearer sense of his next step. His letters at the end of 1915 were filled with images of stasis: ". . . nothing ripens, good nor evil, but goes bitter on the tree, with cold slowness. . . . It is winter with me, my heart is frost-bound." But this, he insisted, was only a temporary death of the heart. "Let me only be still," he told Ottoline, "and know we can force nothing, and compel nothing, can only nourish in the darkness the unuttered buds of the new life that shall be."[100] He wrote in similar vein to Katherine, trying to console her for her distressing Christmas season, ill and alone at Bandol. She had at last "entered into the loss" of her "little brother," she wrote to Jack, "always before that I shrank from the final moment [of Leslie's death]—but now it is past."[101] Lawrence praised the courage of her renunciation:

> I knew you would have to die with your brother; you also, go down into death and be extinguished. But for us there is a rising from the grave, there is a resurrection, and a clean life to begin from the start, new, and happy. Don't be afraid, don't doubt it, it is so.
>
> You have gone further into your death than Murry has. He runs away. But one day he too will submit, he will dare to go down, and be killed, to die in this self which he is. Then he will become a man; not till. He is not a man yet.[102]

These were prophetic words, even though Katherine told Jack that the letter "left [her] cold." For the moment Lawrence's puritan side was in the ascendant, with its dark image of the grain of wheat that must die before it can yield its fruit: life could only be affirmed as correlative with death; creation with destruction. Given the unending psychic and physical struggles of Lawrence's life this may have been a sustaining belief; but how many times could he submit himself to dissolution before his creative resilience would be exhausted? Furthermore, how long could he go on asserting the supreme significance of death, in face of the endless mechanical carnage of the Western Front?

Lawrence also linked his idea of "lapsing" with ancient beliefs about gods who die and are reborn, the seasonal death and renewal of vegetation, and figures who, like Persephone, spend part of the year underground. Man must strike a balance between the conscious and the unconscious, acting and lapsing, with each experience having its own realm: light and the surface for one, darkness and underground for the other. In early December Lawrence was reading Sir James Frazer's *The Golden Bough* and *Totemism and Exogamy* where he found a capstone for his philosophical system: the idea that not only is the form of the universe dualistic, our way of *knowing* it is dualistic too. He wrote enthusiastically of his discovery to Frazer's colleague at Trinity, Bertrand Russell:

> Now I am convinced of what I believed when I was about twenty—that there is another seat of consciousness than the brain and the nerve system: there is a blood-consciousness which exists in us independently of the ordinary mental consciousness, which depends on the eye as its source or connector. There is the blood-consciousness, with the sexual connection holding the same relation as the eye, in seeing, holds to the mental consciousness. One lives, knows, and has one's being in the blood, without any reference to nerves and brain. This is one half of life, belonging to the darkness.

Normally the two forms of consciousness would achieve a self-regulating balance, but the whole force of industrialism, Lawrence believed, worked to destroy it—and he evidently saw Russell himself as an extreme case of the disharmony that resulted: ". . . the tragedy of this our life, and of your life, is that the mental and nerve consciousness exerts a tyranny over the blood-consciousness and that your will has gone completely over to the mental consciousness, and is engaged in the destruction of your blood-being or blood-consciousness, the final liberating of the one, which is only death in result. Plato was the same."[103]

Russell is here type-cast as a cautionary example of one-sided development, a role he also plays as "Sir Joshua Malleson" in *Women in Love.* By criticizing Russell's overdeveloped mental consciousness Lawrence was on safer ground than when he discovered in him a secret blood-lust. Ottoline often deplored Russell's excess of reason too; "It is so sad" she told him, "that you have always to go to the roots of every thing and pull it up and look at it—I *know* you cannot help it—but it takes away the Natural pleasure."[104] Nonetheless, there was an awkward paradox in Lawrence's conscious expression of the need to live unconsciously—and also a recognition that he might in part share Russell's inadequacy. Writing to Katherine on the same day he implicitly admitted it: "Let us be easy and impersonal, not for ever fingering over our own souls, and the souls of our acquaintances, but trying to create a new life, a new common life, a new complete tree of life from the roots that are within us."[105]

Lawrence's idea of "blood-knowledge" created a whole agenda of problems that were to occupy him for the rest of his life, in personal relations, in his philosophy, and in his novels. His letter to Russell explained how blood predominated over mind among primitives, and in the sexual act: ". . . when I take a woman, then the blood-percept is supreme, my blood-knowing is overwhelming. There is a transmission, I don't know of what, between her blood and mine, in the act of connection."[106] The difficulty lies in the precise nature of the "transmission" between lovers: what is the relation between their blood-contact and what they share on other levels of personal or social being—the levels of culture rather than nature? Frazer suggested to Lawrence a possible solution through his study of primitive societies where the two realms had not yet been separated by modern rationalism. In particular, Lawrence found proof of the existence of blood-consciousness in totemism—the cultivation by clans or individuals of a special relation with certain animals or plants:

> All living things, even plants, have a blood-being. If a lizard falls on the breast of a pregnant woman, then the blood-being of the lizard passes with a shock into the blood-being of the woman, and is transferred to the foetus, probably without intervention either of nerve or brain consciousness. And this is the origin of totem: and for this reason some tribes no doubt really *were* kangaroos: they contained the blood-knowledge of the kangaroo.—And blood knowledge comes either through the mother or through the sex—so that dreams at puberty are as good an origin of the totem as the percept of a pregnant woman.

(179)

"Do you know what science says about these things?" Lawrence asked Russell. "It is *very* important: the whole of our future life depends on it."[107] Russell came over to Byron Villas on the twelfth to talk about it. There is no contemporary record of the conversation, though in his autobiography Russell said of Lawrence's theory that it "seemed to me frankly rubbish, and I rejected it vehemently, though I did not then know that it led straight to Auschwitz."[108] This was a grotesque distortion of Lawrence's influence on modern politics, but we *can* say that the theory led straight to various scenes in *Women In Love:* Gerald's beating of his mare, Halliday's fetishes, Gerald and Gudrun's encounter with the rabbit, the wrestling between Gerald and Birkin.

Lawrence expected to work out his new theory in Cornwall and later in Florida, where he still hoped to go in two or three months when Heseltine and a few others were ready to accompany him. Meanwhile he had to visit his family, for the first time since the previous December. Before setting off he arranged for Murry to be a Christmas guest at Garsington as a "homeless infant"—the celebrants of last year's Christmas at Chesham were now either scattered or at odds with one another. Lawrence went up with Frieda to Ada's home in Ripley, Derbyshire, on 23 December. All his close relatives were gathered there: his father, his older brother, George (a rigid nonconformist), his older sister, Emily King, who had come down from Glasgow, a niece, and a nephew. "One's people are the past," Lawrence wrote of the visit. ". . . pure, without mitigation. . . . It is a cruel thing to . . . turn our backs on the future and go back to that which one has been." The experience confirmed his desire for "a new beginning" in Florida. He suffered, also, in contemplating the future of his niece and nephew: ". . . the world seems diabolical to me, with these small, new, fragile, pure children. I can't bear it that the parents should have the children."[109]

Lawrence's reaction to the mining village of Ripley should remind us that he told Russell that blood-consciousness should be recognized as *half* of life, not all of it. What the miners needed, in fact, was more mental or "white" consciousness:

These men are passionate enough, sensuous, dark—God, how all my boyhood comes back—so violent, so dark, the mind always dark and without understanding, the senses violently active. It makes me sad beyond words. These men, whom I love so much—and the life has such a power over me—they *un-*

derstand mentally so horribly: only industrialism, only wages and money and machinery. They can't *think* anything else. . . . They are utterly unable to appreciate any pure, ulterior truth: only this industrial—mechanical—wage idea. . . . That is why we are *bound* to get something like Guild-Socialism in the long run, which is a reduction to the lowest terms—nothing higher than that which now is, only lower.[110]

Guild socialism was becoming intellectually fashionable in 1915; it argued that workers should control their own factories, with the state to be the servant of industry rather than its master. Lawrence's attitude to labor had not changed since July, when he had told Russell "The idea of giving power to the hands of the working class is *wrong.*" At that time, however, he was arguing that supreme power should be reserved for a "body of chosen patricians"; whereas now, having just been raked over the coals by the established system of law, he wanted only to escape domination by either side of the class war. He felt oppressed by the workers in the same way he did by his family—simply because everyone involved knew each other too well:

I love them like brothers—but, my God, I hate them too: I don't intend to own them as masters—not while the world stands. One must conquer them also—think beyond them, know beyond them, act beyond them.

But there will be a big row after the war, with these working men—I don't think I could bear to be here to see it. I couldn't bear it—this last reduction.[111]

After his week in Derbyshire Lawrence was all the more eager to make his next leap into the unknown. "We go to Cornwall on Thursday," he told Ottoline. "There is the beginning."[112]

CHAPTER V

PORTHCOTHAN

"The Brink of Existence"

BY LENDING Lawrence his house J. D. Beresford enabled him
to escape from the social pressures of the London area and to feel
that he could start a new life with a clean slate. For a man of his
temperament this was, of course, an exaggerated hope; still, the
constant friction and excitement of Greatham and Hampstead
had worn him down and he needed relief. More than three
months would pass before the Lawrences saw any of their old intimates. As soon as he arrived in Cornwall Lawrence began inviting them all to come and stay; but the journey from London was
expensive, and the conditions on arrival unpredictable, so none of
the invitations were taken up. Heseltine and Kouyoumdjian came,
but with them the Lawrences had no history of closeness and
conflict. For the next twenty-one months, in fact, the Lawrences
were to have very little direct contact with English intellectual society, and if the authorities had left them to their own inclinations
they would probably have remained cut off until the end of the
war. After the crowded and ultimately unsuccessful social involve-
ments of 1915 Lawrence now entered his term of exile in his own
country.

Beresford's house they took to at once—"a nice old house with
large clear rooms, and such wonderful silence—only a faint sound
of sea and wind. It is like being at the window and looking out of
England to the beyond."[1] The houses where the Lawrences had
lived since 1914 shared a typical English quality of enclosure:
Chesham in the dense greenery of Buckinghamshire, Greatham a
cluster of houses nestled in meadows under the Sussex downs, the
Vale of Health concealed within Hampstead Heath. But Beres-

ford's house commanded a wide view of the treeless landscape of
north Cornwall and of the Atlantic. It was a big, foursquare house
of stone and plaster, standing in its own grounds on a hilltop
overlooking Porthcothan, a hamlet straggling down a valley to the
sea. Padstow was five miles away, but during his stay Lawrence
was seldom well enough to go there. He was seldom well enough
to leave the house in fact; fortunately, it was comfortably furnished and solid enough to resist the violent winter storms on that
part of the coast. By a further stroke of good luck there was a resident housekeeper, a local woman of forty named Emma Pollard.
Lawrence became very fond of her, telling Mrs. Beresford "I like
her presence in the house: which is saying a great deal"; she was
"a good soul . . . and a good cook."[2] Nonetheless Mrs. Beresford
wanted to dismiss her, on the ground that she was too expensive
at five shillings a week—a low wage, according to Lawrence, because she was under a cloud in the village. She had two illegitimate children, ". . . one, the elder, lives at Trevorric farm, with
her parents; the younger lives here. It is a rosy cheeked child of
six. Heseltine says a woman with two illegitimate children must be
good."[3]

All this was a far cry from the "holy family" of Meynells at
Greatham, or the brittle bohemians of Hampstead and Bloomsbury; enough to convince Lawrence, at first, that he had found a
secure refuge from the hysteria and decadence of the capital. The
Cornish people, he imagined, were racially and morally separate
from the English, and uncontaminated by the spirit of war. For
proof, there was the melancholy of Emma's sister-in-law as she
sewed a khaki armlet on her husband's sleeve, in evidence that he
had attested his willingness to join the army when called:

> 'It's come now,' she said. 'We've never had it till now, but it's come now. I'm
> sure, when I look at these buttons, I think "We've got the Kaiser to thank for
> these." Every stitch I put in goes through my heart.'
> Which I think is rather beautiful, showing sincere gentleness and a power
> of love. The English women stitch armlets on freely enough: they have lost
> the power of love. But it does linger here.[4]

"Derby's scheme has wrung their withers," Lawrence commented
ruefully. Still, it had not yet destroyed the special quality of life
here at the end of England. "The women are so soft and so wise
and so attractive" Lawrence told Barbara Low. ". . . so soft, and
unopposing, yet so true: a quality of winsomeness and rare, un-

conscious Female soothingness and fertility of being. I would marry a Cornish woman." Here was his perennial fantasy of being immersed in a warm, nurturing femininity, yet remaining master both of himself and of the sustaining element. Typically, also, the Cornish men were found to be mostly unworthy of this matriarchal paradise, being "detestably small-eyed and mean—real cunning nosed peasants mean as imbeciles." [5]

Lawrence seemed to have found a haven where, after the bitterness of seeing his novel strangled at birth, he could begin again to create in a landscape:

> . . . remote and desolate and unconnected: it belongs still to the days before Christianity, the days of Druids, or of desolate Celtic magic and conjuring; and the sea is so grey and shaggy, and the wind so restless, as if it had never found a home since the days of Iseult. Here I think my life begins again—one is free. Here the autumn is gone by, it is pure winter of forgetfulness. I love it. [6]

He soon began yet another version of his philosophy, which he described as "a maturer and more intelligible Signature. At last, this time, I have got it: the fifth time of writing." [7] To continue the series of good omens, Heseltine arrived within two days, full of enthusiasm for his mentor's pet scheme: a private edition of *The Rainbow*. Nor, for a change, did the financial prospect appear too gloomy; Lawrence still had 100 pounds left from the advance on *The Rainbow* and Ottoline's fund-raising in November; Heseltine enjoyed a small private income and living in Cornwall was cheap. For the first week of his stay at Porthcothan Lawrence rode the crest of a wave of euphoria.

The happiness, so typical of Lawrence's mood on arrival at a new place, was not solidly founded. Though he believed the ordeal of the past year to be over, he was on the verge of a breakdown, perhaps caused by the sudden release of an unbearable tension. Kot seems to have started the trouble. At Christmas Lawrence had urged him to earn enough money to join the Florida exodus, and on arriving in Cornwall he implicitly repeated the invitation in threat-and-promise fashion: "We must begin afresh—we must begin to create a life all together—unanimous. Then we shall be happy. . . . We must cease this analysis and introspection and individualism." [8] Kot's reply has been lost, but it must have contained some home truths of the kind Lawrence was so apt to unleash on his friends; probably it also revealed some of Murry's reservations about joining the Lawrence entourage (he had just left to spend the next three months with Katherine on the Riviera). Lawrence responded with a show of indifference that concealed just how deeply the barb had been planted:

> Well, I am willing to believe that there isn't any Florida—*assez, j'en ai soupé.* I am willing to give up people altogether—they are what they are, why should they be as I want them to be. It is their affair, not mine: English individualists or not individualists, it is all the same to me. I give it up. . . . I admit it all: you are right: there's no *rapport.*
>
> There is my intimate art, and my thoughts, as you say. . . . It is enough, more than enough, if they will only leave me alone.

He wrote in a similar vein to Katherine: she and Jack might come if they liked, but the whole social world with which he had been contending for a year was now "extinguished, like the lights of last night's Café Royal—gone for ever."[9]

All this, however, was no more than a show of self-sufficiency, for Lawrence in fact had reached the limit of his emotional and bodily resources. On the day of his letter to Katherine he fell ill with a "bad cold" which made him feel "queer as if [he] couldn't see any further." As usual he was minimizing his sickness: this attack—successor to a less serious one in mid-December—kept him in bed for two weeks and came close to being fatal. He blamed it, clearly, on the setbacks that had driven him from London; as he told Kot later in the year, "I always feel ill when I feel beaten."[10] He was suffering as much a nervous as a physical breakdown, though it was only to Jack that he revealed its full seriousness:

> I feel now pushed to the brink of existence, and there remains only to fall off into oblivion, or to give in, and accept the ruck: or some way out, as yet undiscovered. I feel absolutely run to earth, like a fox they have chased till it can't go any further, and doesn't know what to do. . . .
>
> You ask "Is there any Florida?" I'm inclined to answer 'No." There is no Florida, there's only this, this England, which nauseates my soul, nauseates my spirit and my body—this England. One might as well be blown over the cliffs here in the strong wind, into the rough white sea, as sit at this banquet of vomit, this life, this England, this Europe. Out of the disciples, there was one Judas. In modern life, there are twelve Judases in the twelve disciples. They are all Judases, one and all, all Judases. Where is one to turn one's face? What good even is death, when life is nothing but this peaked, traitorous meanness? How can death be great, seeing life is such a mean paucity: since they must be counterparts, life and death.

I must own to you, that I am beaten—knocked out entirely. I don't know what to do any more—it seems as if the twilight of all twilights were drawing on, and one could only watch it, and submit: no more hope, nothing further remaining. I could howl with a dog's hopelessness, at nightfall. It seems to be now a case of death, or a miracle. I still believe in miracles—supernatural. I don't believe in human life any more. And failing the miracle, I am finished.

But I'm not going to accept this human life. Foul muck, what have I to do with it.[11]

In the extremity of his despair Lawrence feels himself utterly adrift in the universe. He is able only to howl forth his obsessions: betrayal everywhere, hatred of England, hatred of life itself. His impotent misery is the counterpart to the bright vision of Florida he had conjured up for Jack and Katherine the previous November with such childlike anticipation: "If only it will all end up happily, like a song or a poem, and we live blithely by a big river, where there are fish, and in the forest behind wild turkeys and quails; there we make songs and poems and stories and dramas, in a Vale of Avalon, in the Hesperides, among the Loves."[12] The pendulum of his moods had been swinging progressively farther and faster over the past year, reflecting both the organic process of consumption and the cumulative frustration of seeing all his schemes fail; now it seemed that the real smash had arrived, that his ability to perceive the world coherently had deteriorated beyond repair.

However sympathetic Jack may have been, he was committed to spending the winter with Katherine in Bandol and thus unable to help. Frieda was thrown into a panic and could think of no one better to appeal to than Russell:

I am so worried about Lawrence. He isn't at all well. I really don't know what to do. . . . I feel it such a responsibility, it's too much for me. He might just die because everything is too much for him. . . . Do come, it might do you good and I would be very glad. There are so few people Lawrence can bear the sight of.[13]

Frieda's plea was not phrased in a way likely to move Russell and he refused her invitation. He was himself suffering an acute depression over the war and over Ottoline's coolness. Moreover, he had just returned to London from a similar mission to Torquay, in Devon: when Vivien Eliot suffered a nervous breakdown Russell volunteered to keep her company while she recuperated. Though Vivien was unstable and frivolous—"very second-rate" thought Ottoline—he found her physically attractive, and he admired the poetic talent of her austere husband. The Lawrences, by comparison, no longer intrigued Russell.

Heseltine and Kouyoumdjian were in the house during Lawrence's illness, but they were hardly mature enough to give Frieda much practical support. The cheerful and capable Emma probably did most to pull Lawrence through. Another Good Samaritan also gave assistance: Maitland Radford, the son of Dollie Radford who herself extended so many kindnesses to the Lawrences during the war years. Maitland was a writer about Lawrence's age, with an agreeable personality, and also a doctor. He came down to Porthcothan from London on 24 January, and told Lawrence that his nerves were "the root of the trouble." This was just what Lawrence wished to believe: that his chest inflammation was "*referred* from the nerves" rather than organic.[14] If he could only get over his disappointments of the past year and a half, he convinced himself, his body would heal of its own accord. Radford was no doubt practising bedside diplomacy in allowing his patient to think this, but since the prescribed treatment was simply bed rest, warmth, and a nourishing diet, the formal diagnosis hardly mattered. Even casual acquaintances at this time took it for granted that Lawrence was tubercular, and his phobia about being seen by any doctor who was not a personal friend was a tacit admission of his condition. A diagnosis of nervous exhaustion might at least restrain him from doing anything to aggravate his disease.

Lawrence was seriously ill for nearly a month, feeling "the slithery edge of oblivion" under his feet.[15] Ottoline, herself frequently an invalid, took a kindly interest in his progress; she also sent him a warm sweater, a counterpane, and a supply of special foods. By the first week of February he was definitely on the mend, though still weak and numb down one side of his body:

> . . . now, thank Heaven, it is all getting better, and I feel my old strength coming back, like a pulse that begins to beat and sounds very deep and strong, as if it went to the very heart of the uncreated darkness. I am glad. I have felt very bad, so nearly disintegrated into nothingness. Now I can walk to the sea again and all that fever and inflammation has nearly gone. But I feel very queer after it—sort of hardly know myself.[16]

He continued his convalescence in the warm atmosphere of domesticity that Emma created. Sixty years later one of her children,

Mrs. Lilian Babb, still remembered his attentions, and even the dress he made for her—"brown velvet, embroidered with red hollyberries around the neck." For Dorothy, the younger child who lived at the house, there were "lots of presents—a beautiful leather handbag and a pretty green doll's tea set."[17] Those who were children when they knew Lawrence always seem to have affectionate memories of him.

If the immediate physical crisis was over, and his "soul-sickness after London"[18] in some degree purged by it, nonetheless the events leading up to the suppression of *The Rainbow* had left their mark. Misanthropy, sometimes to the point of mania, became Lawrence's predominant mood during 1916. At the same time, his thinking turned from discursive reasoning toward a different mode of perception. His mind seemed to have come to the end of its tether within the established system; now he must give the world another kind of mental ordering for it to be possible for him to live in it. "I wish there were miracles," he told Ottoline. "I am tired of the old laborious way of working things to their conclusions."[19] Though the idea of "blood-consciousness" dropped from sight for a while after Lawrence's excited rediscovery of it in December 1915, his philosophy of human existence had undergone a further development and he was now germinating a form of expression that would match it. The end product was the distinctive style of *Women in Love,* just as the style of *The Rainbow* matched the shift in Lawrence's consciousness, since *Sons and Lovers,* toward "that which is physic." Not until three months after his illness and nervous collapse did he take up work on *Women in Love;* but the essential mood and themes of this work had already been established by January 1916, and it required only a period of reflection and "crystallization" for them to be articulated in the novel itself.

The Rainbow Books and Music

A FURTHER REASON for delay in turning his energies to *Women in Love* was Lawrence's hope that he might still be able to reissue *The Rainbow.* Three weeks after it was suppressed he broached the plan to Ottoline: "There are so many letters about *The Rainbow,* so many people wanting it. I wonder why it can't be printed privately by subscription—I believe money could be made that way, even."[20] He may have picked up the idea from Clive Bell, whom he had just met, and who was trying to launch a private publishing scheme of his own. Another friend of Ottoline's, Prince Bibesco, obligingly volunteered to get *The Rainbow* published privately in Paris by Conard, a foreign-language publisher. So Lawrence asked Pinker to see if Methuen would waive its rights and sell the plates from which the book had been printed. Nothing came of this approach—the last thing Methuen wanted was a revival of the scandal—so Lawrence then proposed a private edition made up from sheets of Huebsch's American edition, but with the expurgations restored. This fared no better but Lawrence, still undiscouraged, determined to do the whole job himself. His natural collaborator was Jack Murry, who when he had first returned from Bandol in early December had planned to continue *The Signature* and print it on his own press. Such schemes were not necessarily unsound: the highly successful Hogarth Press was begun a year or two later by Leonard and Virginia Woolf on a similar basis, and Lawrence himself was eventually to become well-to-do through the private publication of *Lady Chatterley's Lover.*

At Porthcothan Heseltine eagerly undertook to launch the scheme and also to expand into publishing other books and musical compositions, including his own. Lawrence, with his usual naiveté about business and public taste, decided that Heseltine had some innate talent for these affairs:

> I feel that he is one of those people who are transmitters, and not creators of art. And I don't think we [himself and Murry] are transmitters. I have come to the conclusion that I have no business genius. Heseltine's family have just got that curious touch of artistic genius which will make them perfect dealers in art, I believe. His uncle had one of the best collections or pictures in England—Rembrandt, Watteau, etc.—and he was a stockbroker and very rich.[21]

What Heseltine did have, certainly, was the ability to chime in with Lawrence's rhetoric of disgust, while adding to it some of his own callow trumpet blasts. To an old girl friend, Viva Smith, he wrote unfolding his plans and suggesting that she might become secretary to the organization:

[Lawrence] is a true and amazing philosopher, but, I fear a century out of time—At the present, all but a handful will dismiss him as a riotous lunatic. . . . I am convinced that he is one of the greatest thinkers—as well as being a consummate artist in language—we have ever had, and it is monstrous that his work should not even receive a fair hearing. Oh, this cursed country of mediocrities which spues out all its true teachers and prophets! There is no discrimination, none whatever, and the bloody herd will only read those who uphold them as they are, in their stinking, Christian self-complacency! Books and music alike are trodden under the feet of hogs, *hogs!*[22]

Since Lawrence was too ill during January to do much, Heseltine composed a prospectus and had a thousand copies printed:

THE RAINBOW BOOKS AND MUSIC

Either there exists a sufficient number of people to buy books because of their reverence for truth, or else books must die. In its books lie a nation's vision; and where there is no vision the people perish.

The present system of production depends entirely upon the popular esteem: and this means gradual degradation. Inevitably, more and more, the published books are dragged down to the level of the lowest reader. . . .

It is time that enough people of courage and passionate soul should rise up to form a nucleus of the living truth; since there must be those among us who care more for the truth than for any advantage.

For this purpose it is proposed to attempt to issue privately such books and musical works as are found living and clear in truth.[23]

The first work, naturally, would be *The Rainbow;* the prospectus was vague about what would follow, though in his letter to Viva Smith, Heseltine listed "a sequel to 'The Rainbow,' and a philosophical work, 'Goats and Compasses' (a veritable soul-bomb, a dum-dum that will explode right inside the soul!) by Lawrence, and a novel by Middleton Murry."[24]

The unveiling of the scheme caused an immediate tiff with the Murrys. On 11 February Lawrence had written them about it quite misleadingly: "Heseltine also talks of a publishing scheme. He would combine with you. I myself believe that there is something to be done by private publishing. We can set everything going if you come—at least we can try."[25] Since the proofs of the circular arrived at Porthcothan only six days after this letter, clearly things had been "set going" without even waiting for Jack's approval, still less his arrival. When Jack sent an angry reply, Lawrence tried to disown the project:

> Now don't get in a state, you two, about nothing. The publishing scheme has not yet become at all real or important, to me. . . .
>
> You see it is Heseltine's affair so far . . . I am very glad to have him for a friend. He lived here for seven weeks with us, so we know. Now don't think this friendship hurts ours. It doesn't touch it. You will like him too, because he is real, and has some queer kind of abstract passion which leaps into the future. He will be one with us.[26]

On the same day Lawrence wrote Heseltine, who was trying to drum up support in London, and reaffirmed his own faith in the scheme. He could hardly expect to carry water on both shoulders indefinitely like this, but his rupture with Heseltine, before the Murrys returned to England, saved him from a confrontation.

The bombastic tone of Heseltine's prospectus threatened to give *The Rainbow* a bad name even among those friendly to its author. Ottoline, for example, complained to Russell that it was "such an *odious* Prospectus. It makes me angry—I hate desdain—and contempt."[27] Russell agreed with her, refusing to have anything to do with Heseltine when he came to London. He had also been told by Lawrence to seek help from Beresford, Gertler, Kot, Gordon Campbell, and the Carswells, but even if they had become active, nothing could have saved the scheme after the paltry response to the prospectus. Only thirty people out of the six hundred to whom it had been sent expressed interest in joining. The project therefore died, though Lawrence had by then started work on *Women In Love* and was able to shrug off the fiasco. Heseltine, the supposed business genius, had made the elementary mistake of asking for subscriptions before there was any definite publication being offered. If actual copies of *The Rainbow* had been made available, without the accompanying bombast, they probably would have sold quite well. Either Methuen or the London police might have raised legal obstacles to the book's circulation, but the joint ineptitude of Heseltine and Lawrence ensured the failure of the scheme long before that point.

Writings at Porthcothan

IN SPITE OF his illness and black moods Lawrence was full of literary plans at Porthcothan after two barren months at the end of his stay in London. During January he corrected the proofs of *Twilight in Italy;* he may have made further revisions since this was his custom, but evidence is lacking. Then there was a projected book of poetry. On 16 December 1915 Lawrence had written to his friend T. D. Dunlop, the English consul at Spezia, asking him to forward to England the manuscripts of his prewar poems. They arrived at Porthcothan by 22 January and within nine days Lawrence had put together from them the manuscript of a book *Amores,* enlisting Heseltine's aid as typist. He urged Pinker to circulate the book promptly, reminding him that poetry was now in vogue and that his reputation as a poet was still relatively untarnished. There was some practicality in Lawrence's observations, except that his poems were neither patriotic nor topical, which was what the market called for. He had heard that Sidgwick and Jackson had been doing very well with poetry, so he asked Pinker to try them first—though the reason they had been doing well was because they published Rupert Brooke's poems, whereas Lawrence's were not quite in the same line. They did not fail, inevitably, to point this out: "I had a letter from Sidgwick," Lawrence reported to Pinker at the end of February, "refusing my poems, also giving an unasked and very impertinent criticism of the MS., together with instructions as to how to write poetry. I wrote and told him his letter was impertinent and foolish and presumptuous."[28] Fortunately, Duckworth was still willing to publish the book, as they had his first book of poems, *Love Poems and Others* (1913). "One feels quite mean, Lawrence admitted, "going to somebody else, and then coming back upon refusal. . . . I suppose we shall go trickling slowly on with dear old Duckworth, till the end of the story. . . . But I must say, I *like* Duckworth for sticking to me."[29] After *Amores* and *Twilight in Italy,* however, even Duckworth refused to stick to Lawrence any longer.

The whole business was all the more discouraging in that the poems of *Amores* came from an earlier, more conventional phase

(195)

of Lawrence's career; they were "a sort of inner history" of his emotional entanglements between age twenty and twenty-six, especially with Jessie Chambers and Louie Burrows. But working through his old notebooks at least revived Lawrence's interest and pleasure in poetry, of which he had written little since the start of the war. He was appreciative, too, of poems that Catherine Carswell sent him, though he advised her to be less dependent on regular meter and rhyme: "Write them as they come, the poems. It is like having a child, you can't dictate its form. . . . The essence of poetry with us in this age of stark and unlovely actualities is a stark directness, without a shadow of a lie, or a shadow of deflection anywhere. Everything can go, but this stark, bare, rocky directness of statement, this alone makes poetry, today."[30] Always sensitive to the spirit of place, Lawrence here makes the bare Cornish landscape a model of the style in which he now wishes to write.

Lawrence told Ottoline he wished to dedicate *Amores* to her, and sent her the manuscript for safekeeping at Garsington. But he still had little inclination to write new poems; his lyrical impulses were largely subdued while the war lasted. He was still willing, however, to try his hand at a short story from time to time. Soon after his arrival at Porthcothan he began a story about the oblivion of winter, his first creative response to the isolation of Cornwall. By 9 January he had written the first part of the story, but he then seems to have abandoned it: "I don't know how to go on. You see one must break into a new world and it is so difficult."[31] Probably the manuscript was destroyed before the Lawrences left Cornwall. Something of the spirit of the story may have carried over into "The Blind Man," where the season and setting are partly reminiscent of Porthcothan, and into a much later story, "The Man Who Loved Islands." Closer in time is the "mid-winter oblivion" of the conclusion of *Women in Love,* at the snowbound hotel in the Alps.

Then there was to be a house-party play, written jointly by everyone at Porthcothan, "a comedy for the stage, about Heseltine and his Puma and so on. It will be jolly."[32] The Puma was one of Heseltine's lady friends, and the play seems to have been an elaborate charade. It was never completed, but the substance of it was incorporated into *Women in Love*—though not, by then, in any spirit of jollity.

At the same time, Lawrence was again trying to make a definitive version of his philosophy. His letters for January and February are sprinkled with enthusiastic references to it, and after more than a month's work he felt he had far outdone the version of September 1915, "The Crown":

> My dear Kot, this time at last I have *got* it. Now you would not tell me, if you read it, that I shall write it again. This time, my dear Kot, I have put salt on its tail: I've caught the rabbit: like the old hare in Tartarin. My dear Kot, it is the new word, at last.[33]

Concerning the actual nature of "the rabbit" we must rely on secondhand evidence, since the manuscript has been lost. Early in February the prospectus for *The Rainbow Books and Music* gave it a title, "Goats and Compasses"; this is a common name for English pubs—apparently a corruption of "God Encompasseth Us"—but the connection remains a mystery.[34] When Lawrence sent the text to Ottoline, on 25 February, he described it as:

> . . . the first, the destructive half of my philosophy. Don't read it on a spring day, when the buds are young and tender to unfold. Read it on a black day, when there is a blackness gripping you. Please do this.
>
> I feel my philosophy is real, again a sort of bursting into new seas: when it is finished. There remains the new half to write. But I have crossed the ridge, the new world lies before us.[35]

Evidently the philosophy dealt with the destruction of the "old world"; this had been a preoccupation of Lawrence's since the conclusion of *The Rainbow* and was to become the principal theme of *Women in Love*. Probably he was influenced by two cosmic and nihilistic works he read at Porthcothan, Melville's *Moby Dick* and Dostoevsky's *The Possessed*.*

For the rest we must rely on the evidence of those who read it at the time. Heseltine's description of it as "a veritable soul-bomb" tells us more about him than about the philosophy. Ottoline wrote in her diary:

> It seems to me deplorable tosh, a volume of words, reiteration, perverted and self-contradictory. A gospel of hate and violent individualism. He attacks the will, love and sympathy. Indeed, the only thing that he doesn't revile and condemn is love between men and women. But after all what does sexual love lead to, if there is nothing outside to grow out to? For two people, simply to grow in, and in, into each other, does not satisfy a man for long; perhaps a woman might be content, for women are more possessive. I feel very de-

---

* The title "Goats and Compasses" may relate to the discussion of the compass in "The Needle," chapter 124 of *Moby Dick*.

pressed that he has filled himself with these "evening" ideas. They are, I am sure, the outcome of Frieda. Lawrence writes that "They are more married than ever before." I say, *"Voilà leur enfant."*

She will rejoice that I don't like this philosophy, but I cannot pretend to. How Lawrence, as I knew him, who seemed so kind and understanding and essentially so full of tenderness, could turn round and preach this doctrine of hate is difficult to understand, it seems such a complete contradiction of all I found in him and have heard him say.

But I suppose having accepted Frieda as his wife and finding in her some instinctive satisfaction, he has to suppress his human pity, his gentle and tender qualities, to enable him to fight her and this makes him raw and bitter inside.

To Russell she summed it up, more succinctly, as "rubbish—a child of Frieda's!"[36] Cecil Gray's account, written some twenty years later, asserts: "It struck me, even at that time when I was under the spell of the prophet, as being Lawrence at his very worst: a bombastic, pseudo-mystical, psycho-philosophical treatise dealing largely with homosexuality—a subject, by the way, in which Lawrence displayed a suspiciously lively interest at that time."[37] Some corroboration of Gray's recollections can be found in the suppressed "Prologue" to *Women in Love,* which describes explicitly the physical attraction of Gerald for Birkin; if this was written when Lawrence began the novel in April it may well have been a fictional restatement of theories about homoeroticism already elaborated in "Goats and Compasses." Moreover, the philosophy was written at a time when Lawrence, because of his illness and depression, felt an intense longing for Jack's company. What remains uncertain is how Lawrence connected the themes of homosexuality and the destruction of the old world. The decadent homosexuality of Loerke, in *Women in Love,* is probably the best clue to Lawrence's thinking on this issue.

"A Shameful Affair"

THOUGH the Lawrences habitually asked their friends to live with them, Heseltine was one of the few who actually tried it. He spent nearly two months at Porthcothan, and so learned what intimacy with the Lawrences meant in practice. Within a few days of his arrival on New Year's Day the struggle was on, over what he was and what he should become. Lawrence still professed to like him, but found him "empty, uncreated . . . not yet born. . . . These young individualists are so disintegrated: *are* the young more sound than the old? It seem to me they are much more sick."[38] Sick or not, Heseltine proved reluctant to allow his new mentor to prescribe for him, as he explained to his old mentor, Frederick Delius:

> I don't want to identify myself with [Lawrence] in anything beyond his broad desire for an ampler and fuller life—a real life as distinct from the mere mouldy-vegetable existence which is all that is possible here. He is a very great artist, but hard and autocratic in his views and outlook, and his artistic canons I find utterly and entirely unsympathetic to my nature. He seems to be too metaphysical, too anxious to be comprehensive in a detached way and to care too little for purely personal, analytical, and introspective art. His views are somewhat at variance with his own achievements.[39]

Like many of Lawrence's friends, Heseltine had first been attracted to him by the sensitive realism of works like *Sons and Lovers* and now found his preoccupation with metaphysics and the impersonal distasteful. Nonetheless, he held to the plan of helping to form a nucleus of young people around Lawrence in preparation for the actual founding of a colony, whether in Florida or elsewhere.

The next recruit to arrive at Porthcothan was Heseltine's friend Dikran Kouyoumdjian, on 10 January. Lawrence had seen great potential in Kouyoumdjian in November but now, struggling with extreme sickness and depression, he was less tolerant. The visitor brought with him "the atmosphere of London, most disturbing"; he was antagonistic to Heseltine, and "noisily and offensively" self-assertive. Within a week, Lawrence admitted to Ottoline that she had been "right about Kouyoumdjian—I don't care for him. I shall ask him to go away."[40] Asking, it turned out, was not enough: Heseltine reported to Viva Smith that he "had to expel [Kouyoumdjian] by force, he proved so intolerable to all of us and so impervious to all our hints of displeasure at his presence!!"[41]

In his brief visit to Porthcothan Kouyoumdjian also helped stir up the feud between Frieda and Ottoline. Frieda had long suspected that she was being maligned at Garsington but Heseltine and Kouyoumdjian, having been there in December, were able to give her firsthand proof. In her usual blunt style she confronted Ottoline:

> I know in your heart you have been my enemy. You thought that Lawrence ought to leave me, that I am bad for him, that he does not care for me. . . . But you don't know what we have been to each other in these trying years. . . . You have been very unfair to me, I think, you have tried to put me down as of no account—I could understand that as you must have had to put up with some terrible artists' wives. . . . But you are good and understanding and I do think it's our real desire to be friends! We ought to be in spite of differences in temperament.[42]

Ottoline, however, was still set on playing the role of an injured innocent. She passed on the letter to Russell with the comment: "Isn't Frieda a mad woman!! She would send me mad too. I wonder why she makes this attack on me . . . I have written her an answer as *soothing* as I could—but she puts my back up so!"[43] Ottoline seems to have believed that a grudge had no official existence until it was expressed openly to the one against whom it was directed; so long as a facade of politeness was kept up she did not concede Frieda any grounds for complaint.

Ottoline soon learned from Lawrence that Heseltine was responsible for Frieda's denunciation of her, and she sent him a rebuke for betraying his hostess's confidence. Not abashed, he reminded her of the Homeric motto cited by Samuel Butler in *Erewhon Revisited:*

> Him do I hate even as I hate Hell fire,
> Who says one thing, and hides another in his heart.
> > (*Iliad,* XI, 312–13)

This he followed up with a heavy counterbombardment:

> I am certainly tactless, because I am convinced that tact, so far from providing a cure for misunderstandings, merely suppresses them for a while, after which they break out with renewed virulence.
> After living with the Lawrences for several weeks, I have come to the very definite conclusion that Mrs. Lawrence has been most unjustly maligned behind her back, in several quarters—She has known this for some time past and, very naturally, she is unhappy about it. Am I, therefore, to blame for trying to help her mend matters?[44]

It seemed that Frieda had won the round; but Ottoline, with an impressive grasp of strategy, planned to detach her enemy's ally and turn him around to attack his former base. Though she cordially disliked Heseltine, she realized that he was unstable enough to be manipulated for her own purposes. To understand this, we must go back to Heseltine's overexcited state when he first met Lawrence, in mid-November of the previous year. He was then entangled in an ambivalent love affair with Minnie Channing, a young artist's model known familiarly as "Puma." She was a hanger-on of the bohemian set that frequented the Café Royal, a pretty and wayward opportunist who hoped to get some lasting advantage out of the floating world in which she lived. Heseltine became infatuated with her, and made her into one of the two poles that shaped his adult life. The other was his mother, a rigidly conventional and moralistic woman who dominated him both emotionally and through her control of his allowance of three pounds a week.

Heseltine both despised Puma and despised himself for being sensually in thrall to her. Then, as if to seal their uneasy alliance, she became pregnant; this aroused some sense of obligation in him, but also a strong desire to flee the whole imbroglio—he was, after all, still only twenty-one and entirely dependent on his mother's goodwill for means of support.

When Heseltine visited Garsington in December he added a fresh complication by falling passionately in love with Mlle. Juliette Baillot, the Swiss governess of Ottoline's daughter, Julian. He proposed to her at once, and sent a frantic letter to his friend Boris Khroustchoff, telling him that Puma had defiled his whole life and should be sent packing before he returned to London.[45] Having found a tall, blond, restrained young woman to dedicate his life to, he wished to be rid of the all-too-dark and sensual Puma. But the repulsion did not last, since after a month at Porthcothan he arranged for Puma to come down for an extended visit. When she arrived, on 2 February, the Lawrences failed to see why Heseltine had denounced her previously. "She is a quiet, quite nice little thing really," thought Lawrence, "unobtrusive and affectionate." The trouble, Lawrence told Ottoline, lay in Heseltine's schizoid emotions rather than in any special vice of Puma's:

> He declares he does not like this one, Puma, but he does really. He declares he wants her to go. But he is really attached to her in the senses, in the unconsciousness, in the blood. He is always fighting away from this. But in so doing he is a fool. She is very nice and very real and simple, we like her. His affection

for Mlle is a desire for the light because he is in the dark. If he were in the light he would want the dark. He wants Mlle for *companionship,* not for the blood connection, the dark, sensuous relation. With Puma he has this second, dark relation, but not the first. She is quite intelligent, in her way, but no mental consciousness; no white consciousness, if you understand, all intuition, in the dark, the consciousness of the senses. But she is quite fine and subtle in that way, quite, and I esteem her there *quite* as much as I esteem him.[46]

No doubt Lawrence was speaking out of his own youthful experience of sex, when he was torn between the spiritual Jessie Chambers and the sensual Alice Dax. The solution he proposed was ingenious, but more manageable in a novel than it turned out to be in real life:

Perhaps he is very split, and would always have the two things separate, the real blood connection and the real conscious or spiritual connection, always separate. For these people I really believe in two wives. I don't see why there should be monogamy for people who can't have full satisfaction in one person, because they themselves are too split, because they act in themselves separately. Monogamy is for those who are whole and clear, all in one stroke. But for those whose stroke is broken into two different directions, then there should be two fulfilments.

For myself, thank God, I feel myself becoming more and more unified, more and more a oneness. And Frieda and I become more and more truly married—for which I thank Heaven. It has been such a fight. But it is coming right. And then we can all three be real friends. Then we shall be really happy, all of us, in our relation.[47]

Reading between the lines, one can also see in this advice a message directed to Ottoline: that he accepted the division of her emotional loyalties between her husband and a series of lovers. He was probably also hinting that he no longer imagined any joint allegiance of his own to both Ottoline, as priestess of the spirit, and Frieda as priestess of the flesh—only a simple, undemanding friendship between the three of them. But the more he extolled his marital satisfaction, the more Ottoline lamented that he was being crushed by Frieda's heavy Germanic thumb.

When Heseltine left for London at the end of February, Lawrence suggested to Ottoline that his "terrible cyclonic state" should be allowed to blow itself out:

Heseltine is in a great state of (unjustly) hating the Puma, and looking to Mlle as a white star. He will swing from dark to light till he comes to rest. I believe if he stayed long enough with Mlle *exclusively,* he would hate her: but perhaps not. We can but let him oscillate violently.[48]

The purpose of Heseltine's trip was to promote *The Rainbow Books and Music* and to obtain a medical exemption from military service, after which he could return "free" to Cornwall.[49] But within two weeks he told Robert Nichols that he had changed his mind: "I am not returning to Lawrence; he has no real sympathy. All he likes in one is the potential convert to his own reactionary creed." A later letter to Delius gives some clues as to why he had suddenly come to consider Lawrence his enemy: "Personal relationship with him is impossible—he acts as a subtle and deadly poison. The affair by which I found him out is far too long to enter upon here. . . . The man really must be a bit mad, though his behaviour nearly landed me in a fearful fix—indeed it was calculated to do so."[50]

It seems likely that Heseltine visited Garsington to renew his suit to Mlle. Baillot; once again he wanted Puma out of the way and his plans for her probably resembled Pussum's account of the affair in *Women in Love:*

> He came and cried to me, tears, you never saw so many, saying *he couldn't* bear it unless I went back to him. . . . He made me go back . . . And now I'm going to have a baby, he wants to give me a hundred pounds and send me into the country, so that he would never see me nor hear from me again. But I'm not going to do it. . . ."[51]

Heseltine was also trying, it seems, to keep each woman ignorant of his involvement with the other. Of Lawrence's role we learn something from a letter of Robert Nichols to Cecil Gray in 1933:

> The thorough second-ratedness of D. H. L. in some aspects is shown by D. H. L.'s approval of Puma, and his horrible want of any real insight (for which he is so 'famous') by his attempts to make Puma and Phil resume married life. I think I shall 'give away' how D. H. L. tried hard to prevail on me and then on Phil to enter into relations with a certain girl either marital or extramarital. In this matter he (D. H. L.) played the sentimental sensualist and the whole affair was a typical example of D. H. L.'s utter lack of any real sense of responsibility.[52]

While Lawrence's suggestion that Heseltine should indulge his attraction to two women at once may have been naive, he cannot fairly be accused of irresponsibility in urging his young friend to stay with Puma rather than abandon her while pregnant. Still, it is true that by describing Heseltine's intimate affairs to Ottoline, and implying that he should tell each woman of the nature of his attachment to the other, Lawrence might easily leave Heseltine in a "fearful fix"—even if it was fundamentally of his own making. The rupture between the two men was probably inspired, as Harry T. Moore has already suggested,[53] by Ottoline: her feud with Frieda was working up to a climax, and it would have been consistent with her behavior on other occasions if she had provoked Heseltine by showing him Lawrence's letters about him when he visited Garsington.

By 8 March Heseltine had decided not to return to Cornwall, though when he visited Garsington he still planned to do so because Ottoline gave him two things to take back: a drawing Lawrence had made of Dionysius and the manuscript of "Goats and Compasses." These are the concern of Lawrence's farewell letter to Heseltine:

> Thank you for the Dionysos, which came this morning. By the same post comes Frieda's letter to you, returned by Puma, with a note to the effect that we are both beneath contempt. . . . would [you] send also the MS. of my philosophy . . . I shall be glad when I have that MS. and this affair is finished. It has become ludicrous and rather shameful. I only wish that you and Puma should not talk about us, for decency's sake. I assure you I shall have nothing to say of you and her. The whole business is so shamefully fit for a Kouyoumdjian sketch.
>
> Please send me the manuscript, and we will let the whole relation cease entirely, and remove the indecency of it.[54]

The letter is dated only "Thursday," but was probably sent on 23 or 30 March, since Lawrence already knew by 14 March that Heseltine was not coming back. It is unclear why Puma too was so offended, since the immediate result of the imbroglio was that she and Heseltine were once more united, with Mlle. apparently out of the picture.[55]

Heseltine still had another shot in his locker: instead of sending back the "Goats and Compasses" manuscript he substituted "a page of prophetic reviews of a future book 'D. H. Lawrence, a Critical Study by P. H.,' of which the *Times* will say: 'Reveals the distorted soul of this unhappy genius in all its naked horror,' and the *Spectator* will gloat over 'A monster of obscenity tracked down to its secret lair.' " This callow baiting of his former hero was satisfyingly effective, he told Delius: "Lawrence was quite comically

The Lawrences' wedding photo, July 13, 1914, taken at Selwood Terrace, Kensington, by Gordon Campbell. From Left: D. H. Lawrence, Katherine Mansfield, Frieda Lawrence, John Middleton Murry. *Photo: Humanities Research Center, University of Texas.*

THE CHESHAM CIRCLE

FACING PAGE, TOP: Mark Gertler (center) with E. M. Forster (right), at Garsington. *Photo: Mrs. Igor Vinogradoff.* BELOW: S. S. Koteliansky, c. 1910. *Photo: Mrs. Catherine Stoye.* THIS PAGE, CLOCKWISE: Katherine Mansfield, 1915. John Middleton Murry, 1912. *Photos: Mrs. Mary Murry.* Mary Cannan (formerly Mary Barrie). Gilbert Cannan. *Photos: Mrs. M. Rideout.*

BELOW: Lady Ottoline Morrell. FACING PAGE, TOP: Standing, Augustine Birrell, Clive Bell (?), Frankie Birrell, Aldous Huxley, Lytton Strachey, John Sheppard; sitting, Dorothy Brett, Bertrand Russell, Julian Morrell, at Garsington, c. 1918. BELOW: Suhrawardy, Philip Heseltine, D. H. Lawrence, at Garsington, December, 1915. *Photos: Mrs. Igor Vinogradoff.*

ABOVE: Lady Cynthia Asquith with her son Michael, c. 1917. *Photo: Michael and Simon Asquith.* BELOW: Dorothy Yorke ("Arabella"), painting by D. H. Lawrence. *Courtesy of Beinecke Rare Book and Manuscript Library, Yale University.*

Hilda Doolittle ("H. D."). *Photos: Beinecke Rare Book and Manuscript Library, Yale University.*

c. 1917

1918

ABOVE: Rupert Brooke, in the
uniform of the Royal Naval
Division. BELOW: Manfred von
Richthofen, the "Red Baron".
Photo: Imperial War Museum.

perturbed at the prospect of my revelations. He has practically no friends left."[56] A writer whose reputation and means of livelihood had just been destroyed by the newspaper critics would naturally be perturbed by the threat of further scandalous publicity, but Heseltine was not one who would sympathize. In conducting his intimate relationships he knew no middle voice between adulation or vindictive contempt. Fortunately he did not carry out his threat of publishing an account of his stay at Porthcothan; he even became an admirer of Lawrence again, in 1917–18. That phase ended when he discovered that Lawrence, breaking his written promise of discretion, had caricatured him in *Women in Love* as the squealing degenerate Halliday. He tried to block publication of the novel, and succeeded in forcing Lawrence to make changes in the English edition. It was at this time, apparently, that the manuscript of "Goats and Compasses" ended its picaresque career when Heseltine found it amusing to use it for toilet paper.

It may be tempting to sum up the Heseltine fiasco by turning back on Lawrence his advice to Ottoline, when she complained of his ingratitude: that she should choose her friends more carefully in future. But one of the results of his wartime crisis of health and spirit was precisely that he became less and less capable of choosing his friends wisely, or of keeping his older friendships on an even keel. Even in his self-imposed isolation he longed for a few companions who would share his bleak outlook and his conviction that only a radical transformation could save England. When he found such disciples he became euphoric, convinced that they would be "unanimous" with him in action; but his elation would be replaced by an equally profound rage and depression when the views of his followers diverged in any way from his own. Those who were acclaimed as disciples were, before too long, anathematized as heretics and cast forth. Moreover, this set off a disturbance within Lawrence's network of relationships similar to sequential failure in an electrical system: when he quarreled with one intimate, he was led to demand more support and sympathy from each of those who remained—who were then all the more likely, under this increased strain, to draw the line against his encroachments. The climax of this process was now approaching, as Lawrence sought for a solution to his accumulated miseries in the ideal of a full and mutual commitment between himself, Frieda, and the Murrys.

Exit Russell

FIRST CAME the disintegration of Lawrences' friendship with Bertrand Russell, after scarcely a year's acquaintance. Lawrence had for a while relented from his savage criticism of Russell the previous September. He wrote him two friendly, almost seductive letters after arriving at Porthcothan, asking him down to stay; Frieda also, as we have seen, asked him to help in the crisis of Lawrence's illness. But Russell responded coolly, being wary both of Lawrence's ability to destroy his composure and of his new theory of "blood-consciousness." In London in January he began the lectures on "Principles of Social Reconstruction" that he and Lawrence had once hoped to collaborate on. When it became evident that the series was highly successful, he reported this to Lawrence but lamented that he was nonetheless deeply depressed by his lack of political influence. "He doesn't know why he lives at all," Lawrence told Ottoline, "mere obstinacy and pride . . . keep him alive." Lawrence's mood was quite the opposite. Having just survived a near-fatal illness he scorned Russell's lack of a will to live, and whereas Russell struggled to save mankind from itself Lawrence was feeling, he told Kot, ". . . anti-social . . . everything I do is a shot at these fallen angels of mankind. Wing the brutes. If only one could be a pirate or a brigand nowadays, an outlaw, to rob the angels and hang them on a tree. But long-distance guns has stopped all that jolly game."[57] It was again time, he decided, to dispatch one of his "minatory" letters to his friend:

> I didn't like your letter. What's the good of living as you do, anyway. . . .
> What's the good of sticking in the damned ship and haranguing the merchant-pilgrims in their own language. Why don't you drop overboard? Why don't you clear out of the whole show?
> One must be an outlaw these days, not a teacher or preacher. One must retire out of the herd and then fire bombs into it. . . .
> Do for heavens sake be a baby, and not a savant any more. . . . You had better come and live near us: but not if you are going to be a thinker and a worker, only if you are going to be a creature, an infant.

Lawrence was suffering one of his fits of exasperation at having to leave the Porthcothan house—the Beresfords were coming back—and having no firm prospect of a future home or income. If Russell was once again feeling suicidal, he might at least, Lawrence suggested, provide means for one of his survivors: "I want to ask you, when you make your will, do leave me enough to live on. I want you to live for ever. But I want you to make me in some part your heir." Lack of money, while frightening in itself, was for Lawrence symbolic of a deeper insecurity: the fear that by fleeing to a hill overlooking the cliffs of Cornwall's north coast he had only made it easier for the authorities to corner him and drive him over the brink:

> I feel as if we were all living on the edge of a precipice. Soon I shall be penniless, and they'll shove me into munitions, and I shall tell 'em what I think of 'em, and end my days in prison or a madhouse. But I don't care. One can still write bombs. But I don't want to be penniless and at their mercy. Life is very good of itself, and I am terrified lest they should get me into their power. They seem to me like an innumerable host of rats, and once they get the scent, one is lost.[58]

Lawrence ended by sending his love, but Russell's reply was curt; his patience had run out. Ottoline, however, was still reluctant to write Lawrence off, and she sent Russell a plea that he should not do so either:

> That is a *silly* letter from D H L—but I shouldn't really mind it—He gets obsessed with one idea and can think of nothing else. I suppose he is in a dreadful state because of money and other things—and it is dreadful that he is so obviously *under* Frieda. He is quite unbalanced—and has got this idea of being a Publisher on his brain partly from Frieda and Heseltine but it will pass. I don't think you and he would ever really agree—or agree to differ. He is much too uncivilized for you—I don't think his letter is beastly—It is only detracké! He *is of course really in the Power of the Authorities* in a way we of the upper classes are not. If one reads the account of the Tribunals in London in todays D. News it is awful and I don't wonder he feels demented. Also he is ill. . . . Don't be angry with Lawrence.[59]

But angry Russell was, and remained so long after Lawrence's death. Nonetheless, he *was* shifting course in the direction pointed out by Lawrence. He was ceasing to be a "savant," caring less for mathematics and philosophy and shifting toward writing on social reform for a popular audience—his main occupation for the rest of his life. Though he gave no more money to Lawrence, he gave a substantial sum to T. S. Eliot to support his creative work and help him through his marital troubles. Finally, he was indeed becoming an outlaw: in June 1916 he was to be fined one hundred pounds' for "discouraging enlistment," which led to the loss of his fellowship at Trinity, and the year after he was sent to prison in the same cause. But each man was determined to become an outlaw in his own style, and neither believed any longer that he had anything to learn from the other. If opposition to the war had brought them together it had now, by the seemingly inexorable law that radicals must lacerate each other as much as their opponents, put them forever apart.

The End of Porthcothan

AS HIS FRIENDS dropped off one by one, Lawrence centered his hopes more and more on a reunion with the Murrys. "I have been thinking with much affection and some longing of you two lately," he wrote on 11 February. "I feel you are my only real friends in the world."[60] Recognizing that they hesitated to join their fate with his, he proposed that he and Frieda would take a place alone, or with Heseltine, while scouting around for a cottage for Jack and Katherine. Their mistrust of Heseltine would dissolve when they got to know him, and no one else would come between them as had happened at Hampstead. He rather spoiled the effect of these promises by following them with pages of fevered explication of Dostoevsky, about whom Murry was writing a book. This was Murry's first major critical study, and the prospect of Lawrence breathing hotly over his shoulder while he wrote it was not appealing. Still, the Murrys recognized that their friend was reviving after his January collapse and they had not the heart to flatly dash his hopes.

The Porthcothan group broke camp on 22 February. Heseltine and Puma set off for London, while the Lawrences walked southward in the snow to explore for houses down the coast. Their search ended some fifty miles away, when Lawrence "looked down at Zennor [and] knew it was the Promised Land, and that a new heaven and a new earth would take place." Zennor was then one of the places in all England least touched by the modern world, a "tiny granite village" of seven houses and a church lying below "lovely pale hills, all gorse and heather, and an immense peacock sea spreading all below."[61] It was seven miles south of St. Ives on the road to Lands End; the landscape there is still wild, open, and largely uncultivated, resembling the west coast of Ireland rather than anything else in England. The occasional villages are set inland from the steep cliffs in hollows sheltered from the violent Atlantic storms; a narrow strip of farmland runs between the top of the cliffs and the moors above. The vistas are even more extensive, the trees even fewer than at Porthcothan. By its beauty and remoteness the region satisfied both Lawrence's aesthetic sense and his compulsion to avoid the Moloch of war and industrialism. "The world is so foul," he wrote Pinker, "one is almost suffocated. The only thing is to get away into the furthest corner from the smell of it."[62] Zennor had also the charm of becoming the one place in the English countryside where the Lawrences found a home and paid for it by themselves, without any intervention or charity from friends; because they felt it peculiarly their own they were all the more bitter when driven out a year and a half later.

At first the Lawrences found no house to rent at Zennor, but they were so taken with the village that they returned to Porthcothan for five days only. They probably wanted to be gone before the Beresfords returned. Settling affairs with their host, Lawrence favored Beresford with the confession that they had drunk a bottle of his sloe gin, and with his own final impressions of the local people—Emma, of course, excepted:

> They have got the souls of insects. One feels, if they were squashed, they would be a whitey mess, like when a black beetle is squashed. ... I have thought French peasants vile, like hedgehogs, hedge-pigs. But these people haven't any *being* at all. They've got no inside. ...
>
> The only thing to do is to use them strictly as servants, inferiors: for they have the souls of slaves: like Aesop. ...
>
> It has been a good time, our staying here; a time of getting well, and of discovering a new world of our own. I only wish you could exterminate all the natives and we could possess the land. The barbarian conquerors were wisest, really. There are very many people, like insects, who await extermination.[63]

The immediate occasion of these sentiments was the high cost of renting houses locally, which made Lawrence wonder how he would be able to go on living in Cornwall. Mrs. Beresford was evidently upset by her guest's fulminations, and he quickly sent her an apology (for the gin) and recantation: "You are quite right about the people, too. I wrote in a fit of irritation about them, they all seemed so *greedy*. But it is true, there is in them, as I felt at first, a very beautiful softness and gentleness, quite missing in English people nowadays."[64]

One may extenuate Lawrence's genocidal rhetoric by noting that it was just that: rhetoric, spoken by a sick and desperate man who is remembered in the neighborhood because he enjoyed making dresses for little girls. There is no record of his making even a threatening gesture against local people during the war years. The only actual aggression was directed *against* him, in repeated harrassments by self-appointed spy catchers; apart from this, he seems to have been generally liked and respected by the villagers among whom he lived. Nonetheless, one must recognize that the idea of mass extermination became for him a key fantasy after 1915, one that he pushed to its limit in Birkin's vision of the cleansing of the world by removal of the entire human race.

The diatribe against the people of Porthcothan is a striking reversal of the conclusion of *The Rainbow,* written just a year before, where it is revealed to Ursula:

> that the sordid people who crept hard-scaled and separate on the face of the world's corruption were living still, that the rainbow was arched in their blood and would quiver to life in their spirit, that they would cast off their horny covering of disintegration, that new, clean, naked bodies would issue to a new germination, to a new growth, rising to the light and the wind and the clean rain of heaven.

Men as they exist in England are bound in by a moribund culture, and are therefore vile. In *The Rainbow* they are imagined as unbound, triumphant in a new being; but when Lawrence sees his actual neighbors denying their own condition—and thus even their potential for liberation—he execrates them as a mere infestation of the soil. What is felt to be intolerable, in either case, is that they should continue as they are. In the earlier part of *The Rainbow,* Lawrence showed how successive generations of Midlanders had been shaped by historical change. But as a result of his deracination after 1912, and the general mood of apocalypse after 1914, he ceased to believe in that process. Evolutionary ideas had lost their relevance now that everyone was living "on the edge of a precipice." The very structure of Lawrence's thinking came to be built up from simple positives or negatives, with no allowance for shades or gradations. This may have been a natural evolution for a mind already given to perceiving the world as a vast system of interlocking polarities; but the war moved him further and faster in this direction by imposing on the entire European consciousness just such a system of binary oppositions: for or against, friend or enemy, kill or be killed. Such mutually exclusive categories, which may in peacetime be derided as crude reductions, in war become literal truths and the most practical guide to conduct. In this sense, then, Lawrence did not deny the form of consciousness created by the war; rather, he fully participated in it. His everyday language became saturated with terms of battle: the writer's job is to "fire bombs" into the herd, or to shoot them "with noiseless bullets that explode in their souls."[65] Lawrence's indignant temperament did not permit him to dissociate himself from the war, nor to judge it by the old standards of civility as the pacifists did. Rather, he recognized it as a fundamental shift in man's social relations, and in the mass will that underlay them. If men were to give themselves over completely to hate, he saw no reason why he should not hate the haters—though at the same time refusing all literal participation in the massacres they inflicted on each other. As the level of violence and ruthlessness at the front increased from month to month, so did Lawrence's expressions of hatred for mankind, and even for many of his acquaintances, rise to a higher and higher pitch.

CHAPTER VI

ZENNOR:
The Making of
Women in Love

Higher Tregerthen

ON 28 FEBRUARY the Lawrences left Porthcothan for Zennor where they stayed at the Tinner's Arms, a snug, stone-built public house across the street from the church; its name recalled the mining tradition of the district, though few mines were still being worked. Before leaving Lawrence had sent Ottoline the first half of "Goats and Compasses," the last writing he would do for two months. Enjoying the comfort of the pub during the snowy weather, he occupied himself with reading, writing letters, and combing the neighborhood with Frieda for a suitable house. Always cautious and realistic about accommodations, if about few other things, Lawrence now wanted above all a cheap refuge. He realized the prospects of getting more money for *The Rainbow* were poor and that as a banned author he could not expect favorable terms for another novel. The manuscript of *Amores* had just been rudely rejected by Sidgewick, and although *Twilight in Italy* would be published in the summer it was not the kind of book that was likely to make money. A furnished house, which might cost a pound a week or more, was therefore too heavy a commitment; but an unfurnished cottage could be rented cheaply and made habitable for only a few pounds, since the Lawrences already had some furniture stored in London that could be sent down. They had about fifty pounds left of the money they had collected for their move to America, and by shaving expenses they hoped to last out the war.

After a week, while walking across the fields a mile from Zennor, they discovered a group of vacant buildings called Higher Tregerthen, about a hundred yards above Tregerthen Farm:

> There are three cottages, in a little knot, standing just under a hillside where enormous granite boulders are lodged among the gorse bushes, looking as if they might roll down on us. It is all enormous granite boulders and gorse, above. Below, there are a few bouldery fields, with grey-stone hedges, then the sea. There is one farm in the hollow below. But all is rather windswept and grey and primitive. Yet is has a warm southern quality. When the sun shines, it is wonderful beyond words, so rich.[1]

Tregerthen Farm was run by the Hockings, an old-established local family with whom the Lawrences soon became friends, but Higher Tregerthen belonged to a Captain Short, retired from the merchant marine, who lived in St. Ives. Since the two small cottages were only being used for storage he was willing to rent one of them to the Lawrences for five pounds a year; the other, attached to it, remained vacant during their stay. The one they took had two rooms, a kitchen and scullery downstairs and a bedroom up. There was a small oil stove with no oven, and an outside privy. The cottage had no running water, only a spring on the hillside above. It was literally not much more than a roof over their heads, and sometimes a leaky roof at that, but Lawrence loved its bareness and seclusion. He estimated it could be furnished for another five pounds, after which he and Frieda could live sheltered from war and want "like foxes under the hill." "I look forward very much to the coming days," he told Lady Cynthia. "I need work hardly at all, we shall want so little, and we can do all the things we want to. . . . It isn't scenery one lives by, but the freedom of moving about alone."[2]

Not entirely alone, however, as Lawrence immediately explained to Jack and Katherine:

> What I hope is that one day you will take the long house with the tower, and put a bit of furniture in it: and that Heseltine will have one room in your long cottage; and that somebody else will have the second cot: that we are like a little monastery: that Emma is in your kitchen, and we all eat together in the dining-room of your house: at least, lunch and dinner: that we share expenses.[3]

The "long house" was three cottages knocked into one, standing a few feet from the Lawrences' cottage and at right angles to it. It had been remodeled, complete with ornamental battlements on its little tower, for the popular novelist Guy Thorne ("Ranger Gull"), but he had never taken possession. The rent was only sixteen-pounds a year and it had seven rooms: Jack and Katherine could each have a study, a real luxury for a writing couple. Financially the scheme made good sense: the Lawrences had enough in reserve to live on for some time; the Murrys had Katherine's private income of two pounds a week plus whatever they could earn by writing; Heseltine had his inherited three pounds a week. The total rent of the buildings was less than ten shillings a week. Combining their resources, the group could easily afford to hire Emma as housekeeper and enjoy her excellent cooking—her wages at Porthcothan had been only five shillings a week. Dairy products could be had cheaply from the farm and Lawrence planned to put in a garden. All the men were still exempt from military service on medical grounds so the idea of a little intellectual community, keeping itself apart from the ruin of Europe, seemed both appealing and practical. Lawrence had been reading a book about monasteries, and thought of their settlement as akin to those made by monks in the Dark Ages; there had, indeed, been a line of Celtic monasteries at inaccessible points along the north Cornish coast.

But a common life implied a common purpose, and this was lacking from the start. Though Heseltine had shown himself a devoted supporter of Lawrence's work and a congenial houseguest, the very idea of his presence offended Jack and Katherine. They distrusted Lawrence's new friends on principle. When Heseltine abruptly turned into an enemy the threat of trouble from that quarter was removed, though the loss of his £3 a week was serious. But his defection caused Lawrence to shift the full weight of his longing for friendship onto the Murrys, who for various reasons were reluctant to accept such an overwhelming gift. They were enjoying the happiest period of their life together at the Villa Pauline in Bandol. Jack's abandonment of literary London in order to join Katherine had liberated new creative powers in both of them. He was working eagerly at his first critical book, on Dostoevsky, while she was composing her tribute to Chummie, a long story called "The Aloe" about the scenes of their childhood. Later revised as "Prelude," it is probably her finest achievement. Realizing that at Bandol she had come into full possession of her talent, she was reluctant to return to England—and specially to Cornwall where, in 1914, she had been disgusted by seeing a group of women tormenting a cat. Above all, according to Jack, she "distrusted the very idea of a community."[4]

Lawrence was formally sympathetic to Katherine's reservations, but in the euphoria of finding Higher Tregerthen he felt certain the Murrys too would come to love it. He bombarded them with glowing descriptions, and with promises of harmony: ". . . don't talk any more of treacheries and so on. . . . We are so few, and the world is so many, it is absurd that we are scattered. . . . No more quarrels and quibbles. Let it be agreed for ever. I am *Blutbruder: a Blutbruderschaft* between us all. Tell K. *not* to be so queasy." At last on 16 March, the day before he and Frieda moved from the Tinner's Arms to their cottage, they received letters from Jack and Katherine agreeing to join them; Lawrence had perhaps tipped the balance by telegraphing them that Heseltine had dropped out. Now his joy was complete: "We are so delighted. What a joyful day, when you arrive, and we meet you in St. Ives station, which is on the edge of the sea. I am so frightened that something bad might snatch this from us—but it shan't."[5]

Lawrence at once threw himself into refurbishing Jack and Katherine's quarters, like a fond parent expecting the return of a prodigal. He began sealing damp walls and whitewashing, heavy work for someone of his uncertain health. Then he urged Captain Short to provide a separate privy for the Murrys and to move the existing one away from the room he had chosen for Katherine's study:

> It is a pity it stands there at all, spoiling the only bit of ground. And it would never do to stand another beside it: one might as well, at that rate, live in a public lavatory. I can see Katherine Murry's face, if she saw two W. C.'s staring at her every time she came out of the door or looked out of the window. It would never do.

But these were only minor irritations. "I expect us all to be so happy," Lawrence told Kot. "We have learned some lessons, let us hope, during these two years of misery, and got rid of a great deal of spleen. Now let us be happy: if only the war will end."[6] Jack was expressing equally cheerful hopes: "I think we are going to be very happy with L. in Cornwall. We are, you know, tremendously fond of each other; and for a long time we have been tending towards setting up camp together. And now apparently the time has come. We feel very serene about the future."[7] The person to whom he sent this report was Ottoline; she had not come to Cornwall herself, fearing an exhausting journey and a dubious reception on arrival, but from Garsington she kept a close and far from innocuous interest in the Lawrences' new establishment.

The Long Arm of Lady Ottoline

LAWRENCE, it will be remembered, had saved Jack from a lonely Christmas by getting him invited to Garsington. Ottoline had met him before at Greathan and had not been overly impressed, but this time she was charmed by his stories about life with Katherine:

> I let him talk on and on about her, telling me of their wonderful times together, their transcendental union of soul and body, and the way they 'wisped away together', as he called it—by which, I suppose, he meant flights of thought and talk. It moved me very much hearing of this lovely blending of two beings into one, and the way their minds and imagination flew through the air together.

Ottoline convinced Jack he should return at once to Bandol, and even gave him five pounds for the journey. She ran to the gate and waved to him as he left, a gesture that won over Jack's already susceptible heart:

> I felt at that moment that I knew you, and that I had found a friend—well, I must use our magic word again, for *toujours*. It is only in such a moment that I can speak for both of us with absolute certainty. We go about the world in a kind of terror. We take no roots either in a place or in the hearts of these who call themselves our friends. I am not whining at all—tho' Lorenzo says I do—for it is a fair price to pay for our own secret and transcendent happiness together. But there are times when we suffer terribly, and times when we cannot face the suffering. So we are called impossible. . . . We commit every kind of social crime. It is only our method of self-defence. We dare not let our hearts be open to people who will hurt us cruelly.[8]

(219)

Katherine also began to correspond with Ottoline in a style as rhapsodic as Jack's. The Murrys now became her confidantes and allies: they rejoiced when her mistrust of Heseltine was justified by Lawrence's break with him, and chimed in dutifully with her contempt for Frieda. Before leaving Bandol Katherine wrote an unposted letter to Frieda in which she claimed "you really haven't been right in judging us first the kind of traitors that you did. J. *never* would hear a word against Lawrence."[9] These were weasel words, for if Jack did take Lawrence's side it was against Frieda that he took it.

Jack and Katherine left Bandol on 27 March and arrived in Cornwall for the long-sought reunion on 4 April. Going down on the train Katherine had become "more and more depressed," and in their room at the Tinner's Arms she lamented to Jack "I shall *never* like this place." He felt oppressed by her unhappiness, but she concealed it from Lawrence, so that he sent off cheerful bulletins to their friends: ". . . we all enjoy ourselves. The Murrys are happy with each other now. . . . I find Katherine simpler and better, but Murry not much changed in any way."[10] For a while the pleasures of painting and furnishing carried the two couples along. Jack especially liked this kind of "messing about" after three months of being immersed in his study of Dostoevsky:

> As a companion, Lawrence was a nonpareil. His off-hand, half-schoolmastery way of imparting his amazing range of country lore suited me perfectly; for I made no pretensions in that kind. But it wasn't what the man said, so much as the warm and irresistible intimacy with which he surrounded one, an atmosphere established as it were by a kindly gardener who had, very precisely, decided that you were to grow, and who, by that act, awakened in you the feeling that there was something in you which could grow.[11]

The Murrys had to sleep at the Tinner's Arms for two weeks before their house would be ready so they were still alone for part of each day, which helped ease their transition into the community. But at this delicate point Ottoline again intruded. Just after the Murrys arrived Frieda, for reasons not entirely clear, sent Ottoline her most furious letter yet:

> Now for over a year I was ready to be your friend—but steadily and persistently you have treated me with arrogance and insolence! It took me a long time to realise it. Your last letter to me was again cheap and vulgar—You have told lies about me, you have tried to separate Lawrence and me because you

wanted some sort of unwholesome relation with him—All the time you felt good and holy! . . . . But I have had enough! Either you treat me with ordinary courtesy and respect or I wish neither to hear from you or see you again! . . . Someday it may dawn on you what a good thing you have rejected in my genuine friendship, that I offered you; but I know when you get this letter you will feel as you always do, that an injury has been done to you, while all your feelings and actions have been good and blameless! *That* is so hopeless about you and that *I* am the unreasonable person!

But more than enough![12]

Lawrence's contribution to the row was along the line of "run man! run tiger!" "I am glad she said what she feels," he wrote Ottoline. "That is always best. Then if anything remains, it can begin to grow, free from the weeds."[13] He continued his correspondence with Ottoline for several more weeks, avoiding sensitive topics as if pretending that nothing untoward had happened.

But Frieda's innuendo about Ottoline's sexual interest in her literary lions goaded her into an inspired stroke of mischief: she forwarded Frieda's letter to Jack and Katherine. Jack, having first touched her for the loan of ten pounds, informed her of the sequel:

> Frieda's letter is outrageous. But more outrageous still is the fact that she knows that you sent it to us. Of course what happened is plain. The postman, as usual, brought our letters to the Lawrence's door—we are not yet in our house—and F., seeing your superscription, opened the letter. For, about an hour later, though Katherine and I were perfectly vague and non-committal when taxed about the contents of the letter, Lawrence suddenly said point-blank: "O. sent you Frieda's letter." It was hopeless to deny it.

No doubt if it had not been hopeless Murry would have. He went on to regale Ottoline with an account of the Lawrences' affairs that must have raised his stock at Garsington by several points:

> Lawrence is at present completely on F's side in the quarrel (which isn't a quarrel but an indecent attack), and he spent a long while trying to convince us that for us to remain friendly with you was black treachery to him. It is hopelessly ludicrous, and perhaps we have managed to convince him that there is not the least reason why we should turn and rend you. At all events he has forgotten about it for the moment. F., however, is not likely to forget. I'm afraid, terribly afraid, that we may drift into a final rumpus with her: but we shall try our hardest not to for L.'s sake. I don't quite know how to diagnose the condition of them both for you. In many ways L. seems to me to be much happier, much younger than I have known him for the last two years. On the

other hand he has bought this at a price. I feel he has quite definitely lost something. . . . his present carelessness seems to be due to a despair instead of a superfluity of life, as it used to be. I feel that he will not create anything very much in the future.

F. is *monstrum, horrendum, informe, ingens.* Really, we are frightened of her. She is sure to break out against us sooner or later; if only because she feels that we imperil her present triumph over L. We have tried to like her for three years now and we haven't got any further towards the end. There is in her an ultimate vulgarity which does appal us both. And that is the real reason why she so turned against you, I think. Because she is no longer married to a man who can afford to keep 3 servants, she really does feel herself *déclassé.* Nothing that you could have done would have saved you from her, simply because of this. She despises herself for having thrown up Professor W. for L; and when a woman like that despises herself . . .

You know how much we both love you

Yours ever

J.M.M.[14]

This does not seem an honorable letter to write about one's closest friends, to a woman whom Jack had met only briefly, and Katherine barely at all. But both were fully bent on cultivating Ottoline's favor: Jack because of her social position and also, as we shall see, because he was sexually attracted to her; Katherine because Garsington promised her an escape into freedom, luxury, and sophistication, which one side of her nature hankered after. Their ties with Ottoline remained a bone of contention between them and the Lawrences for several years though, inevitably, Ottoline came to feel that she too had been betrayed by Jack and Katherine.

Blood-brotherhood and *Women in Love*

THE "little monastery" at Tregerthen was founded on 17 April, when Jack and Katherine finally moved into their house. Lawrence had achieved a kind of Rananim after a year of dreaming and plotting, but Frieda remained cheerfully indifferent to his grandiose hopes of life in a community. She was glad to have company in such an isolated spot, and looked no further; in particular, she enjoyed having a woman friend to relieve the tension of living with Lawrence. Though Frieda was ten years older than Katherine, and very different from her in temperament, she found the hours passing easily in her company:

> We had great times doing things together, like making pot-pourri with dried rose leaves and herbs and spices, or painting wooden boxes and having those delicious female walks and talks. She trusted me, I was older and she told me much of her life. And how she could talk. . . . . She had a Dickensish kind of way to give small events a funny twist, and sharp and quick she pounced on anything funny that happened and gave you a swift look, the rest of her face innocent, so that often I had a hard time not to laugh and be rude.
>
> If I had to describe her in one word I would choose the word *exquisite*. She was exquisite in her person: soft shiny brown hair and delicately grained skin, not tall and not small and not thin nor stout, just right. When we went bathing I thought her pretty as a statuette.[15]

Frieda, however, was not aware of some darker undercurrents in her relationship with the Murrys. It was a time of bitter quarrels between her and Lawrence, and Katherine was privately disgusted by the savage side of Frieda that revealed itself in these battles:

> It seems to me so *degraded,* so horrible to see I can't stand it. And I feel so furiously angry: I *hate* them for it. F. is such a liar, too. To my face she is all sweetness. She used to bring me in flowers, tell me how 'exquisite' I was, how my clothes suited me, that I had never been so 'really beautiful'. Ugh! how humiliating! Thank heaven it is over. I must be the real enemy of such a person.[16]

Since both women agreed that Lawrence's belief in an ideal community was foolish, the burden of upholding it fell on his relation with Jack—which was inarticulate, unfilled, and riddled with strife. The crux of their difficulties was Lawrence's erotic feelings toward Jack: he could neither keep them entirely hidden, nor express them in plain words—still less in any direct physical way. Only in his fiction could he wrestle with the dilemma, in the suppressed first chapter of *Women in Love,* which he probably began writing within a week of the Murrys' moving into their cottage. There, Birkin's earlier sexual history is made plain:

> although he was always terribly intimate with at least one woman, and practically never intimate with a man, yet the male physique had a fascination for

him, and for the female physique he felt only a fondness, a sort of sacred love, as for a sister.

In the street, it was the men who roused him by their flesh and their manly, vigorous movement, quite apart from all the individual character, whilst he studied the women as sisters, knowing their meaning and their intents.

Though Birkin suffers deeply from the lack of mutual sexual desire between himself and Hermione, he will never yield to his desire for one of his own sex: "This was the one and only secret he kept to himself, this secret of his passionate and sudden, spasmodic affinity for men he saw. He kept this secret even from himself. He knew what he felt, but he always kept the knowledge at bay."[17]

Lawrence wanted an intimate relation with a man, but mystified the sexual component of his desire by seeking a spiritual brother rather than, simply, a lover. To this veiled proposal Jack responded with his congenital vague deviousness in emotional matters:

> His relation with Frieda left room, and perhaps need, for a relation with a man of something of the kind and quality of my relation with Katherine; and he wanted this relation with me. It was possible only if it left my relation with Katherine intact, and indeed were based on that relation: for I was I only in that relation; or at any rate, only in that relation was I a man who had anything to give to Lawrence.

But when his relation with Katherine was "whole," Jack continued, he "had no need of Lawrence. I could love him tenderly and affectionately, as I believe I did, but I did not depend on him." When Lawrence pressed the issue, Jack instinctively recoiled toward Katherine (whose self-possessed skepticism was proof against any insistence on Lawrence's part); ". . . and as he felt my withdrawal," Jack wrote, "[he] became more urgent to bind me to him. He talked of the blood-brotherhood between us, and hinted at the need of some inviolable sacrament between us—some pre-Christian blood-rite in keeping with the primeval rocks about us. Timidly, I withdrew only the more." Blood sacrifice may have been practiced at the megalithic monuments of ancient Britain; Lawrence seems to have linked it with the custom of warriors swearing mutual devotion by mixing their blood together. Jack feared that he was being inveigled into some "ceremony of black magic to be performed amid the great stones of the eerie Cornish moors" and, not surprisingly, he shrank from the invitation.[18]

Whatever the ceremony Lawrence had in mind, it does not seem to have had an openly sexual purpose; rather, he wanted to create an unbreakable bond with Jack that would make up for the betrayals he had recently suffered in other friendships and for Frieda's qualified allegiance. Before the Murrys arrived, Lawrence hoped for such a bond with both of them; Katherine's aloofness, however, soon disqualified her from the proposed pact. Furthermore, a deep dissatisfaction with women lay somewhere near the heart of Lawrence's impulse, though his fantasy of an eternal and absolute male union revealed, of course, his inexperience of any actual homosexual milieu. Acquaintances like Forster or Keynes could have enlightened him, but his hysterical rejection of any homosexuality but his own esoteric variety prevented any dialogue between them. When his advances to Jack failed he was thrown back, more frustrated than ever, on the old dilemma of his relation with Frieda.

In chapter 20 of *Women in Love* the whole affair is more tentative, and it is not Birkin but Gerald (the surrogate for Murry) who initiates the attempt at comradeship. As the two men lie exhausted after their bout of nude wrestling it is Gerald's hand that closes "warm and sudden over Birkin's"; though the clasp only confirms a shared feeling:

> "One ought to wrestle and strive and be physically close. It makes one sane."
> "You do think so?"
> "I do. Don't you?"
> "Yes," said Gerald.
> There were long spaces of silence between their words. The wrestling had some deep meaning to them—an unfinished meaning.

Lawrence thus imagines, in the novel, a unanimity that never existed at Higher Tregerthen; even so, there remains a realm that the two men tacitly agree to leave unexplored, though Birkin does admit his admiration of Gerald's physical beauty:

> "Yes, that is there to enjoy as well. We should enjoy everything."
> Gerald laughed in his throat, and said:
> "That's certainly one way of looking at it. I can say this much, I feel better. It has certainly helped me. Is this the Bruderschaft you wanted?"
> "Perhaps. Do you think this pledges anything?"
> "I don't know," laughed Gerald.
> "At any rate, one feels freer and more open now—and that is what we want."

There the issue rests, as Birkin's mind "reverts to Ursula"; each man goes on to confirm his relationship with the woman he loves and the final movement of the novel, toward the Alps, begins. Gerald dies because of his failure with Gudrun, though Birkin suggests that if he had fully accepted Birkin's offer of comradeship he might have been saved. The novel is in part a stringent critique of the relation between Jack and Katherine; no doubt Lawrence's treatment of Gerald and Gudrun was colored by his anger at the Murrys for refusing the intimacy he offered them, though their conflicts as a couple were real enough. On the other hand, in describing the final harmony of Birkin and Ursula he was presenting a wishful fantasy rather than the actual state of his marriage in 1916. None of this may change the critic's final assessment of *Women in Love,* but a full knowledge of the facts available to Lawrence's imagination, and the directions in which he changed them, provides a key to his characteristic style of transforming life into art.

The novel itself was probably begun on 24 April, as soon as Lawrence enjoyed a respite from setting up house and felt better in health. At noon on that day in Dublin the Easter Rising began its brief and tragic course; the rebels surrendered five days later and the last executions, of MacDermott and Connolly, took place on 12 May. Lawrence followed the events, but his hatred of the war did not move him to any special sympathy for the Irishmen who refused to fight for England's cause. It was all part of the *danse macabre* of a world gone mad, from which he determined to remain aloof:

> I am doing another novel—that really occupies me. The world crackles and busts, but that is another matter, external, in chaos. One has a certain order inviolable in one's soul. There one sits, as in a crow's nest, out of it all. And even if one is conscripted, still I can sit in my crow's nest of a soul and grin.

Since this was written to Cynthia Asquith, whose father-in-law held final responsibility for crushing the revolt, Lawrence perhaps was trimming his sails to the wind. With Ottoline, whose sympathies inclined to the rebels, he took a different line, recommending to her a biography of Parnell: "It is *very* poignant, now, when the political life, and Ireland, are so torn. . . . In it the passing bell of this present death begins to ring." Only to Forster, now removed to Egypt, did he plainly speak his mind: "[Ottoline] thinks the Irish of the late rebellion all poets and fine fellows. I think them mostly windbags and nothings who happen to have become tragically significant in death. I must say the Irish rebellion shocked me—another rent in the old ship's bottom."[19]

Meanwhile Lawrence himself took refuge in the purity of nature—the only possible antidote, for him, to the vileness of man. Writing to Gertler, in London, he struck a rare note of contentment:

> I am sitting with my back against a boulder, a few yards above the houses. Below, the gorse is yellow, and the sea is blue. It is very still, no sound but the birds and the wind among the stones. . . . Yesterday I saw an adder sleeping on the grass. She was very slim and elegant with her black markings. At last she was disturbed, she lifted her slender head and listened with great delicacy. Then, very fine and undulating, she moved away. I admired her intensely, and liked her very much. . . .
>
> The world is so lovely here, one wonders why men want to exert themselves, having wars . . .[20]

Such radically opposed realities compose the special tone of *Women in Love* —its shifting back and forth between visions of a silent world, purged of human intrusion, and scenes of spectacular emotional violence. But the war itself Lawrence chose to leave out, except as a kind of transparent medium in which the whole action was suspended: "I should wish the time to remain unfixed," he wrote in his Foreword, "so that the bitterness of the war may be taken for granted in the characters."

The basic scheme of the novel dated from *The Sisters* of 1913; only when that book outgrew itself and had to be divided in two in January 1915 did the future *Women in Love* come into separate existence. As Lawrence began writing at Tregerthen, therefore, he probably had on hand a manuscript sequel to *The Rainbow*. But in his usual way he wrote out a complete new text, using the earlier material only when it harmonized with his present mood—which had, of course, changed radically since 1913–14. Hence his description of the new work to Forster as a "sequel to The Rainbow, but *quite* different. Here in this book I am free at last, thank God, and can move without effort or excitement, naturally. I feel rather triumphant in myself, really."[21] One source of freedom, certainly, was the creation of Birkin as hero: through him Lawrence could both express his own impulses directly and open them to countervailing pressures from other characters. Another was Lawrence's withdrawal from the industrial or cultural centers of English society into the pastoral obscurity of Cornwall. He would no longer attempt, as he had done in *The Rainbow,* to show how the individual's quest for fulfillment was shaped by social forces. The four main protagonists of *Women in Love* need reckon only with their own conflicting desires, or their relations with each other. Lawrence was turning away from the English literary tradition toward something more like the American: in Richard Chase's terms, from the *novel* of man confined by social forms to the *romance,* where the individual moves in a less constricted and more symbolic realm—"encountering, as it were, less resistance from reality."[22] Lawrence explained his shift of viewpoint to Ottoline: "When one is shaken to the very depths, one finds reality in the unreal world. At present my real world is the world of my inner soul, which reflects on to the novel I write. The outer world is there to be endured, it is not real—neither the outer life."[23] Being able thus to speak directly, without external hindrance, Lawrence wrote with phenomenal speed, even for him; he reached the point of Ursula and Birkin's marriage in a month, more than four hundred pages in the printed text, and he virtually completed the first draft in another month.

Though Lawrence may have felt that he had broken through into true creative freedom, he was still subject to threats and constraints that could not easily be ignored. The question remained, for example, whether he was writing his novel for anyone but himself, given his frankness about homosexuality in the Prologue:

> already it is beyond all hope of ever being published, because of the things it says. And more than that, it is beyond all possibility even to offer it to a world, a putrescent mankind like ours. I feel I cannot *touch* humanity, even in thought, it is abhorrent to me.[24]

He realized, further, that even if he was no longer interested in society, society was still interested in him. The day after the Murrys moved in at Tregerthen a policeman came with a warrant to arrest Jack for failure to enlist; he showed his medical certificate of rejection, but he seemed certain to be forced into some kind of war work before the year was out. Lawrence was grimly contemplating the same prospect: "They would give me some kind of clerking to do, I suppose. I would like to see the clerking when I had done it. They would have more pain than profit out of me."[25] Meanwhile the rapid work on the novel absorbed his energies; he wrote few letters in May and June, and cared less about life beyond Higher Tregerthen.

Exit Jack and Katherine

WITHIN the "community," however, the strains on all four members were quickly becoming unbearable as Lawrence realized that he could not achieve comradeship with anyone so reluctant and uncertain as Jack. Disappointed on every side, he was losing control of his temper altogether, Katherine reported to Kot:

> Lawrence isn't healthy any more; he has gone a little bit out of his mind. If he is contradicted about *anything* he gets into a frenzy, quite beside himself and it goes on until he is so exhausted that he cannot stand and has to go to bed and stay there until he has recovered. And whatever your disagreement is about he says it is because you have gone wrong in your sex and belong to an obscene spirit. These rages occur whenever I see him for more than a casual moment for if ever I say anything that isn't quite "safe" off he goes! It is like sitting in a railway station with Lawrence's temper like a big black engine puffing and snorting. I can think of nothing, I am blind to everything, waiting for the moment when, with a final shriek, off it will go![26]

On 5 May everything "went off" with a vengeance. It had been a bad week: Lawrence was ill, conscription for married men had been brought in, the Irish rebels were being shot at dawn one after the other. Katherine told Ottoline of the crisis two weeks later; though she toned down the blackness of Lawrence's mood so as to make Frieda the evident villain of the piece:

> It really is quite over for now, our relationship with L. The 'dear man' in him whom we all loved is hidden away, aborted, completely lost, like a little gold ring in that immense German Christmas pudding which is Frieda and with all the appetite in the world we cannot eat our way through Frieda to find him. One simply looks and waits for some one to come with a knife and cut her up into the smallest pieces that L. may see the light and shine again. But he does not want that to happen at all. . . . I only realised this finally about a fortnight ago . . . Frieda asked me over to their cottage to drink tea with them.

(229)

When I arrived for some unfortunate reason I happened to mention Percy Shelley whereupon she said: "I think that his skylark thing is awful Footle." "You only say that to show off," said L. "Its the only thing of Shelley's that you know." And straightway I felt like Alice between the Cook and the Duchess. Saucepans and frying pans hurtled through the air. They ordered each other out of the house—and the atmosphere of HATE between them was so dreadful that I could not stand it; I had to run home. L. came to dinner with us the same evening but Frieda would not come. He sat down and said: "I'll cut her throat if she comes near this table." After dinner she walked up and down outside the house in the dusk and suddenly, *dread*fully—L. rushed at her and began to beat her. They ran up and down out on the road, scuffling. Frieda screamed for Murry and for me—but Lawrence never said a word. He kept his eyes on her and *beat* her. Finally she ran into our kitchen shouting "Protect me! Save me!" I shall never forget L. how he stood back on his heels and swung his arm forward. He was quite green with fury. Then when he was tired he sat down, collapsed and she, sobbing and crying, sat down, too. None of us said a word. I felt so horrified—I felt that in the silence we might all die—die simply from horror. L. could scarcely breathe. After a long time I felt: "Well, it has happened. Now it is over for ever." And though I was dreadfully sorry for L. I didn't feel an atom of sympathy for Frieda. . . . In about half an hour they had almost *recovered*—they were remembering, *mutually* remembering a certain very rich, very good, but very extravagant macaroni cheese they had once eaten . . . And next day Frieda stayed in bed and L. carried her meals up to her and waited upon her and in the afternoon I heard her (I can't think it wasn't intentional) singing and L. joined in . . . Its not really a laughing matter—in fact I think its horribly tragic, for they have degraded each other and brutalized each other beyond words, but . . . all the same—I never did imagine any one to so thrive upon a beating as Frieda seemed to thrive. I shall never be persuaded that she did not take some Awful Relish in it—For she began to make herself dresses and to put flowers in her hair and to sustain a kind of girlish prattle with L. which left Murry and me speechless with amazement *and* disgust—disgust especially!—But I cannot help it—I hate them for it—I hate them for falsity. Lawrence has definitely chosen to sin against himself and Frieda is triumphant. It is horrible. You understand—don't you—that I could not write like this to anyone but you.[27]

In the same letter Katherine claimed that she and Jack were "so happy together—it's like a miracle." Actually, they were about to pass through a crisis of their own, though in a very different style from the Lawrences' sadomasochistic rough-and-tumbles. Katherine's idea of marriage had no common ground with Lawrence's, since she believed neither in the primacy of the sexual bond nor in settling disagreements by confrontation. Irony and evasion were her usual means of coping with difficulties, whereas the Lawrences, she told Beatrice Campbell, were not her kind at all:

I cannot discuss blood affinity to beasts, for instance, if I have to keep ducking to avoid the flat-irons and the saucepans. And I shall *never see* sex in trees, sex in running brooks, sex in stones and sex in everything. The number of things that are really phallic, from fountain pens onwards! But I shall have my revenge one of these days—I suggested to Lawrence that he should call his cottage 'The Phallus' and Frieda thought it a very good idea.

The only real pleasure Katherine took in Tregerthen was when the other three were safely occupied elsewhere. "It is very quiet in the house," she wrote Beatrice, "except for the wind and rain and the fire that roars very hoarse and fierce. I feel as though I and the Cornish Pasty [her kitchen maid] had drifted out to sea—and would never be seen again. But I love such days—rare lovely days. I love above all things, my dear, to be alone. Then I lie down and smoke and look at the fire and begin to think out an EXTRAOR-DINARILY good story about Marseilles."[28]

Though in manner she seemed utterly different from Lawrence, she was seeking by her withdrawal to deny the claims of the outside world and of other people—a state of self-contain ment that Lawrence continually hankered after. Her dilemma, also similar to Lawrences's, was that the *need* for connection kept returning even though it seemed impossible to satisfy. Some years later she explained the problem to Kot: "Often I long to be more *in life*—to know people— even now the desire comes. But immediately the opportunity comes I think of nothing but how to escape. And people have come to see me here—*What* are they? They are not human beings; they are never children—they are absolutely unreal Mechanisms." The last phrase could easily have been written by Lawrence, and in her 1918 *Journal,* after she too had become consumptive, she owned their deep kinship:

My fits of temper are really terrifying. I had one this (Sunday) morning and tore up a page of the book I was reading—and absolutely lost my head. Very significant. When it was over J. came in and stared. 'What is the matter? What have you done?'
'Why?'
'You look *all dark.*' He drew back the curtains and called it an effect of light, but when I came into my studio to dress I saw it was not that. I was a deep earthy colour, *with pinched eyes.* I was *green.* Strangely enough these fits are Lawrence and Frieda over again. I am more like L. than anybody. We are *unthinkably* alike, in fact.[29]

They seem both to have given some credence to the idea of a link between consumption and the exigent, hypersensitive artistic temperament. Nonetheless, Katherine remained at odds with Lawrence because she chose a different way of resolving a similar dilemma. For her, the supreme vocation of the artist was simply to state the truth about life, whereas Lawrence strove continually to tear down the barrier between life and art, exhausting himself in the attempt to remake the world closer to his heart's desire.

Any kinship Katherine may have felt with Lawrence did not affect, therefore, her resolve to wash her hands of the unruly ménage at Higher Tregerthen; moreover, she was again impatient to get away from Jack for a time. "It is not really a nice place," she told Kot. "It is so full of huge stones, but now that I am writing I do not care, for the time. It is so very temporary. It may all be over next month; in fact, it will be. I don't belong to anybody here. In fact, I have no being, but I am making preparations for changing everything." [30] Jack, for his part, was utterly bewildered by the demands Lawrence was making on him. One night he heard him crying out from his bedroom in delirium "Jack is killing me"; but when Jack professed to love him, Lawrence turned on him furiously: "I hate your love, I hate it. You're an obscene bug, sucking my life away." [31] On 14 May, a month after the Murrys had moved in at Tregerthen, Jack explained to Ottoline why they had decided to leave:

> . . . he is really weakened by our being here, instead of gaining the strength he sought. It's very sad: but now quite inevitable. Some where, he is gone all wrong, and with us here, living in reality quite apart from him, the malady is simply aggravated. There have been scenes between him and Frieda which were simply nervous mad, which, having once happened, should have made it inconceivable that they should still live together. But they do live together: and they pretend to be in love—there's something strangely *indecent* about it. But his whole body is sick, so that there's no reason why one thing more than other should be unpalatable.
>
> I think it will be just as bad, when we go away. Somehow, even though he hates us half the time, our presence saves him from facing his real loneliness. If we go—and we shall, very soon, for good—then I think he will probably develop some mania (in the exact and medical sense). But we can't immolate ourselves even to keep him going, and we shan't.
>
> I'm still deeply fond of him: but I respect him much less than I did. That's just animal in me, I suppose,—one always hates a sick man. I neither agree with his ideas, nor am I stimulated by my opposition to them. In almost everything he consciously and deliberately says or does, I detect a taint of illness or hysteria, so that I am compelled to keep silence. To me it is terribly oppressive: it can't be less so to him.

ZENNOR: The Making of *Women in Love*

It's a pity that we, his last hope, should begin to fail. In the main it's his own fault: though that's no comfort to anyone. But the effects of this ghastly lie he lives through F. have become permanent—I don't believe there's the slightest chance of his getting rid of them now. Other things have had their part—the war—and above all this cursed hybrid intellectualism that has warped his real and purely sensitive nature during the last year. . . . because I have loved him very much (I still do) . . . I know I shall desert him sooner, simply because he would kill me. I'm not ill: neither is Katherine. One spends too much in reaching that condition, that it's quite impossible to pretend to spend it again even on your dearest friend. You mustn't think, either, from this, that we're going to have a great quarrel. What's the good? We shall manage it so that our parting will seem necessary for quite other reasons.[32]

To save face on both sides, Jack and Katherine said they could not live on the north coast because it was too bleak. They soon found another cottage some thirty miles away on the south coast, at Mylor near Falmouth. To Ottoline, Lawrence tried to pass off their departure with a sneer—"They should have a soft valley, with leaves and the ring-dove cooing."[33] But his disappointment went far deeper. "Katherine went ahead by train," Murry recalled, "while I remained behind to see our things loaded on the cart. It would have been unlike Lawrence, even at such a moment, not to have lent a hand; and he did. But our hearts were sore. When the last rope was tied, I said good-bye and hoped they would come over to see us. Frieda, who took such incidents lightly, said they would; but Lawrence did not answer. I wheeled my bicycle to the road and pedalled off, with the feeling that I had said good-bye to him for ever."[34] The Murrys had lived at Higher Tregerthen for just two months.

Lawrence, too, saw their parting as something final, the end of a stage in his emotional development: "Murry and I are not really associates. How I deceive myself. I am a liar to myself, about people. I was angry when you [Catherine Carswell] ran over a list of my 'friends'—whom you did *not* think much of. But it is true, they are not much, any of them. I give up having intimate friends at all. It is self-deception."[35] This was a firmer resolution than many Lawrence had made over the past two years. Though he was to have friends and disciples enough until the end of his life, henceforth his attitude to them would always be tinged with irony, or at least reserve. Still, at the end of the war he was to reaffirm his faith in comradeship to Katherine, as if in defiance of the abject failure of the community at Higher Tregerthen:

I do believe in friendship. I believe tremendously in friendship between man and man, a pledging of men to each other inviolably. But I have not ever met or formed such friendship. Also I believe the same way in friendship between men and women, and between women and women, sworn, pledged, eternal, as eternal as the marriage bond, and as deep. But I have not met or formed such friendship.[36]

Though in the practical sense Lawrence recognized the loss of his ideal when the Murrys left Higher Tregerthen, he continued to be preoccupied with it and to devote much of *Women in Love* to the exploration of a possible perfect relation between friends or lovers, one in which their desires for both union and separateness would be equally satisfied. Jack, for his part, admitted only after Lawrence's death that he should have accepted the challenge of working out such a comradeship with his friend:

When he cried out against me at Higher Tregerthen, that I was 'an obscene bug sucking away his life,' my very blood seemed to run thin with horror, I felt that my whole universe was collapsing into a yawning pit; and I fled in terror. I felt that if I stayed at Higher Tregerthen, I should surely die. And the feeling was true. But, now, after many years, I understand what he meant. I *was* 'sucking the life out of him.' Instead of fighting him, I was draining his strength away. I was his negation, and I would not, I could not *be* his negation. I did not know my own responsibility towards Lawrence; I was unconscious of my duty towards him: to wrestle with him to the going down of the sun.[37]

The Compulsion

DESPITE the loss of Heseltine, and now of Jack and Katherine, Lawrence was determined to stay on at Tregerthen until the end of the war. His acute sense of obligation led him to take over at least part of the Murrys' lease. By renting the upper and lower rooms of the adjacent tower he and Frieda would gain a pleasant sitting room (Katherine's old study) and a spare bedroom below. The cost was only five pounds a year more, and paying it would help smooth over Captain Short's irritation at the Murrys' early departure—for which Lawrence felt he should apologize: "I was very sorry about the trouble with Mrs. Murry. But let us all forget it, now it is over. She is not bad, really, only sometimes she is all out of joint with the world, with herself and everybody else."[38] The extra rooms also made it possible for the Lawrences to invite friends from outside to visit. After two years of turmoil, however, he was clearly lowering his sights, for he asked Maitland and Dollie Radford, Barbara Low, and Catherine Carswell: these were the smaller fry of his acquaintances, who would place no great demands on him, nor he on them. Habitually Lawrence grumbled about these friends behind their back, but when actually in their company he would be cheerful and sympathetic, with few of the black moods or violent confrontations he would inflict on such as Murry or Bertrand Russell. This preference for less demanding company was part of his new resolve to "cultivate his garden" more quietly and sensibly than before: "Really, one should find a place one can live in," he told Katherine, "and stay there. Geographical change doesn't help one much. And people go from bad to worse. I think I shall be staring out from Higher Tregerthen when I am a nice old man of seventy."[39] Such an idyllic end, however, depended on staying out of reach of the state, and Lawrence's chance of doing so was now disappearing.

France and Britain had agreed secretly at the turn of the year to mount a great summer offensive, which would make universal conscription in England inevitable. The German attack on Verdun, 21 February 1916, only advanced the date. Between February and the end of June the French were to suffer 315,000 casualties in holding a fort whose importance was purely symbolic; they fed seventy-eight divisions on to the killing ground and by the end their troops were on the verge of mutiny. The pressure on England to fill the manpower gap became irresistible, and the Irish rebellion created a suitable atmosphere of crisis. On 2 May, the day before the execution of the revolt's leader, Padraic Pearse, Asquith announced the extension of compulsory service to married men. Quite typically, Lawrence took the news much harder than the call-up of single men in January. Typically, also, his anger at Britain's loss of liberty was directed more at France's call for help than at their common enemy:

> When I think of the degenerate and insect-like stupidity of the men now, my heart stops beating. That England should go on destroying herself to fight this chimerical Germany, whilst all the time the Allies, like great insatiable

leeches, hang on her body and glut themselves ... this one cannot see, and live.

There is no mistaking now that England represents in the world, and has represented for 300 years the great Christian democratic principle: and that Germany represents the Lucifer, the Satan, who has reacted directly against this principle. But the horrible obscene rats that will devour England and Germany both, these are our noble Allies, our greedy-mouthed, narrow-toothed France, our depraved Russia, our obscene little Belgium. And we give ourselves to be eaten by them: oh God, oh God, it is too much. Can one do nothing?

Despite this outburst—which coincided with another spell of illness—Lawrence was for the time being fatalistic about being drawn into the government's net: "We shall go on here, Murry and I, till we are made to work. One can do no other. I have no conscientious objections." [40]

When at the end of May Lawrence was given notice to report for medical examination he could still jest about finding such a definitive escape from his current annoyances. "I shall go and take my chance of being accepted. If I must be a soldier, then I must—ta-rattata-ta! It's no use trying to dodge one's fate. It doesn't trouble me any more. I'd rather be a soldier than a schoolteacher, anyhow." [41] On 28 June he drove with Frieda over the moors to Penzance, expecting to be examined there, but on arrival he was told he would be sent with a contingent of men to spend the night at Bodmin barracks, fifty miles away. Frieda had to return to Tregerthen alone.

Lawrence's stay at Bodmin gave him a bitter and direct shock that surpassed any experience he had had of the war up to that time: when he wrote the "Nightmare" chapter of *Kangaroo* he began his narrative with the trip to Bodmin, saying little of the two years that preceded it. Even so, he could afford to be mildly humorous and philosophical about the episode, since he was writing six years later in the remoteness of Australia. But the effect on him at the time was unrelievedly painful: "being escorted by train, lined up on station platforms, marched like a criminal through the streets to a barracks. The ignominy is horrible, the humiliation." After an inedible meal he took his rest on a pillow like "an old withered vegetable marrow tied up in a bag"; [42] he had brought no pajamas and was ashamed of being seen in his patched underwear. Lying awake, he pondered the blow that the day's events had already dealt to his ideal of male comradeship. If he had been accepted for service he later told Amy Lowell:

I should have been a stretched corpse in a fortnight: that I knew, at four o'clock in the morning, on that fatal night in barracks at Bodmin. There is something in military life that would kill me off, as if I were in an asphyxiating chamber. The whole thing is abhorrent to me—even the camaraderie, that is so glamorous—the Achilles and Patroclus business. The spirit, the pure spirit of militarism is sheer death to a nature that is at all constructive or social-creative. And it is not that I am afraid or shy: I can get on with the men like a house on fire. It is simply that the spirit of militarism is essentially destructive, destroying the individual and the constructive social being. It is *bad*. [43]

In the morning Lawrence faced his medical board, who treated him with gentlemanly consideration. "I got my complete exemption," he told Barbara Low, "because I was able, spiritually, to manage the doctors ... I said the doctors said I had had consumption—I didn't produce any certificate. I didn't think it fair to Jones." [44] This must have been Ernest Jones, M. D., a friend of Barbara's and later the biographer of Freud. Jones presumably gave Lawrence a certificate to show the doctors at Battersea Town Hall in December 1915; no doubt he was stretching a point by calling him a "former" consumptive. In any case, it must have been evident to any trained eye that Lawrence was physically unfit for service in the army.

Though Lawrence himself had escaped, his experience of compulsion convinced him that it meant the "final fall" of the England he had known; and he prophesied that the "sense, of having chosen wrongly, to the last degree, will haunt and pursue my nation like the Errinnyes pursued Orestes—God save us." [45] What only made it the more tragic, he told Catherine Carswell, was the men's conviction that they were acting in a Christian spirit:

... They are all so noble, to accept sorrow and hurt, but they can none of them demand happiness. Their manliness all lies in accepting calmly this death, this loss of their integrity. They must stand by their fellow man: that is the motto.

For Lawrence, a man's *own* desires were the only valid determinants of his actions. Yet he shunned the hypocrisy of social Darwinism, with its claim that private selfishness would create public benefits and faced unblinkingly the danger that he might be the victim of his enemy's desire:

If all my neighbours chose to go down the slope to Hell, that is no reason why I should go with them. I know in my own soul a truth, a right, and no amount of neighbours can weight it out of the balance. I know that, for me, the war is

wrong. I know that if the Germans wanted my little house, I would rather give
it them than fight for it: because my little house is not important enough to
me. If another man must fight for his house, the more's the pity. But it is his
affair. To fight for possessions, goods, is what my soul *will not* do. Therefore it
will not fight for the neighbour who fights for his own goods.

All this war, this talk of nationality, to me is false. I *feel* no nationality, not
fundamentally. I feel no passion for my own land, nor my own house, nor my
own furniture, nor my own money. Therefore I won't pretend any. . . . If they
had compelled me to go in, I should have died, I am sure. One is too raw, one
fights too hard already, for the real integrity of one's being. That last straw of
compulsion would have been too much, I think.[46]

Lawrence spoke most freely about the war to his women friends,
partly because he considered martial destructiveness to be a typically male passion and partly because they were not personally
under the yoke of compulsion. He did not think it right to try and
convince men either to submit or to resist so he generally avoided
contact with pacifist organizations. Nor would he declare himself
a conscientious objector and seek an exemption from a local tribu-
nal, as Lytton Strachey and other Bloomsbury war resisters were
doing. Lawrence simply reversed the Kantian dogma that one
should act in a way that could serve as a general rule for mankind:
no man, he argued, should expect his actions to justify or impli-
cate the actions of another.

Nonetheless Somers, in *Kangaroo,* recognizes that most people
saw the war as an inevitable duty thrust upon them, and could not
stomach his refusal to share their burden:

All very well, they said, but we are in for a war, and what are we to do? We
hate it as much as he does. But we can't all sit safely in Cornwall.

That was true too, and he knew it, and he felt the most a dreary misery,
knowing how many brave, generous men were being put through this
slaughter-machine of human devilishness. They were doing their best, and
there was nothing else to do. But even that was no reason why he should go
and do likewise. . . .

For, above all things, man is a land animal and a thought-adventurer. Once
the human consciousness really sinks and is swamped under the tide of
events—as the best English consciousness was swamped, pacifist and patriotic
alike—then the adventure is doomed. The English soul went under in the
war, and, as a conscious, proud, adventurous, self-responsible soul, it was lost.
We all lost the war: perhaps Germany least. Lost all the lot. The adventure is
always lost when the human conscious soul gives way under the stress, fails to
keep control, and is submerged. Then out swarm the rats and the Bottomleys
and crew, and the ship of human adventure is a horrible piratic affair, a dirty
sort of freebooting.

This latter degradation of England was just beginning in 1916, since it was only in that year that both sides realized how dearly they would have to pay if they wanted victory. Despite the great battles of 1914 and 1915, the armies of the major belligerents were now much larger and better equipped than they had been when the war began. Military logic therefore demanded a series of horrors like Verdun, to carry on what Lloyd George later called "the bovine and brutal game of attrition." [47] And as the struggle at Verdun intensified the French insisted that the British new army, now mainly composed of the raw volunteers of 1915, must throw its weight into the scale. A joint Franco-British offensive was planned for the Somme, where their two sectors met. Haig described its aims as "relieving the pressure on the French at Verdun and inflicting loss on the enemy." The battle therefore had no clear strategic objectives; even its site was chosen for merely political reasons, for on such firm and undulating terrain the defense would have the overwhelming advantage of good observation posts and solid fortifications. During the last six days of June (the time of Lawrence's stay at Bodmin barracks) there was a great preliminary bombardment by fifteen hundred guns. On 1 July the infantry attacked in perfect summer weather, walking across meadows full of poppies toward the German wire and the machine gunners who had waited out the shelling in deep bunkers. It was the most disastrous day in British military history: 20,000 of the assault troops were killed, 40,000 more wounded. Yet the slaughter was kept up for four and a half months, during which the line was pushed forward a maximum of six miles at a cost of almost half a million casualties. The new army was shattered and the "debate" over conscription lost its meaning: henceforth Britain would fight with a conscript army or not fight at all.

As his country closed ranks for the struggle Lawrence held all the more firmly to his separate resolve. He would refuse utterly to join in the war effort; he would write off his hopes for community and avoid his fellows as much as possible; and he would try to get enough money to safeguard his retired existence at Tregerthen. For this last aim he devoted enormous energy to the rapid composition and revision of *Women in Love*. He completed the longhand text immediately on his return from Bodmin, and suggested to Pinker that on the strength of this Duckworth might be persuaded to give him a set annual income in exchange for rights to all his future work; he mentioned 150 pounds a year as being enough for his necessities. But he realized that few publishers were likely to back him, after the fiasco of *The Rainbow.* The *Times Literary Supplement* had just infuriated him with an "idiotic and false"[48] review of *Twilight in Italy;* after quoting an emotive passage about the "wronged woman" of theatrical tradition, the *TLS* reviewer concluded patronizingly:

> Darkness fell long ago upon all this; and Mr. Lawrence, poet and novelist, should not bring these poor old tatters out again into the light of morning. He owes a new day something better, and could give it. To travesty the kindly, industrious life of those pastoral heights as a riot of voluptuous cruelty, a "white-cold ecstasy," a "raucous, cat-like destructive enjoyment," in a hundred other pretty phrases of the sort, may once have been ingenuous—it is now simply perverse. . . . But Mr. Lawrence is a writer with some sense of style, and it is disappointing to see a good gift so mishandled. . . . He might have written a good book about Italy if he had been content to take things simply, and to see no more than he really saw. But he preferred the easier course of discovering the Infinite.[49]

Pinker at least held firm by lending Lawrence fifty pounds; a welcome addition to his capital, which had dwindled to six pounds. He promised to start writing commercial short stories as soon as the novel was finished; to another friend he explained that he hated to borrow from Pinker, but consoled himself with the thought that "he will make money enough out of me later."[50] Hastening that happy day, he started to type out the final text of *Women in Love* early in July. He hoped that it would be a quick and simple task, but found his endurance at the typewriter limited, so that the manuscript was not completed until the middle of November. Moreover, he fell into his usual habit of revising as he went along, and of writing into the novel current events within his circle of friends. The most important of these new developments concerned Jack and Katherine.

The Murrys Adrift

KATHERINE'S happiness with Jack at Bandol had given way, in Cornwall, to a mood of solitude and skepticism. By the time they moved down to Mylor she was discontented enough to be planning another affair. The narrowness of cottage life oppressed her, and made her impatient with Jack's shortcomings. And she always felt that her New Zealand upbringing cut her off from England and English ways:

> There is the inexplicable fact that I love my typical English husband for all the strangeness between us. I *do* lament that he is not warm, ardent, eager, full of quick response, careless, spendthrift of himself, vividly alive, *high-spirited.* But it makes no difference to my love. But the lack of these qualities in his country I HATE—.... I would not care if I never saw the English country again. Even in its flowering I feel deeply antagonistic to it, and I will never change.[51]

Katherine had been drawn to these spirited qualities in Carco and now, it would seem, hoped to find them again in Mark Gertler—with whom she had already flirted at the memorable Chesham Christmas party of 1914. The facts of their affair are still obscure, but certainly she arranged to meet him at Garsington on 19 June, a few days after she and Jack had moved to Mylor. At the last moment, however, she decided to break her tryst. Gertler confided his disappointment to Kot: "I hardly know how to write to you because I have been so wretched here. When I arrived I found Katherine had already left. She left Monday morning apparently in order to catch a train to Murry in Cornwall! If this is true, and I believe it is, I was not very far wrong when I told you that night that she would go back. But she went back even sooner than I thought." Kot replied that he would have been "simply staggered" had he not already heard the news from Lawrence. "Your maxim about couples once more came true," he told Gertler; presumably that they always fell back on each other.[52] We can only guess at later developments through hints in Lawrence's letters and his use of the affair as grist for *Women in Love,* where Gudrun at the end abandons her husband in favor of the artist Loerke. Lawrence remained fond of Gertler and admired his art, but he makes Loerke a far more sinister figure, "a gnawing little negation, gnawing at the roots of life." Though he is physically repulsive, he appeals to Gudrun as a fellow artist:

> ...the inner mysteries of sensation [were] their object of worship. Art and Life were to him the Reality and the Unreality.
> "Of course," said Gudrun, "life doesn't *really* matter—it is one's art which is central. What one does in one's life has *peu de rapport,* it doesn't signify much."

In the novel Lawrence represented the conflict between Jack and Katherine as being more intense than it really was, and even grafted on to it the physical violence typical of his own struggle with Frieda. To Kot he explained their difficulties in much milder terms:

> I know Katherine is coming to London. I think—well, she and Jack are not very happy—they make some sort of contract whereby each of them is free. She also talks of going to Denmark! But don't mention to her that I have told you anything. She has so many reserves.—But really, I think she and Jack have worn out anything that was between them. I like her better than him. He was rather horrid when he was here.[53]

Though she failed to keep her first assignation with Gertler, Katherine was far from reconciled with Jack; on returning to Mylor she told Kot "Life is so hateful just now that I am quite numb."[54] She returned to London on 8 July to stay with the Campbells and look for rooms where she could live freely, but after a few days, and another visit to Garsington, she went back again to Cornwall. "She wants to run away from herself," Lawrence commented to Kot. "But also from Murry, which complicates matters. I don't know what the upshot will be, how it will end between him and her. To settle that point, of her connection with M., a small sojourn in Denmark might be useful. After that, I do wish she could learn to be still—and alone." The reference to Denmark is enigmatic, though at this time Kot was urging Gertler to make contacts with Continental artists, and it is possible that he and Katherine considered going there together; at the end of *Women in Love* Gudrun goes off with Loerke to Dresden. But we do not know how Katherine's connection with Gertler was resolved. Both were restless and dissatisfied—Gertler was troubled by his fruitless infatuation with Dora Carrington while Katherine had an opposite problem: she wanted to break free from Jack's cloying attachment to her. But in the long run they both proved to have deeper attachments to their "unsatisfying" partners than they had to each other. This, too, was Lawrence's verdict at the time: "I think [Jack and Katherine] should ultimately stick together—but there is so much in their mutual relationship that must pass away first."[55]

Like most of her intimates, Lawrence was vulnerable to Katherine's charm and tolerant of her waywardness. While still keeping his face set against Jack, he wooed her after she left Tregerthen with a letter in his old vein, full of wry local gossip and free from contentious references to sex or other dark powers. He and Frieda also accepted an invitation to Mylor for the weekend of 22–23 July, though the visit did not go smoothly. Lawrence was in one of his exigent moods, and also came close to drowning the four of them in his erratic rowing of Jack's dinghy. Katherine told Ottoline of his prophetic fierceness: "We walked with him as far as the ferry and away he sailed in a little open boat pulled by an old, old man. Lawrence wore a broad white linen hat and he carried a rucksack on his back. He looked rather as though the people of Falmouth had cried to him as the Macedonians did to Paul and he was on his way over to help them."[56]

"Lawrence remembered this visit . . ." Murry recalled, "as one in which I had shown my hostility to him. There was truth in the memory; for though I did not feel exactly hostile, I did feel entirely separate from him. I wanted to be left alone." Jack was also much upset by the prospect of conscription, since he too had been summoned to Bodmin and passed fit for nonmilitary service. On 1 October, therefore, the government would assign him to some menial task; Lawrence had escaped this fate, but was disgusted with Jack for acquiescing to it. "He wrote me a most comminatory letter when he got home [from Mylor]," Jack told Ottoline. "The most violent I have ever had from him, saying that I have the same soul as Sir William Robertson. But I don't feel any the wiser, nor any the less fond of him."[57] The letter has not survived, but probably it resembled the one to Russell telling him he was worse than Tirpitz; Robertson, chief of the Imperial General Staff, believed in wearing the enemy down by a series of set-piece offensives like the Somme. Murry, obviously, was not so bloody-minded. But neither did he have any firm convictions against the war, and once he was "cornered" by his B classification he was willing, as we shall see, to take the line of least resistance.

Jack's old friend from Oxford, Frederick Goodyear, had just chosen a different path. Superficially a lighthearted cynic, he was also in search of some deeper, more convincing experience. When war broke out he returned from India to enlist, and became a weather observer with the Royal Engineers—only to discover that this was as boring as everything else.

When Goodyear came to visit Jack at Mylor in August he had begun the last stage of his quest for meaning by applying for a commission in an infantry regiment, a virtually suicidal act in

1916. Because he never expected to see Goodyear again, Jack reluctantly agreed to his request that they should make a joint visit to Higher Tregerthen:

> Lawrence and Goodyear got on well enough together, and Lawrence was rather surprised to find that Goodyear's knowledge of birds and beasts was greater in its own way even than his own. But he was baffled and disturbed by Goodyear's combination of a fundamental indifference with a delighted interest in things. I see Lawrence squatting like a pitman, in his little kitchen garden with the rough rock wall, uncovering with delicate hands his beetroots from the peahaulm that straggled over them. Goodyear watched him with a quizzical admiration. And I watched them both. Then my eyes turned down the hill to the great still, shining sea below and beyond; and it was all sad and beautiful and beyond understanding.[58]

Even after we discount Murry's purple rhetoric, the encounter seems deeply significant of Lawrence's isolation from the best of his generation, and they from him. He could not understand how anyone could value their lives so lightly as to hurl themselves into the cauldron of the Western Front; there was in England, he told Forster later in the year, "Plenty of the slave courage of death, but no proud courage of life."[59]

Goodyear was killed in action the following May. He was typical, Lawrence felt, of those who had lost hope of the future and turned aside, almost sacrilegiously, from the endless onward flow of life; they thus became thralls of the past, and allowed themselves to be sacrificed to preserve it:

> All those who stand one with the past, with our past, as a nation and a Christian people even . . . must go to the war; but those who believe in a life better than *what has been,* they can view the war only with grief, as a great falling back. . . .
>
> We must have the courage to cast off the old symbols, the old traditions: at least, put them aside, like a plant in growing surpasses its crowning leaves with higher leaves and buds. There is something beyond the past. The past is no justification. Unless from us the future takes place, we are death only.[60]

Surprisingly enough, Lawrence received in August a gesture of understanding and support from an unexpected quarter: the *Times Literary Supplement*. The poems of *Amores* were almost all written before the war, but the *TLS* reviewer focused on a passage that Lawrence had added while revising the collection at Porthcothan:

Oh the miracle of the whole, the widespread, laboring concentration
Swelling mankind like one bud to bring forth the fruit of a dream,
Oh the terror of lifting the innermost I out of the sweep of the impulse of life,
And watching the great Thing labouring through the whole round flesh of the
　world;
And striving to catch a glimpse of the shape of the coming dream.[61]

"The tremendous force of life" [said the reviewer] "and the unreadiness of men to welcome the new idea and make it fruitful for the new dream are the burdens which make much of Mr. Lawrence's poetry gloomy. . . . His attitude to life is that of a man of great vitality but bitter experience; one whose great desires, left unsatisfied, lead to a half-concealed savagery."[62] It was encouraging to find that he still had some literary reputation left; though not enough that he could make a living from his books, or see any other prospect for his future than a simple and obscure existence at Tregerthen.

The Monk of Nitria

IN AUGUST Lawrence withdrew into a still narrower round of contacts. "Here we live very quietly indeed," he wrote Amy Lowell in Boston, "being far from the world. Here we live as if on one of the blessed Isles, the moors are so still behind us, the sea so big in front. . . . It is so lovely to recognise the non-human elements: to hear the rain like a song, to feel the wind going by one, to be thrown against the rocks by the wonderful water. I cannot bear to see or to know humanity any more."[63] By "humanity" Lawrence meant, particularly, his enlightened and intellectual friends such as Ottoline, Russell, and the Murrys. The two former he had already alienated and would never see again; now, after Jack's visit with Goodyear, Lawrence took steps to ensure that he too would keep his distance in future. The occasion was the gift from Jack of his study of Dostoevsky—his first book, and one that made him confident of his powers as a critic. After a cursory reading,

Lawrence sent the proud author a cutting dismissal of both himself and his subject:

> I don't blame humanity for having no mind, I blame it for putting its mind in a box and using it as a nice little self-gratifying instrument. You've got to know, and know everything, before you 'transcend' into the 'unknown.' But Dostoievsky, like the rest, can nicely stick his head between the feet of Christ, and waggle his behind in the air. And though the behind-wagglings are a revelation, I don't think much even of the feet of Christ as a bluff for the cowards to hide their eyes against.
>
> You want to be left alone—so do I—by everybody, by the whole world, which is despicable and contemptible to me and sickening.[64]

This was a broad enough hint that Lawrence wanted to wash his hands of Jack and his metaphysical enthusiasms. Correspondence between the two men became perfunctory, and they did not meet again for more than a year; in the following months Lawrence sprinkled his letters to Kot with insulting references to Jack—though he kept asking for news of his activities. This obsessive use of Jack as a whipping boy continued to the end of Lawrence's life, though after Cornwall there was to be only one more brief period of intimacy between the two men, when Lawrence returned to London at the end of 1923. Eternally bound to Jack by the great expectations he had once had of him, Lawrence greeted every betrayal of these hopes with a fresh outburst of rage, compounded both from disappointment and from jealousy that Jack could still impose on others long after Lawrence had seen through him and proclaimed him a villain. That Frieda continued to tolerate Jack and even to be sexually drawn to him set the final seal on Lawrence's bitterness.

Lawrence now denounced the comradeship that he had so longed for earlier in the year. His letter to Cynthia Asquith on 1 September was made more extreme by the irritation of a "sharp bronchial cold," but he stood by its essentials and made them part of Birkin's intellectual system in *Women in Love:*

> My 'indignant temperament,' as you called it, has done for me, and I am dead to the world. Like the monks of Nitria, I am buried in the desert of Sahara, sit amidst silence like St. Anthony, Avaunt, Woman.
>
> That is the whole story of the present. Of the past, of the world vanquished and forgotten—they gave me a total exemption from military service, otherwise I should be singing with the Cherubim now, instead of sulking amid the sands of Nitria. . . . My blood cribbles with fury to think of it. I am no longer

an Englishman, I am the enemy of mankind. The whole of militarism is so disgusting to me, that—well, well, there is silence after all.

But I hate humanity so much, I can only think with friendliness of the dead. They alone, now at least are upright and honourable. For the rest—pfui!

Here in Nitria there is great space, great hollow reverberating silent space, the beauty of all the universe—nothing more. The few visionary temptations: heather and blackberries on the hills, a foamy pool in the rocks where one bathes, the postman with barbed letters: they are the disordered hallucinations of temporal reality. St. Anthony is not deceived by them. In truth there is vast unechoing space where one goes forth and is free.[65]

Lady Cynthia described this as "a maddish letter," and found the poems in *Amores,* which Lawrence sent with it, "morbid." Yet their friendship continued, and Lawrence still spoke more directly from the heart to her than to almost anyone else: no longer expecting her to change her life, perhaps he now felt all the more secure in using her as a confidante, and as the "sleeping beauty" of his fantasies.

Lawrence's mood ruled out any visit to London in the autumn, even though Jack and Katherine had both returned there and a solitary winter lay ahead of him. His hatred of the capital was reinforced by the notorious "Café Royal incident," which he heard of from Kot on 4 September. The story so impressed him that he used it in *Women in Love* as the confirmation, for Ursula and Birkin, that they should wash their hands of England; but his fictional version differed significantly from the actual event.

The only contemporary account by an eyewitness is a letter from Mark Gertler to Ottoline Morrell written on 2 September, the day after the incident. He had gone to the Café Royal with Kot and Katherine—Jack was probably still in Cornwall—and they found themselves seated next to two "coloured men" and "a long thin white herring of a woman":

Soon to our astonishment they began to talk "Intellectual"—they were University Blacks—using "perfect" English very long words carefully chosen. They talked about Dostoevsky, Russia—the new age, all in a very advanced manner. All this irritated us enough. But imagine our Hatred and Horror when the Red headed peice [sic] of dried Dung produced a volume of Lawrence's poems and commenced to discuss Lawrence with the others, in this perfect English and carefully picked, long words! We had been ragging them all the time, but now we knew something drastic must be done. We sat and thought. Suddenly, Katherine leant towards them and with a sweet smile

(247)

said *"Will* you let me have that Book a moment?" "Certainly" they all beamed back—even more sweetly. Imagine then their horror and utter amazement, when Katharine without a word more, Rose from the table, Book and all, we following most calmly—most calmly and walked out of the Café!!!

We heard them hiss and make various sounds to try and stop us or have us stopped, but every body only stared and no one made the slightest attempt to stop us. So we got away with their book of Lawrence's Poems! What revenge! Outside we simply trembled with excitement. It was indeed a good end.[66]

When Murry described the incident years later he identified the two men as "people who used to visit Lawrence at Byron Villas. . . . one has since become an immensely popular writer."[67] This was almost certainly Kouyoumdjian (Michael Arlen), who could have passed for a "coloured man" to Gertler's jaundiced and no doubt drunken eye; his companion was perhaps Suhrawardy, an Indian whom Lawrence had met the previous December and invited to join the Florida colony. But in *Women in Love* Lawrence makes Philip Heseltine—under the name of Halliday—into the villain of the piece, turning an apparently innocent reading into a public betrayal and substituting for a published book the private letter from Birkin that Halliday reads aloud. Nonetheless Cecil Gray, Heseltine's biographer, had the weight of evidence on his side in his denial that Heseltine was even present when the incident occurred.*

Gertler, in any case, thought of the episode as merely a triumphant prank, but when Lawrence heard of it from Kot he felt that although he had left London he was still being hunted there by proxy:

Your 'Dostoevsky evening' gives me a queer contraction of the heart. It frightens me. When I think of London, the Café Royal—you actually there, and Katharine—terror overcomes me, and I take to my heels, and hide myself in a bush. It is a real feeling of horror. I dare not come to London, for my life. It is like walking into some horrible gas, which tears one's lungs. Really— *Delenda est Carthago.* . . . I must say I hate mankind—talking of hatred, I have got a perfect androphobia. When I see people in the distance, walking along the path through the fields to Zennor, I want to crouch in the bushes and shoot them silently with invisible arrows of death. I think truly the only righ-

---

* CB I, 586–87. The only firsthand evidence against my version of the affair is Arlen's letter in Richard Aldington's *D. H. Lawrence: Portrait of a Genius But* (New York: Collier, 1961), pp. 179–180, where he states definitely that Heseltine was guilty as charged. In weighing Arlen's credibility, however, one should consider that a) he was writing more than thirty years later, and b) he had a score to settle: Heseltine's forcible eviction of him from Porthcothan in January 1916.

teousness is the destruction of mankind, as in Sodom. Fire and brimstone should fall down.

But I don't want even to hate them. I only want to be in another world than they. Here, it is almost as if one lived on a star, there is a great space of sky and sea in front, in spirit one can circle in space and have the joy of pure motion. But they creep in, the obstructions, the people, like bugs they creep invidiously in, and they are too many to crush. I see them—fat men in white flannel trousers—*pères de famille*—and the *familles*—passing along the field-path and looking at the scenery. Oh, if one could have a great box of insect powder, and shake it over them, in the heavens, and exterminate them.

One may partially discount this tirade as just another fit of tubercular rage, directed against those who, unlike himself, were fat and comfortable; still, Lawrence's "perfect androphobia" was now a settled dogma of his philosophy. "If only one had the world *to oneself!*" he concluded. "If only there were not more than one hundred people in Great Britain!—all the rest clear space, grass and trees and stone!"[68] Though Lawrence's grudge against mankind was largely inspired by the war, he seems to have decided, in autumn 1916, that his contempt for his fellowmen justified him in ignoring the slaughter they were inflicting on each other. He considered his rejection for service definite and final, nor did he foresee any other reason why the authorities should concern themselves with him. When his health improved his fits of rage diminished and he limited his concerns to his little household and his novel, which he saw as an anatomy of a sick society that he had once and for all renounced. *Women in Love* would seek to justify Lawrence's autarchy by exposing the nullity of everything "out there" in the Vanity Fair of English social life.

There still remained the possibility, Lawrence told Gertler, that a chosen few might be able to "add [their] spirit together . . . and create a new well-shapen life";[69] but for the present they must patiently submit to a period of retreat. Lawrence argued thus to Ottoline apropos of Bertrand Russell's dismissal from Trinity College as a result of his propaganda for the No-Conscription Fellowship:

It is no good turning upon England in direct attack whilst the war lasts, because the English will be against you. But when the war is over, then, in the debacle, one can hope to shove a stiletto into the stout heart of Britannia.

It is a certain fact, this order of life must go, this organisation of humanity must be smashed. But it is ridiculous to be as innocent as the turtle dove. Now is the time for the wisdom of the serpent. . . . It is not martyrdom we seek. I hate those who seek martyrdom. One wants victory.[70]

No doubt Lawrence was correct in judging that the efforts of the whole band of pacifists would not shorten the war by so much as a day. But his own position was even more dubious: he claimed to hate the existing order, yet insisted that nothing could be done against it—and that those who *did* want to do something were misguided and hateful.

To Katherine Lawrence explained why he wanted a total and metaphysical revolution, rather than a merely political one:

> It is a great and foul beast, this world that has got us, and we are very few. But with subtlety, we can get round the neck of the vast obscenity at last, and strangle it dead. And then we can build a new world, to our own minds: we can initiate a new order of life, after our own hearts. One has first to die in the great body of the world, then to turn round and kill the monstrous existing Whole, and then declare a new order, a new earth.[71]

Taken literally, this may seem pure megalomania, like the "magic thinking" of infants or savages who feel they can create and destroy external reality by a simple exercise of their will. Yet Lawrence was indeed propounding a world-changing idea of salvation through spiritual renewal and erotic fulfillment; and it was the kind of idea that could only prevail "with subtlety," gradually winning acceptance through individual conversions. In retrospect, Lawrence's belief that personal reconstruction had to precede social revolution seems at least as plausible as Russell's schemes for world government and the rule of reason in politics— schemes that often appear devitalized and passé when set against the continuing potency of Lawrence's vision.

The World Outside: Garsington and London

AS LAWRENCE tried not to care about the social world beyond Zennor, he tried also to achieve a similar nonchalance about the recreant Murrys. "Murry is a toad—all right," he told Kot. "With the toad in him I will have nothing to do any more. If there is a decent creature in him also, and that comes forth, then we will accept that and be thankful. I refuse to see people as unified Godheads any more."[72] A new Murry was indeed emerging, as it so frequently did throughout his life, but it was just as well that Lawrence could not observe too closely this next stage of his friend's development.

Jack's B1 classification put him in danger of becoming a noncombatant laborer in France. "Not being in the least degree a C. O.," he told Ottoline, "—for which you must forgive me—I'd far sooner be put into a first line trench." Philip Morrell interested himself in Jack's plight and in August introduced him to John Sheppard, a Cambridge intimate of Lytton Strachey who was now working for military intelligence. Sheppard obtained for Jack a position in his own department, translating foreign newspapers; he started in September at five pounds a week (which he soon doubled) and remained for two and a half years. "What kind of human thing I was in those days, I have no idea," Jack later recalled, with characteristic ingenuousness.[73] Emotionally he may have been a blank but certainly he seized with both hands the chance he had been given, at age twenty-seven, to join the Establishment. As Lea wryly noted in his biography of Jack: ". . . it was good-bye to small magazines, country cottages, flittings, good-bye to Bohemia and poverty."[74] Murry's natural ability and great capacity for work brought him rapid advancement: editor of *The Daily Review of the Foreign Press* in 1917, chief censor 1918, O. B. E. 1920. He somehow found time, also, to supplement his income by writing numerous articles on literature and politics. By 1919, therefore, Jack was well launched on a track that would have made him a major figure in British intellectual or political life had he not turned aside from such ambitions during his emotional vacillations after the war.

Jack and Katherine now plunged into the social round of Bloomsbury and Garsington. They took rooms at the top of J. M. Keynes's house at 3 Gower Street in Bloomsbury; Brett and Carrington shared the floor below, while Keynes, Sheppard, and the economist Gerald Shove lived on the ground floor. Once again they were joining a community—but one very different, in its blend of high-mindedness with emotional promiscuity, from the cluster of cottages set in the rocky fields of Zennor. They both entered into the spirit of their new milieu—Katherine by an ambiguous flirtation with Bertrand Russell and Jack by paying court to the high priestess herself, Ottoline. After visiting Garsington and reaping the fruit of his War Office job, Jack favored his hostess with one of his Dostoevskian declarations:

> I have at times a queer suspicion that I must be in love with you. I don't know. It's very hard to get at what I feel: so rarely do I feel towards persons any emotion more intimate than amusement or blank terror. . . . I think you are beautiful in ways in which beauty has never appeared to me before. I think that your personality is so real that I carry the memory of it with me as evidence that the world is not all a wilderness nor all men and women trivial liars. I love also to contrast you with the people who revolve about you and to think that you know how petty and conceited and dead most of them are. . . .
>
> I cry for the moon, surely. But the moon is near to hand and tangible compared to what I cry for. And then I do not cry. I just wonder, and try to hold my own true meaning . . .[75]

Reading this wonderfully typical effusion, one should perhaps not claim to understand Jack better than he understood himself; his infatuation was probably in part genuine, in part tinged with opportunism and with the desire to be revenged on Katherine for *her* infidelities. Though Ottoline was sixteen years older than Jack she was still an attractive woman, despite her bizarre mannerisms, and he was often attracted to women of more definite personality and wider sexual experience than his own. Jack continued to press his suit through the autumn, though nothing seems to have come of it except that Katherine became considerably irritated at both of them. Ottoline, however, was sufficiently responsive to Jack's flattery that in the following summer he was moved to spread the word in London that *she* was infatuated with *him*. This so upset Ottoline that thereafter she felt for Jack a settled mistrust and contempt—once again he had made an enemy of someone who had begun by greatly admiring him.*

Katherine helped to stir the pot by making up to Bertrand Russell, which gave her both an eminent confidant and an opportunity to strike back at Ottoline. She did not consummate the affair, perhaps because of Russell's involvement at the time with Colette

---

* In a letter to Ottoline of 2 November 1928 (TxU) Jack recalled the "happy—and miserable times" they had shared at Garsington, and added: "I don't think it was our fault that things were not 'lastly as at firstly well.' I think the whole war years were devilish, and responsible in themselves for exasperated nerves and misunderstandings." Ottoline wrote on the back of this effusion: "This is just one of J. M. Murry's lies—and self-deceits."

O'Neill, though he apparently did not object to having Katherine
for a mistress too. But without being technically unfaithful to Jack
she was able at least to sideswipe Ottoline, as Russell has recalled:

> Her talk was marvellous . . . but when she spoke about people she was envi-
> ous, dark, and full of alarming penetration in discovering what they least
> wished known and whatever was bad in their characteristics. She hated Otto-
> line because Murry did not. . . . I listened to all that [she] had to say against
> her; in the end I believed very little of it, but I had become able to think of
> Ottoline as a friend rather than a lover. After this I saw no more of Katherine,
> but was able to allow my feeling for Colette free scope.[76]

Outsiders as they were, the Murrys had sufficient charm and talent to make an impressive debut in Bloomsbury; but they seemed
driven to play elaborate double games that were inevitably found
out—it was not a milieu where secrets could be kept for long—and
that alienated almost all their new friends within a few years. Jack
especially suffered from this odium, which was most scathingly
expressed in the caricature of him as Birlap in Huxley's *Point
Counter Point*.

Though Lawrence kept asking Kot for news of Jack and Katherine (which he would then greet with ribald contempt), he was
far enough away from them not to be totally exacerbated by their
vagaries. Insofar as Gerald in *Women in Love* represents Murry, he
is Murry magnified and still possessing, up to the final catastro-
phe, the potentiality of becoming a noble and genuine comrade-
in-arms for Birkin. Hermione, similarly, has more stature in the
novel than Lawrence was willing to concede to Ottoline in actuality. However vehemently he might consign them to outer darkness as dilettantes and false friends, in the novel he needed to
make them adequate foils for Birkin, lest that character decline
into a mere solipsistic ranter. He was therefore genuinely surprised at the violence of Ottoline's rage at his portrayal of her as
Hermione, when she came to read the book.

Frieda, too, remained blithely unaware of how deeply she had
offended Ottoline. Early in September she planned a visit to London to see her children; she took this as an opportunity to be restored to Ottoline's good graces, so sent her a naive but generous
apology:

> Have you forgotten my nasty letter of the spring? I wrote it chiefly because I
> was disappointed that we could not be friends. Few people I have met have
> moved me so deeply, I could feel how sad so much in your life had been and

how you had kept on so courageously, I seemed to have to weep your unwept tears for you—Very likely it was my fault to a great extent, I was very overwrought, things had been too much for me—You say, we are both too old to alter I dont think so—You are not happy and I know we both want new things to happen, new good things . . .[77]

Frieda went on to suggest a meeting in London or, failing that, a visit by Ottoline to Zennor. She may have been encouraged by Lawrence to eat humble pie, but more likely the impulse was her own. Lawrence had another spell of chest trouble shortly before she wrote, and she must have been alarmed to see him bedridden before winter had even arrived. When he was desperately ill the previous January Ottoline's gifts had helped to pull him through. That was in the relative comfort of Porthcothan, and with a reserve of money from *The Rainbow;* now they faced a winter living in a primitive cottage in one of the bleakest and most isolated spots in England, and without any reliable source of income. Nor could they expect much support from London, since most of their friends were either alienated or unable to afford the fare of two pounds ten shillings to visit them. Though Lawrence kept up a bold front, Frieda was looking for a way out.

Ottoline, however, was not to be placated and no meeting took place. Frieda arrived in London on 16 September and stayed for about a week. She was able to meet her children at a lawyer's office and hoped to preserve her ties to them, though Lawrence still disapproved: ". . . she should leave the children alone," he told Dollie Radford, "till they are men and women. Then, if there *is* love, if there *is* a connection, it is undeniable: if there *be* no active love, nothing can create it."[78] Her other contacts were more awkward, except for the always reliable Dollie whose guest she was in Hampstead. Relations with Jack and Katherine were still strained; it is not clear if they even met, but Frieda and Kot compared notes and realized how the Murrys had been slandering them behind their backs. Kot, especially, felt betrayed in his deep attachment to Katherine. "You see," Frieda explained to him, "Jack has a terribly jealous nature. He was jealous of Katherine, pretended like the sneak that he is to be your friend, and his hate worked underneath all the time. There is a very great cowardice in Jack, I still feel very bitter about them both." Frieda realized that the Murrys worked in concert against outsiders while simultaneously using them as pawns in their own intimate conflicts, and she suggested to Kot that they should combine to force Jack and Katherine to "become simple, as we all must learn to be":

> [Lawrence] wrote to Jack: "You, Jack, are a little phenomenon of meanness." . . . Yet there is so much that is good in them, must one not *fight* their dishonesty? I have had so many good hours with Katherine, for that I owe her to *make* her more honest with me. . . . They are as mean as they can be to everybody, *then* they turn round and say: "Aren't people vile?" And Katherine never opposes Jack's vileness, but rather enjoys it. To me they have been so mean, especially Jack; wherever they have been, they have turned people against me, tried to regard me as a *quantité negligeable.* Well, from my point I am not going to put up with it a minute longer. . . . I am no angel myself, but they have done me infinitely more harm than ever I did to them.[79]

Frieda carried out her threat to give Jack a piece of her mind but as usual he evaded any recognition that the complaint might be justified. Katherine merely served it up to Ottoline as another tidbit of Lawrentian gossip:

> Frieda sent Murry a tremendous "biff" yesterday—"Now I am going to have my say"—It was just the same "Ach du hässliche Augustine" as usual. Sooner or later all Frieda's friends are bound to pop their heads out of the window and see her grinding it before their door—smoking a cigarette with one hand on her hip and a coloured picture of Lorenzo and Nietzsche dancing 'symbolically' on the front of the barrel organ. Murry, yesterday, very wisely slammed the window down and refused to listen, but *I* hung on every note . . .[80]

If Ottoline had known the kind of picture Katherine was painting of *her* behind her back, she would have been less inclined to relish the caricature of Frieda. But "sooner or later" Katherine's chickens all came home to roost too.

Frieda's Return

WHEN FRIEDA arrived home in late September she found the weather dreary and her husband sick and depressed; the prospect of a winter at Higher Tregerthen looked bleaker than ever and she tried to arrange with Dollie Radford a loan of her cottage at

Hermitage, in Berkshire, where the climate was milder. But the plan fell through, as did Lawrence's truly farfetched proposal to Ottoline that he and Frieda should come to stay at the bailiff's cottage at Garsington. Uncertainty about their future probably contributed to a climactic quarrel soon after Frieda's return though the immediate cause, Catherine Carswell believed, was the old trouble about the children. After the first onslaught Lawrence thought the battle was finished, so he went into the scullery to wash up:

> While he was thus engaged, with his back to the living-room door, singing quietly to himself . . . Frieda came in from the living-room carrying one of the stone dinner plates. His unconcerned roundelay after what had just passed . . . so wrought upon her that her wrath boiled up afresh. Down on the singer's head she brought the dinner plate.
>
> It hurt him very much and might, of course, have injured him seriously. But he was as far from bearing Frieda a grudge as from turning the other cheek. "That was like a woman!" said he. . . . "No man could have done such a thing when the quarrel was over, and from behind too! But as you *are* a woman," he added ruefully, "you were right to do as you felt. It was only lucky you didn't kill me. You might have."[81]

This assault finally made the Lawrences swear off such dangerous encounters—or so Lawrence told Jack in a letter announcing a radical shift in the terms of his marriage: "Frieda and I have finished the long and bloody fight at last, and are at one. It is a fight one has to fight—the old Adam to be killed in me, the old Eve in her—then a new Adam and a new Eve. Till the fight is finished, it is only honourable to fight. But, oh dear, it is very horrible and agonising."[82]

Lawrence used the quarrel in *Women in Love,* but gave it a very different context and meaning. Birkin is assailed by Hermione rather than Ursula, and she strikes him twice with a paperweight of lapis lazuli in a deliberate attempt to murder him. Though Birkin admits the validity of her hatred he breaks off his intimacy with Hermione after the episode and withdraws, first into the solace of nature and later into a phase of self-containment and disillusion with love. In real life the attack led to reconciliation; in the novel it produces Birkin's misanthropic isolation. Yet Lawrence could not sustain either response in the long run: he could neither be at peace with Frieda nor live apart from her, but found himself doomed to struggle with her, to no final end.

When Catherine Carswell came to visit Higher Tregerthen at

the beginning of October Lawrence and Frieda were enjoying an interlude of calm, both having been purged by the violence of their recent battle. Catherine was the same age as Frieda—thirty-seven—also divorced and recently remarried; she was trying to establish herself as a novelist, which had given her and Lawrence their first common ground. Unlike many of Lawrence's younger, more gifted and unstable friends, she gave him from first to last a steady sympathy. On the other hand, it must have been tacitly accepted that as a writer she could be no more than a pupil to Lawrence, and that as a woman she would be neither critic nor rival to Frieda. Lawrence praised her for fitting into the routines of cottage life more pleasantly and unobtrusively than his London friends: "I think one understands best without explanations," he observed to her, adding that he believed the Scots had a special gift for such quiet comradeship. The only awkward moment in her visit came when she began to undress for bed then returned to the upper room of the tower to get a book, and found the Lawrences still sitting there:

> I had brought no dressing-gown with me, but there seemed to me no impropriety in my costume—an ankle-length petticoat topped by a long-sleeved woollen vest! Lawrence, however, rebuked me. He disapproved, he said, of people appearing in their underclothes. No doubt, if I had not privately believed my négligé to be attractive as well as decent, I might neither have ventured to appear in it nor have felt so much abashed as I did by Lawrence's remark. So essentially, Lawrence was right after all![83]

The puritan side of Lawrence's temperament showed also in his constant habit of work. Mrs. Carswell mentions that after buying a damaged shawl for Frieda he devoted two entire days to mending it, working far into the night:

> When I say I never saw Lawrence idle, I do not mean that he was that wretched thing, a time-haunted man. He was that as little as he was the Shavian 'writing machine'. He did not seem to be 'driven,' either by clocks or conscience. He worked more as a bird works, eagerly and unceasingly till the job on hand was finished. But he certainly valued time as any good worker must, and he was shocked in a light passing way when he noticed other people dilly-dallying or spending their hours on trivialities or lying unduly long in bed of a morning.

When Catherine lamented how barren she felt by comparison he replied, simply but poignantly, "Ah, but you will have so much longer than I to do things in![84]

The Merry-Go-Round

AT THIS TIME, Lawrence kept in touch with London and the world of the arts mainly through Mark Gertler. During Frieda's September visit to London she had found Gertler good company, perhaps because they both spoke with an accent and were looked on as "Huns" by the jingoes, despite their British citizenship. Always friendly to anyone who liked Frieda, Lawrence decided that Gertler was one of the chosen few who might still be capable of transforming themselves. But when Lawrence received a photograph of Gertler's new painting *The Merry-Go-Round* he was excited by an achievement much greater than anything he had expected. Till then Gertler had been an accomplished artist, but one whose subjects were relatively innocuous: portraits of East End Jews, landscapes, and still lifes. But in the spring and summer of 1916—the time of Verdun and the Somme—he labored at a giant new canvas, five feet by six, that he called a *"very unsaleable* picture of 'Merry-Go-Rounds'." He was acutely aware of the contradiction between what he *wanted* to paint and what he was *obliged* to paint in order to support himself. He was also worried by his vulnerability as a young and single man: "I have never felt more passionately a desire to paint than now," he told Kot. "You can't think how many wonderful ideas I have for future work. Yet at any moment I may be dragged away into this war. What a nightmare it is to me!" When he completed the painting in the autumn St. John Hutchinson, a Bloomsbury lawyer who had defended many pacifists against conscription, warned him against exhibiting it:

> It will of course raise a tremendous outcry—the old, the wise, the professional critic will go mad with anger and righteous indignation—and what strikes me is that these symptoms may drive them to write all sorts of rubbish about German art and German artists in their papers and may raise the question acutely and publicly as to your position.[85]

The previous November, indeed, Gertler's *Creation of Eve*—an idyll in the tradition of Blake and Gauguin—had caused a scandal at the London Group show: the *Morning Post* derided its "Hunnish indecency," and a spectator put a "Made in Germany" sticker on Eve's nude belly. Gertler planned to include *The Merry-Go-Round* in the autumn 1916 London Group show, but the owner of the Goupil gallery refused to have anything more to do with the group until it was purged of "enemy aliens, conscientious objectors or sympathizers with the enemy."[86] It was April 1917 before Gertler could show the painting; it did prove unsalable, as he had feared, and for many years it remained in his studio.

The literal subject of *The Merry-Go-Round* was a group of servicemen and their girl friends enjoying themselves at a fun fair; Gertler had often witnessed such scenes on Hampstead Heath near his studio. But the painting savagely satirized the prevailing war spirit. When Lawrence saw the photograph, he recognized in it a summing-up of the disintegration of the West:

> Your terrible and dreadful picture has just come. This is the first picture you have ever painted: it is the best *modern* picture I have seen: I think it is great, and true. But it is horrible and terrifying. I'm not sure I wouldn't be too frightened to come and look at the original.
>
> If they tell you it is obscene, they will say truly. I believe there was something in Pompeian art, of this terrible and soul-tearing obscenity. But then, since obscenity is the truth of our passion today, it is the only stuff of art—or almost the only stuff.[87]

The obscenity of *The Merry-Go-Round* lies in its atmosphere of bisexual violence. The heads and necks of the horses resemble giant phalluses, ridden by soldiers and women whose sexual attributes are confusedly interchangeable; they are all in pursuit of the horse's hindquarters on the left of the painting—which resemble the buttocks of a man bending over rather than a real horse. The sexuality of the picture is utterly impersonal and sterile: though the riders are filled with desire, it is all channeled into an endless round of mechanical futility.

But Lawrence saw much more in the painting than perverted sexuality. The riders' circuit is enclosed by a design suggesting a military helmet, perhaps even a medieval hell-mouth, so that the emotional violence of the scene proclaims the link between individual and mass passions in this age of iron:

> . . . in this combination of blaze, and violent mechanised rotation and complete involution, and ghastly, utterly mindless human intensity of sensational extremity, you have made a real and ultimate revelation. . . . Also I could sit down and howl beneath it like Kot's dog, in soul-lacerating despair. I realise

(259)

how superficial your human relationships must be, and what a violent maelstrom of destruction and horror your inner soul must be. It is true, the outer
life means nothing to you, really. You are all absorbed in the violent and lurid
processes of inner decomposition: the same thing that makes leaves go scarlet
and copper-green at this time of year. It is a terrifying coloured flame of
decomposition, your inner flame.—But dear God, it is a real flame enough,
undeniable in heaven and earth.—It would take a Jew to paint this picture. It
would need your national history to get you here, without disintegrating you
first. You are of an older race than I, and in these ultimate processes, you are
beyond me, older than I am.[88]

For Lawrence, the Jews are forerunners: the oldest race of mankind, they are therefore the first to arrive at the cul-de-sac of
modern culture and to warn those behind them: "At last your race
is at an end—these pictures are its death-cry. And it will be left for
the Jews to utter the final and great death-cry of this epoch: the
Christians are not reduced sufficiently. I must say, I have, for you,
in your work, reverence, the reverence for the great articulate extremity of art."[89]

In *Women in Love* the sculptor, Loerke, "the wizard rat that
swims ahead,"* follows the path of degeneracy through an excess
of mental sensation. Lawrence feared that Gertler himself might
be consumed by the very extremity of his vision, and he urged
him to visit Zennor from time to time to recuperate:

Only take care, or you will burn your flame so fast, it will suddenly go out. It is
all spending and no getting of strength. And yet some of us must fling ourselves in the fire of ultimate expression, like an immolation. Yet one cannot as-
sist at this *auto-da-fé* without suffering. But do try to save yourself as well. . . .
You seem to me to be flying like a moth into a fire.[90]

The warning illustrates the interplay between Lawrence's immediate perceptions of his friends and the use his fictional imagination made of them, for he is here paraphrasing a scene from
chapter 13 of *The Trespasser* in which a Lawrentian figure, Hampson, warns the novel's hero, Siegmund:

'If you have acquired a liking for intensity in life, you can't do without it. I
mean vivid soul experience. It takes the place, with us, of the old adventure,
and physical excitement.'

* In the 1916 text, however, Lawrence did not suggest that Loerke was Jewish; this was
done during revisions in 1917.

> Siegmund looked at the other man with baffled, anxious eyes. 'Well, and what then?' he said.
>
> 'What then? A craving for intense life is nearly as deadly as any other craving. You become a *concentré;* you feed your normal flame with oxygen, and it devours your tissue.'

Hampson is hinting that Siegmund may become tubercular, like himself, if he does not change; Siegmund ignores the advice, is unable to cope with divided loyalties to his wife and his mistress, and commits suicide. Gertler, four years after Lawrence's warning, contracted tuberculosis; in 1939, depressed by the state of his health, his marriage, and his career, he killed himself. The circuit between reality and fiction was closed.

Completion of *Women in Love*

GERTLER'S PAINTING of *The Merry-Go-Round* was the last important happening within Lawrence's circle to be used in *Women in Love,* even though it would be another four years before the novel was published. When Lawrence received the photograph on 9 October he had typed about half of his handwritten manuscript, revising as he went along; his reaction to Gertler's achievement undoubtedly contributed to the portrayal of Loerke in the latter part of the novel. On 13 October he complained to his former typist, Mrs. Clayton, that the work was a strain and asked her to do the rest for him; she agreed, but in the meantine Lawrence accepted an offer from Pinker to have it done free. Between then and 31 October he finished writing this version in longhand, working at phenomenal speed, even for him. He sent this off to Pinker to be typed, keeping on hand two copies of the part that he had already typed himself. Almost any other writer would have taken a vacation at this point, but Lawrence immediately began to add further handwritten revisions to the typescript he had retained; Frieda helped him by transcribing his revision onto the second typed copy. On 6 November more typescript (of the second half of the novel) began to arrive from Pinker, so that during the first three weeks of November Lawrence was able to add handwritten revisions to two copies of a complete "original" typescript. He was in a dark mood at this time and his additions made Hermione, in particular into a more unpleasant and grotesque figure. On 20 November, having completed his revisions, Lawrence sent a complete copy of the typed manuscript to Pinker—the one with revisions in his own hand.[91] He still expected to round out the novel with a short epilogue that he would not write until the manuscript was actually sent to the printer. At some point he wrote a page of it: Gudrun has severed relations with Loerke and is living with her six-month-old son by Gerald in Frankfurt.[92] Perhaps Lawrence wanted to await the final outcome of Katherine's period of restlessness in order to work it into the novel, but he never completed the epilogue nor did he incorporate the changes in Katherine's life after 1916.

When sending Pinker a section of *Women in Love* in October, Lawrence accurately predicted its fate, in the short run at least: "It is a terrible and horrible and wonderful novel. You will hate it and nobody will publish it." When he received the neat typescript he was more optimistic, a reaction any writer will recognize: "The novel is really rather wonderful: something quite new on the face of the earth, I think. I wonder what it will seem to you. . . . I don't think this book is likely to be suppressed for *immorality,* like *The Rainbow.* God knows how it will go."[93] In order to give it a clearer run, Lawrence sent the second copy to Catherine Carswell so that her husband could check it for potentially libelous passages. Then, at last, he allowed himself to rest—and to wait.

The composition of *Women in Love* had been achieved in seven months of concentrated work: the manuscript ran to 666 pages of typescript, and Lawrence had done three substantially different drafts in that brief period. He had begun in the springtime while he still hoped that he, Frieda, and the Murrys might be the nucleus of an idyllic community of artists at Tregerthen. By the time he finished Jack and Katherine had long departed to London; they were now connected with the Lawrences only by the sneers relayed back and forth by third parties. Conscription had taken Jack for war work, and conceded Lawrence his liberty only at the government's pleasure. With winter closing in, his prospects seemed as bleak as the moors above his cottage. The autumn had been cold and rainy, inflicting on him repeated bouts of illness;

now he faced several months of hardship on an inadequate wartime diet and in a house without central heating or any utilities. Though Lawrence was not one to harp on the desperate state of his health, he must have realized that he might not survive to see the spring. When he heard from E. M. Forster in Alexandria, Lawrence poured out the full bitterness of his situation in reply:

> I get sick of giving people my books, or even of writing. People today want their senses gratified in art, but their *will* remains static all the time with the old, and they would rather die than face a conclusion out from the senses to the mind. There ought to be a flood to drown mankind, for there is no health in it. . . . I am sure, that even if *this* war ends in our lifetime, war in the same sort will go on. The process of violent death will possess humanity for many a generation yet, till there are only a few remaining of all these hordes: a slow, slow flood of death will drown them all. I am glad, for they are too corrupt and cowardly.

This somber prophecy was just the prelude to a flood of disgust for Lawrence's countrymen, who had so humiliated him over the past two years:

> One writes, one works, one gives ones hand to people. And the swine are rats, they bite one's hand. . . . I think it would be good to die, because death would be a clean land with no people in it: not even the people of myself. . . . *I* believe in a free, proud happiness. But how can one be happy with rats biting one. How to get away from them? They are everywhere, they cling on to one, they carry one down with their weight.[94]

As a literal description of Lawrence's situation, this was almost hallucinatory: he had been buried in the country for almost a year, sometimes staying home for weeks at a time without even going to St. Ives, seven miles away. But as a writer, he considered his relation to his audience to be as organic and mutually binding as any personal intimacy. His art had never been for art's sake but for everyone's sake, so when it was jeered at and suppressed this was to him a foul and calculated ingratitude.

If he could again exile himself from England, Lawrence hoped to renounce entirely the literary world that had become such a bane to his spirit. "I am going to write saleable short stories now," he told Forster, "so that I may have a little money, and may not be trapped in by the rats of the world. Money is the only mail they won't bite through. Then I think I shall go to Italy. I am so weary of mankind. If it speaks a foreign language, I don't notice it so much."[95] But it would not be easy to make his escape in this way, and the alternative—to give up the struggle and be pulled down into the "river of dissolution"—had become terribly enticing. When Lawrence had written his equally bitter letter to Jack the previous January, he had still resisted the idea of death as a way out of his troubles: "What good even is death, when life is nothing but this peaked, traitorous meanness? How can death be great, seeing life such a mean paucity: since they must be counterparts, life and death." Now, however, lying sick in bed overlooking the fields and the Atlantic, he saw death as perhaps the only consolation for all the bitterness of the past years: "Really, one looks through the window into the land of death, and it *does* seem a clean good unknown, all that is left to one. But it is so *sure*, death, that one is always strong in it. It is so sure, one is free to live, whatever the world may be, having death as a certainty, a free, honorable land, inevitable."[96]

Lawrence's exile in Cornwall and his writing of *Women in Love* both served the same purpose: to get him clear of that intellectual society into which he had been drawn as a result of being detained in England by the war. "One sheds one's sicknesses in books," he had remarked of *Sons and Lovers;* if in that novel he had fought free of his devouring mother, in *Women in Love* he was similarly casting off the incubus of a devouring mother country. Though the rejection cost him dearly, he had always believed in the creative possibilities of struggling against old ties, old habits. Only a day after his apocalyptic letter to Forster he was encouraging Kot to fully accept the truth "that people and the world *are* foul and obscene"; only then, he argued, could one act boldly and carelessly. "I have done with the Murrys, both, for ever," he proclaimed, "—so help me God. So I have with Lady Ottoline and all the rest. And now I am glad and free. Now we must wait for the wheel of events to turn a little, so that we can escape out into the open, to the Rananim. That is all."[97]

CHAPTER VII

ZENNOR:
The Buried Life

A Change of Regime

AS THE LAWRENCES' FUNDS dwindled that autumn 1916 Frieda made a private appeal to Amy Lowell, who sent them early in November the generous gift of sixty pounds. Having so much cash on hand set Lawrence dreaming of travel though the difficulties of moving, especially to a foreign country, were still great. The shifting balance of political forces in England held out some hope of peace, but Lawrence admitted to Cynthia Asquith that letters received from Frieda's sisters in Germany showed they were "still resistant and rather ugly in spirit. I must say, judging from these, I can't feel that Germany wants peace yet, any more than England does. Their fulfilment is still in this ugly contending. . . . The whole show is too nasty and contemptible, essentially."[1] When Lady Cynthia objected to his cynical view of the struggle, Lawrence conceded that he should stop preaching about "war in the abstract" as he had done during his spell of political activism in 1915:

> I will only say, in the particular, that for *me* the war is utterly wrong, stupid, monstrous and contemptible . . . But—here I submit—I am only myself. At last I submit that I have no right to speak for anybody else, but only for my single self. War is for the rest of men, what it is, of this I can say nothing. . . .
>
> And it comes to this, that the *oneness* of mankind is destroyed in me. I am I, and you are you, and all heaven and hell lies in the chasm between. Believe me, I am infinitely hurt by being thus torn off from the body of mankind, but so it is, and it is right. And believe me that I have wept tears enough, over the dead men and the unhappy women who were once one with me. . . . Therefore I am sorry for all my generalities, which must be falsities to another man, and almost insults. Even Rupert Brooke's sonnet, which I repudiate for my-

self, I know now it is true for him, for them. But for me it is *not* true, and nothing will ever make it so: least of all death, for death is a great reality and seal of truth: my truth, his truth. It is terrible to think there are opposing truths—but so it is.[2]

The logical consequence of these beliefs, Lawrence felt, was that he should leave for Italy as soon as possible; but since he could not get free of England he yielded for a while to the mental exhaustion that followed the completion of his novel. "This is a kind of interval in my life," he told Kot, "like a sleep. One only wanders through the dim short days, and reads, and cooks, and looks across at the sea. I feel as if I also were hibernating, like the snakes and the dormice."[3] Before long, though, he was bestirring himself in yet another attempt to further the cause of peace.

Early winter was the season for peace feelers and for political maneuvering. By 19 November the Battle of the Somme had run its course. The Allies had suffered 630,000 casualties, most of them British, and the Germans 660,000; the furthest Allied advance was five miles, and no major offensives could now be expected until spring. Lawrence had been living like a hermit during the last phase of the battle, completing his novel, but on 22 November he went to St. Ives for the first time in nine weeks. Soon afterward he asked Cynthia Asquith: "When are we going to have a shot at preparing this nation for peace? Peace and war lie in the heart, in the *desire,* of the people—say what you will. . . . I think that Germany—peace terms—allies—etc.—*do not matter.*"[4] He asked her if the police would let him speak publicly against the war and meanwhile inquired about the peace movement to Barbara Low: "Can you tell me if anything is being done in London or anywhere? You might send me any newspaper or such that shows any interesting attitude towards the war. . . . I feel the time drawing near when I must issue out of my little lair and howl in the teeth of the world."[5]

But a political crisis intervened before Lawrence could make a move. For several months Asquith's opponents had been complaining that he was too dilatory and old-fashioned to prosecute the war effectively. The lack of definite success on the Somme brought matters to a head and Lloyd George demanded that the day-to-day conduct of the war be entrusted to a war committee of three, not including the prime minister. Lloyd George, a brilliant minister of munitions and secretary of state for war, was clearly the rising man. He was backed by a cabal of hardline conservatives within the coalition, notably Bonar Law and Sir Edward Carson. Before the war they had denounced Lloyd George as a pro-Boer, a socialist, and a traitor to the British cause in Ireland but now they saw him as England's best hope for victory. Over the past year Lloyd George had proclaimed his nationalist and authoritarian views in a style that made Asquith seem a mere ditherer when it came to modern warfare. When the crunch came Asquith's support had so eroded that he was forced to resign on 5 December. After Bonar Law failed to form a government Lloyd George became prime minister, on 7 December; he was to hold office for nearly six years. Asquith, stripped of power and influence, became leader of the Opposition.

To Lady Cynthia, Lawrence professed dismay at the waning of her father-in-law's power; but with Gertler he had no need to equivocate for the sake of politeness:

> Though I think Asquith is by far a more decent man than Lloyd George or any of the others, yet I wish he would clear out, and leave them to it. The debacle would come the quicker. It is bound to come, the great smash-up in this country—and oh, oh God, if it would only come quickly. But it will never take place while Asquith holds the Premiership. He is too much the old, stable, measured, *decent* England. Alas and alack, that such an England must collapse and be trodden under the feet of swine and dogs. But so it is, by the decree of unalterable fate.

In Cornwall, Asquith's fall was taken as proof that England was on its last legs. ". . . in Penzance Market," Lawrence told Lady Cynthia, "farmers went about with wonderstruck faces, saying, 'We're beaten. I'm afraid we're beaten. These Germans are a wonderful nation, I'm afraid. They are more than a match for us.'" Nonetheless, Lawrence was convinced that his "countryful of swine" looked forward to the rout: "They want in their vile underneath way of working to scuttle the old ship and pitch everybody into water. Well, let them. Perhaps when we've all had a ducking in the sea of fearful disaster, we shall be more wholesome and truthful."[6]

Lloyd George's first major speech convinced Lawrence that England was headed for chaos and horror: "The man means nothing, stands for nothing, is nothing: and he mechanically does what Germany does, and the nation vociferously cries 'Hear, Hear.'" Typically enough, though Lawrence also scorned those who opposed the new prime minister's policies of blood and iron. After reading the papers she had sent him, he told Barbara Low that "if one is to do anything real in this Country, one must eschew all connection with Fabianism, Socialism, Cambridgeism, and advancedism of all sorts, like poison. It is a nasty form of dry rot in the human species. One must go out on one's own, *unadhering.* I would rather, myself, appear in the Morning Post than anywhere: but of course it is unthinkable."[7] The *Morning Post* took a jingoistic line on the war and opposed women's suffrage but Lawrence had long respected its gentlemanly tone, "such a relief after the majority of newspaper filth." The liberal reformers, on the other hand, were "our disease, not our hope. . . . Fusty, fuzzy peace-cranks and lovers of humanity are the devil. We must get on a new track altogether."[8]

Lawrence's politics amounted to this: that the pacifists were wrong because they invoked an ideal version of "what the people wanted," and that Lloyd George was wrong because he pandered, all too skillfully, to the actual "currish desire" of the bottom dog. In either case it was accepted that "the people" set the standard of value. What England really needed, Lawrence told Dollie Radford, was:

> . . . a republic based on the idea of extrinsic equality and intrinsic inequality. . . . We are only equal in so far as that every man should have equal opportunity to come to his own fulfilment. But that every man should come to the same fulfilment is mere rubbish, and that every fulfilment is equal to every other is mere meaningless words.—What the world needs to learn, today, is to give due honor to those who are finer in spirit, and to know the inferiority of those who are mean and paltry in spirit.

The question remained, how was the world to be taught its lesson? Living in Cornwall, Lawrence had become even more unrealistic—if that were possible—about the practical methods of politics. With persuasion and organization he would have nothing to do; he would only issue manifestos when the spirit moved him, then howl against the wind when no one responded. Fundamentally, he did not want to state his views publicly at all. He told Dollie that peace was likely within six months but his recipe for achieving it showed why his political initiatives were bound to end in failure and farce: "Let us gather our souls and bring it to pass, by prayer or whatever it is. I firmly believe that the pure desire of the strong creates the great events, without any action: like the prayer of the saints. I firmly believe that." [9]

To take any action on the war, however quixotic, Lawrence would have had to return to London; for a month or so after receiving the sixty pounds from Amy Lowell he planned to go there, but whenever it came to the point of actually leaving he could not do it. His move to London the previous August had turned out so disastrously that he wanted some favorable sign before he would leave the country again, and Lloyd George's access to power was nothing of the sort. "I can conceive myself down here, still waiting," Lawrence told Gertler. "An old, hook-nosed, benevolent old man, living on crusts and charity. So be it—its very nice down here, much nicer than anywhere else." [10] He determined therefore to postpone his political schemes and continue to lie low. But even his quiet corner would not remain undisturbed.

The Reception of *Women in Love*

THOUGH LAWRENCE would not reenter the social world in person the manuscripts of *Women in Love* were received there as a disturbing token of his presence. Sending a copy to Catherine Carswell, he ventured a little allegory of its fate: "I wrote this [letter] during a great hail-storm—that is the storm of abuse and persecution. Now the sun shines sweetly on the MS. —that is the light of victory." [11] But he very soon discovered that the hailstorm was likely to continue, and to blow from more than one quarter simultaneously. Only three weeks after he had sent a copy to Pinker he learnt that Methuen would not exercise their option on the book. Lawrence's next hope was that "faithful Duckworth"—who had recently published *Twilight in Italy* and *Amores*—would "rise up and be noble." [12] But both books had been commercial failures, and if Duckworth took *Women in Love* it would have to reckon with the additional danger of another police raid. Pinker impressed on Lawrence how commercially handicapped the novel was by this risk; his response was to seek aristocratic protection for the book, "in the 18th-century fashion." Cynthia Asquith was the obvious person to ask for suggestions: "Do you know anybody of any weight or importance, who would take it under his, or her, protection, so far as to accept a serious dedication? It is a much finer book than *The Rainbow,* and I would rather it were never published at all than insulted by petty dogs as that was." A week before, Lawrence had asked if she would accept the dedication of a book of poems, and he was perhaps hinting that the novel was similarly available. But the Asquiths themselves were as vulnerable to the "newspaper curs" as Lawrence was; Lady Cynthia must have pointed out to him the folly of his scheme for in his next letter he apologized for being the kind of person who was "always asking of [her] something [she] couldn't do."[13] He soon realized, in any case, that it would take more than aristocratic patronage to get England to accept his novel.

While Pinker negotiated with publishers, the private circulation of the other manuscript of *Women in Love* was spawning fresh intrigues. At first Lawrence wanted to keep the book away from the Garsington grapevine: "I want you and Carswell to read it," he told Catherine, "and *please* make any corrections necessary, and tell me any discrepancy. *Don't let anybody else read it.* . . . Ask Don if he thinks any part libellous—e.g. Halliday is Heseltine, the Pussum is a model called the Puma, and they are taken from life—nobody else at all lifelike." Just a few days later, however, Lawrence received a letter from Ottoline, "saying she hears she is the villainness of the new book. It is very strange how rumours go round." It is hard to believe that he would be surprised at "Hermione Roddice" being taken as a portrait of Ottoline, yet he consistently denied the resemblance. Had he not made changes from his actual relation with Ottoline—having Hermione attack Birkin with the lapis lazuli paperweight, for example? So far as he was concerned, such changes meant that Hermione was not a "lifelike" representation of Ottoline; he failed to see that many of them would only increase the novel's offensiveness to her. Above all she must have been shocked that Lawrence made Hermione Birkin's mistress, for Ottoline was acutely sensitive to gossip that made her into a kind of intellectual Catherine the Great, inveigling handsome young artists into her boudoir.

By coincidence Lawrence reveived just at this time a copy of Gilbert Cannan's novel *Mendel,* which was closely based on Gertler's actual career. "Gertler, Jew-like, has told every detail of his life to Gilbert," Lawrence told Catherine Carswell. "—Gilbert has a lawyer's memory and has put it all down."[14] To Kot, Lawrence expressed more sympathy for Gertler: "it is, as Gertler says, journalism: statement, without creation. This is very sickening. If Gilbert had taken Gertler's story and *re-created* it into art, *good.* But to set down all these statements is a vulgarising of life itself."[15] The formula may have satisfied Lawrence, but it was not likely to satisfy those who felt betrayed by the way he used his friendship with them in his fiction.

It seems, then, that Lawrence was acting in good faith when he told Ottoline he would send her the manuscript of *Women in Love* to show her that her fears were unjustified. The novel first passed through the hands of Barbara Low and Esther Andrews, and reached Ottoline about New Year's Day. She was, of course, appalled by it. "Lawrence has sent me his *awful* Book," she told Russell, "It is so loathesome one can not get clean after it—and a most insulting Chapter with *minute* photograph of Garsington and a horrible disgusting portrait of me making me out as if filled with cruel devilish *Lust.* Isn't it a shame After having been friendly but it is of course Frieda's revenge."[16] Ottoline claimed in her memoirs that until this moment she had no idea Lawrence held any resentment against her; perhaps she was overly impressed by his refusal to intervene in her quarrel with Frieda. In any case, she was shocked by the depth of his malice:

> I was called every name from an 'old hag', obsessed by sex-mania, to a corrupt Sapphist. He described me as his own discarded Mistress. . . . In another scene I had attempted to make indecent advances to the Heroine, who was a glorified Frieda. My dresses were dirty; I was rude and insolent to my guests. . . .
>
> On I read, chapter after chapter, scene after scene, all written, as far as I could tell, in order to humiliate me. The only assuagement to the shock was that all the worst parts were written in Frieda's handwriting.[17]

Frieda had done no more than transcribe revisions from the other copy of the manuscript; still, these revisions showed that Lawrence was inclined to paint Hermione in much darker colors in November than he had done in the earlier version of July and August. Though he had little contact with Ottoline during the intervening months, he may have been incensed by her chilly response to the apologetic letter Frieda sent her in September. Nor could he have been happy to hear that Jack and Katherine were being drawn into Ottoline's orbit. Whatever his motives in portraying Ottoline as Hermione, he was certainly not inclined to disown his work, as he defiantly announced to Catherine Carswell: "Ottoline Morrell was in a frenzy over the novel: I told her it was her own fault, there was nothing to be in a frenzy over. So now I expect we are enemies for ever. I don't care. I don't care if every English person is my enemy—if they wish it, so be it."[18]

So far as Lawrence was concerned the duel was over, but Ottoline did not consider her honor satisfied. Her bitterness was sustained by the dreadful suspicion that Lawrence might indeed have perceived a truth about her that she could not herself admit: "Was I really like that, I wondered, and for many months the ghastly portrait of myself, written by someone whom I had trusted and liked haunted my thoughts and horrified me."[19] But such doubts did not affect her concern to rally to her side anyone who had been friendly with both herself and the Lawrences. Though Brett had been ecstatic about Lawrence in autumn 1915, and would be so again, she now declared a cautious allegiance to Ottoline; Katherine Mansfield also gave support and practical advice:

> Dearest I hardly know what to write about Lawrence. Brett has told me [word illegible] and all about the book and I can imagine how bad it is. There is no doubt about it: left to himself Lawrence goes mad. When he is with people he expands to the warmth and the light in them—he is a Darling and often very wonderful, but left to himself he is cold and dark and desolate. Of course Frieda is at the bottom of it. He has chosen Frieda and when he is with real people he [finds?] how fatal that choice is. But his cursed obstinacy eggs him on in his loneliness with her to justify his choice, by any means—by even the lowest methods. I feel I understand him so well and the whole huge unreal fabric that he builds up as his 'house' against the world. And I am *sure* there is only one way to answer him. It is very cruel but it's the only weapon to prick his sensitive pride. It is to laugh at him—to make fun of him—to make him realise that he has made a fool of himself. *Anything* else will only make him feel like Christ whipping out the temple mongers. I have always realised that he needs to be laughed at more than anything. It cures his madness. At the time it makes him furious but then quite suddenly he sees himself spinning round on one toe and he laughs, too. But he ought not to be allowed to go on. He *must* be stopped. I think it is really *fatal* that such books should be published.[20]

Apart from the psychological analysis of Lawrence—which was of dubious value, since Ottoline was in no laughing mood— Katherine's letter gave plain encouragement to Ottoline to take legal action against the novel. For a time, however, she held her fire; meanwhile the manuscript was making the rounds of one publisher after another. They all refused it, "dear old Duckworth" included. "I don't wonder at it, if no one will publish the novel," Lawrence told Pinker. "When I read the newspapers, I see it would be vain. It does not matter very much—later will be better. It is a book that will laugh last." "It is not that it is so 'improper,'" he explained to Eddie Marsh, "but that it is too directly in antagonism with the existing state of squilch."[21] The only hope seemed to lie in Kot's offer to translate the novel into Russian; Lawrence devoted a good deal of time and enthusiasm to this plan, though Catherine Carswell thought it was largely a device whereby Kot hoped to induce his needy friend to accept the loan of ten pounds!

By the middle of February Lawrence had virtually given up hope of getting *Women in Love* accepted; then Ottoline came to fire her shot into the corpse. She sent Philip to warn Pinker that "if [the novel] was published as it stood he should bring action against the Publishers for libel."[22] When Lawrence heard the news he was already so worn down by the novel's other difficulties that he was more disgusted than angry:

> Really, the world has gone completely dotty! Hermione is not much more like Ottoline Morrell than Queen Victoria.... Ottoline flatters herself. There is a hint of her in the character of Hermione: but so there is a hint of a million women, if it comes to that....
>
> But it doesn't matter. It is no use trying to publish the novel in England.... The novel can lie by till there is an end of the war and a change of feeling over the world. And poor vindictive old Ottoline can be left to her vanity of identifying herself with Hermione. What does it all matter![23]

Indeed, Lawrence had drawn on Ottoline for the "shell" of Hermione while for her inner qualities—her lack of sexual spontaneity, her violence toward Birkin—he had also borrowed a good deal from Jessie Chambers and from Frieda herself (in her hostile aspect). But it would not have been easy to explain that to a jury.

Two months later Lawrence gave Cynthia Asquith a fuller version of Philip Morrell's dealings with Pinker (who was, of course, not his publisher but his agent):

> [Lawrence] said he had not made a portrait of Ottoline in his new novel. His woman was infinitely superior, but the Morrells were so furious at the supposed lampoon that Morrell wrote—inconceivable as it sounds—to the pub-

lisher, asking him to come down [to Garsington] and to identify the character as his wife, and Ottoline asked Lawrence to return an opal pin she had given him. Fancy calling in that worm of a publisher as detective![24]

This must have seemed a perfect stroke of irony to Lawrence, given that just over a year before Morrell had been working with Pinker *against* the suppression of *The Rainbow;* the volte-face was so complete that it must have seemed an act of deliberate malice. David Garnett, indeed, recalled that "we thought very badly of Ottoline for suppressing *Women in Love*";[25] by "we" one takes him to mean Bloomsbury, especially the Duncan Grant and Vanessa Bell axis. Ottoline's behavior may be explained, if not excused, by two nasty shocks she had just suffered. First, Bertrand Russell had decided to "shake her off," in part because he was now deeply in love with Colette O'Neil; he did so with considerable cruelty, telling her that her hair was turning gray and she was "very uninstinctive." When he complained of her making him unhappy, she replied: "Perhaps after all Lawrence's view of me in his book is partly True. (It is a far worse onslaught on me than his Letter to you—and Trumpeted forth to the Public)."[26] Then came an even harsher blow: she learned that Philip—whom her smart friends made fun of, and who had tolerated so many of her own sexual vagaries—had been unfaithful to her. Regardless of the "justice" of the affair, the news caused her to suffer a severe nervous breakdown; Philip's draconian measures against *Women in Love* were, it would seem, the product of both his own sense of guilt and a real concern for his wife's sanity if she were exposed to public ridicule. One may therefore condone his apparent betrayal of his liberal principles; but what is one to make of Katherine Mansfield's role? She was simultaneously encouraging Ottoline to sue Lawrence and encouraging Bertrand Russell to discard Ottoline; while Jack, five years later, would review the English edition of *Women in Love* in terms almost as provocative and tendentious as those applied to *The Rainbow* by the harshest critics of 1915.

One definite result of the whole tawdry affair was Ottoline's resolve to sever all ties with Lawrence. "I never saw [him] again," she wrote, "although he made several attempts through our mutual friends to see me. I did not think it would be possible for me to behave naturally or unself-consciously in his presence. The hurt that he had done me made a very great mark in my life." Her

(276)

antipathy was reinforced when she heard, later, "that Lawrence and Frieda had spread terrible and horrible stories about me—a mixture, I suppose, of his bad conscience and perversity and her victorious spite." The kernel of these stories, probably, was Frieda's claim that Ottoline had "played Salome to Lawrence's John the Baptist"; that a Cavendish-Bentinck should be accused of trying to entice into her bed the son of a local collier must have seemed the unkindest slander of them all.[27]

Escape to the West?

THOUGH LAWRENCE freely proclaimed *Women in Love* "a masterpiece," he recognized that its reception in London marked, for the time being at least, the end of his career as a novelist. In the social world, furthermore, his vendetta with Lady Ottoline cut him off from the only substantial group of British artists and intellectuals who opposed the war. For all his contempt for the Bloomsbury set, he knew that they were able to protect conscientious objectors from the worst malevolence of the authorities, and to find them tolerable jobs doing "work of national importance." They had done just that for Jack. Until recently, also, Lawrence could expect his friendship with Lady Cynthia to shield him from official persecution; but Asquith's fall removed that comfort (which was mostly an illusion, anyway). Lawrence was therefore displaying a sober realism when, toward the end of 1916, he revived his plan of a year before to move to America.

His decision became firm during the visit to Higher Tregerthen in early November of two young American journalists, Robert Mountsier and Esther Andrews. Lawrence was obsessed at the time with the hope of escape, and Mountsier seemed able to help him. He had first met Lawrence at the time of *The Rainbow* troubles, and was now eager to act as his advance man in New York. A week before, Lawrence had hoped to move to Italy to escape the "terrible moisture" of the Cornish autumn but now, under the influence of his recent visitors, he told Catherine Carswell (in strict confidence) that he had decided to go westward instead:

> I *know* now, finally: (a) That I want to go away from England for ever. (b) That I want *ultimately* to go to a country of which I have hope, in which I feel the new unknown. In short, I want, immediately or at length, to transfer all my life to America. Because there, I know, the *skies* are not so old, the air is newer, the earth is not tired. Don't think I have any illusions about the people, the life. The people and the life are monstrous. I want, at length, to get a place in the far west mountains, from which one can see the distant Pacific Ocean, and there live facing the bright west. But I also think that America, being so much *worse,* falser, further gone than England, is nearer to freedom.[28]

After the deception of the past year, Lawrence was stepping with extreme care through the thicket of personal relationships. Though he liked Mountsier very much, he did not make of him a white hope like the now disgraced Heseltine. The Carswells were invited to join him and Frieda in America, but only when they were themselves convinced that the time had come to leave England. "I *know* my Florida idea was right," Lawrence told Catherine. "It was quite right, all save the people. It is wrong to seek adherents. One must be single. . . . Above all, conserve yourself, and live only in marriage, not elsewhere."[29] Though Lawrence had many "adherents" in the remaining thirteen years of his life, his attitude toward them was almost whimsically tolerant, even patronizing: the defections of Jack, of Heseltine, and of so many others, had at last convinced him to limit his hopes of Rananim to a partnership of convenience rather than an outpost of the New Jerusalem.

The move to America also seemed financially promising since *Seven Arts,* a New York magazine, had offered Lawrence a cent a word for any short stories he cared to submit. Amy Lowell's gift of sixty pounds would pay the Lawrences' fare to America and help them get settled though Lawrence cagily told Amy, and Lady Cynthia also, that he would use the money to move to Italy for the winter. He hoped to hurl the thunderbolt of *Women in Love* against his false friends then quietly slip away in the midst of the confusion. For two months, then, Lawrence kept his counsel while waiting for Mountsier to return to America and prepare the way for him. But the fall of Asquith in early December began a run of ill luck that soon convinced Lawrence that the quicker he set out for America the better. Lloyd George's accession made it impractical to work privately for peace, the first rejection of *Women in Love* came in the middle of the month, and Pinker could not sell the story "The Mortal Coil"—which Lawrence had sent him a month earlier—probably because of its morbid subject and German setting. Lawrence had planned to write only "salable" short stories, but now it seemed that in England he could not succeed even in that modest aim. "I am sick of poking about in a corner, up to the neck in poverty. It is enough. I think America is my untilled field."[30]

Lawrence prepared for his departure by inviting Mountsier and Esther Andrews to come down again and spend Christmas at Zennor. He had planned to come to London in December, but canceled the trip when he realized just how unappetizing the political atmosphere would be, and how little he really wanted to see people like Jack or Gordon Campbell. "What an ugly farce Christmas is this year," he told Catherine. "Will anybody *dare* to sing carols, etc. Pah, it all stinks. What a pity you cannot poison Mrs. Carswell [her mother-in-law]."[31] The first Christmas of the war Lawrence had spent gaily enough with his circle of friends at Chesham; by the second he had fallen back on his family in the Midlands; now he wanted to see only the two Americans who could help him leave England altogether. For six months—from October 1916 to April 1917—they were the only people from outside Cornwall that Lawrence saw at all.

As if to seal Lawrence's conviction of "the end of England," a police sergeant from St. Ives cycled the seven miles out to Tregerthen on the rainy night of Christmas Eve to question Mountsier and check his papers; he returned later with a military officer, for more interrogation. Still, the Lawrences went ahead with their planned celebrations. They invited four of the Hockings to come up from the farm: William Henry, his brother Stanley, and his sisters Mabel and Mary. All sat at a round table in the upper room of the tower, and Lawrence proclaimed that "Everyone here shall be equal tonight." After dinner Stanley played his accordion and they all sang, with Frieda drawing on her repertoire of German folk songs, some learned when she was a child from the soldiers of the garrison at Metz. But Lawrence was glad when it was over he told Catherine; he felt "smothered and wreary, and buried alive in the world," and Christmas only seemed to mire him deeper in despondency.[32]

When Mountsier returned to London at the end of the week—leaving Esther Andrews behind at Tregerthen—Lawrence was jolted from his apathy. According to the account in *Kangaroo,* Mountsier was "arrested, and conveyed to Scotland Yard: there examined stripped naked, his clothes taken away. Then he was kept for a night in a cell—next evening liberated and advised to return to America." Lawrence was of course outraged by the episode but he felt some *schadenfreude* also, since Mountsier had upset Frieda by his eagerness for America to enter the war against Germany: "I am glad the British lion, which you have always held such an admirable beast, has pawed you about a bit in its bestial and ugly fashion: now you will know the enemy, and where he lies. These ancient nationalities are foul in the extreme." What a pleasure it would be, he fantasized, to "just say to the fools 'Yes, I am the cleverest spy in the universe,' and set them ransacking nothingness to its farthest corners." But failing this, the best thing was for them all to escape across the Atlantic in February: "I have *finally* decided," Lawrence told Mountsier, "that it is only possible to live out of this world—make a sort of Garden of Eden of blameless but fulfilled souls, in some sufficiently remote spot—the Marquesas Islands, Nukuheva. Let us do that. I am sick to death of the world of man—had enough. Why should one go on, beyond the nausea." [33]

Samoa, Tahiti, Nukuheva were for Lawrence "places with the magic names . . . the sleep and the forgetting of this great life, the very body of dreams"; Nukuheva specially fascinated him as the setting for Melville's *Typee,* which he read in early December. Already when reading *Moby Dick* the previous February he had wanted to "go a long voyage into the South Pacific," but Melville's sunnier first book appealed to him even more: "Melville found in Typee almost what he wanted to find, what every man dreams of finding: a perfect home among timeless, unspoiled savages. There, in Nukuheva, the European psyche, with its ideals and its limitations, had no place. Our artificial ethical laws had never existed. There was naked simplicity of life, with subtle, but non-mental understanding, *rapport* between human beings." [34]

Lawrence promptly set about clearing the way for his voyage to Cythera. "I cannot get a single thing I write published in England," he told Eddie Marsh. "There is no sale of the books that *are* published. So I am dished." He asked Eddie to find him some obscure government post, "away off in one of the Pacific islands, where we could both live in peace. I don't want to have anything to do whatsoever with quarrelling nations. If I could have some little peaceful job to do, I would do it and be thankful. But not in England—I couldn't stand it."[35] As Asquith's secretary for civil list pensions Eddie had been able to get the Order of Merit for the dying Henry James and a grant of one hundred pounds for the impoverished James Joyce. But when Asquith fell in December Eddie fell with him, down to a menial clerkship in the basement of the Colonial Office. He continued his literary patronage through his private means but Lawrence, with his banned novel and his German wife, was not a credible candidate for a government job.

Still, Lawrence felt he must pull every string to get to America, or suffer a nervous collapse like that of the previous January at Porthcothan. "I *can't* go on living here on a miserable pittance which Pinker. . . . will allow me," he complained to Lady Cynthia. "It is too insulting."[36] In Cornwall he felt like a fox cornered by hounds, like Laocoön crushed by snakes, like a man buried alive. His letters at this time are filled with images that point to his fear of another bronchial crisis like the one that almost killed him a year before: "Here, the very physical atmosphere, consisting of hydrogen and oxygen and nitrogen and God knows what, hurts, starves, injures my spirit by being breathed into my lungs and blood. . . . I can't breathe here."[37] Fortunately, he passed through the crucial period of December to February with only a minor cold, even though that winter was one of the worst in living memory; probably the isolation of Higher Tregerthen protected him from more dangerous infections.

Lawrence's relatively good health seems also to have benefited his nerves, except for one apocalyptic letter when Mountsier requested an article on the wartime recruitment of women into traditional male occupations. Lawrence replied that he hadn't "the guts" to write it:

> All I can say is, that in the tearing asunder of the sexes lies the universal death, in the assuming of the male activities by the female, there takes place the horrid swallowing of her own young, by the woman. . . . I am sure woman will destroy man, intrinsically, in this country. But there is something in me, which stops still and becomes dark, when I think of it. . . . I am sure there is some ghastly Clytemnestra victory ahead, for the women. . . .
>
> I don't want to think about it any more. . . . My way is elsewhere. It is not I

who will stay to see Medea borne up on a chariot in heaven. That belongs to the tearing asunder, of which I have had enough. I am going now out of this Sodom.[38]

He found something particularly sinister in women controlling machinery and taking over traditionally masculine jobs.* In part this was a private obsession that may be traced back to his sexual humiliation by a gang of girl workers at Haywood's surgical factory, when he was a sensitive youth of nineteen; in part it was a general distaste for the female emancipation that came as a side effect of the war.

Still, England's fate seemed of little moment so long as only a few formalities prevented the Lawrences' departure for America. Eddie Marsh wanted assurance that he would not be politically embarrassed if he supplied a reference for the passport office, so Lawrence again dissociated himself from the antiwar movement:

> Have I showed any public pacifist activity?—do you mean the Signature?—At any rate, I am not a pacifist. I have come to the conclusion that mankind is not one web and fabric, with one common being. That veil is rent for me. I know that for those who make war, war is undeniably right, it is even their vindication of their being. I know also, that for me, war, at least this war, is utterly wrong, a gastly and unthinkable falsity. And there it is. One's old great belief in the oneness and wholeness of humanity is torn clean across, for ever.[39]

In short, Lawrence was not renouncing his opposition to the war but he renounced any attempt to influence others against it. He asked Pinker to confirm his reasons for going: ill health, lack of money, and a desire to arrange the publication of *The Rainbow* and *Women in Love* in New York. Gordon Campbell he asked for legal support, if necessary. Campbell's father, the lord chief justice of Ireland, had just been made a baronet; Lawrence, as usual, was counting straws in the wind but failing to realize the limits of personal influence.

On 12 February Lawrence and Frieda learned that the endorsements were denied. The Foreign Office was apparently willing to let them go, but the military authorities would only allow people to leave for a purpose that served the national interest. One suspects, however, that in this case the refusal was more than just a routine assertion of the state's power to control labor. In early

---

* He returned to this theme in the story "Tickets Please" (1919), about a maenadlike crew of women tram conductors who mob their male superintendent.

1917 a diplomatic crisis was brewing over America's possible entry into the war, and the British government was highly sensitive to American public opinion. Mountsier had come to England to write articles for the American press and was probably arrested because of his contact with Frieda; not only was she under routine surveillance as a "person of hostile origin," she was also known to be in contact with her family via Switzerland—a family whose name was now becoming a household word in Britain through the exploits of her cousin Manfred von Richthofen, the "Red Baron." After Mountsier's arrest, Lawrence suggested he should make contact with Bertrand Russell and the leadership of the Union of Democratic Control; this would certainly have created further suspicion if the intelligence services got wind of it.

As if to complete Lawrence's feeling of entrapment, on 31 January Germany declared a blockade of the British Isles through unrestricted submarine warfare, which meant that neutral ships could be sunk if they approached England. "The world is one slab of horror," Lawrence told Mountsier, "It can't go on: this is really breaking-point. . . . If America declares war, I think I shall die outright." Meanwhile there was the immediate shock of submarine warfare right at their doorstep:

> Yesterday two ships were submarined just off here: luckily we didn't see them: but Stanley [Hocking] watched one go down, and the coastwatchers saw the crew of the other struggling in the water after the ship had gone: all drowned: Norwegians I believe. My sister writes a ghastly story from Glasgow, of a new and splendid submarine on her trial trip in the Clyde: she dived and never came up, all watching expected her. But I cannot bear it, it makes me tremble. It can't go on, it is the maximum of evil. . . . There is a kind of fiendishness triumphant over the earth.[40]

The situation looked so bleak that Lawrence could imagine no recourse but to try again, in a little while, for permission to leave. "You mustn't think I haven't cared about England," he told Lady Cynthia. "I have cared deeply and bitterly. But something is broken. There *is not* any England. One must look now for another world. This is only a tomb." But to Catherine Carswell, who was neither aristocratic nor English, he was able to vent his full bitterness at being held back from the New World:

> I curse my country with my soul and body, it is a country accursed physically and spiritually. Let it be accursed forever, accursed and blasted. Let the seas

swallow it, let the waters cover it, so that it is no more. And let it be known as accursed England, the country of the damned. I curse it, I curse England, I curse the English, man, woman, and child, in their nationality let them be accursed and hated and never forgiven.[41]

So ended Lawrence's hopes for America. *Women in Love* had been such a full and measured indictment of English society that it seemed supremely appropriate for its author to go into exile on completing it; the ultimate irony, then, was for the England he had so excoriated to refuse to let him go. During the remainder of the war period Lawrence seems to have lost his role both as a man and as an artist; demanding a "new sky" over him before he can freely create, he feels stifled by the same narrow horizon of his native country. His writings become smaller in scale and more cramped, the voice of a fettered muse.

Stories, Poems, and *The Reality of Peace*

AFTER SENDING OFF the manuscript of *Women in Love* Lawrence told Kot he was not working and needed books to read, mainly about America and Italy since he hoped to be living in one country or the other before long. He was particularly impressed by Melville's *Typee* and Fenimore Cooper's *Deerslayer* which helped inspire, later in 1917, his next major creative work: *Studies in Classic American Literature*. But his first writings after the novel were stories that he thought of as simple potboilers. In late summer T. D. Dunlop had sent him some manuscripts that he had left behind at Lerici in 1914. They included a story of German military life, "The Mortal Coil"; Lawrence sent it to Pinker but no English magazine would take it. He followed it up, on 6 November, with "Samson and Delilah," a story dashed off in the midst of final revisions to *Women in Love*. The story, about a woman whose husband deserted her and then came back to claim her after fifteen years in America, was probably based on an actual episode and its setting resembled "The Tinner's Arms" at Zennor. It was published in March 1917 by the *English Review,* though when it ap-

peared Lawrence professed not to care for it. Around the middle
of December he sent off a third story, "The Miracle"; this was set
in the Midlands and may also have been quarried from the Italian
manuscripts since it has no reference to the war. No one would
publish it, a failure that seems to have convinced Lawrence that it
was futile to seek popularity by turning out "salable" items. In
1921, however, he revised it for the collection *England, My England;* now renamed "The Horse-Dealer's Daughter," it became
one of his most famous stories.

Lawrence also turned his attention to poetry again while waiting to leave for America. Cynthia Asquith had sent him a collection of her husband's poems, on which he rendered a relatively
diplomatic verdict:

> At any rate he is not a deader, like Rupert Brooke: one can smell death in
> Rupert: thank heaven, not really here: only the sniff of curiosity, not the great
> inhalation of desire. (You won't mind what I say.) I think Herbert Asquith is a
> poet—which is after all the most valuable thing on earth. But he is not writing
> *himself* at all here—not his own realities. Most of this is *vieux jeux.* [42]

Some two weeks later Lawrence sent Lady Cynthia a "tiny book"
of his own poems which he wanted to dedicate to her, a gesture
that implied a subtle rivalry with her husband. When the collection was eventually published as *Bay* in 1919 it included eighteen
poems, almost all written during the war and attempting to catch
the atmosphere of the Home Front. Most of them, however, seem
sketchy and unconvincing; exceptions are "Bread upon the Waters" and "Obsequial Ode," poignant addresses to soldiers who
have "achieved their fate" in death.

But the work on *Bay* was only the prelude to finishing a more
vital record of Lawrence's emotional development: the gathering
of all the poems he had written about himself and Frieda from
their first meeting in March 1912 down to the present. "It is a sort
of final conclusion of the old life in me" he told Catherine Carswell, "—'and now farewell,' is really the motto. I don't much want
to submit the MS. for publication. It is very intimate and vital to
me." [43] Lawrence's working title at this time was "Poems of a Married Man." When he sent the completed manuscript to Catherine,
just after he was denied permission to go to America, the title had
become "Man and Woman." "I wonder what it will seem to you,"
he asked her, "—this book of poems. It will either seem much, or

very little."[44] Lawrence held back for six weeks before sending the poems to Pinker on 3 April. Reluctant as he was to expose his love for Frieda to the inevitable jeers, he needed to keep his name before the public and earn whatever small sums he could by writing.

Look! We Have Come Through!—as the collection was finally called—was largely made up of prewar poems, many of them written at Villa Igea on Lake Garda in 1912–1913. But a few date from the war years, notably three long poems that give a philosophical summation of the Lawrences' love affair and marriage: "New Heaven and Earth" (written at Greatham), "Manifesto," and "Craving for Spring." The probable date of "Manifesto" is early summer 1916, after the Murrys had left Tregerthen and Lawrence was working out, through Birkin, his doctrine of "singleness" in love. The early sections of the poem tell how the poet has satisfied his basic needs: for means to live, for knowledge, for sexual fulfillment, and for the love of one woman. Yet still something lies beyond:

To be, or not to be, is still the question.
This ache for being is the ultimate hunger.
And for myself, I can say "almost, almost, oh, very nearly." . . .
I know her now: or perhaps, I know my own limitations against her. . . .
It is that one comes to.
A curious agony, and a relief, when I touch that which is not me in any sense,
it wounds me to death with my own not-being; definite, inviolable
    limitation, . . .

Love and sexuality are for Lawrence the keys to the central problem of how to define the boundaries of the self. Because of his special intimacy with his mother and his abnormal sensitivity to other people's emotions, Lawrence seemed to live as intensely outside himself as he did in the more introspective world of the personal ego. This talent, quickly recognized by critics, brought him early success as a writer; but in the war years he came to feel that it was a tainted gift. His earlier sense of oceanic union with humanity changed, now that hatred and destruction prevailed everywhere, into a state of paranoid exacerbation in which he was constantly fearful and "sick of mankind." Now he wanted Frieda to help him build up higher the walls of his ego instead of trying to merge with him:

(286)

ZENNOR: The Buried Life

She has not realised yet, that fearful thing, that I am the other,
She thinks we are all of one piece.
It is painfully untrue.

I want her to touch me at last, ah, on the root and quick of my darkness
and perish on me, as I have perished on her.

Then, we shall be two and distinct, we shall have each our separate being.
And that will be pure existence, real liberty.

Since everything must rely on its opposite for definition, the differences between men and women must be kept sharp lest both be left suspended in the void of nonbeing.

"Manifesto" ends with a vision of universal solipsistic vitalism. Here, as so often in Lawrence, metaphysics is grounded in biology: the poet embraces even the harshest implications of Darwinism and finds them good, in a complete inversion of Tennyson's Victorian fear of nature "red in tooth and claw," at strife with both itself and God:

Every man himself, and therefore, a surpassing singleness of mankind.
The blazing tiger will spring upon the deer, undimmed,
the hen will nestle over her chickens,
we shall love, we shall hate,
but it will be like music, sheer utterance,
issuing straight out of the unknown,
the lightning and the rainbow appearing in us unbidden, unchecked,
like ambassadors.
We shall now look before and after.
We shall *be, now.*
We shall know in full.
We, the mystic NOW.

If this should seem like a paean to mere bloodthirstiness, one should recall that Lawrence was not one of those who, like Tennyson or Kipling, viewed war as a bracing purge for a society gone slack; wars, he believed, were caused by too much repression of instinct rather than too little.

Look! We Have Come Through! ends with poems on Autumn, Winter, and "Craving for Spring," the last one probably written in February 1917 as Lawrence was completing the manuscript. The poem offers one of his typically inconclusive conclusions, filled with intense longing for a renewal of both nature and society.

In the prefatory "Argument" to *Look! We Have Come Through!*
Lawrence asserts that the man and woman, after their long conflict of love and hate, "transcend into some condition of blessedness"; but the last poems express desire rather than fulfillment.
Though the poems, together with *Women in Love,* helped to clarify
the struggle between Lawrence and Frieda they did not necessarily bring that struggle any closer to resolution.

One other literary project in the period just after *Women in Love*
was a series of lectures on American literature that Lawrence
hoped to deliver when he arrived in New York. After Christmas
he asked Mountsier to send him a shelf of American classics so
that he could start; but work on *Look! We Have Come Through!* intervened and by the time it was finished, on 18 February,
Lawrence and Frieda had been denied permission to travel. So he
set aside the American lectures. Instead, he rapidly wrote seven
philosophical essays on "The Reality of Peace." "Philosophy inter-
ests me most now," he told Murry later in the spring, "—not
novels or stories. I find people ultimately boring: and you can't
have fiction without people. So fiction does not, at the bottom, interest me any more. I am weary of humanity and human things.
One is happy in the thoughts only that transcend humanity." [45]

"The Reality of Peace" reiterated the message of "Craving for
Spring": that the "mass of mortification" now stifling the war-torn
world should be purged away in a cosmic drama of renewal. The
essays were frankly propagandistic, though they were as unsuccessful in this aim as Lawrence's recent "money-making stories"
were at making money. Nonetheless, he had the usual high hopes
of them: "They are very beautiful and, I think, very important.
. . . We must think *hard* about their publication. *We must begin now
to work for a new world, a creative peace.*" [46] Four of the essays were
published by the *English Review* but Austin Harrison, the editor,
refused the last three and they were subsequently lost.

Lawrence again explained the war as a subconscious desire of
the masses for death, a process that would not be complete until
England had a civil war as sequel to the Great War. But he now
renounced both the socialism and the authoritarianism that he
had espoused earlier: *all* political struggle, as a product of the
organized will, destroys the free play of impulse that makes for
life. Though in 1915 Lawrence had embraced the doctrine of
Heraclitus that "all things come into being and pass away through
strife" he now sought relief from such an eternal conflict of op-

posites. The solution lay neither in a willful commitment to one side, nor in a denial of the conflict, but in the full "realisation" of our intrinsic, inevitable duality:

> We are not only creatures of light and virtue. We are also alive in corruption and death. It is necessary to balance the dark against the light if we are ever going to be free . . .
>
> If there is a serpent of secret and shameful desire in my soul, let me not beat it out of my consciousness, where I cannot follow it with my sticks. Let me bring it to the fire to see what it is. . . .
>
> I shall accept all my desires and repudiate none. It will be a sign of bliss in me when I am reconciled with the serpent of my own horror, when I am free both from the fascination and the revulsion. For secret fascination is a fearful tyranny.[47]

Though the argument is that the repression of *any* desire is harmful, the imagery in these passages—of putrescence, snakes, the marsh—points to a special concern with anality and homosexuality. Lawrence implies, further, that those who have come to terms with their darkest impulses make up a small group of *illuminati* who are the true makers of history. They are opposed by two kinds of people. On one side are the false initiates: those like Loerke in fiction, or J. M. Keynes in actuality, who know something of the secret doctrine but pervert it into purely destructive ends. Such men figure in Lawrence's obsession with the Judas figure, whom he often imagines as a decadent homosexual. On the other side are the torpid and egotistical masses; Lawrence's great fear was that this "flock which counts me part of itself compresses me and squeezes me with slow malice to death." "The slaves have got the upper hand," he proclaimed, so the initiates should "go forth with whips, like the old chieftain." Implicitly, he welcomed the war as a completion of the task the whips had begun:

> Smash, beautiful destructive death, smash the complete will of the hosts of man, the will of the self-absorbed bug. . . . They have defied you so long. They have even, in their mad arrogance, begun to deal in death as if it also were subjugated. They thought to use death as they have used life this long time, for their own base end of nullification. . . . Let there be no humanity; let there be a few men. Sweet death, save us from humanity. . . . Let me derive no more from the body of mankind.

The only regrettable aspect of the war is that it may kill some of those who bear within them the seed of the new life.

Only in the fourth essay did Lawrence begin to speak of peace, though he still asserted that "it is not of love that we are fulfilled, but of love in such intimate equipoise with hate that the transcendence takes place." No doubt he explored his idea of "transcendence" in the missing essays—and also, one hopes, struck a more genial note to compensate for the murderous rhetoric of the earlier parts. He showed no pity for those who fought because he believed that they had willingly enrolled in the ranks of death; whereas a conflict between lovers allowed for the free interplay of love and hate and held out at least the possibility of a transcendence into "blessedness." But contemporary readers must have been appalled by Lawrence's contempt for the warriors who were now bracing themselves for the Flanders campaign of 1917, and even the loyal Austin Harrison probably cut short publication of the series because he thought Lawrence had gone too far. Lawrence, however, seems to have been quite unaware of having given cause for offence. He planned even to approach the National Council for Civil Liberty to see if they would issue his essays as a book; they had sent him Sir Norman Angell's influential attack on war, *The Great Illusion,* and he hoped to follow in its footsteps. In fact, "The Reality of Peace" sank without a ripple: the reality of 1917 was Vimy Ridge and Passchendaele, not "the glad absolution of the rose" that Lawrence darkly extolled. Yet Lawrence for a while hoped that the essays might succeed where *The Signature* had failed, and thought of leaving Cornwall to further this aim:

> We *must* have done entirely with the half-truths of actual life. They are leeches hanging on our souls. I feel like starting something somewhere: but hardly know yet where to begin. I believe there are peace demonstrations every Sunday in the Victoria Park. I think I am almost ready to set out preaching also, now: not only cessation of war, but the beginning of a new world.[48]

Lawrence's plan was inspired by his anger at the new, more comprehensive Military Service Act, under which he faced another medical examination and possible reclassification. "If they bother me," he told Kot, "I will go to prison. I *will not be compelled:* that is the whole of my feeling. I should very much like to do something to get a better government. This Parliament must be kicked out: it is a disgusting fraud. It is time we had a living representative government here. How can we tolerate such a grunting *schweinerei?*"[49] If Lawrence had mounted a soapbox to preach the overthrow of parliament he would undoubtedly have been given a humiliating lesson in practical politics, but fortunately he held back. Frieda had equally wild ideas about her husband's potential influence—she even suggested to Kot that "The Reality of Peace" might be awarded a Nobel Prize for Peace. Regardless of such fantasies, political events had taken a turn that ensured there would be no peace in 1917.

Return to the World

SHORTLY AFTER Lawrence completed "The Reality of Peace" Czar Nicholas II abdicated; his fall set off the struggle between liberals and radicals that would end in the Bolshevik Revolution and Russia's withdrawal for the war. Three weeks later, on 6 April, America finally declared war on Germany after some of her merchant ships had been sunk by German submarines. Yet these changes in the balance of forces only encouraged both sides to fight on, in the hope of turning the new situation to their advantage. In February Lawrence had threatened that if America joined the war he would "die outright," yet when the dreadful event occurred he said only "America is a stink-pot in my nostrils, after having been the land of the future for me."[50] He transferred his hopes, in some measure, to Russia; but in the short run he gave up all prospect of moving to America or of political change within England. Since exile was impossible, there remained only silence and cunning—though neither would come easily to one of Lawrence's temperament.

At the end of March Lawrence finally decided to take stock of affairs in the outside world. Frieda had made one trip to London during the past sixteen months, while Lawrence had not left Cornwall at all. The return fare was so high—three pounds ten shillings in 1917—that they could only travel when some winfall came their way; this time it was Amy Lowell who sent five pounds for some poems of Lawrence's in the *Imagist Anthology*. Frieda promptly left, on 23 March, for a week in London at Dollie Radford's. She probably went alone because of a quarrel with Lawrence: in February she had arranged to see her children before leaving for America, and this had stirred up the old bitterness. Two weeks later Lawrence was ready for his own excursion. Before leaving he approached Murry for the first time in six months, to suggest meeting in London. But this cautious move toward reconciliation was balked when the note was not forwarded from Gower Street—which Jack had left—in time for him to reply. Lawrence thought himself snubbed and made no effort to seek out Jack in London. It is doubtful in any case that a meeting would have been successful, for Jack was totally immersed in his work at the War Office; he had even separated from Katherine, since they had been unable to find a suitable flat where they could live together. But after he returned to Cornwall Lawrence did begin to correspond with Jack again, for a time.

When Lawrence left Higher Tregerthen on 14 April he first went to spend four days with his sister Ada at Ripley; Emily also came down from Glasgow for the occasion. He had not seen his family since Christmas 1915, when he had felt it "a cruel thing to go back into the past." The account in *Kangaroo* suggests that this visit was equally disturbing. First there was Somers' long journey by rail halfway across the country: "He loved it so much. But it was in the grip of something monstrous, not English, and he was almost gripped too."

At Derby he got on a bus jammed with drunken young miners, whose melancholy singing seemed to him only a prelude to revolution—the "great smash-up" that would follow the war:

> As they tore their bowels with their singing, they tore his. But as he sat squashed far back among all that coated flesh, in the dimmest glim of a light, that only made darkness more substantial, he felt like some strange isolated cell in some tensely packed organism that was hurling through chaos into oblivion. The colliers. He was more at one with them. But they were blind, ventral. Once they broke loose heaven knows what it would be.

This final unleashing of the working class was one image of the apocalypse that Lawrence could never contemplate without fear.

Lawrence's stay with Ada was marred by Emily's falling ill with intestinal flu, but he appreciated the help and affection of the old Eastwood circle as his more recent friends dropped away. From Ripley he went to visit Willie and Sallie Hopkin at Eastwood, and invited them to come down to Cornwall. He arrived in London on 19 April and stayed with Kot, since Dollie Radford was also flu-ridden at her country cottage at Hermitage. His first business was with Pinker, to discuss the prospects for *Look! We Have Come Through!* and "The Reality of Peace." Some of the more "impersonal" poems from the former book Lawrence promised to Austin Harrison of the *English Review;* this, we should remember to its credit, was the only English periodical that published anything by Lawrence in the war years—except for two poems in *The Egoist.*

On the day after he arrived Lawrence saw the two women friends with whom he still felt at ease, Catherine Carswell and Lady Cynthia Asquith. He favored Lady Cynthia with a few home truths, telling her that her autistic son John could be cured if she would get off the "false unreal plane" of her social life; that Beb would not be killed at the front if she didn't want him to be; and that she should not "subscribe to the war" by working in a hospital. One supposes that Lawrence's personal charm took the edge off such comments; a note in Lady Cynthia's diary gives a hint of this: "How amazingly unlike he is to his books, in which there is no gleam of humor." Another reason for Lady Cynthia's docility was her habit of collecting extraordinary people of every kind, and taking each at his own value. The day after a "delightful" visit to the zoo with Lawrence she took equal pleasure in lunching at the Berkeley with Bernard Freyberg, V. C., who at age twenty-seven had just become the youngest brigadier in the British army. One of the great heroes of the war—he was wounded more than twenty times—Freyberg was militarism incarnate: "He ate Homerically," Lady Cynthia noted, "laying down his fork to exclaim: 'How I love fighting!' . . . He was a wonderful contrast to Lawrence in point of view. I felt very much in sympathy with both. I wonder if it is a good thing to be so fluid."[51]

After only three days in London Lawrence suddenly collapsed with the endemic intestinal flu and Kot had to nurse him until he was well enough to go and stay with Dollie Radford at Hermitage. He was depressed by finding so many people ill, and by the apparent fruitlessness of his two weeks away from Tregerthen. He had found all his family and friends mired in their old habits, and the political scene was more hopeless than ever. The people in London were "chastened and helpless," the government "quite, quite, incompetent, yet determined to prosecute the war indefinitely.

The military authorities are in the filthiest state of blood-thirstiness, it is all just a hopeless mess." Still, Lawrence convinced himself that Germany, Austria, Russia, and Italy were sufficiently war-weary that peace had to come within a few weeks; though when it did, he told Sallie Hopkin, things would only get worse:

> ... there are bound to be labour insurrections, *purely selfish* on the part of labour, caring *not* for life, but only for labour. ... It is impossible to believe in any existing body, they are all part of the same evil game, labour, capital, aristocrat, they are the trunk, limbs, and head of one body of destructive evil. ... One can only stand far aside, and wait till there is a showing of a good spirit of resurrection in the hearts of people. But they have the last stages of death to go through yet: and it will not be a lovely process.[52]

Lawrence probably never visited the National Council for Civil Liberties to recommend to them "The Reality of Peace"; once he was taken ill—he blamed his illness, characteristically, on "the evil influence of aggregate London"—he seems to have cared for nothing but escape, first to Hermitage and then back to Zennor:

> as far as peace work, or *any* work for betterment goes, it is useless. ... I feel that people *choose* the war, somehow, even those who hate it, *choose* it, choose the state of war, and in their souls provoke more war, even in hating war. So the only thing that can be done is to leave them to it, and to bring forth the flower of one's own happiness, single and apart.[53]

It was an agenda for self-sufficiency in his little cottage, where he now expected to remain until the war ended.

Outside the Whale

LAWRENCE returned to Higher Tregerthen on 27 April to find a guest keeping Frieda company, Esther Andrews. When she stayed with the Lawrences the previous January, after her lover Mountsier had returned to London, the three of them had become close enough that she was given the nickname "Hadassah" (Hebrew for Esther) and expected to come along on the expedition to Nukuheva. Nonetheless, she and Frieda got on each other's nerves so badly that she had to leave after a few days. Back in London, she felt herself treated badly by Mountsier, who was on the point of leaving for America. "There is something very nice and lovable in [Mountsier]," Lawrence told Catherine Carswell. "But also underneath is the old worldly male, that is bent on this evil destructive process, and which battens on the ugliness of the war. There is a great ugliness and vultureness underneath, quite American."[54]

Esther was still fretting over her broken romance when she came to Tregerthen in April, and in her vulnerability she now became infatuated with Lawrence—an infatuation that was still present when she set down her impressions of him for Mabel Dodge Luhan in 1922:

> But what you want to know particularly, I suppose, is what he is as a human being. He is one of the most fascinating men I ever met. The first time I ever saw him, he talked for a whole afternoon, almost steadily. He will do this at once and without the slightest self-consciousness if he feels a sympathy in his listener. . . .
>
> But at the slightest touch of adverse criticism or hostility, Lawrence becomes violent. His vituperation is magnificent. I have never heard its equal. . . . He says he has no friends that he has not quarrelled with. . . . In the marvellously sweet side of his nature, he is inarticulate. And yet he is the gentlest, kindest person in all human relations that anyone could be on this earth. The peasants around where he lived in Cornwall adored him, blindly. . . .
>
> Lawrence lives the life of a workman. . . . He is very frugal, with all the thriftiness of his working-class background, but he would share whatever he had with another without a thought. The little spotless sunny house in Cornwall had the most beautiful simplicity that I have ever seen. . . .
>
> People are always making pilgrimages to him. He hates it, but is infinitely sweet to them. His awareness of other people is unbelievable. When you are with him, you feel that there is not a corner of your mind or spirit or whatever you have that Lawrence doesn't see and be tolerant of. And he bares himself perfectly frankly. When a mood or an impulse is in him, there is no such thing as repression. It all comes out in a mighty gust.[55]

She was at Higher Tregerthen for nearly two weeks after Lawrence returned and during most of this time Frieda was wretchedly ill with colitis. At some point—presumably near the end of her stay—Esther made sexual advances toward Lawrence. Whether or not they were reciprocated depends on whom one chooses to believe. According to Mabel Luhan, Esther was "the only woman with whom—Frieda told me later—Lawrence was ever 'unfaithful' to her! . . . She forced Lawrence to tell her about it and then showed the girl the door. It had, or at least so he told her, been a miserable failure, anyway."[56] Catherine Carswell called this story "both misleading and incorrect. At the time I heard the particulars from both Lawrence and Frieda." What really happened, she claimed, was entirely one-sided:

> [Esther Andrews] was unhappy, and in the strength of her unhappiness could not resist attaching herself to Lawrence and trying to match her strength against Frieda's—disastrously to herself. Yet she took away with her, when she left later that summer, an enduring admiration. And I dare say she would now assert that her visit to Cornwall was the least disastrous episode in her life.[57]

Mrs. Carswell certainly was closer to the events than Mabel Luhan, but her account is still a vague, secondhand version of an episode that seems to have inspired an embarrassed reticence in the two persons immediately concerned, Lawrence and Esther. It was obviously in Lawrence's interest to minimize the affair; all that seems definite is that he was unable or unwilling to make love to Esther, that she left Higher Tregerthen because of Frieda's hostility, and that Lawrence felt he had been worsted by Frieda. For the next several months he turned his face away from her—in part, we may assume, because he felt humiliated by the whole imbroglio. Esther never met the Lawrences again, and her later fate is obscure.

Though Lawrence had given up on England and America in that early summer 1917, he was roused by the crumbling of the czarist autocracy in Russia: he may have called for the founding of new dictatorships, but established ones he generally despised. "When I think of the young new country there," he told Kot, "I love it inordinately. It is the place of hope. We must go, sooner or a little later. But let us go gently. I feel a violent change would be the death of me."[58] Kot was gathering English contributions for Maxim Gorky's revolutionary paper *New Life* and Lawrence, no doubt attracted by the title, agreed to write for it, and even planned to learn Russian himself. But his interest faded as he came to realize how far removed were the concerns of Russia from his own, and Kot himself soon became depressed by the course of events there. After the Bolsheviks seized power Lawrence's interest in Russia became purely clinical; as with the

English class struggle, "stand aside" was his motto. "It must go through as it is going," he told Kot. "Nothing but a real smelting down is any good for her: no matter how horrible it seems. You, who are an ultraconscious Jew, can't bear the chaos. But chaos is necessary for Russia. Russia will be all right—righter, in the end, than these old stiff senile nations of the West."[59]

In May Lawrence realized that even the revision of "The Reality of Peace" was taking too much out of him. "Suddenly," he told Catherine Carswell, "I felt as if I was going dotty, straight out of my mind, so I left off. One can only wait and let the crisis come and go."[60] It seemed futile to go on writing when no one was reading, and for the next few months he had little interest in doing so. He found gardening a much more pleasurable occupation, spending long hours outside in the sunshine while the young lambs frolicked in the fields, though he was not amused when they ate up his broad beans. With his usual domestic resourcefulness he meant to raise food on a large scale, for England at this time was in serious danger of being starved out before the war could be fought to a conclusion. If only he and Frieda could be self-sufficient and free from troublesome intruders, he would not pine for his lost America: "War, and militarism," he told Catherine, "and the whole whale of authority, seems to have swum off from me and left me alone on a small peaceful island."[61]

Even the official summons for another medical examination, which arrived the first week in June, left him relatively unperturbed at first. He sent in a request for exemption, enclosing a certificate from the local Dr. Rice; when the authorities denied it he made a quick trip to London to see a Harley Street specialist. This time he was able to meet Jack, at Dollie Radford's house. "He looked tired and ill," Jack recalled, "but virtue flowed out of him. I noticed, again with the old admiration, how completely he was surrendered to the simple task, so rarely performed by men, of making others happy."[62] But the mission was otherwise a waste of time and money; it proved only how eager Lawrence was to avoid repeating his horrid visit to Bodmin barracks of a year earlier. Yet when he finally had to obey the summons, the ordeal seems to have been less than he feared:

> This time things went much more quickly. [Somers] was only two hours in the barracks. He was examined. He could tell they knew about him and disliked him. He was put in class C-3—unfit for military service, but conscripted for light non-military duties. There were no rejections now. Still, it was good

enough. There were thousands of C men, men who *wanted* to have jobs as C men, so they were not very likely to fetch him up. He would only be a nuisance anyhow.

Lawrence was thus safe from the military for at least another year, though his third and worst examination was yet to come.

That summer he at last took seriously his own advice to Gertler, when he had complained of nervousness and depression: "Can't you put your soul to sleep, and remain just superficially awake, drifting and taking no real notice, just amuse yourself like a child with some sort of play work? . . . busy and happy while one's soul of contention sleeps."[63] He spent whole days at Lower Tregerthen farm, which appealed to him as the Chambers farm had when he was a boy: a place of warmth and simple tasks, and a refuge from the moral conflicts that made life uneasy at home. Time passed easily in giving young Stanley Hocking French lessons—as he had fifteen years earlier to Jessie Chambers—or sitting by the stove, filching Mrs. Hocking's fried potatoes. Then there were the long days of hay-making and harvesting, in the fields overlooking the Atlantic. Lawrence thought of himself as a regular farm worker, though unpaid, and claimed in *Kangaroo* that "work went like steam" when he was on the job. Stanley Hocking, however, took this with the disdain of the professional for the dilettante: "That's a good one. We had another workman besides Lawrence, and Lawrence was only considered a boy compared to this other workman. Work 'went like steam' not because Lawrence was there. There were many days when he wasn't there, and work went on as usual."[64] Lawrence wasn't very strong by local standards; moreover, he worked only if the weather was fine and it suited him to do so: "If he was helping us in the fields and something occurred to him, he would drop whatever he was doing immediately, and go in and write for the next two or three hours. He had a typewriter, and after he had left a nearby field, we would sometimes hear the typewriter tapping away."

With the wartime shortage of labor, any farmer would have been glad of help, however casual, but gratitude was inevitably tinged with resentment of those who were free to help or not as the whim took them. Added to this was the perennial Cornish mistrust of the citified outsider. The Hockings' hired man, noting the difference in vigor and social status between Frieda and her husband, jeered that "she must have found him in a Lucky Bag!"

(a bag of candies and trinkets sold to children for a halfpenny). Lawrence's fantasy of becoming "one of them," of subduing his intellectual nature to work on the farm, was evidently not taken seriously by those whom he wanted to join.

That summer the Lawrences found their first local friend who could claim to be their social and intellectual equal. When Lawrence came back from his April visit to London he discovered to his chagrin that Philip Heseltine had showed up as a guest at the "Tinner's Arms" and then rented a bungalow on the moors between Zennor and Penzance.* Lawrence professed not to like him any more, but the bitterness of the previous spring had abated enough for the two men to drift back into a guarded and intermittent friendship. Then Cecil Gray appeared on the scene: a friend of Heseltine's who decided also to settle in the neighborhood. He was a year younger than Heseltine and of similar background and tastes. A musician, he lived on an allowance (of two hundred pounds a year) from his wealthy mother and hated the war, from which he was kept safe by a medical exemption. Gray came down from his native Edinburgh to live in London during the war, where for a time he shared a flat with Heseltine; later he found the atmosphere of London hysterical and sought refuge by renting for five pounds a year a house at Gurnards Head, on the other side of Zennor about two miles from Tregerthen.

Lawrence soon got on friendly terms with his new neighbor, though he should perhaps have realized that any intimate of Heseltine's was likely to be something of a neurotic. Gray envisioned a life of romantic isolation on his cliff top, in the spirit of Nerval's "El Desdichado," but Lawrence explained to him the more mundane necessities of life at Zennor. Before Gray moved down from London Lawrence bought furniture for him in St. Ives and supervised the workmen who were renovating his house, Bosigran. He did much more, though an upper-class snob like Gray was unable to appreciate it:

* Heseltine was in flight from Minnie Channing ("Puma"), who had borne his son the previous year and whom he had married, for reasons he explained to Phyllis Crocker: "I, for my part, would never permit the paws of officialdom to mess about with any relation that really existed between me and any human being—So when I was badgered by our mutual friend [Puma] (with whom I had never had and could never have any but a purely bestial relation) to make her a final present of forty shillings worth of respectability in a 'certificate of marriage', I made no objection, seeing that the ceremonial meant no more for me than to make a mock of what was already a mockery." (PH/PC, 19 April 1917, BL).

> [Lawrence] even insisted on scrubbing and polishing the floors for me—he had always, indeed, a strange predilection for such domestic activities, which I was far from sharing, and I was therefore only too glad to leave them to him. In retrospect, however, I am inclined to suspect that in addition to his genuine fondness for such occupations there was also a certain streak of mystical self-abasement involved. But . . . at the time I was not aware of this Dostoievskian element in the situation.[65]

The obvious differences in temperament between Gray and Lawrence would led in time to another feud. But in summer 1917 Lawrence was in a relatively tranquil state; he did not pressure his young friend into becoming something he was not, but was glad simply to enjoy the company of a cultured neighbor who also deplored militarism and official busybodies. In *Kangaroo* Gray appears as "James Sharpe," a young musician who "insisted, like a morose bird, that he wanted to be alone. But he wasn't really morose, and he didn't want really to be alone." If this was true of Gray, it was equally true of Lawrence himself; the two "hermits" and Frieda visited back and forth constantly, to the increasing suspicion of the locals. They also made the acquaintance of an even more scandalous pair of outsiders who had taken a cottage a mile from Tregerthen at Treveal:

> There are near some herb-eating occultists, a Meredith Starr and a Lady Mary ditto: she is a half-caste, daughter of the Earl of Stamford. They fast, or eat nettles: they descend naked into old mine-shafts, and there meditate for hours and hours, upon their own transcendent infinitude: they descend on us like a swarm of locusts, and devour all the food on the shelf or board: they even gave a concert, and made the most dreadful fools of themselves in St. Ives.[66]

Though such antics were an irresistible target for Lawrence's wry humor, he was not altogether hostile to occult tradition. As a young man he had frequented the Theosophical Society in Nottingham with Willie Hopkin, and the presence of the Starrs seems to have revived his interest. Heseltine too, at his retreat up on the moors, was deeply and murkily involved in magical pursuits. Lawrence asked a new correspondent, Waldo Frank, whether he was a theosophist; and a month later, on 25 August, he was recommending theosophy to his friend Dr. David Eder—as a substitute for Judaism!:

> Have you read Blavatsky's *Secret Doctrine?* In many ways a bore, and not quite real. Yet one can glean a marvellous lot from it, enlarge the understanding

immensely. Do you know the physical—physiological—interpretations of the esoteric doctrine?—the *chakras* and dualism in experience? The devils won't tell one anything, fully. Perhaps they don't understand themselves—the occultists—what they are talking about, or what their esotericism really means. But probably, in the physiological interpretation, they do—and won't tell. Yet one can gather enough. Did you get Pryce's *Apocalypse Unsealed?* [67]

It is hard to trace the direct influence of occultism on Lawrence's work of the period, though by the time of *Fantasia of the Unconscious* (1922) it was quite evident. He was skeptical about occult doctrines insofar as they represented the wisdom of the past, but approved of their insistence that the highest knowledge should be reserved for an elite. The task of the moment, therefore, should be to create a secret wisdom relevant to mankind's future: "There should be again a body of esoteric doctrines," he told Frank, "defended from the herd. . . . It needs *this,* before ever there can be any new earth and new heaven. It needs the sanctity of a mystery, the mystery of the initiation into pure being." [68] In *Kangaroo* and *The Plumed Serpent* Lawrence imagined political leaders gifted with arcane powers, but in his personal life he did not seek to assemble any body of initiates over whom he might exercise total control. His temperament was too open and volatile for him to become the master of a cult.

Rather than gathering associates at this time, Lawrence was alienating those he still had. Up to now Kot had remained his most faithful friend in London, but after three years of intimacy Lawrence suddenly decided to make an issue of his Jewishness. When they last met (probably when Lawrence came to London in June), they must have discussed the persistence of antisemitism in the "new" Russia, which Lawrence seems to have defended as part of the awakening of the true Russian spirit. He was forming a theory that the Americans and the Jews were kindred races—and therefore, in 1917, leaders of the destructive forces in world history. "Russia," he told Kot, "seems to me now the positive pole of the world's spiritual energy, and America the negative pole." It followed that the Jewish spirit was really the *negation* of true religion:

Why humanity has hated Jews, I have come to the conclusion, is that the Jews have always taken religion—since the great days, that is —and used it for their own personal and private gratification, as if it were a thing administered to their own importance and well-being and conceit. . . . This is abominable. With them, the conscious ego is the absolute, and God is a name they flatter

themselves with.—When they have learned again pure reverence to the Holy
Spirit, then they will be free, and not slaves before men.*

Though Kot was a secular humanist, he was still close enough to
his origins to find Lawrence's comments offensive; he did not
reply to the letter, and a break ensued that was not healed until
the Lawrences moved to London in October.

That Lawrence was possessed by more than a mere fit of irritation is proved by a letter to Waldo Frank the same month. Frank
was editor of the American magazine *Seven Arts,* which in 1917
printed two stories by Lawrence, "The Mortal Coil" and "The
Thimble"; it was vital for Lawrence to develop an American market for his writings, yet he went far out of his way to offend Frank
over the same issue:

> I hear Huebsch is a Jew. Are you a Jew also? The best of Jews is, that they
> *know* truth from untruth. The worst of them is, that they are rather slave-like,
> and that almost inevitably, in action, they betray the truth they know, and
> fawn to the powers that be. . . . The material world dominates them with a
> base kind of fetish domination. . . . I have got Jewish friends, whom I am on
> the point of forswearing for ever.[69]

Presumably the friends would be Kot, Gertler—with whom
Lawrence had not corresponded since April—and perhaps Barbara Low. David Eder he did not want to forswear, but he did
warn him against going on a Zionist mission to Palestine: "Why do
you go with the Jews? They will only be a mill-stone round your
neck. Best cease to be a Jew, and let Jewry disappear—much best."
When Waldo Frank wrote back in defense of Judaism, Lawrence's
anger over the issue finally boiled over:

> So Judas was a Super-Christian! And Jews are Super-Christian lovers of
> mankind! No doubt it is true. It makes me dislike Judas and Jews very much.
> . . . I believe in Paradise and Paradisal beings: but humanity, mankind—*crotte!*
> We shall disagree too much, from the root. Better let it be an *Ave atque Vale—
> jamque Vale.* God, I *don't want* to be sane, as men are counted sane. It all
> stinks.[70]

---

*CL 516–517. Compare the following from Madam Blavatsky, whom Lawrence was
reading about this time: "the Jews . . . knew little of, nor would they deal with, the real
divine Occultism, their national character being averse to anything which had no direct
bearing upon their own ethical, tribal, and individual benefits" (*The Secret Doctrine* (Pasa-
dena: Theosophical University Press, 1974) I, 230).

This was the end of Lawrence's involvement with Frank, and with *Seven Arts;* three very lean years would pass before another American magazine, *The Dial,* began to print Lawrence's contributions. It is likely that Lawrence at this time also revised *Women in Love* to identify Loerke as probably "a Jew—or part Jewish"; yet when his antisemitic fit abated he again became friendly with Kot and the rest. A year and a half later, in fact, he was eager to join Eder in Palestine!

At the end of September Lawrence was already mending fences. "You should never mind my onslaughts," he told Kot. "Go on as if they hadn't taken place: why answer them, they're no better for it." This showed some appreciation by Lawrence of how dissociated his spells of rage were from their ostensible targets; typically enough, when his anti-Semitic phase was at its height there cannot have been any actual Jews for miles around. Still, Lawrence followed his indirect apology with the injunction to "Please unlearn all the social lessons. I have learnt to be unsocial entirely, a single thing to myself." And if Kot were to take him at his word, what basis could there be for their friendship? Perhaps Lawrence wanted him as a last witness of the time, only two or three years ago, when they had been a little group united against the world: "Murry wrote me once or twice—but it fell off again. Katherine wrote once or twice—that too falls off again. The past is past. So little of it has survived into the present.—I am fond of the people at the farm."[71] Kot seems not to have replied either; so, by autumn 1917, Lawrence's circle had narrowed to Frieda, his neighbors, Cecil Gray, Catherine Carswell, and scarcely anyone else.

"Pure Abstract Thought"

HAVING progressively discarded his friends, Lawrence found that he had discarded with them the desire to write more novels or stories; there was no market for his fiction in any case, so it hardly seemed worthwhile to make the effort. If he was to write at all, he would write only for himself. "I am tired of emotions and squirmings and sensations," he told Gertler. "Let us have a little pure thought, a little perfect and detached understanding." [72] After his seven philosophical essays on "The Reality of Peace" in March he wrote at least two more in similar vein, hoping that they might all be gathered in a book. The essays were "Love" and "Life"; Lawrence set them aside when the proposed book fell through, but in October Catherine Carswell reminded him of them and he sent them to the *English Review*. They appeared there in January and February 1918.

"Love" is the more important of the two essays, though it is in parts hasty and muddled. "Love is not a goal; it is only a travelling," Lawrence asserts, since it is created by the desire of opposites to unite and final success would destroy the desire. It can be either sacred or profane; these can only be combined in the love between man and woman, "the greatest and most complete passion the world will ever see. . . . the perfect heart-beat of life, systole, diastole. . . . It is the melting into pure communion, and it is the friction of sheer sensuality, both." The counterpart to sacred love in the social realm is brotherly love, the desire for the union and perfection of all mankind. But this ideal, if pursued too exclusively, turns back on itself: "I shall persist in representing a whole loving humanity, until the unfulfilled passion for singleness drives me into action. Then I shall hate my neighbour as I hate myself. . . . In the name of brotherly love we rush into stupendous blind activities of brotherly hate." The remedy, as always in Lawrence's thought, is to balance the two impulses: an ideal society will allow its members to be as unsocial as they wish, relying on their countervailing desire for connection and unanimity to keep individualism from turning into Hobbesian destructiveness. In love, similarly, the desire to separate from the beloved must be fulfilled equally with the desire to unite.

"Life" provides a valuable gloss on one of Lawrence's finest poems, "Song of a Man Who Has Come Through," which uses the romantic metaphor of man as an aeolian harp vibrating to the wind of time. The essay argues that man stands between the chaos of the primal unknown and the completeness of the created world; he must not think of himself as "self-contained or self-accomplished," but as one whose vitality enters him from outside:

ZENNOR: The Buried Life

We shall never know how it comes to pass that we have form and being. But we may always know how through the doorways of the spirit and the body enters the vivid unknown, which is made known in us. Who comes, who is that we hear outside in the night? Who knocks, who knocks again? Who is that that unlatches the painful door?

The great sin against life is to deny entry to the stranger—to strive to petty, self-contained ends rather than allowing the impersonal life force to flow freely through us.

Probably this was the theme of Lawrence's next "philosophy," which he worked at slowly and sporadically from May 1917 until late August, calling it "At the Gates" (which may refer to the strangers at the door in "Life"). "It is based upon the more superficial *Reality of Peace*," Lawrence told Pinker. "But *this* is pure metaphysics, especially later on: and perfectly sound metaphysics, that will stand the attacks of technical philosophers. Bits of it that might be very unpopular, I might leave out."[73] This was his *real* last word, Lawrence explained to Kot, the culmination of a three-year effort that had begun with the *Study of Thomas Hardy.* None of these writings had brought him more than a few guineas, most failed even to be published and those that did appear had no discernible influence except perhaps to damage Lawrence's already shaky reputation. Even Frieda, who was blamed by Ottoline Morrell for fostering these writings, eventually lost patience; according to Stanley Hocking she burned a batch of them in 1917, shouting: "There you are, Lorenzo, they've all come back again. Your writings are all philosophy and bosh and nobody wants them!"[74] Nobody wanted "At the Gates," certainly; the manuscript was probably returned by Pinker in February 1920 when he ceased to be Lawrence's agent, and some time afterward it was lost or destroyed. That Lawrence allowed so many of his philosophical writings to perish suggests that, whatever his initial enthusiasm for them, he cared little for their fate once they had served their purpose of clarifying the successive stages of his thought.

It is likely that Lawrence also made his last major revision of *Women in Love* during summer 1917. When Kot suggested in December 1916 that the novel might be published in Russian Lawrence had no copy on hand to send him, but he arranged with Pinker for two more copies to be typed, one to be sent directly to Kot and one to be kept at Tregerthen. These were completed at the end of March, and they incorporated the extensive revisions that Lawrence had added in longhand to the original typescripts. Early in March Lawrence told Ernest Collings that the novel had been rejected by numerous publishers, and Collings suggested that his friend Cecil Palmer might be able to publish it. Nothing happened for several months, but at the end of June Lawrence told Pinker that Palmer wanted to see the manuscript. He was encouraged by this show of interest to make further handwritten revisions to his typed copy, before sending it off to Palmer around 12 July.[75] Palmer kept the manuscript until the end of August then returned it, with his regrets that he could not afford to publish it privately. Though Lawrence was disappointed, he realized that private publication was the most likely means of getting *Women in Love* into circulation, and for the next two years he continued to look for some wealthy patron who might undertake it.

Meanwhile, his correspondence with Waldo Frank had revived his interest in America, both as a civilization and as a place to live. "If the rainbow hangs in the heavens," he told his new acquaintance, "it hangs over the western continent. . . . Europe is a lost name, like Ninevah or Palenque." *Women in Love,* he explained, was the record of how Europe had become lost to him, thanks to the war: ". . . it is purely destructive, not like *The Rainbow,* destructive—consummating."[76] From Lawrence's emotional oscillations one would expect the reappearance of a scheme of creation emerging from destruction, and this is indeed the underlying plan of his next major work, *Studies in Classic American Literature.* He had done some preliminary reading for it the previous winter; now, at the end of August 1917, he began to write.

Lawrence's belief in the American spirit was, however, far more sober than his utopian fantasies about England's regeneration in early 1915. What he most desired was to escape, if only in imagination, from the established form of society in Europe; though American social forms had no appeal for him either, he was drawn westward by the vision of an uncorrupted landscape and a reborn humanity:

> Do you think I imagine your Yankee-land Paradisal?—The last word of obscene rottenness contained within an entity of mechanised egoistic *will*—that is what Uncle Sam is to me.—But there is a quality in your sky, a salt in your earth, that will, without the agency of man, *destroy you all,* and procreate new beings—not men, in our sense of the word.—Oh, for a non-human race of man![77]

Though Whitman and Twain had lamented the end of the open road and the disappearance of the American Adam, Lawrence still hoped to revive them, and to convince the Americans of today to turn back in search of what they had lost.

The original title for the book was "The Transcendental Element in Classic American Literature"; by this Lawrence meant the *hidden meaning* of texts that had been generally taken, especially in Europe, as mere children's literature. The meaning he found was so deep, indeed, that it was largely hidden from the authors themselves; but Lawrence was not at all upset by this discrepancy, which he justified with his famous maxim "Never trust the teller, trust the tale." His interest in theosophy at this time inclined him to look for a "secret doctrine" behind the received texts of a culture, though Lawrence pressed hardest on the author's deference to convention or his fear of his own creation. The pervasive influence of *Studies in Classic American Literature* on later critics is a tribute to the brilliance Lawrence displayed in inventing and applying this method.

When Lawrence's essays began to appear in the *English Review* at the end of 1918 the first of them, and the one that established the book's major themes, was "The Spirit of Place."[78] A more exact title would be "The Spirit of Race," for the essay has more to do with the imagined qualities of various peoples than with geography. Lawrence's ruling assumption is that the English, in migrating to America, experienced a spiritual mutation that has been obscured by the superficial similarities between the two cultures today. This new reality can be apprehended by deciphering the two meanings of the "art-speech" of American literature: "first, the didactic import given by the author from his own moral consciousness; and then the profound symbolic import which proceeds from his unconscious or subconscious soul, as he works in a state of creation which is something like somnambulism or dreaming."

The surface meaning of the settlement of America is that millions of Europeans sought in the West a religious liberty and a material prosperity that they could not enjoy at home. Lawrence, however, looks deeper. The established axis of Europe, he argues, used to be the polarity running north and south between Germany and Italy, but during the Renaissance the peripheral races of the west—the Celts and Iberians—succeeded in establishing a great new polarity running from east to west. No doubt Lawrence imagined his own residence in Cornwall, facing the Atlantic, as belonging to that polarity. Though the Pilgrim Fathers were not Celts, he included them in the broad movement of "mystic opposition, even hatred, of the civilising principle of the rest of Europe." The Pilgrims did not really want to establish liberty in the west but to indulge "a gloomy passion. . . . to destroy or mutilate life at its very quick, lusting in their dark power to annihilate all living impulses." It is Lawrence's old theme of the conflict between being and knowing; the westward movement is a reaction against the sensuous humanism of the Renaissance, "the will of man rising frenzied against the mystery of life itself, and struggling insanely to *dominate,* to have the life-issue in unutterable control, to squeeze the mystic thing, life, within the violent hands of possession, grasp it, squeeze it, have it, have unspeakable power over it."

America, for Lawrence, is therefore "the great field for the lust of control in the modern world," and the American social and industrial system the visible expression of that lust:

> The New Englanders, wielding the sword of the spirit backwards, struck down the primal impulsive being in every man, leaving only a mechanical, automatic unit. In so doing they cut and destroyed the living bond between men, the rich passional contact. And for this passional contact gradually was substituted the mechanical bond of purposive utility.

"Lust of control" is a motif that links all the essays in the book, though it may take quite disparate forms in Franklin, in Poe, or in Melville's Ahab. In American history, Lawrence argues, this control has been progressively extended and tightened, but he expects America eventually to reverse its course out of sheer reaction against the completeness of its achievement. The American is like the Jew "in that, having conquered and destroyed the instinctive, impulsive being in himself, he is free to be always deliberate, always calculated, rapid, swift, and single in practical execution as a machine." But when the "new, soft, creative wind" blows, the iron ships of American will "put forth vine and tendril and bunches of grapes, like the ship of Dionysos in full sail upon the ocean. . . . Meanwhile. . . . we can listen to the sad, weird utterance of this classic America, watch the transmutation from men into machines and ghosts, hear the last metallic sounds."

In Cornwall, Lawrence was still under the spell of his boyhood fantasies about life on the frontier and his urgent desire to remove himself from war-torn England. A faith in the coming "mystic transubstantiation" of America helped him to endure his present plight; critical as he was of America, he believed that even its excesses were making a contribution to a fundamentally positive development. When he came to rewrite the book at Taos in 1922–23 he was reacting bitterly against his disastrous stay with Mabel Dodge Luhan—having come to America to pray, he remained to jeer.

William Henry

LAWRENCE spent many days with the Hockings during summer 1917 but was really intimate with only the eldest son of the family, William Henry, who was two or three years older than himself. William Henry's restlessness on the farm had set him at odds with his mother—the head of the family—and his sisters. Frieda wanted to marry him off to some sympathetic woman; Lawrence scorned this solution, and suggested instead (to Barbara Low) that this Hardyesque misfit should make a trip to London to widen his horizons:

> He is *really* interested in things: but he hasn't enough mental development, mental continuity. That is the terrible fate of those who have a high *sensuous* development, and very little mental: centuries of sensuous culture, and then sprung into mental life, in one generation, and flung into the seethe of modern intellectual decomposition. . . . And he suffers *badly,* and his people hate him—because he *will* take the intellectual attitude, and they want only the vague sensuous non-critical. He ought to live away from them.

Meanwhile Lawrence found himself cast in the role of saviour, much against his own inclination: "He looks to me as if I could suddenly give him wings. . . . I wish one didn't always find a petty tragedy on one's doorstep. . . . one *does* avoid him, he *is* rather a burden. He has never been inside the house yet, and for some reason, I cannot invite him."[79]

(309)

ZENNOR: The Buried Life

Lawrence decided not to arrange the London visit, since it seemed unfair to impose William Henry on his friends, but by autumn 1916 he had become more at ease with him, and more appreciative of his positive qualities:

> If you go right to the root of the matter with him, he is most marvellously understanding. He has thought deeply and bitterly. "I have always dreamed," he says, "of a new order of life. But I am afraid now I shall never see it." And again "Yes, there's something one wants, that isn't money or anything like that—But shall I ever get it?—I want it—" he puts his hand to his chest with a queer, grasping movement,—"I can feel the want of it here—but shall I ever get it?—That's what I begin to doubt. Lately, I begin to doubt it." There is something manly and independent about him—and something truly *Celtic* and unknown—something non-christian, non-European, but strangely beautiful and fair in spirit, unselfish.[80]

The friendship does not seem to have developed further for several months; William Henry came for Christmas dinner with his brother and sisters, but as a rule Lawrence would visit the farm at will without making his home similarly open to the Hockings. Each side seemed fixed in its social station: the Lawrences outsiders and intellectuals, the Hockings tied to the land. William Henry was doubly tied, in fact, because if he stopped working on the farm he would at once have been conscripted and sent to the trenches. A further barrier to intimacy was Frieda's foreignness and her aristocratic manner; for all her joviality, the locals could never really feel at ease with her as they could with Lawrence, who was so much closer to being "one of them."

In summer 1917, however, Lawrence again immersed himself in the primitive and Celtic powers that he sensed around him at Zennor, as he had done the year before when seeking blood-brotherhood from Murry. He tells how Somers, in *Kangaroo,* "no longer wanted to struggle consciously along, a thought adventurer. He preferred to drift into a sort of blood-darkness, to take up in his veins again the savage vibrations that still lingered round the secret rocks, the place of the pre-Christian human sacrifice." As Somers tries to discard his conscious, intellectual self he is drawn into comradeship with "John Thomas," the phallic pseudonym that Lawrence gave William Henry:

> Somers stayed above all day, loading or picking, or resting, talking in the intervals with John Thomas, who loved a half-philosophical, mystical talking

about the sun, and the moon, the mysterious powers of the moon at night, and the mysterious change in man with the change of season, and the mysterious effects of sex on a man. So they talked, lying in the bracken or on the heather as they waited for a wain. . . . And the farmer, in a non-mental way, understood, understood even more than Somers. . . .

Poor Harriet spent many lonely days in the cottage. Richard was not interested in her now. He was only interested in John Thomas and the farm people, and he was growing more like a labourer every day. . . . She was driven back on herself like a fury. And many a bitter fight they had, he and she.

Lawrence had several reasons for turning his face against Frieda. His completion of *Look! We Have Come Through!* the previous February still left the question of what they had come through *to,* and the poem "Manifesto" showed that he wanted something from Frieda—an instinctive reverence of his maleness—that she refused to yield him. For good measure, she had humiliated him by scotching his tentative love affair with Esther Andrews in May; and there is some evidence that she may have rubbed salt into the wound by herself carrying on an affair with Cecil Gray while Lawrence was occupied on the farm. And Lawrence still feared in Frieda the "devouring mother," the moon goddess who feeds on her sons; Birkin's stoning of the moon in chapter 19 of *Women in Love* was a powerful expression of this hostility. Lawrence returned to the issue in August 1917 with his Freudian friend Dr. Eder: "I should like to talk to you also about the lunar myth—the lunar trinity—father—mother—son, with the son as consort of the mother, the *magna* Mater. It seems to me your whole psycho-analysis rests on this myth, and the physical application. And it seems to me this myth is the mill-stone of mill-stones round all our necks."[81] Through William Henry, then, Lawrence sought a connection with ritual powers—of Druidism or human sacrifice—that could repel the female power of the moon and establish a countervailing polarity to that between himself and Frieda.

So far as Catherine Carswell is concerned, that is *all* Lawrence wanted from his friendship with the young farmer:

A working man and a Celt, a man with a subtly pagan face, born in the shadow of these Druidical stones, yet English too, might, surely must, have some wordless understanding of one of the oldest of all human rites. I have heard Lawrence say that sexual perversion was for him "the sin against the Holy Ghost," the hopeless sin. But he cherished the deep longing to see revived a communion between man and man which should not lack its physical symbols. He even held that our modern denial of this communion in all but idea was largely the cause of our modern perversions.[82]

But a letter from Frieda to Jack Murry in 1953 hints that Lawrence did indeed taste the forbidden fruit, most likely with William Henry: "If he had lived longer . . . you would have been real friends, he wanted so desperately for you to understand him. I think the homosexuality in him was a short phase out of misery—I fought him and won—and that he wanted a deeper thing from you. I am aware so much as I am old, of the elements in us, that we consist of." Frieda added, in letters to other people: "Murry suggests that L. had homosexual feeling for him, I know he never did. . . . Murry and he had no 'love affair.' But Lawrence did not disbelieve in homosexuality."[83] If there was a physical consummation with William Henry it must have been in the style of Whitman's "Calamus"—which was for Lawrence a great key to the mystical comradeship he desired:

But just possibly with you on a high hill, first watching lest any person for miles
    around approach unawares,
Or possibly with you sailing at sea, or on the beach of the sea or some quiet
    island,
Here to put your lips upon mine I permit you,
With the comrade's long dwelling kiss or the new husband's kiss,
For I am the new husband and I am the comrade.

When Lawrence wrote his essay on Whitman the following year, he accepted him as a guide to the mysteries of pure maleness, beyond procreation:

    Acting from the last and profoundest centres, man acts womanless. It is no longer a question of race continuance. . . . Acting from these centres, man is an extreme being, the unthinkable warrior, creator, mover, and maker.
    And the polarity is between man and man. Whitman alone of all moderns has known this positively. Others have known it negatively, *pour épater les bourgeois*. But Whitman knew it positively, in its tremendous knowledge, knew the extremity, the perfectness, and the fatality.[84]

In "The Reality of Peace" Lawrence had proclaimed that "I shall accept all my desires and repudiate none." The problem was how he could act out these desires without violating other injunctions

(312)

that he had laid upon himself. By the negative polarity between men he meant the whole realm of homosexual rituals, from Oscar Wilde to Keynes to the "fatal glamor" of comradeship in war; everything about this world filled him with horror, as a sterile "extinction of all the purposive influences." With Jack Murry and with William Henry he sought to create some new, untainted ritual—a blood-brotherhood without what he considered the decadent affectations of people like Keynes and Frankie Birrell. But his demands were so personal and esoteric that he could not find any spontaneous way of winning over the bewildered objects of his affection.

Not satisfied with his ambition to create a wholly new mode of sexuality, Lawrence wanted also to reconcile it with his pledges to Frieda. A few years later, when his friend Godwin Baynes was suffering in a troubled marriage, Lawrence recommended that he should look to Whitman: "I find in his Calamus and Comrades one of the clues to a real solution—the new adjustment. I believe in what he calls 'manly love,' the real implicit reliance of one man on another; as sacred a unison as marriage: only it must be deeper, more ultimate than emotion and personality, cool separateness and yet the ultimate reliance."[85] Though comradeship was a step beyond marriage, both must coexist if the male relation is not to become "purely deathly." This had been a recurrent motif in Lawrence's emotional life, curiously similar to the love triangle in Shakespeare's sonnets between the poet, his ideal friend, and his aggressively sexual dark lady (as in the sonnets, also, Lawrence would later be shattered to discover a sexual bond between his friend and his lady). When he and Frieda were unhappy together Lawrence would seek love from a male friend, but he vacillated between seeing the comrade as a *solution* to his marital problems, and as an outright *alternative* to marriage. Cecil Gray asserted of Lawrence: ". . . his sexual potentialities [were] exclusively cerebral. . . . It might not be true to say that Lawrence was literally and absolutely impotent . . . but I am certain that he was not very far removed from it."[86] This is either a malicious lie (as is possible) or a report of what Gray was told by Frieda in 1917–18; if we give it any credence, it supplies a further motive for Lawrence to seek with William Henry a fulfillment he could not achieve with Frieda.

Three years later—around the time of his advice to Baynes—

Lawrence apparently confided to Compton Mackenzie a similar emotional dilemma:

> What worried him particularly was his inability to attain consummation simultaneously with his wife, which according to him must mean that their marriage was still imperfect in spite of all they had both gone through. I insisted that such a happy coincidence was always rare, but he became more and more depressed about what *he* insisted was the only evidence of a perfect union.
>
> "I believe that the nearest I've ever come to perfect love was with a young coal-miner when I was about sixteen," he declared.[87]

Mackenzie was over eighty when he wrote this memoir of a conversation of forty years before; he had tangled with Lawrence for satirizing him in "The Man Who Loved Islands," but this does not seem sufficient reason to deny him credence altogether. Probably Lawrence was not referring to a young miner but to a farmer: Jessie Chambers' brother Alan, who was three years older than himself. In summer 1908 he spent two weeks bringing in the hay with Alan and his brothers, rejoicing in the sensuousness of farm life; he made Alan the model for George Sexton in *The White Peacock,* where the chapter "A Poem of Friendship" celebrates their affection. The nude bathing scene between George and Cyril Beardsall (the Lawrence figure) suggest the kind of ideal homoeroticism that Lawrence dreamed of:

> [George] saw I had forgotten to continue my rubbing, and laughing he took hold of me and began to rub me briskly, as if I were a child, or rather, a woman he loved and did not fear. I left myself quite limply in his hands, and, to get a better grip of me, he put his arm round me and pressed me against him, and the sweetness of the touch of our naked bodies one against the other was superb. It satisfied in some measure the vague, indecipherable yearning of my soul; and it was the same with him. When he had rubbed me all warm, he let me go, and we looked at each other with eyes of still laughter, and our love was perfect for a moment, more perfect than any love I have known since, either for man or woman.

Lawrence's homoerotic fantasies often seem to involve his being held and soothed by a stronger, usually older man, a desire that might have more to do with his need for security and affection than with any active homosexuality. But he demanded as much from the men he loved as from the women and it is not surprising that, on the terms he offered, he found no man to cast his lot in with him as Frieda had done. In *Kangaroo* we see John Thomas

(314)

shying away from Somers when he becomes too importunate, by deliberately keeping him waiting for two hours at St. Ives:

> Somers . . . knew that this was a sort of deliberate insult on John Thomas' part, and that he must never trust him again.
>
> It was well after seven when the fellow came—smiling with subtle malevolence and excusing himself so easily.
>
> "I shall never come with you again," said Somers quietly.

The friendship between Lawrence and William Henry was not broken off entirely, but it became clear that the Cornishman had drawn back from the intimacy that had been too insistently thrust on him. A year later, after the Lawrences had left Cornwall, Lawrence heard that William Henry had married. Offended in some way by the news, he cast him aside with the other fallen idols: "W. H. is rather a fool, and bores me. I feel distressed for the old ewe—his mother. If he had any decency he would go and live with Mary Quick in my cottage and leave his mother on the farm. When they write to me I'll tell them that. But he'll be too 'big,' I know."[88] So the episode ended; and Lawrence, having failed to achieve a homoerotic solution to the painful and exhausting conflicts of his sexual life, would never be so close to a man again.

The Expulsion

WE WILL NEVER KNOW the precise roles of the various civil and military authorities in harassing the Lawrences during the war years; but certainly they were never left in peace for long, while at times rival agencies were stumbling over each other in their eagerness to keep their prey on the hop. In keeping Frieda under surveillance the Home Office acted through the police rather than the military. Cornwall was a coastal defense zone, so that coast watchers and military intelligence also came to take an interest in the Lawrences' affairs. Then there were the local people who made accusations about them to the police, who were obliged to investigate.[89] During 1916 all this amounted to no more than mild harassment, but after Mountsier's Christmas visit the Lawrences came under a steadily darkening cloud of suspicion. Then came the German proclamation of unrestricted submarine warfare on 31 January 1917. For the first few months of the offensive the British navy had no effective antisubmarine strategy and U-boats ranged freely in the western approaches sinking dozens of ships each week. If they had continued at the same rate Britain would have had to capitulate within a year for lack of food and supplies. Locally, three ships were sunk in February and March off the coast between Lands End and St. Ives; the coast watchers became ever more zealous as the situation worsened and the German successes led to absurd rumors—that they had a secret fuel dump in a cove below Zennor and so forth.

The rising fame of Manfred von Richthofen, the "Red Baron," also played its part in drawing attention to the Lawrences. On 29 April 1917 he shot down five British planes in one day, one of them his fiftieth kill. He was only a distant cousin of Frieda's and she had never met him, but anyone linked to such a German hero would acquire a reflected notoriety. Secure, as she thought, in her British citizenship, Frieda was indiscreet and at times provocative both in her dealings with authority and in her contacts by mail with her relatives; the local postman was a leading jingo and he cannot have relished delivering the *Berliner Tageblatt* to Higher Tregerthen. When Heseltine and Gray arrived in early summer, it began to seem that conspiracy was afoot—here were three apparently healthy young men and an obviously German woman, none with any regular occupations, and living in houses overlooking the sea. After the war, Gray learned that he had almost been disposed of by vigilantes in 1918:

> On one occasion an expedition of local worthies, armed with scythes and pitchforks, set out to march on my house at Bosigran with the intention of murdering me and throwing my body over the cliffs; but . . . the gallant host, as they drew nearer to their objective, gradually melted away, one by one, until only two of them were left by the time they reached their destination; whereupon they decided to postpone operations until some later and more auspicious occasion.[90]

Though Lawrence was a marked man in the neighborhood, he would not trim his sails to the wind—if anything, he seems to have spat into it:

[Somers] refused to be watchful, guarded, furtive, like the people around, saying double things as occasion arose, and hiding their secret thoughts and secret malignancy. He still believed in the freedom of the individual. . . . he hated the war, and said so to the few Cornish people around. He laughed at the palpable lies of the press, bitterly. And because of his isolation and his absolute separateness, he was marked out as a spy.

Impressive as Lawrence's devotion to principle may have been, it was not an attitude that would pass unnoticed or unpublished in 1917.

By August Lawrence suspected that his letters were being tampered with, which may account for the scarcity of references to war or politics in his 1917–18 correspondence. Self-appointed intelligence agents watched him and Frieda by day and eavesdropped on them by night, hiding under an overhanging boulder a few feet from their scullery window. When they tarred a chimney, when they hung curtains of different colors, when Frieda went out to the privy at night with a flashlight, they were suspected of signaling to enemy submarines. Frieda was stopped by two coast watchers and her bag searched for a camera—which turned out to be a loaf of bread. Around the end of the month came the most serious clash with authority yet, when the Lawrences went to stay overnight with Gray at Bosigran:

> . . . after supper, when it was already dark, we were sitting around the fire amusing ourselves by singing German folk-songs (it must have been a horrible noise) when suddenly there came a peremptory hammering at the front door. I went to open it, but even without waiting for me to do so, the door was flung open and in marched half a dozen or so men with loaded rifles, who proceeded to search the house, saying that lights had been noticed flashing out to sea from my windows. Finding nothing incriminating on the premises, the intruders withdrew, with operatic gestures like a Verdi chorus, and blood-curdling threats to the effect that I would hear more of the matter.[91]

Gray was charged under the Defense of the Realm Regulations with negligence in showing a light; he received "a vindictively heavy fine"—given as twenty pounds in *Kangaroo*—and a lecture on serving his country instead of "skulking in an out-of-the-way corner."

Though he suffered under the same odium that Lawrence did, Gray later developed a bitter enmity toward him that led him to condone the official harassment of them both:

[Lawrence] was foolishly lax and indiscreet in speech when in the company of people whom he may sometimes wrongly have supposed to be trustworthy; and at that time he more than once expressed to me—and to others, no doubt—his intention of initiating a disruptive, pacifist and nihilist campaign in the industrial North, with a view to bringing about a speedy end to the War. I remember vividly an occasion in his cottage at Tregerthen before the eviction, when he declared that he had definitely determined on this course of action and asked me whether I would be willing to accompany him: a suggestion to which I agreed unhesitatingly, such was the extent of his influence over me in those days.[92]

The only corroboration for this story is in a letter from Lawrence to Gray in June 1917, which ends with the phrase: "Remember the revolution." This was at a time when both men were facing unpleasant medical reexaminations—Gray was a C2, Lawrence a less vulnerable C3—and Lawrence was usually at his most bitter when faced with this threat (he told Eddie Marsh this time that he "should like to flourish a pistol under the nose of the fools that govern us").[93] But any plans he made to work actively against the war were probably no more than spasmodic—as Gray put it, "mere hot air, and as often as not entirely forgotten the next day." For all his fulminations against Lloyd George, the "little Welsh rat," Lawrence recognized that his regime would act more firmly and nastily against dissenters than Asquith had ever done. He was thus technically correct in assuring Lady Cynthia that he and Frieda were "as innocent even of pacifist activities, let alone spying of any sort as the rabbits in the field outside";[94] but it was an innocence born from caution and in his heart Lawrence longed to sabotage the war machine.

Gray, however, believed that Lawrence had a real and sinister talent for political agitation. Like Bertrand Russell, he was ashamed that Lawrence had once influenced him so strongly, and made up for it by exaggerating the wickedness of his erstwhile mentor:

Lawrence, in fact, could easily have become a British Hitler. Apart from many striking similarities of doctrine between them, which have become increasingly evident in the passage of the years, there was in Lawrence also the same dark, passionate, fanatical power, the same capacity for casting spells and captivating the sympathies and imagination of the common people, and especially the underdog. Fortunately he, and we, were saved from this fate by the strength of his artistic genius, in virtue of which his revolutionary impulses

(318)

received expression in his writings instead of in the field of politics and direct action.

The fact remains that Lawrence was a potential Hitler, and Scotland Yard may well have shown more psychological penetration than appeared at the time, in vaguely apprehending in him a subversive force such as was to emerge in due course elsewhere.*

The authorities certainly distrusted Lawrence and Frieda from the beginning of the war, but they took little direct action against them until summer 1917, when the war was going badly for the Allies and both the populace and the government were more eager than ever to find scapegoats on the Home Front. Some pressure to tighten up British security came from France, where widespread mutinies in May had raised the threat of a general insurrection and forced the army to go on the defensive. In June the young hero and poet Siegfried Sassoon issued a public statement against the war, assisted by Bertrand Russell and Jack Murry, and if Robert Graves had not arranged for Sassoon to be certified a victim of shell shock he would have become a *cause célèbre*. But the immediate cause of action against the Lawrences was most likely the fluctuations of submarine attacks. From March through July the coast near Zennor had been a relatively quiet zone and the success of the convoy system, introduced in June, must have given hope that it would remain so. In August, however, two ships were sunk between Lands End and St. Ives, and in September the toll suddenly jumped to six. This was just a random variation, but it must have led to increased vigilance along the coast.

On Thursday 11 October, while Frieda was at Gray's house and Lawrence in St. Ives, the cottage at Higher Tregerthen was searched by three men who took away—according to the account in *Kangaroo*—manuscripts, letters, and Lawrence's address book. They returned the next morning: a young army officer, two detectives, and the police sergeant from St. Ives. The policeman read them an order from Major-General Western of the Southern Command, Salisbury, ordering them to leave Cornwall within three days; to report to the police within twenty-four hours after finding a new residence; and to stay out of Class 2 prohibited

---

*Musical Chairs, 130–131. To put this in perspective it should be noted that Gray himself became one of the first British fascists in the early 1930s, though he later claimed that it was a mere foolish interlude.

areas—about one-third of England, comprising all coastal regions and major ports. The detectives searched the house again, taking some letters in German from Frieda's mother, and the whole party then took their leave. No grounds were given for the order, though the officer claimed that more was involved than the simple fact of Frieda's German birth; nor was there any means of appeal, since the order was made under section 14B of the Defense of the Realm Regulations. Ironically enough, the most prominent victim of such an order had been Bertrand Russell, who on 1 September 1916 had been forbidden to enter prohibited areas without special permission from the War Office. The action was inspired by Russell's summer tour of South Wales, where he had made antiwar speeches to large and receptive audiences of miners and steelworkers. The War Office generals conceded that Russell was not a German spy, but they pointed out to him that under section 14 they could also exclude anyone suspected "of acting, or of having acted, or of being about to act, in any manner prejudicial to the public safety of the Defence of the Realm."[95] This was enough to restrict Russell's movements until May 1918, when they were further restricted by putting him in Brixton prison—a fate that never seriously threatened Lawrence, for all his intransigence.

The Lawrences' expulsion order had come on Friday morning, so they had to be out of Cornwall on the following Monday. The financial blow alone appalled them: they had nearly six months still to run on their lease, which they had paid in advance, and nowhere else could they hope to find such cheap housing. Indeed, with their tarnished reputation and uncertain income they would find it hard to rent any accommodations, nor would they have the garden and farm produce that had kept their expenses low at Tregerthen. Finally, whatever money Frieda had been receiving from Germany could not be counted on in the future.

But far worse was the moral shock of being expelled from the place that they had thought was a refuge from militarism and social disintegration. Lawrence simply could not accept the idea that his whole way of life, created by eighteen months of dogged effort, had been summarily destroyed by a power against which there was no recourse—the same power that had suppressed *The Rainbow* two years before:

> Somers, so sick of things, had a great fire of all his old manuscripts. They decided to leave the house as it was, the books on the shelves, to take only their

personal belongings. For Somers was determined to come back. Until he had made up his mind to this, he felt paralysed. He loved the place so much. Ever since the conscription suspense began he had said to himself, when he walked up the wild, little road from his cottage to the moor: shall I see the foxgloves come out? If only I can stay till the foxgloves come. Then it was the heather— would he see the heather? And then the primroses in the hollow down to the sea: the tufts and tufts of primroses, where the fox stood and looked at him.

Lately, however, he had begun to feel secure, as if he had sunk some of himself into the earth there, and were rooted for ever. His very soul seemed to have sunk into that Cornwall, that wild place under the moors. And now he must tear himself out.

Cornwall had given Lawrence, who was always so finely attuned to his natural surroundings, as much peace and happiness as he could find anywhere in an England given over to the collective martyrdom of the war. Its lonely, treeless vistas had chimed perfectly with the creative impulse of *Women in Love,* that valedictory portrait of lovers, of a whole society, in extremity. If Lawrence had not succeeded in founding his little cloister of refugees from war there, he had at least been spared the strain of trying to reconcile himself with an intellectual society that ever tantalized him with partial assent to his deepest convictions. Now he must confront them again, be cast back into the maelstrom of London, to him "foul" and "sickening." But there was nowhere else to go.

CHAPTER VIII

LONDON
and HERMITAGE

LONDON: 44, Mecklenburgh Square

THE HOCKINGS loyally helped Lawrence and Frieda to pack up and drove them to St. Ives on Monday morning, 15 October. Cecil Gray, and perhaps William Henry too, gave them some money to get started in London. Lawrence assured William Henry they would meet again, though silently he doubted it. Then came the moment of departure, as Stanley Hocking recalled it fifty years later: "The military officer and the police sergeant were there at the station to see that they got on the train. I remember that. The officials just stood there and said nothing. Nobody spoke. All these people are dead now."[1] The Lawrences would never see Zennor again.

Richard Somers, in *Kangaroo,* sits on the train "perfectly still, and pale, in a kind of after death, feeling he had been killed. He had always *believed* so in everything—society, love, friends. This was one of his serious deaths in belief. So he sat with his immobile face of a crucified Christ who makes no complaint, only broods silently and alone, remote." Harriet, however, is happy to have escaped being interned and refuses to share in her husband's passion: "She had far less belief than he in the goodness of mankind. And she was rather relieved to get out of Cornwall." The bleak, inhuman quality of the Cornish landscape had soothed Lawrence, but to Frieda it meant only loneliness and hardship. She would be glad to have friends again and be close to her children, while the hostility of the locals at Zennor had deeply frightened her, as a German, in a way Lawrence seems not to have felt at all.

When the Lawrences arrived in London Dollie Radford made

them welcome in her little house at 32 Well Walk, Hampstead, though she was ailing and had to cope with the intermittent insanity of her husband. Lawrence reported their new residence to the police, and before long they again began to be questioned and followed by detectives. The day after arriving in London he went to ask Lady Cynthia for help in getting the expulsion order lifted; her diary entry shows that she felt she had little to offer except sympathy:

> His health doesn't allow of his living in London and all the money he has in the world is the *prospect* of eighteen pounds for the publication of some poems all about bellies and breasts which he gave me to read. People should either be left in peace *or* interned at the country's expense. I promised to do what I could in the matter, but doubt whether it will be much—after all, the woman *is* a German and it doesn't seem unreasonable.[2]

Whatever power her family still possessed was being used in the *cause célèbre* of Lady Angela Forbes, who had set up a network of troop canteens in France but had just been refused permission to return there by the British army. She was accused of drunkenness and immorality: for example, she had washed her hair in a kitchen sink, and a clergyman had heard her say "Damn!" while serving tea and sandwiches to ten thousand soldiers at five o'clock in the morning. It was the kind of family squabble much relished by the aristocracy; Lady Cynthia's father, Lord Wemyss, was a former lover of Lady Angela's and he arranged a face-saving compromise in the House of Lords. But for all her formidable backing she was not able to impose her will on the army; and the Lawrences, of course, had much less chance of doing so. Lawrence asked Gordon Campbell and Montague Shearman (a friend of Gertler and Kot) to attempt legal action, though this was futile when the government had acted under DORA. There remained only the hope that the military might change their mind; for some time Lawrence expected this happy turn of fortune, and only over several months did he gradually give up the dream of returning to Higher Tregerthen.

"Bid Me to Live"

MUCH AS he appreciated Dollie Radford's hospitality Lawrence found it "prison and misery" to be a long-term house guest, so after a week he and Frieda accepted the loan of Hilda Aldington's spacious bed-sitting room at 44, Mecklenburgh Square, on the eastern edge of Bloomsbury. (Hilda was staying near Richard Aldington's training camp at Lichfield, Staffordshire.) During their stay in London the Lawrences became part of Hilda's circle. Lady Ottoline and Russell were now anathema, and the whole previous "generation" of friends from Chesham had also become *non grata* at the time of Lawrence's return. Murry had collapsed from overwork at the War Office and was convalescing in the very citadel of the enemy, Garsington. Katherine had been living apart from Jack since the spring, but they kept in close touch and often visited Garsington together, so she too was out of favor. Kot was temporarily estranged because of Lawrence's attitude to the Jews. Whether Gertler was involved in the quarrel is unknown, but he was in any case a regular guest at Garsington; moreover, his unhappy affair with Carrington had left him nervous and easily depressed and he found intimacy with Lawrence a threat to his stability. Gordon Campbell, becoming richer and more respectable, apparently wanted to keep the contentious Lawrences at arm's length. Gilbert and Mary Cannan were separated; he was now living with a younger woman and had begun to show signs of the megalomania that caused him to be permanently confined to a mental home within a few years. The Carswells, finally, were away in Edinburgh, where Donald was in a military hospital; they returned to London before the Lawrences left, but were preoccupied with how to make a living—Donald had just been discharged from the army and Catherine was expecting a child in May.

Lawrence was thus open to forming new ties, and Hilda Aldington responded to his need. A year younger than Lawrence, she had been born Hilda Doolittle, the daughter of a professor of astronomy at the University of Pennsylvania. While a student at Bryn Mawr she joined the circle of literary young people around

Ezra Pound, and for a while they were unofficially engaged. Another member of the group, William Carlos Williams, has recalled Hilda's self-consciously poetic temperament. On one occasion, he warned her of an approaching thunderstorm:

> Instead of running or even walking toward a tree Hilda sat down in the grass at the edge of the hill and let it come.
> "Come, beautiful rain," she said, holding out her arms. "Beautiful rain, welcome." And I behind her feeling not inclined to join her in her mood. And let me tell you it rained, plenty.[3]

Miss Doolittle began to write poetry under the pseudonym H. D. by which she is commonly known. She came to London in 1911 and again lined up with Pound, becoming a founding member of the Imagist group of poets; in October 1913 she married Richard Aldington, another Imagist, who was six years younger than she.

The Aldingtons first met Lawrence on 30 July 1914 at Amy Lowell's dinner celebrating her sponsorship of a new Imagist anthology—a tactical victory in her struggle with Ezra Pound, wherein Pound had genius but no money, Amy the reverse. Lawrence mentioned in a letter to Harriet Monroe the next day that "Mrs. Aldington has a few good poems."[4] They became friends a year later when the Lawrences and the Aldingtons were both living in Hampstead, and shortly after moving to Porthcothan Lawrence asked Dollie Radford, whom he had introduced to H. D., to ask her if she wanted a cottage in Cornwall. She and Richard went to Exmoor, in north Devon, instead; Richard did not want to be exposed at close quarters to the Lawrences' stormy marriage, nor even to visit Zennor. Still, Lawrence and H. D. corresponded regularly and exchanged writings.[5] He considered her the only good poet among the Imagists, and touted her work to such arbiters of taste as Eddie Marsh; though he once joked about her poems: "She is like a person walking a tight-rope: you wonder if she'll get across."[6] Richard Aldington has pointed out that Lawrence was in some degree influenced by H. D.; his poem "Autumn Rain," written at Zennor, is almost a pastiche of her manner in *Sea Garden* (1916). Though the two poets shared a gift of quick and vivid response to nature, their fundamental concerns were very different: the voice one hears in *Sea Garden* is almost spectrally clear and disembodied, with none of the stark emotional urgency that stamps almost all of Lawrence's poems. One sees this opposition of temperament in H. D.'s criticism of *Look! We Have Come Through!*: ". . . they won't do at all: they are not *eternal*, not sublimated: too much body and emotions."[7] Nor did she like or understand *Women in Love* when he sent it to her early in 1917.

Despite these artistic conflicts, a special closeness had developed between them by autumn 1917. It began when H. D. was grieving over a miscarriage in 1915; Lawrence came to see her at Hampstead a number of times while Richard was away, and seemed to her the only one who really understood what she had suffered. The course of their relationship can be inferred from her autobiographical novel, *Bid Me to Live,* where the Lawrences figure as Elsa Frederick and "Rico," the Aldingtons as Julia and Rafe Ashton. After Aldington was conscripted, Lawrence apparently invited H. D. to join one of his projected colonies, telling her "we must go away where the angels come down to earth". The time cannot be set exactly but was probably when Lawrence hoped to live in the Marquesas—November 1916 to February 1917. It was, of course, not unusual for Lawrence to make such proposals to a married woman; but this time H. D. was willing to establish a bond with him, though only "in her purely emotional-cerebral dimension."

To understand H. D.'s attitude to Lawrence we must take into account the troubled state of her marriage. An illuminating and, it would seem, substantially accurate account of it is given in John Cournos' *roman à clef, Miranda Masters* (1926). The heroine, Miranda, refuses to sleep with her husband after having had a miscarriage, for fear of another pregnancy, but does not want to give him up. Her solution is to "Get someone to release his flesh and his soul shall be yours. . . . But no harlot! No common creature!" Meanwhile she herself becomes passionately attached to various other men, artists or writers, arousing their desires but stopping just short of satisfying them. The narrator of the novel, Gombarov (standing for Cournos himself), is one of these chosen ones for a while; though a friend warns him that Miranda is only "a spiritual hetaira." When a friend of Gombarov's, Winifred Gwynne, rents a room in Miranda's house she picks on her as a suitable companion for her husband: "What she lacks in spirit she makes up in the loveliness of her body. So that she cannot possibly be my rival." But her husband soon tells her that he loves Winifred and wants to live with her. Miranda laughs hysterically and cries out "By all means let us be sensible. Let us forget blessed madness, sacred passion, ecstasy of gods. . . . Let us be as other people with their commonplace habits and petty lusts."

This is how the affair stood when the Lawrences came to live at Mecklenburgh Square. The Aldingtons were away, as we have seen, but Richard had started an affair with the original of "Winifred," an American girl of his own age named Dorothy Yorke, known to her friends as Arabella. An attractive and fashionable bohemian, she worked sporadically as a decorator in Paris and in London. She had previously had an affair with John Cournos, and came to live in his room at Mecklenburgh Square when he went to Russia shortly before the Lawrences arrived. In *Aaron's Rod* Lawrence was to draw her portrait as "Josephine Ford," "a cameolike girl with neat black hair done tight and bright in the French mode. She had strangely-drawn eyebrows, and her colour was brilliant." In *Bid Me to Live* she is Bella Carter, the girl upstairs with whom Julia (H. D.) maintains an uneasy friendship, knowing that she is her husband's mistress.

When Rico and Elsa (the Lawrences) arrive on the scene in *Bid Me to Live,* Julia soon draws them into her network of intrigue by adding herself onto their relationship:

> she and Rico would burn away, cerebralistically, they would burn out together.
> Julia existed, parasitically, on Rafe, and Rico lived on Elsa. But once alive, fed as it were from these firm-fleshed bodies, they were both free, equal too, in intensity, matched, mated.[8]

The apparent symmetry of this pattern, however, obscures the fact that Julia casts herself as the central figure who enjoys an intense spiritual connection with both men. The two other women merely have to satisfy the men physically so that they will accept Julia on her own terms.

One need hardly stress the pitfalls that awaited anyone who became intimate with H. D., yet by accepting the loan of her room Lawrence tacitly admitted that he wanted their relationship to develop further. He recognized, also, that after his Cornish exile he needed more contact with people if he was to write fiction again. So, two weeks after arriving in London, he renounced for a while his homesickness for Zennor: "I am not anxious to come back just now," he told Gray, "One seems to be, in some queer way, vitally active here. And then, people, one or two, seem to give a strange new response."[9] Consciously or not, he was assembling the cast of another novel.

The Lawrences got on well from the start with Dorothy Yorke, and their friendship was to be a long and relatively tranquil one. Then H. D. returned from Lichfield for a visit, during which the three women slept in her room while Lawrence used Dorothy's. In *Bid Me to Live,* Julia records her first impression of "Rico":

> The mud was still stuck to his rough ploughman boots, his corduroy trousers were tucked in at the tops. He had not even had time to shake, as it were, the dust off his feet. Cornwall was still with him. The sea-tan, sun-tan, had not withered from his face; but for all that, one felt the pallor beneath it. Soon he would be white and drawn, as he had been the first time she saw him, visibly an invalid, with his narrow chest, his too-flaming beard, his blue eyes.

As if Julia's scenario were not complex enough, on their first evening together Elsa adds another term to the equation:

> Rico said, "You are there for all eternity, our love is written in blood," he said, "for all eternity." But whose love? His and Elsa's? No—that was taken for granted. It was to be a perfect triangle. Elsa acquiesced.
> "This will leave me free," she muttered in her German guttural, "for Vanio."

"Vanio" corresponds to Cecil Gray, whom the Lawrences familiarly called "Grigio"; but Julia, in the novel, cannot tell how serious Elsa and Rico are about their proposal:

> obviously he and Elsa had it all fixed up between them. . . . Elsa had or would have or had had a young friend (lover?), a musician; this fitted in with Rico's great goddess-mother idea of her and did not break across their own relationship. Elsa had fed Rico on her "power," it was through her, in her, and around her that he had done his writing.

During both her marriages Frieda had indulged in casual affairs with younger men, so it is likely enough that she might have done so with Gray—perhaps out of pique at Lawrence's attachment to William Henry. Nonetheless, Lawrence remained on friendly terms with Gray and looked forward to seeing him in London. When Gray arrived, then, he and Frieda would be free to resume their affair, since Lawrence would be occupied with H. D.

So, at least, Julia assumes when she finds herself alone with Rico the next day. Like "a child waiting for instruction" she moves her chair to his elbow:

> Now was the moment to answer his amazing proposal of last night, his "for all eternity." She put out her hand. Her hand touched his sleeve. He shivered, he seemed to move back, move away, like a hurt animal. . . . It was not she who had started out to lure him. It was himself with his letters, and last night his open request for this relationship. Yet even this touch (not heavy on his sleeve) seemed to send some sort of repulsion through him. She drew back her hand. There were voices at the door.

She wonders if Rico withdrew because he sensed the approach of visitors, or because of "personal repugnance, some sort of *noli me tangere*"; but the latter seems more plausible, since Rico takes no further initiative and the much-heralded affair between him and Julia is never consummated. The novel gives no clear reason for this, but a conversation recorded elsewhere by H. D. sheds some light on the affair:

> Frieda said that she had had a friend, an older man, who had told her that "if love is free, everything is free." There had been the scene the night before or shortly before, in which Lawrence said that Frieda was there for ever on his right hand, I was *there* for ever—on his left. Frieda said when we were alone, "but Lawrence does not really care for women. He only cares for men. Hilda, *you have no idea of what he is like.*" [10]

Typically enough, Frieda's affectation of extreme frankness disguises a deeper reticence. The "older man" sounds like her former lover Otto Gross, a psychiatrist whose theories of sexual and political liberation anticipated the more famous work of Wilhelm Reich; by taking Gray as a lover Frieda could feel that she was striking a blow for a new era, and also nurturing yet another creative young man. Her dark warning about Lawrence's sexual nature reflected her belief that only a women of extraordinary strength of character, like herself, could cope with his unnamable vagaries.

Lawrence's version of the episode differs from those of Frieda or H. D., but does not contradict them. When Gray taunted him about living in such an equivocal ménage, and likened his female adorers to Mary Magdalene washing Christ's feet, he retorted that "If Jesus had paid more attention to Magdalene, and less to his

disciples, it would have been better. It was not the ointment-pour-
ing which was so devastating, but the discipleship of the twelve."
  Instead of Pharisaically criticizing his dealings with women—
which were "not so Philippically filthy either"—Frieda and Gray
should recognize that he was seeking a new kind of relation between the sexes:

> your hatred of me, like Frieda's hatred of me, is your cleavage to a world of
> knowledge and being which you ought to forsake, which, by organic law, you
> must depart from or die. And my 'women,' Esther Andrews, Hilda Aldington,
> etc. represent, in an impure and unproud, subservient, cringing, bad fashion,
> I admit—but represent none the less the threshold of a new world, or un-
> derworld, of knowledge and being. And the Hebridean songs, which repre-
> sent you and Frieda in this, are songs of the damned: that is, songs of those
> who inhabit an underworld which is forever an underworld, never to be made
> open and whole. And you would like us all to inhabit a suggestive underworld
> which is never revealed or opened, only intimated, only *felt* between the initi-
> ated. —I won't have it. The old world must burst, the underworld must be
> open and whole, new world. You want an emotional sensuous underworld,
> like Frieda and the Hebrideans: my 'women' want an ecstatic subtly-intellec-
> tual underworld, like the Greeks—Orphicism—like Magdalene at her feet-
> washing—and there you are.[11]

Lawrence seems to associate Gray and Frieda with the decadent
sensuality of Gudrun and Loerke, whose "whole correspondence
was in a strange, barely comprehensible suggestivity, they kindled
themselves at the subtle lust of the Egyptians or the Mexicans."
The Hebridean folk songs that Gray liked to sing belonged, similarly, to an outmoded phase of history; and the relation between
Gray and Frieda seemed to Lawrence "an inflamed darkness of
sensation" and a denial of life.
  With H. D. Lawrence was groping for a different kind of connection. It was still imperfect because her subservience to him
conflicted with the ideal of "free, proud singleness," but he shared
with her an interest in the Orpheus legend as a guide for their
quest. H. D. had been working on a poem called "Eurydice," in
part as a way of "sublimating" her recent unhappy experiences:
Eurydice's descent into the underworld corresponds to her miscarriage, the descent of Orpheus to her reconciliation with Richard, the separation of Orpheus and Eurydice to Richard's departure for the war and his affair with Dorothy Yorke. The poem
ends with Eurydice abandoned in the underworld, yet more content there than in the upper world that her husband enjoys:

At least I have the flowers of myself
and my thoughts, no god
can take that;
I have the fervour of myself for a presence
and my own spirit for light.

This is the "ecstatic subtly-intellectual underworld" that Lawrence proposes to share with her. His own mention of the Orphic cult implies that their union would be a mutual devotion in asceticism: the Orphics believed that man had a dual nature and tried to purge themselves of their sensual part—the Titan inheritance—in order to cultivate their divine nature, derived from Dionysus. But Lawrence's categories were so esoteric that even so sensitive a person as H. D. could not tell what he really wanted from her; one can only assume that he was again trying to establish some relationship different in quality from his marriage, and thus counterbalancing it—this time, however, with a woman rather than a man. Yet at the same time, according to *Kangaroo,* he was writing "passionately" to William Henry and hoping that he would join in founding a new colony. It is probably just as well that his plans to reorganize his close relationships remained tentative and incomplete.

The Next Step?

HAVING once again formed a circle of friends, Lawrence naturally turned his mind to the old vision of an ideal community somewhere far to the west of Europe. He had resumed his friendship with Dr. David Eder, who kindled his imagination with stories about visiting his uncle's Colombian plantation in 1898. In those days Eder had been a great adventurer, collecting zoological specimens in the wildest parts of Colombia, Bolivia, and Brazil. Lawrence wrote to Gray right away about this new opportunity: "The Andes become real and near. Dr. Eder will come— something *right* in him. . . . He has relatives who have big estates in Colombia. We can get as far as these estates—rest there—then move on to find our own place. The Eder plantations are in the Cauca Valley, Colombia—towards the old Spanish Town of Po-payán, which is inhabited now only by Indians."[12] He also invited the Carswells (though admitting that her pregnancy was "a complication"), giving them a complete cast of characters:

> There will be Frieda and I, and Eder, and Mrs. Eder, and William Henry and Gray, and probably Hilda Aldington, and maybe Kot and Dorothy Yorke. We shall go to the east slope of the Andes, back of Paraguay or Colombia. Eder knows the country *well*. Gray can find one thousand pounds. The war will end this winter. In that case we set off in the spring—say March.[13]

It seems appropriate that such a motley company should be aimed toward Paraguay, whither Candide had voyaged before them, telling his skeptical companions: "We are going to a different world, and I expect it is the one where all goes well. . . . It is undoubtedly the new world that is the best of all possible universes." But of course they never came close even to buying tickets. Gray had no thousand pounds to set the ball rolling; in any case, as he recalled, "the idea of spending the rest of my life in the Andes in the company of Lawrence and Frieda, filled me with horror—the combination of the mountain heights and the psychological depths was more than I could sanely contemplate."[14] Nor did he relish playing second fiddle to a Lawrence surrounded by "a worshipping circle of attractive female disciples." The two men continued to squabble by letter, until Lawrence had to admit that their friendship had exhausted itself:

> I don't care what you accept or don't, either: it bores me a bit. But don't go throwing about accusations and calling me a liar gratuitously. Look, we have come through—whether you can see it or not. —Perhaps you are right to resent the impertinence of the "Look!" None the less, we have come through. —But enough of this—we can leave it alone henceforth, and abstain, me from underworlds etc., you from calling me a liar.[15]

The other prospective colonists also ruled themselves out: William Henry could not leave his farm, Kot would not leave his house, the Eders had not really believed in the project, and so forth. Anyway, none of the men could leave England while the war lasted. By summer 1918 Lawrence was already looking back on it nostalgically, as yet another fading dream: "Do you remember this time last year we talked of the Andes?" he wrote

Gray. "—and you used to say you were not *ready*. There won't be any Andes. And I don't suppose any of us were ready."[16]

While living at Mecklenburgh Square Lawrence had told Gray that he could not read or write at all, only try to learn Greek "faintly and fitfully"—probably because of a shared interest with H. D. in Greek mythology. He exaggerated, of course; despite all the comings and goings in H. D.'s room, *Bid Me to Live* is sprinkled with vignettes of Rico writing in the midst of everything: "He had spread the note-book open on his knee and was scribbling away, simple all-there, like a little schoolmaster setting an examination or correcting an exercise, she thought, the true artist working with no apparent self-consciousness." Lawrence seems to have suspended work on *Studies in Classic American Literature* while he was in London, but he agreed to write an article for Wilbur Cross of the *Yale Review* on "The Limits to the British Novelists," in response to an article by a Mrs. Gerould in a previous issue. Since so few periodicals were willing to buy his work he could hardly refuse the fee of ten guineas; yet he remarked, presciently, that he would only write for Cross "if you let me say what I liked, which you wouldn't." Cross ran true to form by rejecting Lawrence's piece on the grounds that it would be out of date by the time he could print it and it has unfortunately been lost.[17]

A few years later Lawrence was able to shy coconuts freely at his rivals, in his sparkling essays on the modern novel. But whatever his opinion of their literary merits, in December 1917 he was willing to seek the patronage of Bennett and Galsworthy if it would enable *Women in Love* to appear. Pinker served as intermediary, since Bennett was his client and he was friendly with Galsworthy; the idea, apparently, was for the two of them to put up the capital for a private printing. Pinker invited Galsworthy and Lawrence to lunch together on 13 November; Galsworthy described the "provincial genius" in his journal as "Interesting, but a type I could not get on with. Obsessed with self. Dead eyes, and a red beard, long narrow pale face. A strange bird."[18] Nor was Lawrence inclined to admire Galsworthy's self-assurance and worldly fame. He had already dismissed him as boring and "vieux-jeu," and before the war he had told Edward Garnett that he did not want to write like Galsworthy even if he could. Neither Galsworthy nor Bennett, of course, agreed to pay for printing *Women in Love*. By the time Lawrence heard this he was not much disappointed, anyway, for he was again pursuing the will-o'-the-wisp of trade publication. His contact this time was Joseph Hone, a young Irish writer whom he met through Gordon Campbell. Hone had provided financing for Maunsel and Co., publishers, of Dublin, and Lawrence hoped that he might induce them to take *Women in Love*. Hone, the future biographer of Yeats and George Moore, was also a friend of James Joyce's from the Martello Tower days and a man of integrity; but the firm he backed was another matter. Its manager, George Roberts, had agreed in 1909 to publish *Dubliners* then subjected its struggling author to a shameful ordeal of harassment and prevarication. In 1912 Maunsel finally printed the book, but then took fright and destroyed the entire edition; Joyce considered whether to shoot Roberts, then settled on the more prudent course of leaving Ireland the next day and never returning. Fortunately for Lawrence, matters never progressed so far that *Women in Love* had to run the gauntlet of Irish prudery.

Hone also suggested to Lawrence that Maunsel might publish the latest version of his philosophy, "At the Gates." Heseltine was now living in Dublin, trying to evade both his wife and the military authorities. He had again changed course on Lawrence and now considered "The Reality of Peace" to be "the supreme utterance of all modern philosophy."[19] In January Hone went to Dublin, where Lawrence hoped he would join forces with Heseltine to get the philosophy into print; but, once more, nothing was achieved. Meanwhile George Moore had read *Women in Love* and his verdict got back to Lawrence: "[he] says it is a great book," Lawrence told Catherine Carswell, "and that I am a better writer than himself."[20] The praise was welcome, even if it could not be converted into any more tangible benefit.

The publication of *Look! We Have Come Through!* in mid-November by Chatto and Windus turned into another painful disappointment. Its reception was summed up in Bertrand Russell's barbed witticism: "They may have come through, but why should I look?" The only early review, buried at the back of the *Times Literary Supplement,* was cast in the depressing mould that had become familiar over the past three years. The reviewer conceded Lawrence his skillful handling of *vers libre,* but deplored his "orgies of extreme eroticism" and "quasi-tragic despairs." By way of summation he described the poem "She Looks Back" as "excited morbid babble about one's own emotions which the Muse of poetry surely can only turn from with a pained distaste."[21] Telling this to Amy Lowell, Lawrence observed wryly: "I feel as if I had affronted a white-haired old spinster with weak eyes. But I don't really care what critics say, so long as I myself could personally be left in peace. This, it seems, cannot be. People write letters of accusation, because one has a beard and looks not quite the usual thing: and then one has detectives at one's heels like stray dogs, not to be got rid of. It is very hateful and humiliating and degrading."[22] Even if the hounds could be thrown off the scent, to live in peace required money, and the failure of *Look! We Have Come Through!* made Lawrence's financial prospects bleaker than ever. The eighteen pounds advance he never saw, because it went directly to reduce his debt to Pinker; he had two articles forthcoming in the *English Review* and a book barely started—*Studies in Classic American Literature*—for which he had no contract. *Women in Love* had now been making the rounds for a year, without any firm prospect of publication. Though Lawrence held to his vocation as a writer he seemed to be disqualified from making a living at it, for as far ahead as he could see.

London at War

DESPITE the complications of life at Mecklenburgh Square, Lawrence took a certain relish in mixing with the fashionable world of London after nearly two years of Cornwall. With casual acquaintances he could still be a charming and light-hearted companion, and by December Lady Cynthia was noting that he was "obviously *much* happier and saner for his visit to London."[23] He and Frieda went regularly to the opera; for *Aida* on 13 November Lady Cynthia had been lent Lady Cunard's box and set out to fill it with "the most comic concentration of human beings ever seen." Besides the Lawrences, the party included Augustus John— another "provincial genius," but one who knew better how to trade on his eccentricities—and Ivo Grenfell. The latter was the youngest son of Lord Desborough, a handsome eighteen-year-old recruit in the blue uniform of the Household Cavalry. His eldest brother, Julian, was a famous scholar-athlete who had captured the spirit of 1915 with his poem "Into Battle," and had written home from Flanders: "I adore war. It's like a big picnic without the objectlessness of a picnic. I have never been so well or so happy."[24] Before long he was shot in the head at the second battle of Ypres; three months later the middle brother, Billie, was killed too. By 1917 Lady Cynthia had become inured to the daily horrors of war but she still found young Ivo a touching figure, now threatened by the fate of his two brothers. The evening at the opera, however, did not let her indulge these tender feelings: "The most piquant features," she noted, "were the conjunction of two red beards and of the young guardsman to the Pacifist's Hun wife. She would talk about the war to Yvo and tell him how very much smarter the German regiments were! She was draped in a Chinese shawl and Lawrence had trimmed his beard for the occasion." Lawrence himself, at the end of the affair, "announced that he would like to howl like a dog."[25]

Before this night at the opera Lady Cynthia, trying to promote a friendship between the two "red beards," had inveigled the Lawrences to John's studio, where she was sitting for a portrait. Though Lawrence "admired the large designs," for the most part he repeated his performance at Duncan Grant's studio in 1915. "He charged John," Lady Cynthia wrote, "to depict 'generations of Wemyss disagreeableness in my face, especially the mouth,' said disappointment was the keynote of my expression, and that what made him 'wild' was that I was 'a woman with a weapon she would never use! Let the dead paint the dead.' . . . He thought the painting of Bernard Shaw with closed eyes very true symbolism." John took all this imperturbably and even asked Lawrence to sit for a portrait sketch, but this unfortunately never came about. Next day Lawrence told Lady Cynthia he liked John, but he was "a drowned corpse"; he added that John couldn't "paint you— very boring, his attempts."[26] Their acquaintance, not surprisingly, went no further, though when Lawrence's paintings were seized by the London police in 1929 John signed a letter of protest and volunteered to testify that they were "serious works of art."

At Mecklenburgh Square Lawrence was able to enjoy a more casual social life than in Lady Cynthia's fashionable world. He liked to organize charades; in one of them casting himself as God the Father and Frieda as the Serpent in Eden. H. D.'s opaque and brooding recollections of the group are counterbalanced by the lighter mood that prevails in Brigit Patmore's sketches of it:

> Everyone burned with a different incandescence. Frieda in a sun-drenched way, wild, blonde hair waving happily, grey-green eyes raying out laughter, her fair skin an effulgent pale rose. Lorenzo, as if he had drunk fire and was quite used to it. Hilda, a swaying sapling almost destroyed by tempests, all the blueness of flame gone into her large distracted eyes. Cecil Gray was a shaded candle, he held his intelligence watchfully behind spectacles. Arabella [Dorothy Yorke], the only dark one among us, smouldered under her polished hair. She was cross once because Lorenzo compared her to a lacquer box, but she *was* imprisoned in something and disliked our mental prankishness. Richard flickered with the desperate gaiety of the soldier on leave and unresolved pain. He had the most robust body and therefore its broad strength showed none of our febrile agitations.[27]

Brigit herself hovered on the fringe of the circle. A beautiful woman of about Lawrence's age, she was drawn to the artistic life but her stockbroker husband wanted her to remain at their suburban house with their two young children. Later she was to break away, living with Richard Aldington in the late 1920s and becoming a published writer. Lawrence met her when he was first shown around London by Ford Madox Ford, but it was not until 1917 that they became close friends. She was the kind of fine lady that he liked to weave romantic fantasies about, though without making any serious demands of her; he was content to enjoy her stylishness, her Irish charm, and her striking looks. Her memoirs of him often show Lawrence in the cheerful, irreverent mood that he could still slip into when the moment was favorable. One day, for example, when Frieda was ill he set off with Brigit for lunch at a smart restaurant, wearing his usual velvet jacket and corduroy trousers:

> The waiters were shocked in their vulgar consciousness of Lorenzo's unconventional clothes and they did not disguise it. I refused table after table with the nonchalant impertinence they take for good manners. Lorenzo did not seem to notice their rudeness, but I felt like a watch-dog. . . .
> Back in Mecklenburgh Square we found Frieda sitting up in bed by the side of the fire.
> "Well, Frieda, are you all right? Do you feel better?"
> "Yes. *So* much better, Lorenzo. So lovely and *warm* here. But *such* a stupid book. No *reality,* no *feeling.* How stupid people are! I can't *bear* it."

"Of course we're never stupid, are we? The woman thinks she's perfect, does she? Well, well." Putting a fresh glass of lemonade on the table by Frieda's pillow. "Brigit took me to the Elysian Fields. Think of that. And the waiters didn't approve of Brigit's guest so she turned very haughty and great lady. She wanted to drink claret and I wouldn't let her."

"How *like* you, Lorenzo. Such a *bully*. Poor Brigit, he would go against you just to exercise his power. You *must* not give way."[28]

Though Lawrence enjoyed being lionized by ladies of fashion he always retained a wry awareness of how superficial his excursions into that world would remain. When Aaron Sisson reflects on his distaste for London, in *Aaron's Rod,* he probably expresses a good deal of Lawrence's own feelings about his stay at Mecklenburgh Square:

He was flattered, of course, by his own success—and felt at the same time irritated by it. . . . Wherever he was he liked to be given, tacitly, the first place—or a place among the first. Among the musical people he frequented, he found himself on a callow kind of equality with everybody, even the stars and aristocrats, at one moment, and a backstairs outsider the next. . . . There was a certain excitement in slithering up and down the social scale, one minute chatting in a personal tête-a-tête with the most famous, or notorious, of the society beauties; and the next walking in the rain, with his flute in a bag, to his grubby lodging in Bloomsbury. Only the excitement roused all the savage sarcasm that lay at the bottom of his soul, and which burned there like an unhealthy bile.

Beyond all the dining-out and opera-going, moreover, there ran always the dark counterpoint of the war, now passing through one of its worst phases for England. The British summer offensive in Flanders had opened with some encouraging local successes, but in the October rains it was reaching its dreadful anticlimax. Until now, the war's great image of horror for England had been an ironic one: the carnage of the first day of the Somme, with its incongruous setting of a perfect summer's day in a "vast garden of scarlet wild poppies." But Passchendaele stripped away any glamor, any contrast between mass death and natural beauty. There was no more "field" of battle, all vegetation had been smashed by artillery, the slaughter took place on a landscape all of whose features reduced to a single word: mud. Leon Wolff's description of the attack of the 66th Division on 9 October shows the three remaining elements of the war: the machine gun, the mud, and the victims:

(341)

As the British walked forward the classic drama of the Western Front was again enacted, in this instance even more graphically—the scene that will forever haunt Western civilization—for as they did so the rain perversely stopped and in perfect visibility German machine gunners began to play upon the advancing waves of men, their bullets lashing and spurting from the pillboxes and from behind parapets. In the flame and clamor and greasy smoke the British slogged forward deliberately, almost unhurriedly. . . . As the British walked, some seemed to pause and bow their heads; they sank carefully to their knees; they rolled over without haste and then lay quietly in the soft, almost caressing mud. Others yelled when they were hit, and grabbed frantically at limbs or torso, and rolled and tumbled. In their fear of drowning beneath the slime they tried to grip the legs of their comrades, who struggled to break free.[29]

To all this Lawrence affected a stony indifference. Yet when on 17 October he wrote to Cecil Gray at Zennor, he was barely able to keep the horror of Flanders from overwhelming him:

But oh, the sickness that is in my belly. London is really very bad: gone mad, in fact. It thinks and breathes and lives air-raids, nothing else. People are not people any more: they are factors, really ghastly, like lemures, evil spirits of the dead. What shall we do, how shall we get out of this Inferno? . . .

'To every brave cometh test of fire,' . . . It's like that—only should be 'cometh test of mud.' It is like being slowly suffocated in mud. Nevertheless, we will come out somehow. But I have never known my heart so pressed with weight of mud.[30]

In his war novel *Death of a Hero* Richard Aldington describes how life in England becomes spectral for his soldier-hero: only the Front, whatever its horrors, is real. He had written Lawrence in February 1918, concerning the tangled web at Mecklenburgh Square: "These human relationships which now seem so important will, I know, soon become trivial, almost nothing. For . . . in a short time I shall inevitably be sent to France."[31] But Lawrence felt only contempt for Aldington's attitude, since his own was precisely the opposite. Rawdon Lilly, in *Aaron's Rod*, expounds this view to Aaron after having been visited by a veteran who obsessively repeats the horrors he has seen:

"The war was a lie and is a lie and will go on being a lie till somebody busts it." . . .

"But the war did happen, right enough," smiled Aaron palely.

"No, it didn't. Not to me or to any man, in his own self. It took place in the automatic sphere, like dreams do. But the *actual man* in every man was just ab-

sent—asleep—or drugged—inert—dream-logged. . . . I *knew* the war was false
. . . The Germans were false, we were false, everybody was false."

"And not you?" asked Aaron shrewishly.

"There was a wakeful, self-possessed bit of me which knew that the war and
all that horrible movement was false for me. And so I wasn't going to be
dragged in. . . . I would like to kill my enemy. But become a bit of that huge
obscene machine they called the war, that I never would, no not if I died ten
deaths and had eleven mothers violated."

As the war became more horrible, the normal reaction was to
become more obsessed by it, even against the promptings of one's
"better self." But for Lawrence, the worse it got the more he felt
bound to deny it a foothold in his emotions, since for him consciousness meant complicity; not until years afterward could he
speak from the heart of what the war had done to him.

Clearly, he could be less conscious of the war if he left London.
Since 30 November he and Frieda had moved to 136, Earl's Court
Square, where Cecil Gray's mother had the lease of a flat.
Lawrence loathed it on sight, he told Lady Cynthia: "The middle
classes, and the whitewashed devil of middle class-dom sends me
mad. . . . I hate this milieu. It makes Cornwall seem *very* desirable."[32] But their return was still blocked. The only practical
recourse, for the moment, was to accept Dollie Radford's offer to
lend them her cottage at Hermitage in Berkshire. Shortly before
Christmas they set out for the country; they would never again
live in London—or, for that matter, any large city—for the rest of
their married life.

HERMITAGE: Chapel Farm Cottage

HERMITAGE is a small village in Berkshire about five miles
north of Newbury, on the edge of the Chilterns. Its houses are
scattered along a wooded hillside, but the views from them are not
extensive; the landscape is trim and enclosed in the style of the
Home Counties, utterly unlike the bare wildness of Zennor.
Chapel Farm Cottage is actually two attached houses, each laid

out in the usual rather cramped two rooms up and two down, though there is a pleasant hedged garden with trees overhanging. Hermitage was too like Chesham for Lawrence to be really content there: once again he was buried in a countryside too tame for his mood, at an impasse in his career, suffering from bad health in an uncomfortable cottage. In some ways the Lawrences were even worse off than they had been at Chesham for they lacked money, friends, and even food and fuel. Furthermore, the police came by regularly to check up on their affairs. The worst hardship, perhaps, was the moral one of occupying the house on Dollie Radford's charity; Lawrence's letters from Hermitage are sprinkled with splenetic outbursts against her—especially when she reclaimed the cottage for short visits, so that he and Frieda had to take rooms in the village. At Zennor the grandeur of the scenery had conferred glamor even on their straitened existence, but Hermitage must often have seemed no more than a mean and inglorious cul-de-sac.

Nonetheless, Lawrence had learned the uses of patience since 1914; he was always soothed by any kind of countryside, and his emotional life during this first stay of four months in Berkshire seems less feverish than at any previous period during the war. It was futile to plan any new Rananim when clearly the fighting was going to continue for at least another summer; most of his acquaintances, anyway, had settled into a gloomy inner state of siege. In November Katherine Mansfield had caught a chill while visiting Jack at Garsington; soon she was found to be suffering from active tuberculosis, and forced to follow an invalid regime. She went alone in January to Bandol for several months of convalescence, since Jack could not leave his War Office job. It is not certain when Lawrence learned of her broken health, but the bitterness ran too deep on both sides for even this blow to produce any immediate reconciliation.

One positive step, however, was Lawrence's renewed friendship with Kot after the break caused by his anti-Semitic letters of the summer. Once again Kot became Lawrence's agent in London, called on to escort his sister Ada from Marylebone to Waterloo, to supply books, or to negotiate with Leonard and Virginia Woolf a possible sublet of Higher Tregerthen. Rather than knowing the Woolfs the Lawrences knew of them, thorugh such mutual acquaintances as Kot, E. M. Forster, and Katherine. Though

Lawrence was intrigued (and Frieda even more so) by the idea of exchanging Higher Tregerthen for the Woolfs' house in Richmond, nothing came of the proposal, either at this time or when it was revived in May 1919. So Lawrence was again forced to sue for help in getting a roof over his head. He first went to stay with his sister Ada for the New Year, where it was suggested she might pay the rent for a cottage near Ripley for him and Frieda. He was reluctant to shelter so closely under the family tree—a cottage in Berkshire would have suited him better—but eventually this was what he was forced to accept. Meanwhile he could only return cap in hand to Pinker:

> Do you think that Arnold Bennett or somebody like that, who is quite rich out of literature, would give me something to get along with? It is no use my trying to delude myself that I can make money in this world that is. But there is coming a big smash-up, after which my day will begin. And as the smash-up is not far off, so I am not very far off from a walk-in.[33]

Lawrence did not know that Bennett had already made him an anonymous load of forty pounds via Pinker in November 1915 as a discreet mark of sympathy over the banning of *The Rainbow*. This time Bennett committed himself to a subsidy of three pounds a week, but only if H. G. Wells and John Galsworthy did the same. They refused, as he could probably have anticipated. When told by Pinker that Lawrence was insulted, Bennett "confined [his] assistance to the preaching of Lawrence's dazzling merits." What Lawrence actually told Pinker was: "If Arnold Bennett will help, why the devil must he wait for others to keep him in countenance. And if he won't, why then so be it."[34] Given that Lawrence's assets totaled six pounds nineteen shillings his remarks were pointed rather than insulting; but Bennett, by his own account "dazzled" by Lawrence, was wary of burning his fingers in the flame. In his heart he seems to have acknowledged—or feared—that a greater man than himself had emerged from the Midlands, but 10,000 pounds a year and the veneration of the great public were not to be jeopardized by too violent an espousal of Lawrence's cause.

The final crisis of penury was averted by Montague Shearman and Kot, who each sent Lawrence ten pounds at the end of February. Both were Jewish, yet Lawrence was not moved by their generosity—nor that of Dr. Eder, who had given him money the previous October—to stop grinding his anti-Semitic axe. The most he did was pay Shearman the backhanded compliment of telling him he was not one of the "damnable people like Pinker, my agent, who dangle a prospective fish on the end of a line, with grinning patronage, and just jerk it away. . . . . I've got quite a lot of murder in my soul: heaven knows how I shall ever get it out."[35] Soon afterward Lawrence received nine guineas from the *English Review* for his essays on "Love" and "life," so he was able to keep Kot's check uncashed and eventually return it to him in July. The long-run outlook, though, was as bleak as ever unless *Studies in Classic American Literature* became a money-maker—which was unlikely—or the war ended and Frieda could get some money from her family. Lawrence had complained to Pinker that "one can't begin taking one's hat off to money, at this late hour of the day."[36] But the hard fact was that he and Frieda had been living mainly on charity for some time, and would have to go on doing so even after the end of the war. It was not until 1920, when the American market began to open up and Lawrence acquired a reliable English publisher in Martin Secker, that he was again able to support himself. The hue and cry after *The Rainbow* cost him almost five years of penury.

Life or Work?

THOUGH the Lawrences' existence at Hermitage was undramatic and they were often pinched for necessities, they were at least removed from the "evil influence" of London; "our simple life in the cottage," Frieda recalled, "healed [Lawrence] a lot."[37] Increasing shortages of food and fuel made it awkward for people to pay visits: apart from the Radfords, only Barbara Low came to stay. For several weeks in January and February Lawrence was bedridden with colds and the bronchitis that he had escaped during the previous winter; he could do little but gaze out the window and muse on the change in his situation:

There is a field—the thatched roof of a cottage—then trees and other roofs. As the evening falls, and it is snowy, there is a clear yellow light, an evening star, and a moon. The trees get dark. Those without leaves seem to thrill their twigs above—the firs and pines slant heavy with snow—and I think of looking out of the Tregerthen window at the sea. And I no longer want the sea, the space, the abstraction. There is something living and rather splendid about trees. They stand up so proud, and are alive.

When Lawrence got better, Frieda has recalled, "we would go for long walks over the fields and get mushrooms if there were any, and in the spring through the woods we found clearings where big primroses grew and pools of bluebells. In the spring we also got baskets full of dandelions and made dandelion wine." [38] His mood was gentle enough that he lived quite companionably with the Brown family, who had the attached cottage. Lawrence would help Mr. Brown in the garden, or use Mrs. Brown as the model for an evening dress he was making for Ada, but he specially liked their seven-year-old daughter Hilda. Many years later she remembered the evenings she would spend with them:

> With his wife I would sit quietly, supposedly reading or doing homework, but really watching the (to me) incredible speed at which he wrote.
> Suddenly he would put down his pen, enquire what I had done that day, and decide it was time to eat the evening meal which had been prepared earlier. He would invite me to share their meal (As I grew older, this fact amazed me), and after the meal we would sit round the fire and sing songs. [39]

After three soldiers were billetted on the Browns Hilda was given a bedroom in the Lawrences' cottage, so that she became almost an adopted child to them.

Though the Lawrences made other friends in the village, they seem to have been looked on as conspicuous aliens. The police suspicion of them must have been noted, as well as Frieda's being obviously German. Cecily Lambert Minchin, who became the model for Banford in "The Fox," gives an idea of how they appeared to the locals:

> I was amazed to see coming towards me a most astounding spectacle—a tall, very slender creature clad in drainpipe khaki trousers, light shirt, scarlet tie, and what appeared, in the distance, to be a blue dressing jacket, but on closer acquaintance turned out to be a butcher blue linen coat. Above this shone the reddest beard I have ever seen, vivid and startling, a very pale gauntish face with deep blue penetrating eyes, and a shock of mousey blonde hair topped with a white floppy child's hat of cotton drill. Following a few yards behind was a very plump, heavily built woman, with strong features and blonde hair. [40]

(347)

In 1975 Mr. Albert Rouse recalled how the village children used to follow after Lawrence and call him "Walking Jesus"—because "we were told that Christ was ginger."[41]

Lawrence had consciously chosen to live in isolation at Hermitage, and he no longer gave vent to violent outbursts of misanthropy as he had done in the early months in Cornwall. But he also recognized that his vocation as artist was not by itself enough to sustain him; hence the dilemma that he described to Gertler:

> I think the old way of life has come to an end, and none of us will be able to go on with it. We must either get out into a new life, altogether new—a life based neither on work nor love—or else we shall die. . . . But my heart shuts up against people—practically everybody—nowadays. One has been so much insulted and let down.[42]

Gertler was passing through a crisis of his own: his long and tormenting relationship with Carrington seemed irreparably shattered when he found that she was planning to live permanently with Lytton Strachey at Tidmarsh—only nine miles from Hermitage. They moved in there, actually, on almost the same day that the Lawrences moved to Hermitage, but there was no contact between the two households—by now any dealings between the Lawrences and Bloomsbury were conducted by such intermediaries as Gertler or Kot. So Lawrence and Frieda spent Christmas 1917 alone in their little cottage, while at Tidmarsh Strachey enjoyed turkey and claret with Carrington and his wealthy patron Harry Norton.*

On 14 February Gertler ran into Carrington and Strachey at a London party given by Mary Hutchinson; drunk and bitter, he ambushed Strachey afterward and pummeled him. No great damage was done and the episode was closed by an apology a few days later, but Gertler was deeply depressed and consoled himself by going off to Garsington to paint. "There is a limit to how much one can suffer," he told Kot. *"Work is my only salvation."*[43] He wrote in the same vein to Lawrence who, as one would expect, argued that he was not going the right way to be saved:

> I *don't* think that to work is to live. Work is all right in proportion: but one wants to have a certain richness and satisfaction in oneself, which is more than

---

* The Lawrences spent August 1919 at Rosalind Pophan's cottage in Pangbourne, only a mile from Tidmarsh—where Strachey was quietly working on *Queen Victoria*. But no meeting is recorded.

anything *produced*. One wants to *be*. I think we need, not to paint or write, but to have a liberation from ourselves, to become quite careless and free. And we need to go away, as soon as we can, . . . you and Campbell and Kot and Shearman and Frieda and me . . . and in some queer way, by *forgetting* everything, to start afresh. . . . But it is no good, if work, or love either, seems to you the be-all and the end-all. Work and love are subsidiary.

A month later, though, even an ideal community appeared to Lawrence impossibly restrictive:

> I feel like a wild cat in a cage—I long to get out into some sort of free, lawless life—at any rate, a life where one can move about and take no notice of anything. . . . I *hate* and *abhor* being stuck on to any form of society.[44]

His desire to be a gypsy was an equal and opposite reaction to Frieda's desire to settle down, which had been intensified by seeing two nearby cottages for rent. One recalls Lawrences's youthful dream of living in a cottage with Louie Burrows as he describes the charm of one of them, at Hampstead Norris: "down in a little village, fast asleep for ever; a cottage just under the hill, under the hazel-woods, with its little garden backing to the old churchyard, where the sunny, grey, square-towered church dozes on without rousing." Already at Hermitage he was learning "to lapse along pleasantly with the days," but he was appalled to think he might yield altogether to inanition, oblivious to the war and all his past wrongs. "I believe I could go into a soft sort of Hardy-sleep, hearing the church chime from hour to hour, watching the horses at the farm drink at the pond, writing pages that *seemed* beautifully important, and having visits from people who *seemed* all wrong, as coming from the inferior outer world."[45]

Lawrence's mood was not benevolent enough to make peace with Ottoline and Russell, however, let alone Jack Murry. When undertaking a new book of poetry he had occasion to contact Ottoline, for the first time since late 1916, asking her to send him manuscripts that had been stored at Garsington. But when he thanked her for them, on 1 April, he made no conciliatory move—only observing, wryly: "Perhaps we shall meet in some sort of Afterwards, when the laugh is on a new side."[46] Toward Russell he was even more unbending, and unmoved by his former friend's conviction on 9 February of making "statements likely to prejudice His Majesty's relations with the United States of America," for which he was sentenced to six months in jail.

Lawrence explained to Kot why he continued to set his face against his comrades of 1915:

> I know the Ot. is very nice, somewhere. I once was *very* fond of her—and I am still, in a way. But she is like someone who has died: and I cannot wish to call her from the grave. She is good and, in a way, I love her, as I love someone who is dead. But not for life.
>
> I too am sick of the world builders—*à la* Lansbury. I want their world smashed up, not set up—all the world smashed up. These Lansbury and Bertie Russell world-builders are only *preventers* of everything, the negators of life.[47]

Writings at Hermitage

AFTER A MONTH of settling in at Hermitage Lawrence again began to write prolifically, undeterred by the endless setbacks of the past three years. He first took up the *Studies in Classic American Literature* which he had laid aside after the expulsion from Cornwall; by mid-February he was working on the sixth essay, on Poe, and the last, on Whitman, was completed in early June. He saw these essays as his only hope of income for the next year or two, as he explained to Kot when asking him to type them out:

> . . . do read them through *very* carefully for me, before you type them. And then, if you see anything that would be best left out, from the publishing point of view, do leave it out. I very much want to sell these essays. I know how good they are in substance. Yet I know it will be difficult to get them accepted. I want to make them acceptable to a publisher, if it is in any way possible.[48]

Lawrence also saw the essays as the end of the cycle of his philosophical writings since 1914. "I shall never write another page of philosophy—or whatever it is—when these are done," he told Cecil Gray. "Thank God for that. Yet it is absolutely necessary to get it out, fix it, and have a definite foothold, to be *sure*." [49]

At Hermitage Lawrence also returned for a while to novel-writing. In May 1917 he had told Jack Murry that he found "people ultimately boring: and you can't have fiction without people." [50] But the new circle of friends at Mecklenburgh Square revived his interest, and while he was still staying there he began the book that would be completed in 1921 as *Aaron's Rod.* On 21 February 1918, at Hermitage, he told Gertler that he was writing "very spasmodically, another daft novel. It goes slowly—very slowly and fitfully. But I don't care." A month later he reported the completion of 150 pages, all "as blameless as Cranford. It shall not have one garment disarranged, but shall be buttoned up like a Member of Parliament. Still I wouldn't vouch that it is like *Sons and Lovers:* it is funny. It amuses me terribly."[51] This is the last reference to the novel until after the war; one assumes that its first plan resembled the *Aaron's Rod* of three years later, though no early drafts have survived.

The flight of Aaron Sisson from job, home, and family would have been a natural outgrowth of Lawrence's claustrophobic mood at Hermitage, when he wanted to simply wander off like a gypsy. Another impulse behind the novel was the desire to transpose the marital deadlock of *Sons and Lovers* from a tragic into a comic mode. Unlike Ernest Morel, Aaron does not allow himself to be slowly ground down by his bourgeois wife, but escapes with his magic wand—the flute that gives him entry to the bohemian world of London and Florence. In some degree Lawrence may have wanted to "make amends" to his father for the critical treatment of him in *Sons and Lovers,* but his contrition can scarcely have been profound for the prevailing tone of the novel is one of emotional detachment, often to the point of flippancy. Probably his main concern was to explore, through the character of Aaron, his own fantasies of insouciant freedom through repudiation of the marriage bond. But not wanting to leave Aaron entirely unconstrained, Lawrence makes him confront Rawdon and Tanny Lilly, who are close replicas of himself and Frieda. Lawrence thus externalized his self-division by distributing it between two characters, instead of working out the marital conflict directly as he had already done in *Women in Love.*

His work on *Aaron's Rod* coincided with the floating of yet another scheme to publish *Women in Love.* When he told Lady Cynthia of his financial problems in February she thought of approaching Prince Antoine Bibesco, whom she had recently met in his capacity as the lover of her young sister-in-law Elizabeth Asquith (they married in 1919). Bibesco was a rich Rumanian diplomat resident in London, a man of the world and a dedicated womanizer. He also had cultural pretensions, having been a friend of Proust in Paris, and seemed open to the idea of subsidizing Lawrence's novel. A lunch was arranged to discuss the scheme to which Lady Cynthia also invited her friend Desmond McCarthy, the drama critic of the *Sunday Times,* but she did Lawrence no favor by including him. "Unfortunately," she noted in her diary, "Desmond McCarthy, who might be helpful, takes Lady Ottoline seriously as a friend and wishes her protected from the pain the (according to him) obvious lampoon of her would inflict. . . . [He] spoke of Lawrence as indisputably a genius, but *no* artist."[52]

A week later Lawrence came to London to carry forward the plan, not realizing that McCarthy had already scotched it. The manuscript of *Women in Love* was then in the hands of C. W. Beaumont, a bookseller and small publisher on Charing Cross Road. Lady Cynthia knew of him as a friend of her younger brother Yvo before he was killed in 1915, so she volunteered to act as an intermediary between Beaumont and Prince Bibesco; Lawrence thereupon went home, relying on Lady Cynthia's influence to outweigh his own tarnished reputation. From Hermitage he outlined the business details to her: an edition of a thousand copies would cost three hundred and seventy-five pounds to produce, and would sell for a guinea. If Bibesco would provide one hundred and fifty pounds to start production the work could be advertised and advance subscriptions would cover the remaining costs; in return Lawrence would dedicate the novel "To Prince Antoine Bibesco, whose liberality has enabled this book to appear." As for Ottoline, Lawrence reported that a friend—probably Gertler—was approaching her "to know how she feels. I know she would like the thing to appear, for self-advertisement—and her sheep-faced fool of a husband would like to denounce it, for further self-advertisement. Pah, people make one sick." But Ottoline turned out to be adamantly opposed to the novel's appearing, so that Lawrence was again left with nothing but sour grapes for his portion: "As for the Ott," he told Gertler, "—why should I bother about the old carrion? If I can publish, I shall publish. But ten to one I can't, and I don't care a straw either way."[53]

In London, furthermore, the usual snags were arising. Beaumont did not want his name on the book, since he feared prison, nor did Bibesco want to accept the dedication. Lady Cynthia herself was having doubts, after Beaumont told her that "of course parts of it had merit—but it was worse than *The Rainbow*." When she received the actual manuscript, on 22 March, her doubts grew stronger: "Surely he is delirious," she noted in her diary."—a man whose temperature is 103°? or do I know nothing about human beings? It is all so *fantastic* to me and 'unpleasant'—morbid to a degree."[54] A month later the novel was back in its author's hands, returned by Bibesco without comment. From Lady Cynthia's diary it is evident that what Bibesco really wanted was to have an affair with her, and so long as she refused him he would not play Maecenas to her deserving author—even if he had liked the book, which he obviously did not.

Lawrence's last word on the subject came at the beginning of 1919, when he heard from Kot that Gertler had been invited to Bibesco's to see his Cézannes and had hopes of some patronage: ". . . although these buffoon-princes have money and pretensions, they are just like the Bennetts and Wellses and Selfridges and Lyons of this world ... they will only pay for their own puffing-up. Tell Gertler that there is nothing doing in the Bennett-Bibesco quarter." This proved to be the last of Lawrence's efforts at publishing by himself *Women in Love* or *The Rainbow,* and his account of it shows how deep a wound the three years of futile effort had inflicted on him:

> I knew that it was Desmond MacCarthy who had put a stopper on Prince B., moaning on Ottoline's outraged behalf. I knew that. And I knew that Prince B. had not the courage to say a word either to me or to Cynthia Asquith, but returned the MS. wordless. And I knew that Desmond MacCarthy was quite pleased with himself for having arse-licked Ottoline and the Prince both at once, both of them being pretty sound benefactors of Desmond, who rather enjoys his arse-licking turns. All these things, my dear Kot, I knew and know: in fact I know very many things which I prefer to leave, like manure, to rot down in my soul, unspoken, to form the humus of a new germination.[55]

So the plan for Beaumont to produce *Women in Love* collapsed, and its failure may well have contributed to Lawrence's temporary abandonment of work on *Aaron's Rod.* But the connection did bear one small and tardy fruit. In December 1916 Lawrence had sent Lady Cynthia the manuscript of a "tiny book of poems" that he wished to dedicate to her, but he then decided not to submit them for publication because they were "ironical and a bit wicked."[56] Now Beaumont asked him for a few poems to be hand-printed in a limited edition so he agreed for the collection to appear, under the title *Bay*. Beaumont would pay ten pounds for the rights; it was not much, but Lawrence stipulated that after six months he should be free to sell individual poems to magazines for whatever he could get. When he signed the agreement on 22 May Lawrence expected the small but tasteful volume to make a prompt appearance; however, it took Beaumont eighteen months to print the eighteen poems, and when he did finish he made a series of blunders in the book's format. As the months of delay dragged on he became a target for the invective that Lawrence reserved for those who failed to honor their commitments: he was a "bewildered chicken," he printed on "Japanese vellum-rubbish," he was "dear, foetid little Beaumont."[57] By the time the book came out the war had ended: it had thus lost its topicality and seems not to have been reviewed at all, though Lawrence was at least able to place about half the poems in *English Review, Poetry,* and other journals during 1918 and 1919.

As an offshoot of *Bay,* however, Lawrence decided to compile another hybrid volume of old and new poems. He wrote to Cecil Gray at Zennor for two notebooks containing poems, and also retrieved some manuscripts from Garsington. By 22 May he had made a collection that he called "Choir of Women," though when he sent it to Pinker on 18 June the title had become "Coming Awake." "I think there is nothing in it to offend anybody," Lawrence noted. "—tell me . . . if you think there is anything that would be better left out. . . . At first I had it in two little separate books, one called 'In London,' the other 'Choir of Women.' I can split it up again if you think publishers would rather have it that way."[58] The final title was the sober *New Poems.* But even this was misleading: though Lawrence had revised and rearranged the poems, almost all had been conceived before the war. His situation in 1918 provided little inspiration for poetry.

The material for short stories, however, was more promising. Lawrence had done nothing in the genre for at least a year, but some vignettes of country life began to catch his eye at Hermitage. The Brown family next door had a corporal billeted with them who was pursued by several of the local girls; this was probably the germ of the story "Monkey Nuts," on one of Lawrence's favorite themes: a reluctant man being claimed by an aggressive woman. A more substantial work derived from the Lawrences' friendship with two cousins, Cecily Lambert and Violet Monk, who were tenants of Grimsbury Farm at nearby Long Lane. The idea of two women running a farm by themselves must have piqued Lawrence's interest, for he and Frieda went over to visit without being introduced. They became constant visitors, and Lawrence would help to milk the goats and do other farm chores. Miss Lambert's brother Nip, a soldier on leave from East Africa, also spent some time at the farm. From this household Lawrence developed his long story "The Fox." As usual, his models were not best pleased by the use he made of them. Miss Lambert considered the tale "sheer fantasy," and complained that "it was execrable taste to belittle me for no fault of my own while accepting my hospitality." She must indeed have been shocked by Lawrence's portrayal of her as a dog-in-the-manger closet Lesbian who tries to destroy her friend's romance with the young soldier who comes to stay, especially since it was really her cousin who was the "possessive and jealous" one.[59] But Lawrence had other concerns than giving a fair or faithful portrayal of the household at Grimsbury Farm. It is probable, for example, that he wanted to make a fictional study of William Henry Hocking: the soldier in "The Fox" is named Henry and is Cornish—and his captain is named Berryman, after Katie Berryman who ran the store at Zennor.

Leaving Hermitage

AT THE BEGINNING of March Lawrence and Frieda had to consider seriously how they were to get through the year. Their February crisis had been relieved by Shearman's ten pounds and other small gifts or payments, but they had no prospect of a steady income. On 8 March Lawrence told Captain Short he could not renew the lease of Higher Tregerthen since there was no way of telling when he might be allowed to live there. Nor could they stay at Chapel Farm Cottage, since the Radfords wanted it from May onward. So Lawrence had to fall back on his sister Ada's offer to pay the rent of a house for a year, provided it was close to her own home at Ripley. He told Willie Hopkin that he was reconciled to the idea of returning to the Midlands:

> I should really like to come back now, and be not far away from all the old people. . . . any little place, nice and separate, would do. I can't be jammed in among people any more. Frieda and I have lived so much alone, and in isolated places, that we suffer badly at being cooped up with other folk. Ada takes it very much amiss that we don't go and stay with her, to look round. But it is real purgatory to be in her little house, with everybody and everything whirling round.[60]

For the second week of April Lawrence went up to Derbyshire by himself to look for a house, while Frieda enjoyed a visit with her children in London. Lawrence and Ada found a suitable bungalow on the outskirts of Middleton-by-Wirksworth, near Cromford, Derbyshire; after he returned to Hermitage she took it on a one-year lease for sixty-five pounds furnished. This was, of course, quite beyond Lawrence's own means. Having thus assured himself of lodging, he promptly planned an escape route by asking Captain Short if he could still renew his lease on the small cottage at Tregerthen for five pounds a year; he told Short he would like to leave his furniture there so that he could return as soon as the war ended.

Though Lawrence had solved the immediate problem of subsistence, it was at the cost of accepting his sister's charity and leaving Hermitage, of which he had become quite fond. When he wrote to Gertler just before leaving Berkshire he was again filled with the bitterness of defeat:

> I am getting through day after day—and becoming very weary. One seems to go through all the Ypres and Mount Kemmels and God knows what. In some blind and hypnotic fashion I do a few bits of poetry—beyond that, I am incapable of everything. . . . My soul, or whatever it is, feels charged and surcharged with the blackest and most monstrous 'temper,' a sort of hellish electricity—and I hope soon it will either dissipate or break into some sort of thunder and lightning, for I am no more a man, but a walking phenomenon of suspended fury.[61]

Mount Kemmel was a French stronghold in Flanders, taken by the Germans three days before (on 25 April) as their great spring offensive approached its climax. By making a separate peace with Russia they had been able to transfer fifty divisions back to the

Western Front, whereas the Americans had only been able to put the equivalent of six on the field when the Germans opened their attack on 21 March. Once again a German victory seemed imminent, or at best a long period during which the Allies would have to remain on the defensive. Walking through the woods, Lawrence had an encounter that symbolized, in some way he could not define, the savage hopelessness of it all: "I found a dead owl, a lovely big warm-brown creature, lying in the grass at my feet, in the path, its throat eaten by weasels. It sticks in my mind curiously—as if something important had died this weekend—though what it can be I don't know."[62] With this mysterious augury the Lawrences took leave of Hermitage at the end of April, to return to the region they had eloped from together just six years before.

CHAPTER IX

MIDDLETON-BY-WIRKSWORTH

Photo: Notts County Library

Exile's Return

NOTTINGHAMSHIRE, his native country, was to Lawrence the mundane heart of the Midlands: collieries, red-brick villages, fields never far removed from the traces of industry. But across the Erewash River from his home at Eastwood lay Derbyshire, stretching to the west and north; this was holiday country, away from the grim influence of the mines. Here the villages were of gray stone and the landscape still unspoiled; its dark, narrow, wooded valleys lying under the high "bare country of stone walls, which he loved."[1] The Beardsalls, Lawrence's mother's family, lived at Wirksworth and his sister Ada had moved to Ripley when she married; now, with her husband in the navy, she was delighted to have her older brother close to home. The house she had leased for him and Frieda was just on the outskirts of the small village of Middleton-by-Wirksworth, perched on the brink of a steep little valley and with a view of the hills opposite. A bit more spacious and up-to-date then Higher Tregerthen, it nonetheless had a fairy-tale quality of lostness and seclusion to which Lawrence responded strongly; he spoke of himself as buried "in the darkish Midlands, on the rim of a steep deep valley, looking over darkish, folded hills—exactly the navel of England, and feels exactly that." Later in his stay he described to Katherine Mansfield the hollow beneath the cottage: "Last evening at dusk I sat by the rapid brook which runs by the highroad in the valley bed. The spell of hastening, secret water goes over one's mind. When I got to the top—a very hard climb—I felt as if I had climbed out of a womb."[2] This image of an engulfing, female landscape reflects his uneasiness at being drawn back to his origins, to the scenery—and the family and friends—of his youth. He must have felt deeply, as he attempted this reconciliation, the two great absences from that time: his dead mother, and Jessie Chambers—who had married John Wood in 1915 but was still nursing her reproachful silence.

When they first moved in, on 2 May, the Lawrences felt only the menacing loneliness of their new home. "The place is beautiful," he wrote Lady Cynthia, "but one feels like Ovid in Thrace. . . . I wish we could have gone back to Cornwall. . . . I feel as if I were on a sort of ledge half-way down a precipice, and did not know how to get up or down." He worked around the house and read Gibbon, which reinforced his end-of-the-world mood; to Amy Lowell he spoke of having "come home, in these last wretched days—not to die, I hope. . . . The future seems utterly impenetrable, and as fathomless as the Bottomless Pit, and about as desperate."[3] But when his family began to descend on him he showed them a surprisingly genial face. This was partly a quirk of temperament: though generally ill at ease when staying in someone else's home, he eagerly encouraged visitors to his own—he was born a host rather than a guest. He seems also to have realized, on returning to the Midlands, how vulnerable and isolated he had become after breaking so many friendships over the past three years, yet how much goodwill remained in those to whom he was still "our Bert." After Willie Hopkin and his daughter Enid had come over from Eastwood for a weekend, Lawrence wrote wistfully to Mrs. Hopkin:

> It was so jolly when we were all together. And it is the human contact which means so much to one, really. . . . I quite suffered when they had gone away on Monday—and usually I am so glad to be alone. . . . I find, for myself, nowadays, that change of scene is not enough—neither sea nor hills nor anything else; only the human warmth, when one can get it, makes the heart rich.[4]

As the German offensive came closer and closer to Paris, Lawrence looked to old ties and familiar faces to shelter him from the crisis. His sisters offered some security, though many of the old family tensions still lingered. Emily was a devout Wesleyan whom Lawrence nicknamed "Pamela, or Virtue Rewarded"; years later, still resisting her influence as an older sibling, he remarked wryly: "I am really not 'our Bert.' Come to that, I never was."[5]

Ada he had a soft spot for, as the baby of the family, but Frieda mistrusted her, and each woman was jealous of the other's influence. He had an untroubled affection for his sisters' children, fortunately, so that he and Frieda were happy to become substitute parents for several weeks. Emily had a nine-year-old daughter, Peggy, and Ada a little son named Jack, of whom Lawrence remarked:

> [he] is only three years old, and therefore quite decent. . . . I am surprised how children are like barometers to their parents' feelings. There is some sort of queer, magnetic, psychic connection—something a bit fatal, I believe. I feel I am all the time rescuing my nephew and my niece from their respective mothers, my two sisters; who have jaguars of wrath in their souls, however they purr to their offspring. The phenomenon of motherhood, in these days, is a strange and rather frightening phenomenon.[6]

To complete the family circle Lawrence's father, now seventy-two, also came to visit; Lawrence had little to say of him but perhaps his attitude to Eastwood, where he spent a day in June, provides a clue: "For the first time in my life I feel quite amiable towards it—I have always hated it. Now I don't."[7] Even his mother's sister Ada came, later in the summer; Lawrence found her boring but enjoyed talking to her husband, Fritz Krenkow, a professor of Oriental studies, and asked him to visit again. From the south, however, there was only one visitor that summer: Dorothy Yorke, who stayed for two weeks in June. She had now begun a ten-year attachment to Richard Aldington, who was back at the Front; the Lawrences became "very fond of her" during her visit, while she left at the end "in tears and grief."[8] On the day she went Lawrence had a fit of depression himself, over his endless difficulties with money and his utter lack of prospects; he must have been seriously troubled, for he asked Gertler about a possible healing of the Great Schism: "I suppose you are at Garsington now? Is it nice? . . . How is Ottoline now? Do you think she would like to see us again? Do you think we might be happy if we saw her again—if we went to Garsington?" Gertler confided to Kot that the letter put him in a very difficult position, and that "Ottoline particularly objects to Frieda." After having made the first move, Lawrence was infuriated at not getting a generous response: "I got such a stupid answer from [Gertler]," he told Kot. "—vague and conditional like Mr. Balfour discussing peace terms. To Hell with Ott.—the whole Ottlerie—what am I doing temporising with them."[9] Their estrangement would continue for ten more years.

With the Murrys, however, there was a better chance for reconciliation. When Katherine returned from Bandol in April 1918 Jack scarcely recognized her; her tuberculosis had progressed rapidly, and she had been held up for three weeks in Paris in an acute state of anxiety when the Germans had got close enough to bombard the city with seventeen-inch "Big Berthas." On 2 May her divorce from George Bowden was made absolute and on the next day she and Jack were married at the same South Kensington registry office where they had stood witness for Lawrence and Frieda four years before. The Lawrences were not invited, and apparently did not even know of the step the Murrys were taking in London. Two months later, however, a major obstacle to the rapprochement of the two couples was removed when Jack fell out with Ottoline over his review of Sigfried Sassoon's *Counter-Attack and other Poems.* Typically enough, Jack had been charmed by Sassoon in 1917 and had helped him with his protest against the war; but his review savaged the book as "verses— . . . not poetry," and the author as one whose "mind is a chaos."[10] Ottoline, who was at that time infatuated with Sassoon, was enraged. From then on she had a settled mistrust of Jack and, in lesser degree, of Katherine too. Since the Murrys could no longer serve as cat's-paws in Ottoline's campaign against the Lawrences, the way was open for them to make a fresh start, for the first time since their falling-out at Zennor.

An Application for Relief

IN MARCH Lawrence had told Lady Cynthia that the idea of being a householder with servants oppressed him: "He would like two hundred pounds to banish worry—no more."[11] He did manage to get something like that amount in 1918 but the worry lay in the getting it, for he had to beg the money he could no longer earn by writing. In 1918 he published one book, *New Poems,* a tiny paperbound volume that sold for two shillings sixpence.

Lawrence's advance was only six pounds five shillings. This was his eleventh book and at thirty-three he should have been drawing a steady income from his works, but after the suppression of *The Rainbow* sales of his other books were reduced to a trickle. His whole income from writing in 1918 was no more than about thirty pounds. In the spring he received two major gifts: from Ada the year's rental of Mountain Cottage plus twenty pounds in cash, and from Amy Lowell forty pounds. But this was not enough to carry him and Frieda through the year.

Lady Cynthia was herself living from hand to mouth, but she exerted what influence she could on Lawrence's behalf. Charles Whibley, a Cambridge don and successful essayist had been in love with her for years—though since he was nearly sixty and ugly she found his advances distressing. When asked to help Lawrence he told her that he opposed publication of *Women in Love,* but "could probably get him one hundred pounds from the [Royal] Literary Fund, only . . . [with] a tacit understanding that he should write something—and that, not inevitably censorable."[12] Lawrence agreed to accept the money, and vouched for the innocence of the novel he was working on, *Aaron's Rod.* On 10 June Whibley recommended Lawrence to the Fund as "a poet of considerable distinction, and the author of some excellent stories"; he made no mention of Lawrence's novels—calculating, no doubt, that the less said about *The Rainbow* the better. Lawrence then had to fill out an application form; "I was not very polite and cringing," he told Gertler, "so probably shall get nothing. Curse them, that's all—curse them once more, fat fleas of literature that they are."[13] His actual letter to the Fund contained no curses, only the flat statement that the war had reduced his earnings from 450 to 500 pounds (an overstatement) to less than 100 pounds. "There is no prospect," he continued, "of my receiving anything worth mention, in the future as I see it now. So I am at a loss. Nevertheless it is with considerable chagrin that I fill in forms of application for help. I don't want to importune the Royal Literary Fund." He added, in answer to a query from the Fund's secretary, Llewelyn Roberts: "I have not tried to obtain work in any Government department, because my health does not allow me to undertake any regular employment."[14]

Much as he disliked doing so, Lawrence realized that he should do some quiet lobbying for his case. He renewed correspondence with Mary Cannan, who had used her influence with the dramatist Alfred Sutro to get Lawrence fifty pounds from the Fund in October 1914. His letter was spiced with nostalgic memories of Cholesbury and with sympathy for Mary over Gilbert's abandoning her, but the kernel of it was an unabashed plea for her to help him out of the "very painful" situation of having to live on Ada. He named Pinker and J. D. Beresford as referees. Pinker told the committee that "His work is not of the character that makes a popular appeal, and as it is not possible for a man of his artistic temperament to adapt his work to the general taste he has for some time past been dangerously near to penury, in spite of the fact that his habits are of the most frugal"; Beresford reinforced the point that "his genius appeals to a very small public, and every lover of letters must applaud his courage in refusing to write anything less than his best."[15]

As the day of decision approached, Lawrence's resentment of the Fund's trustees rose higher: "I hope the dogs and swine will have sufficient fear of God in their hearts: *fear,* that is the only thing that will do them any good: fear of the wrath of the Lord." Whatever it was that did the trick, Lawrence was able to tell Kot on 12 July that he had just received "a miserable fifty pounds from that dirty Royal Literary Fund"—and could therefore return uncashed the check for ten pounds that Kot had sent him a month earlier. Though he and Frieda were now solvent for a while longer, he felt more than ever at the mercy of his rulers, and his grudge against them burned deeper. They made him stay in the country, but expelled him from his chosen home; they took away his livelihood by banning *The Rainbow,* then gave him a few months charity once he admitted his destitution. "Oh my dear Kot," he exclaimed, "for these months and years of slow execution we suffer, I *should* like my revenge on the world."[16]

Writings at Mountain Cottage

LAWRENCE'S first literary work at Mountain Cottage was the completion of the last four or five essays of *Studies in Classic American Literature.* By 20 June he was done, telling Kot that he had "a complete blank" in front of him, and Gertler that: "I don't work—don't try to—only just endure the days."[17] In August the essays were sent to Pinker and began the usual round of rejections, except for the publication of eight of them in the trusty *English Review*. By the time the book finally appeared in 1923 Lawrence had reached America, and had revised the essays to reflect his disillusion with it. The 1918 text was much more fresh and enthusiastic; it was also Lawrence's first success, outside *Women in Love*, at combining abstract philosophizing with quick, instinctive response. Its stature as a seminal work on the American tradition may justify Lawrence's laborious working-out of his philosophy in 1914–18.

It would be a digression from the story of Lawrence's wartime experience to give a full analysis of *Studies in Classic American Literature*, but two of its themes should be mentioned briefly. One is the apotheosis of male comradeship in the eassay on Whitman. By summer 1918 Lawrence's intimacy with William Henry Hocking had crumbled, yet he still held by the ideal that he had hoped to fulfill in it. The other theme is Lawrence's concern with the mystical geography of the body in the essay "The Two Principles" (omitted from the 1923 text). The body, he argues, is divided horizontally at the diaphragm: the lower part is the seat of blood consciousness, the upper of mental consciousness. He even asked Mrs. Eder for an anatomical map of the human nervous sytem, so that he could give a scientifically correct account of the upper, spiritual consciousness; but he held that this was only a partial truth that needed the truth of blood knowledge to be made complete. This "double truth" was a tacit abandonment of his earlier ambition to construct a complete and rigorous philosophical system. From now on he would simply assert against the "facts" of science a separate and higher reality based on his immediate sense of the way things were.

As he completed the *Studies in Classic American Literature* Lawrence pondered what he might do next to earn a living. Since neither fiction nor poetry nor philosophy would pay, he could only fall back on his three years' experience, as a schoolteacher and his connection with Vere Collins, an executive of the Oxford University Press in London, suggested a use for this skill. When *The Rainbow* was prosecuted Collins had offered to help him with a private edition; they became friends, and the Lawrences stayed at Collins' house in Hampstead shortly before leaving for Cornwall. After the move to Hermitage their acquaintance was renewed. Collins admired the breadth of Lawrence's knowledge and proposed that he might write a textbook of European history for use in schools. The project was probably first discussed early in 1918, and taken up seriously by Lawrence in June when he was thrown on the mercy of the Royal Literary Fund.

In April Lawrence had begun to read Gibbon, perhaps with an eye to the history book. He found in him an antidote to his disgust with current events: "I am quite happy with those old Roman emperors," he told Gray, "—they were so out-and-out, they just did as they liked, and *vogue la galère,* till they were strangled."[18] On 3 July he reported that the Oxford University Press would give him the assignment, not "a formal, connected, text book, but a series of vivid sketches of movements and people"; he would be paid fifty pounds for an acceptable manuscript. Though this was in a sense hackwork, Lawrence was not too proud to take the commission—nor was it without interest to him:

> I feel in a historical mood, being very near the end of Gibbon. The chief feeling is, that men were always alike, and always will be, and one must view the species with contempt first and foremost, and find a few individuals, if possible—which seems at this juncture not to be possible—and ultimately, if the impossible were possible, to *rule* the species. It is proper ruling they need, and always have needed. But it is impossible, because they can only be ruled as they are willing to be ruled: and that is swinishly or hypocritically.[19]

Lawrence finds the dynamic of history in this tension between rulers and masses, and between energy and destruction: "If Attila or some other barbaric villain hadn't squashed the cities of the Adriatic head, we should have had no Venice. . . . Is Attila a reprehensible savage, or a creator in wrath?"[20] The invasions spilled over from the "great reservoirs of human life" beyond the Rhine when the Romans had become too effete to resist them; two of the most compelling set pieces in the *History* are the chapters on "The Germans" and "The Huns," where Lawrence revels in the fierce spontaneity of the invaders.

In 1914 Lawrence had invoked a similar physiological theory of history to excuse, if not justify, the expansionism of the "adolescent" German nation. By 1918 he no longer cherished illusions about German imperialism, but he found in Gibbon an approach to history that helped him to bear the destructive horrors of the world war. Lawrence's eulogy of the Dark Ages was a step beyond such totally misanthropic visions as Birkin's fantasy of the extirpation of mankind. Still, this shift had its darker side in the emergence of a new ruling idea: that the chaos and degradation of the general run of mankind could only be transcended if they would submit themselves to a ruthless and inscrutable leader.

A week after telling Gray he might do the *History* Lawrence had completed the first chapter, on "Rome"; by the end of July he had done three, which he sent off to the Press as samples. They were taken more or less directly from Gibbon, since he had no access to other authorities. Nonetheless he expected the Press to dislike the style, which he designed to "convey the true historic impression to children who are beginning to grasp realities. We should introduce the deep, philosophic note into education: deep, philosophic reverence."[21] Having submitted the chapters, Lawrence seems to have set aside the *History* until December, when the Press authorized him to complete the work. To help him prepare the manuscript they assigned Mrs. Nancy Henry, a free-lance editor whose husband, a music critic, had been interned in Germany for the duration of the war. She asked Lawrence, in turn, for assistance in publishing some poems that her husband had sent her from his camp. With his usual readiness to collaborate, Lawrence rapidly made a little book from forty-two of the poems, titled it "Poems of a Prisoner," and sent it off to Pinker. He also gave Mrs. Henry advice on a story she had written and suggested that he might rewrite it himself, though nothing came of these literary projects. Her friendship smoothed the way for Lawrence's *History* but she disappeared from his life once it was well launched.

Lawrence made another positive step toward assuring his future as a writer at Mountain Cottage, though he did not realize it at the time. He had sent his collection of poems, "Coming Awake," to Pinker in June, dedicating it to Amy Lowell (his other three wartime books of poetry had been dedicated to Ottoline, to Frieda, and to Cynthia Asquith). When Chatto and Windus, publishers of *Look! We Have Come Through!,* showed no eagerness to continue their association with Lawrence he agreed that the young publisher Martin Secker should have his new book. Secker managed to get off on the wrong foot with Lawrence by insisting on the "decidedly false" title of *New Poems,* but thereafter he proved himself to be that long-sought jewel: a publisher who was reliable and who believed in Lawrence's work. Not until the 1920s, though, did Lawrence gain any substantial income from this association.

The Crisis Approaches

AT THE BEGINNING of June Lawrence had asked Sallie Hopkin whether she expected a crisis that month. He meant, of course, in the war, for the Germans had crossed the Marne for the first time since September 1914 and were less than sixty miles from Paris. But he was also near the end of his tether in his personal life, plagued by poverty and another notice to report for medical examination. "I feel very desperate," he told Kot, "and ready for anything, good or bad. I think something critical will happen this month—finally critical. If it doesn't I shall bust." [22] Even the staunch Kot seemed to be disintegrating too; he suffered a nervous collapse late in June and Lawrence's letters to him are full of warnings that he might "metamorphose into a sort of rock," and of pressing invitations to Mountain Cottage. Kot's prospects of earning a living were meager because he had become more and more reluctant to leave his house—a mild form of agoraphobia that progressed into severe depressions for which he was hospitalized later in his life.

If Kot's characteristic response to unhappiness was to become "rooted and immovable," Lawrence's was to pace restlessly about—at least so far as the length of his tether would permit. His desire for some transformation in his fortunes was intensified by the sudden change in the course of the war, which was turning into one of movement and surprise after so many months of static bloodletting. The French had begun their counteroffensive on 18 July, sending the Germans back four miles on the first day; then, to pinch off the German salient, the British attacked to the north on 8 August. Massing two thousand guns and four hundred tanks they advanced on the Somme, a few miles to the east of their disastrous repulse of two years before. This time the black day was for the Germans, and their defeat was so decisive that Luden-dorff, the supreme commander, offered his resignation to the kaiser three days later. It was not accepted, but the Kaiser conceded that the war must be ended soon since Germany had almost reached the limit of its powers of resistance. Only three months of battle remained.

Lawrence spent most of those three months away from Mountain Cottage. Once he had completed the sample chapters of his *History* at the end of July he planned a visit to London with Frieda, who had been granted permission to see her children again. They arrived on 12 August to stay with Kot at 5 Acacia Road, bringing with them their meager rations; the visit was uneventful, in part because they steered clear of the Murrys' new establishement at 2 Portland Villas in Hampstead. They did see one friend from former days, Gordon Campbell, though Lawrence later told Kot he was "a bit disgusted with him. . . . But I must see him again, if only to abuse him."[23]

The Lawrences interrupted their stay at Acacia Road to spend a weekend at Mersea with Barbara Low and her sister, Mrs. David Eder; they went to Hermitage on 23 August and three days later to the Forest of Dean, in Gloucestershire, where they had arranged to spend a short holiday with the Carswells. After they had left London Kot sent Gertler another of his perennial complaints about their marriage:

> The idea of Frieda coming here again irritates me and gives me a kind of stubborn muddle-headed anger. If she disappeared L. would be saved, because she is devouring him bit by bit, gradually, permanently. We had a few more quarrels and she shed profuse tears, but, I think, she weeps only to benefit her digestion. Tears to her seem to be a kind of purgative, after which she eats with an increased appetite and gusto. . . . How I wish Frieda disappeared. Lawrence is most interesting and of the real few who matter.[24]

When Lawrence proposed another visit to Kot he tried to shrug off the conflict by telling him that "Frieda quite loves you since open enmity is avowed"[25]; but Kot must have put them off with an excuse for their next time in London was spent at Dollie Radford's.

Catherine Carswell remembers Lawrence's prevailing mood while on holiday with them as "extraordinary gaiety, serenity and youthfulness, such as we never saw again in him." They were housed in the roomy stone vicarage of Upper Lydbrook, on the edge of the Forest of Dean; their days were devoted to excursions through the woods, their evenings to singing and charades. As they went through the countryside Lawrence cut an even more striking figure than usual in panama hat, green-and-red blazer, and a shrunken pair of flannels—the only ones he owned—that revealed his thin ankles. To complete the effect, Frieda wore "the largest and brightest of cotton checks," and the Carswells had a homemade hammock for their three-month-old son John. "It pleases me that we carried the child about," Lawrence wrote Donald Carswell afterward. "One has the future in one's arms, so to speak: and one *is* the present." [26]

At Lydbrook Lawrence conceived the story "The Blind Man" and used the vicarage for its setting, though he seems also to have drawn on memories of the house at Porthcothan with its attached farm. Catherine recognized something of herself in Isabel Pervin, the story's female protagonist, and Bertrand Russell had usually been considered the model for Bertie Reid, the old family friend who comes to visit Isabel (who is pregnant) and her blind husband, Maurice. The basic triangle of the story, however, is much closer to Cynthia Asquith's situation: though her husband was not blinded in the war, he was wounded and shell-shocked, and had a temperament akin to Maurice Pervin's intense reserve—he sometimes became so remote that Cynthia felt she was "hammering on layers of thick felt." [27] Lady Cynthia herself was of Scots origin, like Isabel, and had just taken a position as private secretary to her countryman Sir James Barrie—the principal model, I believe, for Bertie Reid. Reid, in the story, "was ashamed of himself, because he could not marry, could not approach women physically"; Barrie had married, but because of his impotence his wife had left him to marry Gilbert Cannan. Lawrence of course knew the story through his friendship with the Cannans at Cholesbury.

The dénouement of "The Blind Man" Lawrence called "queer and ironical": Maurice is at first jealous of Bertie, but by touching his face he comes to know him intimately and feels that he has found a lifelong comrade who will complete his marriage. Isabel does not oppose the bond between the two men, for she knows that Bertie wants only to escape from Maurice: "He could not bear it that he had been touched by the blind man, his insane reserve broken in. He was like a mollusc whose shell is broken."

Lawrence commented on the story, to Katherine Mansfield, "I realise *how* many people are just rotten at the quick";[28] he was outraged that a popular idol like Barrie should camouflage his sexual inadequacy by hiring a society beauty to serve as the "flower in his buttonhole."

The Nightmare

AFTER FIVE DAYS in the Forest of Dean the Lawrences returned to Mountain Cottage, where Lawrence again took up *Aaron's Rod,* that much-interrupted novel. Then, on 11 September, he received a summons for a medical reexamination at Derby. It was his thirty-third birthday—"sacred year," he commented wryly—and as usual he was outraged and "determined to do nothing more at the bidding of these swine."[29] The next day, again as usual, he recognized that he had little choice. His second medical board, at Bodmin in June 1917, had put him in category C3—the lowest class, fit only for light, nonmilitary duty. But all manpower was now under conscription so someone like Lawrence, who was not doing "work of national importance," could at anytime be assigned to a job. The usual job for C3's, according to Cecil Gray, was cleaning out lavatories; when he himself was called for service in August 1918 he simply "hid" in the Reading Room at the British Museum until the war ended. Lawrence preferred to get a job that would exempt him from service, but he knew this would not be easy.

Meanwhile, in his fury at the authorities he again longed for a political revenge:

> It is time I had an issue. . . . But there is no spirit of resistance or freedom in the country, and I have only a contempt for martyrs. If only men roused up and stiffened their backbones, and were men. I wouldn't mind how much I risked myself. But offer myself as a martyr of self-sacrifice I couldn't do, it is too shoddy, too late.[30]

To Kot, Lawrence proposed a definite plan: he and Frieda would come to live at Acacia Road for some weeks, sharing expenses, so that he could make contact with Robert Smillie, Philip Snowden, Mary Macarthur, and Margaret Bondfield. These were leaders of the pacifist left: Smillie the head of the Scottish Miners Federation, Snowden the chairman of the Independent Labour Party, Mary Macarthur (later Anderson) founder of the National Federation of Women Workers. Lawrence had probably met several of them in his youth, when Willie Hopkin brought them to Eastwood in support of socialist or feminist causes. They represented one of two political forces still opposed to the Lloyd George government, the other being the liberal-intellectual pacifists grouped around Clifford Allen of the No-Conscription Fellowship. With these latter Lawrence would make no common cause: "I hate the reformers worst," he told Kot, "and their nauseous Morrellity. But I count them my worst enemies, and want my revenge on them first."[31] However, he was not close enough to the antiwar movement to realize that his division of it into radical sheep and liberal goats was superficial: Robert Smillie, for example, had stepped forward in 1916 to read a speech by Bertrand Russell at Glasgow after Russell had been excluded from the area, and intellectuals mingled amicably with labor leaders in such groups as the progressive "1917 Club" in Soho. Lawrence felt at this point that only the workers had both power and will to change England; he had been forced to recognize that the right had no real quarrel with the status quo, since their only distinguishing mark was the jingoism that Lloyd George had now taken over to serve his own ends. Nonetheless, he explained to Kot that he did not favor the path Russia had taken: "I don't think chaos is any good for England. England is too old. She'll either have to be *wise,* and recover her decency—or we may as well all join Eder in Jerusalem." What was certain was that he, personally, must find an escape from the trap he was in: "I had rather be hanged or put in prison than endure any more. So now I shall move actively, personally, do what I can. I am a desperado."[32]

When the "desperado" arrived at a school in Derby for his medical exam on 26 September he confronted an equal desperation in his inquisitors. The sudden German collapse at the end of October was brought about by weeks of steady hammering in which the British and Commonwealth armies—fresher than the French, more seasoned than the Americans—spearheaded the Allied attack and took the heaviest losses. The last British offensive, which began on 8 August, cost about 350,000 casualties; though the death of the poet Wilfred Owen a week before the Armistice may seem a trick of fate, there were thousands who died so close to the end of it all. Casualties in this final push were heavier than Passchendaele and were exceeded only by the Somme in 1916. Any medical board in late 1918 would have showed hostility to those who seemed on the verge of escaping the war scot-free. Lawrence, for his part, had known since his last exam the bitterness of being expelled from his home and reduced to living on charity.

The account of the examination in *Kangaroo* is so saturated with contempt that Lawrence often loses control of the fictional tone and yields to pure rage. But two recurrent images hold the narrative together: the "big collier, about as old as himself" who goes through the process with Somers, and the "incomprehensible joke at the expense of the naked" that keeps going round the big schoolroom. The climax does not come with Somers' claim that he has been "threatened with consumption," though Lawrence never came closer to admitting he was tubercular, but with what immediately follows:

> "Turn round," said the puppy. "Face the other way."
> Somers turned and faced the shameful monkey-face at the long table. So, he had his back to the tall window: and the puppy stood plumb behind him.
> "Put your feet apart."
> He put his feet apart.
> "Bend forward—further—further—"
> Somers bend forward, lower, and realised that the puppy was standing aloof behind him to look into his anus. And that this was the source of the wonderful jesting that went on all the time.

The collier, who comes next, does not understand what is happening and squats on his haunches instead of bending over; Somers finds him "terrible. . . . [his] snub-nose had gone quite blank with a ghastly voidness, void of intelligence, bewildered and blind. It was as if the big, ugly, powerful body could not *obey* words any more." He is an image of pure subjugation, a man so cowed that he cannot even be conscious of what is being done to him.

The examination completed, Somers is allowed to dress and wait for his classification:

> Yes, they were running him to earth. They had exposed all his nakedness to gibes. And they were pining, almost whimpering to give the last grab at him, and haul him to earth, a victim. Finished!

> But not yet! Oh, no, not yet. Not yet, not now, nor ever. Not while life was life, should they lay hold of him. Never again. Never would he be touched again. And because they had handled his private parts, and looked into them, their eyes should burst and their hands should wither and their hearts should rot. So he cursed them in his blood, with an unremitting curse, as he waited.

For Lawrence, to touch another person is a gesture of recognition—and one that creates a mutual responsibility if it is accepted. But when the doctor lays his hand on Somers he wants only to humiliate him, to show him that even the secret recesses of his body are at the disposal of the authorities. Somers will abandon his home rather than admit this claim: "He hated the Midlands now, he hated the North. They were viler than the South, even than Cornwall. They had a universal desire to take life and down it: these horrible machine people, these iron and coal people."

It may seem that all this is a hysterical overreaction to a relatively minor annoyance and that Lawrence, because of repressed homosexuality or some other freak of temperament, refuses to recognize that he has suffered much less from the war than most Englishmen of his generation. In the chapter following "The Nightmare" he justifies his violent response as coming directly from "the instinctive passional self" that is heedless of rational argument:

> The conscription, all the whole performance of the war was absolutely circumstantially necessary. It was necessary to investigate even the secret parts of a man. Agreed! Agreed! But—
>
> It was *necessary* to put Richard Lovat [Somers] and the ugly collier through that business at Derby. Many men were put through things a thousand times worse. Agreed! Oh, entirely agreed! The war couldn't be lost, at that hour. . . .
>
> And there you are. But—. He was full of a lava fire of rage and hate, at the bottom of his soul. And he knew it was the same with most men. He felt desecrated.

If the conduct of the war was necessary and logical; if a German victory would have made things even worse; then why, Somers asks, "why will men not forgive the war, and their humiliations at the hands of these war-like authorities? Because men were *compelled* into the service of a dead ideal. And perhaps nothing but this compulsion made them realise it *was* a dead ideal." The ideal was "Love, Self-sacrifice, Humanity"; in Lawrence's Joachite theory of history these were the virtues of the Christian era, now superseded by the dawning antidemocratic era of the Holy Spirit.[33] The soldiers sacrificed themselves for an ideal that could not inspire any new life that might have made the sacrifice worthwhile. They were left only with a bitter sense of having been "sold" and a craving for revenge on the rulers who deceived them.

Still, Lawrence realized he would have to wait to enjoy his share of that revenge. Shocked by his helplessness before the authorities at Derby, he renounced his plan of seeking out those opposed to the government and sought, above all, to escape further humiliation. "I've had enough of the social passion," he wrote when he returned home. "Labour and military can alike do their dirty businesses to the top of their bent. I'm not going to squat in a cottage feeling their fine feelings for them, and flying for them a flag that only makes a fool of *me*. I'm out on a new track—let humanity go its own way—I go mine. But I *won't* be pawed and bullied by them—no."[34]

The Last Days

LAWRENCE decided to move to London without notifying the police; once there, he would seek employment that would exempt him from any call to service. He immediately set about pulling such strings as were still within reach. To Pinker he suggested another approach to Arnold Bennett, who was now supervising British propaganda to all friendly countries for the Ministry of Information. Of course, the prospect of Lawrence lending a hand with such work was plainly ludicrous. To Lady Cynthia he made a slightly more plausible proposal:

> I really know something about education. I want a job under the Ministry of Education: not where I shall be kicked about like an old can: I've had enough of that. You must help me to something where I shall not be ashamed. Don't you know that man Fisher? He sounds decent. Really try and get me introduced and started fairly. I need a start—and I'm not going to be an under-servant to anybody: no, I'm not. If these military canaille call me up for any of their filthy jobs—I am graded for sedentary work—I shall just remove myself, and be a deserter.[35]

H. A. L. Fisher, the historian and cousin of Virginia Woolf, was at that time president of the Board of Education and sponsor of the Education Act of 1918; he would hardly have recommended Lawrence for a senior position on the strength of his three years of teaching at Croydon, or of his reputation as a writer. Moreover, Fisher believed in a wider extension of educational opportunity, while Lawrence wanted more elitism and segregation by ability. So nothing came of Lawrence's vision of being a real-life Birkin, the rising young man in the educational hierarchy.

Lawrence and Frieda came to London on 7 October, staying at Dollie Radford's in order to avoid friction with Kot. Lawrence first consulted Pinker about his career, which was continuing its usual modest trickle: *New Poems* just out in a small edition, *Studies in Classic American Literature* beginning to appear monthly in the *English Review*. Pinker must have made it clear that there was no feasible way of improving Lawrence's fortunes. The only gleam of hope Lawrence discovered for himself: a subeditor of *The Times* named Freeman agreed that he might submit some articles to the *Times Educational Supplement,* and perhaps to the *TLS* as well. At this point, however, he had to pay heed to Frieda's health; soon after arriving in London she had caught cold, which then turned to influenza (the great pandemic of 1918 was reaching its peak). Hoping that Frieda would feel better in the country, they went down to Hermitage on 22 October, only two weeks after their arrival in London.

The major event of this brief stay was Lawrence's reconciliation with Katherine Mansfield. She was deeply changed from the flighty and sardonic young woman that he had last seen at Mylor, in June 1916. Her real talent was a writer was just beginning to declare itself in "Prelude," published by the Hogarth Press in autumn 1918; and the acceptance of another fine story, "Bliss," by the *English Review,* had brought her a wider public. She had sealed her relation with Jack by marriage and had lost her mother, of whom she was deeply fond. Just as she was entering her maturity as a woman and as an artist there had come the shock, at the end of 1917, of discovering that she had consumption. Shortly before the Lawrences came to London she and Jack had moved into a house they called "The Elephant" at 2, Portland Villas, on Heath Road in Hempstead. It overlooked the Vale of Health, where the Lawrences had lived in 1915, and lay only a few hundred yards from their current lodgings with Dollie Radford. Lawrence came regularly to visit Katherine while Jack was safely away at the War Office and Frieda sick at home; Katherine described to Brett how he had again become the ideal companion of prewar days:

> For me, at least, the dove brooded over him, too. I loved him. He was just his old, merry, rich self, laughing, describing things, giving you pictures, full of enthusiasm and joy in a future where we become all "vagabonds"—we simply did not talk about people. We kept to things like nuts and cowslips and fires in woods and his black self *was* not. Oh, there is something so loveable about him and his eagerness, his passionate eagerness for life—that is what one loves so.[36]

Surely Lawrence had consciously resolved to charm Katherine, for he must have seen at once how ill she was. Sylvia Lynd, visiting her at this time, found her "frail and very subdued . . . . and very thin. Her rings slid up and down her fingers as she made the tea."[37] Lawrence was always sensitive to ill health in others, having suffered so much from it himself. His reunion with Katherine caught her at a crucial moment, when she had just consulted two doctors about her condition. One of them, an English cousin of hers, took his leave by remarking "Well, dear, of course you won't make old bones"; she found this typical of the Beauchamps' cheerful insensitivity. The other, a famous specialist, saw her on her thirtieth birthday, 14 October. He told Jack: "There's one chance for her—and only one. If she goes into a *strict* sanitarium immediately. . . . If she will go somewhere for a year and submit to discipline, then she has about an even chance. If not, she has two or three years to live—four at the outside."[38] But Katherine convinced herself that a sanitarium regime, which would forbid her to write, would kill her, and her moral ascendancy over Jack enabled her to gain his acquiescence. She never entered a sanitarium and lived just over four years, during which much of her finest work was done.

Who can say that she chose wrongly? Certainly Lawrence, who was confronted with a similar choice for years, would have agreed with her decision—for reasons that Jack explained after both were dead: "Katherine also wanted to believe, and *did eventually come to believe,* that her disease was spiritual, not physical. . . . It's quite horrible that when Lawrence and K. were seeing a good deal of each other in 1918, and I was seeing nothing of L., K. encouraged him and herself to believe it was not physical at all." The most Katherine would do was to "live the sanatorium life" in her own home. On Jack's income they could afford two servants, one of them a full-time nurse; she would follow a strict diet and "have a separate bedroom *always* and *live* by rule." The idea of "being alone, cut off, ill with the other ill" she could not bear, but she needed also to protect herself from Jack's moodiness and self-pity. So he only met Lawrence once that October: "I remember arriving home one afternoon," he recalled, "when Lawrence and Katherine were talking gaily together. I felt that I weighed on them like a lump of lead. It was the old gay talk of a new life in a new country, in which we used to find our solace years before. But I was out of it. I was trying, in vain, to digest the hard sentence of the specialist on Katherine, of which she did not know." [39] For his part, Lawrence still looked askance at Jack, who was prospering and advancing his name as a critic while his former mentor languished in penury. Though Lawrence wrote regularly to Katherine from then on, he pointedly excluded Jack.

While taking up the threads of one relationship Lawrence was dropping another, that with Cecil Gray. Gray had returned to his Cornish house in February and Lawrence corresponded with him amiably enough. But he said nothing about H. D., who had gone there to live with Gray, hoping to make a definite break with her tangled emotional life in London. Her connection with Gray remains obscure, but it seems to have been largely compounded of opportunism on his part and escapism on hers—not motives that Lawrence would be likely to approve. Still, he kept in touch with Gray about the local gossip until the end of July, after which no more letters have survived. The immediate reason for the break was no doubt Gray's decision to go "underground" after being classified C3; he abruptly left Zennor and spent the rest of the war in London (H. D. remained in Cornwall). He did not see Lawrence there, nor in Italy, where they both went in 1919 as soon as they were free to travel. Their friendship had been founded on a chance association rather than on any strong affection or community of interest; in time, Gray became one of Lawrence's most savage critics, even long after his death.

When Lawrence took Frieda down to Hermitage to convalesce the end of the war was obviously close at hand. His bitterness over the medical exam died down as he realized that they need only await the end quietly, with little risk of trouble from the local police. Though food and fuel were scarce, they could begin to breathe freely and to renew their acquaintance with the world as it had been before the deluge:

> Men were working harder than ever felling trees for trench-timber, denuding the land. But their brush-fires were burning in the woods, and when they had gone, in the cold dusk, Somers went with a sack to pick up the unburnt faggots and the great chips of wood the axes had left golden against the felled logs. Flakes of sweet, pale gold oak. He gathered them in the dusk, in a sack, along with the other poor villagers. For he was poorer even than they. Still, it made him very happy to do these things—to see a big, glowing pile of wood-flakes in his shed—and to dig the garden, and set the rubbish burning in the late, wistful autumn—or to wander through the hazel copses, away to the real old English hamlets, that are still like Hardy's *Woodlanders*.

Sustained by this foretaste of peace Lawrence began to write steadily again, having done little since his work on *Movements in European History* in July. He first tackled the pot-boiling articles on education that the *Times* had commissioned, but found that he was simply unable to get them going. Instead, he wrote the play *Touch and Go,* apparently in just six days. The play shows him wrestling with things he had once put behind him, but which he had encountered again in 1918: the mining community of his youth, and his friendship with Katherine and Jack. Unfortunately, the result is an awkward mixture of two different conflicts, between a pair of lovers and between capital and labor. Furthermore, Lawrence adds a spokesman for his own views, Oliver Turton, who can only hover ineffectually at the fringe of the dramatic action; if such a figure was to be present at all he should have been formidably present, like Captain Shotover in *Heartbreak House*.

Touch and Go can also be seen as a sequel to *Women in Love,* but without a counterpart to Ursula. Gerald Crich is now Gerald Barlow, still the scion of a mining dynasty; Gudrun is Anabel Wrath; Birkin becomes the more pallid and ironic Oliver Turton. Like Gudrun (and Katherine herself) Anabel has lived with Gerald, has left him for an affair with a foreigner, and has now come back hoping to reestablish their connection on a truer basis. She had left partly through jealousy of Oliver: "Gerald loved you far too well ever to love me altogether," she now tells him, ". . . . You don't know his sneering attitude to me in the deepest things—because he shared the deepest things with you. He had a passion for me. But he loved you." Oliver, however, no longer wishes to be the third point of a triangle with them. Yet even without this outside pressure Gerald and Anabel are at odds; in a reversal of the situation in *Women in Love,* she wants him to "be a bit gentle and peaceful and happy with a woman," whereas he wants to prove his manhood by driving to the wall both Anabel and the three thousand men who work for him.

The miners' leader is Job Arthur Freer, who starts out toadying to Gerald then is transformed, after Gerald has given him a kicking, into a violent revolutionary. These two are thus locked in a pure battle of wills; against them Lawrence sets two men who want an alternative: Willie Haughton, a utopian socialist modeled on Willie Hopkin, and Oliver the skeptical outsider. "All our lives would be better," Oliver proclaims, "if we hadn't to hang on in the perpetual tug-of-war, like two donkeys pulling at one carrot. The ghastly tension of possessions, and struggling for possession, spoils life for everybody." Not surprisingly, Lawrence succeeds much better at dramatizing the conflict between miners and owners than he does in his exhortations to "leave off struggling against one another, and set up a new state of things." The way out, he suggests, would be for the miners to choose better leaders, men of vision like Haughton rather than blinkered fighters like Job Arthur. But the play ends with no real change of heart on either side; nor are we convinced that there should be one, given the portentous vagueness of Lawrence's vision of a farsighted leader to whom both should submit. In his political thinking, Lawrence has not progressed beyond the shallow critique of democracy that he had pressed on Russell three years before.

Lawrence told Lady Cynthia that he wanted *Touch and Go* to be a success on the stage so that it might have a real influence on the industrial front, which was bound to become turbulent when wartime controls were lifted. "I have written a play out of my deep and earnest self," he wrote her, "fired up my last sparks of hope in the world, as it were, and cried out like a Balaams ass. I believe the world yet might get a turn for the better, if it but had a little shove that way. And this is my attempt—I believe the last I am capable of—or the first, perhaps—at a shove." [40] Lawrence realized, correctly, that he had a better chance of giving the world a shove through artistic creation than through direct involvement in politics. But he invariably underestimated the time it would require for his message to be heard; and in the case of *Touch and Go* he would find that the play was too flawed dramatically for its message to have any impact at all.

The completed Manuscript of *Touch and Go* was sent to make the rounds of Lawrence's woman friends; first Katherine—whose only recorded comment was that it looked *"black* with miners"[41]— then Catherine Carswell and Lady Cynthia. To the latter Lawrence joked that he was imagining himself as "a second Sir Jas. [Barrie], with a secretary"; but he does seem to have expected the play to succeed, and to have wanted to part company with Pinker before it did. "I have an idea that you would rather not be bothered any longer with my work," Lawrence wrote him on 5 November, "which certainly must be no joy, nor profit, to you. Will you let me know if this is so. I remember you said when we made the agreement that it might be broken if either was dissatisfied."[42] Pinker's response is unknown, for there is a six-month gap in their correspondence following this letter. But Lawrence could not yet bring himself to make a definite break and their uneasy partnership continued for another year. Lawrence disliked asking Pinker for loans that he had no way of repaying, and he was now placing most of his work through his own, rather than his agent's, initiative. Yet he was obliged to pay Pinker 10 percent on all his meager earnings. It seemed to Lawrence that Pinker was too much the conventional literary businessman to ever find a niche for his work, so he would be better off doggedly pursuing the course he himself believed in—even if no one else did—and trusting to the future for vindication.

From the other side of the Atlantic, meanwhile, Amy Lowell was urging on him an opposite strategy:

> . . . although I regret sincerely that you cut yourself off from being published by an outspokenness which the English public does not understand, I regret it not in itself . . . but simply because it keeps the world from knowing what a great novelist you are. I think that you could top them all if you would be a little more reticent on this one subject. You need not change your attitude a particle, you can simply use an India rubber in certain places, and then you can come into your own as it ought to be.

This must have raised a weary grin from Lawrence, who had tried often enough during the past four years to write innocuous and salable fiction. "No, Amy," he replied, "again you are not right when you say the india-rubber eraser would let me through into a paradise of popularity. Without the india-rubber I am damned along with the evil, with the india-rubber I am damned among the disappointing. You see what it is to have a reputation. I give it up, and put my trust in heaven."[43] Nonetheless, he started to write "The Blind Man," giving yet another hostage to fortune.

As the Lawrences left London for the seclusion of Hermitage the German war machine had begun to seize up. Five days after they arrived the commander in chief, Ludendorff, resigned and two days later, on 29 October, the German fleet mutinied. Rumors of peace circulated in Hermitage on 6 November; then came, at last, the eleventh hour of the eleventh day of the eleventh month. "Everybody suddenly burst out singing," said Siegfried Sassoon's poem; but what most people who were in the front lines remembered was the strange silence of the hour. Bertrand Russell, in London, "felt strangely solitary amid the rejoicings, like a ghost dropped by accident from some other planet"; Jack Murry, in a mood of suicidal despair over the sentence of Katherine, took no comfort from the celebrations; in Wales a shell-shocked young captain, Robert Graves, went "walking alone along the dyke above the marshes of Rhuddlan . . . cursing and sobbing and thinking of the dead."[44]

Nor were Lawrence and Frieda inclined to rejoice. On the afternoon of 11 November they were in London, where Monty Shearman's rooms became a central meeting place for the band of artists and intellectuals who had held out against the war spirit that possessed their countrymen. Most of the inner circle of Bloomsbury were there: Clive Bell, Roger Fry, Lytton Strachey and Carrington, Duncan Grant, Maynard Keynes with his future wife, Lydia Lopokova. The other guests, not less distinguished, included Osbert and Sacheverell Sitwell, Diaghilev, Massine, Lady Ottoline and Gertler. Ottoline was not present at the same time as the Lawrences, which was probably just as well: but they did see David Garnett, for the first time since 1915. Garnett has recalled that Lawrence "looked ill and unhappy, with no trace of that gay sparkling love of life in his eyes which had been his most attractive feature six years before. I greeted him warmly, but he only nodded, said: 'So you're here,' and went on talking. Frieda gave me a squeeze and a look of pleased astonishment in her yellow eyes which made up for his lack of warmth." Lawrence's grimness no doubt owed something to his distaste for Bloomsbury and for the general mood, at the party and all over London, of dionysian revelry; but, beyond such ephemeral irritants, he was determined to bear witness among the joyful crowd to his own bitter experience of the war years. Later, when Garnett and an attentive circle had gathered round, he told them the lesson they should draw from the "Great War for Civilisation," as it was officially called:

> "I suppose you think the war is over and that we shall go back to the kind of world you lived in before it. But the war isn't over. The hate and evil is greater now than ever. Very soon war will break out again and overwhelm you. It makes me sick to see you rejoicing like a butterfly in the last rays of the sun before the winter. The crowd outside thinks that Germany is crushed forever. But the Germans will soon rise again. Europe is done for: England most of all the countries. This war isn't over. Even if the fighting should stop, the evil will be worse because the hate will be dammed up in men's hearts and will show itself in all sorts of ways which will be worse than war. Whatever happens there can be no Peace on Earth."
>
> There was a sombre joy in the tone in which he made these fierce prophecies of evil, and I could see that he was enjoying being the only man in the room who was not rejoicing because the fighting was over. It was the last time that I saw Lawrence, or spoke to him.[45]

In *Kangaroo* nothing is said of the party at Shearman's. Perhaps Lawrence omitted it because he was so set against the spirit of the gathering; when given a chance to be reconciled with Ottoline, David, and the rest, he only retreated further into his scornful isolation. The vignette of Armistice Day in *Kangaroo* shows the Somers alone at Hermitage, instead of with the revelers in London:

> He and Harriet sat and sang German songs, in the cottage, that strange night of the Armistice, away there in the country: and she cried—and he wondered what now, now the walls would come no nearer. It had been like Edgar Allan Poe's story of the Pit and the Pendulum—where the walls come in, in, in, till the prisoner is almost squeezed. So the black walls of the war—and he had been trapped, and very nearly squeezed into the pit where the rats were. So nearly! So very nearly. And now the black walls had stopped.

When the war began Lawrence had been separated from Frieda, away on his walking tour of the Lake District with Kot. Now that it was over he insisted on going back to Mountain Cottage to work on his history, which had just been accepted by Oxford; though Freida refused to go North and remained in London with Dollie

Radford. Apart from her dislike of the hardship and isolation of Middleton-by-Wirksworth, they were at odds over her grief at Germany's defeat. Lawrence, characteristically, refused either to celebrate with the victors or to commiserate with the vanquished. Katherine Mansfield, who had seen Lawrence several times during Armistice week, sent Lady Ottoline a barbed little sketch of his mood:

> He is gone off to the Midlands today—still without Frieda. He seems to have quite forgotten her for the time—merely saying: "she wants me to become a german and I'm *not* a german"—and so dismisses her. But I wonder why he is taken in by the most impossible charlatans—I am afraid he will never be free of them. Perhaps his whole trouble is that he has not a real sense of humour. He takes himself dreadfully seriously nowadays: I mean he sees himself as a symbolic figure—a prophet—the voice in the wilderness crying 'woe'.[46]

So those who four years before had acclaimed Lawrence as a genius now dismissed him, in his lonely Derbyshire cottage, as a gull and a crank. Lawrence, for his part, would willingly have dismissed all his countrymen. He would be obliged to stay in England for another full year before he could get permission to leave, another year of poverty and sickness (he barely survived a severe case of influenza in February 1919); but once he was able to cross the channel, on 14 November 1919, he never lived in England again.

At the end of Amistice Day David Garnett went to the home of Keynes, the most worldly-wise of the Bloomsberries, and listened, over wine and sandwiches, to his verdict on the day's celebrations: " 'What is really important,' Keynes said, 'is that we can't go back on this. Whatever may develop neither side can start the war up again. The troops would not fight and the people would not work.' This was a more common-sense argument than Lawrence's and with it in my mind I went to bed and fell fast asleep."[47] More than ten million had died; but who except Lawrence could foresee, or accept, that the Nightmare was not over?

EPILOGUE

From Introduction to
Memoirs of the Foreign Legion

THERE ARE certain things which are *so* bitter, *so* horrible, that the contemporaries just cannot know them, cannot contemplate them. So it is with a great deal of the late war. It was so foul, and humanity in Europe fell suddenly into such ignominy and inhuman ghastliness, that we shall *never* fully realize what it was. We just cannot bear it. We haven't the soul-strength to contemplate it.

And yet, humanity can only finally conquer by realizing. It is human destiny, since Man fell into consciousness and self-consciousness, that we can only go forward step by step through realization, full, bitter, conscious realization. This is true of all the great terrors and agonies and anguishes of life: sex, and war, and even crime. . . . Knowledge, true knowledge is like vaccination. It prevents the continuing of ghastly moral disease.

And so it is with the war. Humanity in Europe fell horribly into a hatred of the living soul, in the war. There is no gainsaying it. We all fell. Let us not try to wriggle out of it. We fell into hideous depravity of hating the human soul; a purulent small-pox of the spirit we had. It was shameful, shameful, shameful, in every country and in all of us. Some tried to resist, and some didn't. But we were all drowned in shame. A purulent small-pox of the vicious spirit, vicious against the deep soul that pulses in the blood.

We haven't got over it. The small-pox sores are running yet in the spirit of mankind. And we have got to take this putrid spirit to our bosom. There's nothing else for it. Take the foul rotten spirit of mankind, full of the running sores of the war, to our bosom, and cleanse it there. Cleanse it not with blind love: ah no, that won't help. But with bitter and wincing realization. We have to take the disease into our consciousness and let it go through our soul, like some virus. We have got to realize. And then we can surpass. . . .

It is the only help: to realize, *fully,* and then make up our minds. The war was *foul.* As long as I am a man, I say it and assert it, and further I say, as long as I am a man such a war shall never occur again. It shall not, and it shall not. All modern militarism is foul. It shall go. A man I am, and above machines, and it shall go, forever, because I have found it vile, vile, too vile ever to experience again. . . .

Man perhaps *must* fight. Mars, the great god of war, will be a god forever. Very well. Then if fight you must, fight you shall, and without engines, without machines. Fight if you like, as the Romans fought, with swords and spears, or like the Red Indian, with bows and arrows and knives and war paint. But never again shall you fight with the foul, base, fearful, monstrous machines of war which man invented for the last war.

Abbreviations
Notes
Index

ABBREVIATIONS

[For abbreviations of periodicals, see *MLA International Bibliography,* vol. 1 (1976)]

ABR I: *The Autobiography of Bertrand Russell: 1872–1914* (New York: Bantam, 1968).
ABR II: *The Autobiography of Bertrand Russell: 1914–1944* (New York: Bantam, 1969).
AD: *Lady Cynthia Asquith: Diaries 1915–1918,* ed. E. M. Horsley (New York: Knopf, 1969).
Alpers: Antony Alpers, *Katherine Mansfield: A Biography* (New York: Knopf, 1953).
Aspects: E. M. Forster, *Aspects of the Novel* (New York: Harcourt Brace, 1927).
Bedford: Sybille Bedford, *Aldous Huxley: A Biography* (New York: Knopf, 1974).
BL: British Library, London.
BRA: Bertrand Russell Archives, McMaster University, Hamilton, Ont.
BTW: *The Autobiography of John Middleton Murry: Between Two Worlds.* (New York: Julian Messner, 1936).
Burnet: John Burnet, *Early Greek Philosophy* (New York: Meridian, 1957).
CB: *D. H. Lawrence: A Composite Biography,* ed. E. Nehls. 3 vols. (Madison: University of Wisconsin Press, 1957–59).
CH: *D. H. Lawrence: The Critical Heritage,* ed. R. P. Draper, (London: Routledge & Kegan Paul, 1970).
CL: *The Collected Letters of D. H. Lawrence,* ed. Harry T. Moore (New York: Viking, 1962).
Clark: Ronald W. Clark, *The Life of Bertrand Russell* (London: Jonathan Cape and Weidenfeld & Nicolson, 1975).
CP: *The Complete Poems of D. H. Lawrence,* ed. V. de Sola Pinto and W. Roberts (New York: Viking, 1971).
Darroch: Sandra Jobson Darroch, *Ottoline: The Life of Lady Ottoline Morrell* (New York: Coward, McCann & Geoghegan, 1975).
Delavenay: Emile Delavenay, *D. H. Lawrence: The Man and his Work. The Formative Years: 1885–1919* (Carbondale and Edwardsville: Southern Illinois University Press, 1972).
DHLR: *The D. H. Lawrence Review.*
FF: David Garnett, *The Flowers of the Forest* (London: Chatto & Windus, 1955).
FLM: *Frieda Lawrence: The Memoirs and Correspondence,* ed. E. W. Tedlock, Jr. (New York: Knopf, 1964).
GLD: E. M. Forster, *Goldsworthy Lowes Dickinson* (London: Edward Arnold, 1945).
Gossip: Beatrice Lady Glenavy, *Today We Will Only Gossip* (London: Constable, 1964).
Hardy: G. H. Hardy, *Bertrand Russell & Trinity: A College Controversy of the Last War* (Cambridge: Cambridge University Press, 1942).
Hassall: Christopher Hassall, *A Biography of Edward Marsh* (New York: Harcourt Brace, 1959).
Holroyd: Michael Holroyd, *Lytton Strachey: A Biography* (Harmondsworth: Penguin, 1971).
Hux: *The Letters of D. H. Lawrence,* ed. Aldous Huxley (London: Heinemann, 1932).
InH: H. T. Moore, *The Intelligent Heart: The Story of D. H. Lawrence* (New York: Farrar, Straus & Young, 1954).

ABBREVIATIONS

Keynes: J. M. Keynes, *Two Memoirs* (London: Rupert Hart-Davis, 1949).

Kinkead-Weekes: Mark Kinkead-Weekes, "The Marble and the Statute: The Exploratory Imagination of D. H. Lawrence," in *Imagined Worlds: Essays on Some English Novels and Novelists in Honour of John Butt,* ed. M. Mack and I. Gregor (London: Methuen, 1968), pp. 371–418.

KMJ: *The Journal of Katherine Mansfield 1904–1922* (London: Constable, 1962).

KML: *Katherine Mansfield's Letters to John Middleton Murry: 1913–1922* (London: Constable, 1951).

Lacy: *An Analytical Calendar of the Letters of D. H. Lawrence,* by G. M. Lacy (Ann Arbor: University Microfilms, 1971). Unpublished letters are cited by their number in this calendar.

Lea: F. A. Lea, *The Life of John Middleton Murry* (New York: Oxford University Press, 1960).

LKM: *The Letters of Katherine Mansfield* (London: Constable, 1929).

LL: *Lawrence in Love: Letters to Louie Burrows,* ed. James Boulton (Nottingham: University of Nottingham, 1968).

Lon Mag II: Mark Schorer, "I Will Send Address," *London Magazine* 3 (February 1956): 44–67.

Marwick: Arthur Marwick, *The Deluge* (Boston: Little, Brown, n.d.).

MGL: Noel Carrington, ed., *Mark Gertler: Selected Letters* (London: Rupert Hart-Davis, 1965).

Mizener: *The Saddest Story: A Biography of Ford Madox Ford* (New York and Cleveland: World, 1971).

MLM: *Katherine Mansfield: The Memories of L. M.* (Leslie Moore) (London: Michael Joseph, 1971).

MOM: *Memoirs of Lady Ottoline Morrell 1873–1915* (New York: Knopf, 1964).

MOM II: *Ottoline at Garsington: Memoirs of Lady Ottoline Morrell 1915–1918,* ed. R. Gathorne-Hardy (London: Faber & Faber, 1974).

M Russ: *D. H. Lawrence's Letters to Bertrand Russell,* ed. Harry T. Moore (New York: Gotham Book Mart, 1948).

Musical Chairs: Cecil Gray, *Musical Chairs* (London: Home & Van Thal, 1948).

NIBW: Frieda Lawrence, *"Not I, But the Wind"* (New York: Viking, 1934).

Num. People: Edward Marsh, *A Number of People* (New York: Harper, 1939).

Peter Warlock: Cecil Gray, *Peter Warlock: A Memoir of Philip Heseltine* (London: Jonathan Cape, 1934).

Phoenix: D. H. Lawrence, *Phoenix* (London: Heinemann, 1936).

Phoenix II: D. H. Lawrence, *Phoenix II* (New York: Viking, 1970).

Pioneer: J. B. Hobman, ed., *David Eder: Memoirs of a Modern Pioneer* (London: Victor Gollancz, 1945).

PL: *The Priest of Love: A Life of D. H. Lawrence,* by H. T. Moore (New York: Farrar, Straus and Giroux, 1974).

RDHL: J. M. Murry. *Reminiscences of D. H. Lawrence* (London: Jonathan Cape, 1933).

RDP: Lawrence, *Reflections on the Death of a Porcupine* (Bloomington: Indiana University Press, 1963).

RLC: John Dickinson, "Katherine Mansfield and S. S. Koteliansky: Some Unpublished Letters," *Revue de Littérature Comparée* 45 (1971): 79–99.

RLF: Royal Literary Fund Archives.

Ross: Charles L. Ross, "The Composition of *Women in Love:* a History, 1913–1919," DHLR 8, no. 2: 198–212; "The Revisions of the Second Generation in *The Rainbow,"* RES, n.s. XXVII, no. 107 (1976): 277–295.

SCAL: D. H. Lawrence, *Studies in Classic American Literature* (New York: Doubleday, 1951).

SFD: S. Foster Damon, *Amy Lowell: A Chronicle* (Boston: Houghton Mifflin, 1935).

SM: Armin Arnold, ed., *The Symbolic Meaning: The Uncollected Versions of Studies in Classic American Literature* (New York: Viking, 1964).

SP: Catherine Carswell, *The Savage Pilgrimage: A Narrative of D. H. Lawrence* (London: Chatto & Windus, 1932).

ABBREVIATIONS

Spender: Stephen Spender, ed., *D. H. Lawrence: Novelist, Poet, Prophet* (London: Weidenfeld & Nicolson, 1973).

STH: Lawrence, *Study of Thomas Hardy,* in *Phoenix.*

TxU: Humanities Research Center, University of Texas.

Vittoz: Roger Vittoz, *Treatment of Neurasthenia by Teaching of Brain Control* (London: Long-
mans, Green, 1911).

Williams: John Williams, *The Home Fronts: Britain, France and Germany 1914–1918* (London: Constable, 1972).

Zyt: *The Quest for Rananim: D. H. Lawrence's Letters to S. S. Koteliansky,* ed., G. Zytaruk
(Montreal and London: McGill-Queen's University Press, 1970).

NOTES

[Where references have been consolidated, they are given in the same order as the quotations appear in the text.]

CHAPTER I

1. See CL 122, Spender 39, and CB I, 179 (David Garnett has confirmed that Frieda had an affair with Harold Hobson at this time: conversation with the author, 30 June 1973).
2. CL 130.
3. CL 171.
4. CL 282.
5. Delavenay 144.
6. CL 272.
7. FLM 190; ? February 1914.
8. CL 281.
9. To E. M. Forster; Lacy 1142.
10. CB I, 145.
11. CL 287. For a fuller account of these revisions see Keith Cushman, DHLR 8, 176, and Brian Finney in SB 28 (1975), 321–332.
12. Marsh, one should note, was sentimentally drawn to men but worshiped only from afar; in adolescence he had been rendered impotent by a severe attack of German measles. See Christopher Hassall, *A Biography of Edward Marsh* (New York: Harcourt Brace, 1959), pp. 17–18, 23.
13. CB I, 235.
14. Lacy 640.
15. CL 309.
16. Kinkead-Weekes, 373.
17. Hux 219.

CHAPTER II

1. CL 289.
2. SCAL 137.
3. CL 516.
4. SFD 271.
5. Royal Literary Fund archives.
6. Letter to Hewlett, 12 September 1914. Unpublished: RLF archives.
7. Lacy 677.
8. SFD 247.

NOTES

9. STH 407.
10. Hux 209.
11. CB I, 242.
12. SFD 278.
13. CL 291, 295.
14. BTW 305.
15. Lacy 640.
16. CL 299.
17. Conversation with the author.
18. CB I, 258.
19. JMM/Catherine Carswell: 14 June 1931, unpublished, TxU.
20. Lawrence opposed contraception from the start of his relations with Frieda (CL 120), but they may have taken precautions for fear of problems with the divorce case if Frieda became pregnant.
21. Holroyd 537.
22. MGL 34.
23. MGL 63.
24. Alpers, 145. Beauchamp, a leading financier, was knighted in 1922. As Alpers explains, Beauchamp was wary of giving money to Katherine to do as she liked with: her allowance at this time was one hundred pounds a year, which was barely sufficient for necessities. But he spent lavishly within his household; in 1903, for example, he chartered the entire passenger accommodation of a 10,000-ton liner to take his family to Europe.
25. FLM 410.
26. CL 293.
27. D. Garnett, Conversation with the author: cf. CB I, 210.
28. SFD 271; Hux 208.
29. CL 309, 310.
30. On 17 November Lawrence wrote to Harriet Monroe in Chicago: "Today came the War Number of *Poetry,* for which also I thank you. It put me into such a rage—how dare Amy [Lowell] talk about bohemian glass and stalks of flame?—that in a real fury I had to write my war poem, because it breaks my heart, this war" (CL 294). In the files of *Poetry* is preserved a handwritten ms. "Passages from *Ecce Homo,*" consisting of excerpts from a draft of the poem later called "Eloi, Eloi, Lama Sabachthani?" But neither draft appeared in *Poetry.* It is possible that Harriet Monroe was making an expurgated version, without some of the erotic descriptions of violence such as: "Like a bride he took my bayonet, wanting it,/ Like a virgin the blade of my bayonet, wanting it,/ And it sank to rest from me in him,/ And I, the lover, am consummate" (CP 742). Certainly Amy Lowell objected to the "pure, farfetched indecency" of the poem when it appeared in the special Imagist issue of *The Egoist* for 1 May 1915 (SFD 306). See Alvin Sullivan, "D. H. Lawrence and *Poetry:* The Unpublished Manuscripts," DHLR 9, no. 2 (1976), pp. 266–277.
31. The Phoenix was also, of course, a symbol of Christ. Lawrence was struck by the description of it in Mrs. Heather Jenner's *Christian Symbolism,* which he read in December 1914 (CL 304). Cf. James C. Cowan, "Lawrence's Phoenix: An Introduction," DHLR 5, pp. 187–199.
32. See David Kleinbard, "D. H. Lawrence and Ontological Insecurity," PMLA 89 (1974), p. 155.
33. CL 290.
34. CL 298.
35. STH 479.
36. Written in January 1913; Hux 95.
37. STH 398.
38. At Metz, in May 1912; David Garnett, "Frieda and Lawrence," in Spender 38.
39. STH 406, CL 347.
40. Williams 23. In effect the Act suspended civil rights and put Britain under martial law for the duration of the war. The original DORA was extended by a long series of "Defense of the Realm Regulations."
41. STH 403.
42. STH 436.

43. The description of Tom Brangwen's work as a mine manager comes at the end of Ursula's Lesbian relationship with Winifred Inger, an episode that Lawrence added in December 1914 or later (Kinkead-Weekes 379). The "Industrial Magnate" chapter would have been completed around late summer of 1916.

44. CL 298.

45. STH 405, 406, 403.

46. CL 318.

47. STH 443. Weininger argues that everyone is bisexual in varying degrees; his book was translated into English in 1906 and Lawrence probably read it. His influence is discussed by Delavenay (308, 348), though he probably overrates it. Lawrence's example of the total male is Shelley, on the grounds that he is utterly spiritualized and almost bodiless (STH 459).

48. STH 445.

49. "Surgery for the Novel—or a Bomb?" (1923); *Phoenix* 520.

50. CL 295.

51. CL 296.

52. CL 299.

53. NIBW 81.

54. From the story "Je ne Parle pas Francais."

55. KMJ 63.

56. BTW 321.

57. MGL 77.

58. MCL 79

59. CL 307.

60. *Gossip* 99.

61. Letter of? January 1919; Lacy 1461: *Pioneer* 121.

62. Letter of Jessie Chambers to Emile Delavenay, September 1933; Delevenay, *D. H. Lawrence: L'Homme et la genèse de son oeuvre* (Paris: Klincksieck, 1969), p. 665.

63. FLM 370.

64. InH 179; Lon Mag II 47.

65. CB I, 263.

CHAPTER III

1. OM/BR, 31.12.14. All Ottoline's letters to Russell are in the Bertrand Russell Archive, McMaster University. ". . . that muddled stuff of Woolfe": Virginia Woolf's first novel, *The Voyage Out.*

2. CB I, 240.

3. MOM 10.

4. MOM 66.

5. CL 306.

6. CB I, 240; CL 305.

7. MOM 275, 274.

8. MGL 81.

9. Lacy 721; 28 January 1915.

10. CL 308.

11. 27 January 1915; the words are omitted from the text of the letter in CL 308, as is a sentence saying Lawrence has burned Ottoline's letter.

12. CB I, 273.

13. An advance copy; Forster's favorable review of the novel appeared in the *Daily News and Leader,* April 8. Lawrence judged it "interesting, but not *very* good—nothing much behind it." (Lacy 746).

14. CL 315.

15. Lacy 721;? 28 January 1915.

16. CL 180.

17. Lacy 721.

NOTES

18. Lacy 721. Lawrence's mention of "withdrawing himself" may refer to the doctrine of "dual mortification" that he had described to Murry at Chesham: ". . . very often when he wants F. she does not want him at all . . . he has to recognize and fully allow for this." (CB I, 256).

19. FLM 196; Lacy 732, 3 February.

20. CL 323, 316.

21. CL 251.

22. CL 319.

23. Terminal Note to *Maurice*. However, Forster seems to have been writing "indecent" short stories on homosexual themes since about 1907: *The Life to Come and Other Short Stories* (New York: Avon Books, 1976), p. xiv.

24. CL 323.

25. 12 February 1915; TxU.

26. 20 February 1915; King's College. Though he is not named, the letter almost certainly refers to Lawrence.

27. Included in *The Life to Come*.

28. See, for example, Robert H. Stoller, "Sexual Excitement," *Archives of General Psychiatry*, August 1976; J. Gagnon and W. Simon, *Sexual Conduct* (Chicago: Aldine, 1973).

29. Quoted in *The Life to Come*, xvii.

30. Lacy 746, ?24 February 1915.

31. GLD 123.

32. *Aspects* 143.

33. GLD 38.

34. CL 800; Lacy 2452, 19 February 1924.

35. CL 315 (where the letter is misdated; more likely ?24 January).

36. CL 313.

37. Lacy 729.

38. MOM 275.

39. TxU; dated by Frieda 12 February, but Forster arrived on the 10th.

40. Lacy 738; ?11 February 1915.

41. 13 February 1915; BRA.

42. Lon Mag II 49.

43. *Gossip* 63. Thirty-seven years later Murry found the letter again and sent it to Campbell.

44. Zyt 27; CL 314.

45. *Gossip* 80.

46. ?24 Feb.; DHLR 6, no. 1, p. 5.

47. BTW 326–327.

48. BTW 338.

49. CL 321.

50. BTW 333.

51. BTW 340.

52. CL 313.

53. Lawrence's phrase; see William Gerhardi, *Memoirs of a Polyglot* (New York: Knopf, 1931), p. 234.

54. ABR I, 276.

55. BR/OM, nos. 1063, 1065.

56. BR/OM; no. 1150, 20 November 1914.

57. BR/OM; no. 1204, 21 January 1915.

58. CL 314.

59. CL 311.

60. CL 317.

61. CL 320.

62. STH 408.

63. Lacy 738; ?11 February 1915.

64. Clark 256; BR/OM, no. 1237, ?13 February 1915.

65. CL 325.

66. CL 326.

NOTES

67. CL 324.

68. Presumably a pun on both "The Gay Saviour" and Nietzsche's *The Gay Science*.

69. DHLR VI, 4, no. 1; ?24 February 1915.

70. CL 328; he enclosed his well-known drawing of a rainbow arching over a grimy scene of houses and collieries—see my article in DHLR 8, no. 1.

71. Hux 219.

72. CL 322.

73. Kinkead-Weekes 379. See also Ross, *passim*.

74. p. 71 above; cf. *The Rainbow*, 463.

75. Letter to Francis Birrell, August 1915, quoted in Holroyd, 591.

76. BR/OM; no. 1233, 6 March 1915.

77. BR/OM; no. 1234.

78. CB I, 302.

79. CL 324.

80. Holroyd 198.

81. BR/OM; no. 1234.

82. Ibid.

83. Keynes 79.

84. Clark 257; BR/OM, no. 1234.

85. Hux 236.

86. CL 331; "W. D. C." is an error for U. D. C., the Union of Democratic Control.

87. CL 329.

88. Hux 238; Keynes's name added from ms.

89. Hux 238. About this time Lawrence also attacked Eleanor Farjeon for admiring Dostoevsky: "You're all making a mistake. You all think he is concerned with God. *Can't you see* that his only concern, his only interest, *is in sin?*" (CB I, 293).

90. CL 332.

91. Lon Mag II; BR/OM, no. 1244, 3 April 1915.

92. BR/OM, no. 1244.

93. BR/OM; no. 1245, 6 April.

94. Hux 237; last two sentences added from ms.

95. CL 331.

96. BR/OM; no. 1286, 11 June.

97. Hux 237.

98. Hux 234.

99. FF 52–54; he did however visit the Lawrences in Hampstead in the fall of 1915. *Texas Quarterly* vol. 9, no. 3, p. 32.

100. Interview with the author, 30 June 1973.

101. Zyt 39.

102. CL 332, with additions from ms.

103. CL 337.

104. See the description of these revisions in Kinkead-Weekes and Ross.

105. Hux 234.

106. Lacy 772, 773, conflated; 20 April 1915.

107. CL 333.

108. CL 334.

109. FF 37.

110. BR/OM; nos. 1258, 1261.

111. Vittoz 77, 83. Cf. *Women in Love* (New York, 1920), 151.

112. CL 335.

113. CL 334.

114. CL 336.

115. CL 336; BR/OM, no. 1261, 1 May 1915.

116. CL 337.

117. CL 337. Larwrence had met Brooke socially and heard about him from David Garnett.

118. Hassall 287.

119. CL 338.

120. CB I, 296.
121. Lacy 805; 6 June 1915.
122. See Colin Simpson, *Lusitania* (London: Longman, 1972); though his conclusions have been challenged.
123. CL 340.
124. SFD 247.
125. Reply to a question by Leicester Harmsworth, 9 November 1915; cited in a letter to the *Daily News* by Sylvia Pankhurst, 15 December 1915.
126. CL 344.
127. FL/EMF, 5 February 1915, King's College; FLM 195, 196.
128. FLM 193; Lacy 772; 20 April 1915.
129. FL/OM; TxU, 20–28 April 1915.
130. CB I, 288.
131. Marwick 51, Mizener 251; it eventually became the Ministry of Information in 1918, under Lord Beaverbrook.
132. Mizener 250–251.
133. CL 323.
134. FLM 389.
135. Mizener 202.
136. CB I, 209; Mizener 282; FLM 389.
137. FLM 208, 201.
138. FL/OM; Lacy 785, TxU.
139. CB I, 306.
140. AD 18; 11 May 1915.
141. CL 341.
142. OM/BR; 27 April, 7 May.
143. CL 347.
144. Lacy 826; 26 July 1915.
145. Examples from pages 418, 442, and 444 of the Methuen edition.
146. CL 345.
147. Hux 222.
148. FL/OM, TxU, 20–28 May, 1915; Lacy 785.
149. Lacy 801, 785.
150. Hardy 27, 29.
151. CL 346.
152. BR/OM, no. 1281, 31 May; CL 347.
153. Lacy 799; 2 June 1915.
154. M Russ 49.
155. BR/OM, nos. 1287, 1295, and 1306; 12, 21, and 25 June 1915.
156. CB I, 310.
157. MOM II, 36.
158. MOM II, 37.
159. AD 45; 21 June.
160. FL/OM; TxU, ?21 June 1915.
161. OM/BR; 18 June.
162. BR/OM; no. 1306, 21 June.
163. CL 350.
164. CL 350.
165. BR/OM; no. 1306, 21 June.
166. CL 354; the section of this letter marked [P.S.] is actually a separate letter, probably of 7 July.
167. M Russ 8off.
168. Hux 240.
169. BR/OM; no. 1302, 8 July 1915.
170. ABR II, 58, 59.
171. CL 353.
172. CL 352.
173. Burnet 136, 137.

174. CL 353–354.
175. CL 354. The word "must" was underlined fifteen times, much to Russell's annoyance.
176. CL 355.
177. CL 355.
178. CL 356.
179. CL 351, (misdated ?5 July; should be ?19 July); AD 58, 25 July.
180. Hux 242.
181. CL 351.
182. Lacy 813, ?20 June; passage omitted in CL.
183. AD 37, 5 June.
184. Quotations are from the first version of the story, published in the October 1915 *English Review*.
185. CL 357.
186. Hux 242.
187. CL 358.

CHAPTER IV

1. CL 360.
2. AD 80.
3. CL 361.
4. CL 362.
5. "Note to The Crown" in RDP.
6. CL 363.
7. Lacy 829.
8. *Twilight*, p. 15; revised from the sketch "Christs in the Tirol."
9. Delavenay 341.
10. *The Futurist Manifesto* (1909), CL 280.
11. CL 362.
12. Hux 257, with additions from ms.
13. BTW 352; CL 363.
14. M Russ 57.
15. Hux 257, with additions from ms.
16. Lacy 867, 28 September.
17. CL 368; Mrs. Dax was the model for Clara Dawes in *Sons and Lovers*.
18. Lacy 865.
19. CL 365.
20. Quotations from the reprint of the article in *Justice in War Time* (Chicago: Open Court Publishing Co., 1917).
21. CL 367.
22. ABR II, 13; BR/OM, no. 1320, ?19 September.
23. Hux 254.
24. M Russ 61; CL 470.
25. "Note to the Crown" in RDP.
26. CH 90.
27. CH 92.
28. BTW 351.
29. AD 86.
30. AD 85; CL 370. For the offending passage see *Signature* I, 14.
31. *Signature* III, 3.
32. *Signature* I, 4.
33. *Signature* I, 10.
34. *Signature* II, 9.
35. RDP 32.

36. *Signature* II, 10.
37. RDP 74, *Signature* III, 7.
38. CL 360, RDP 79.
39. *Signature* III, 4.
40. RDP 83.
41. RDP 98–99.
42. AD 89.
43. CL 371; Zyt 54.
44. CL 373.
45. AD 94.
46. CL 374–376.
47. See D. Farmer, "D. H. Lawrence's 'The Turning Back': the Text and its Genesis in Correspondence," DHLR 5, 121–131. Lawrence, hoping to influence American opinion, submitted the poem to *Poetry* (Chicago); but it was not accepted.
48. CL 377.
49. Lacy 889; ?17 October.
50. CH 93–95.
51. CH 96–97.
52. Lacy 901.
53. D. MacCarthy, "Obscenity and the Law," in *Experience* (Freeport, N.Y.: Books for Libraries Press, 1968), p. 141.
54. Delavenay 239.
55. Holroyd 605.
56. Hux 269; CL 376.
57. From Lawrence's portrait of her as "Miss James" in his story "The Last Laugh."
58. CB I, 337.
59. Dismissed by Lawrence, in a letter to Ottoline, as "words—literature—bore" (Hux 237)
60. Letter to D. Garnett, quoted in Holroyd 607.
61. CL 377.
62. Delavenay 238, 240.
63. FL/OM, 8–10 November 1915, TxU.
64. CL 378–79.
65. Hux 279.
66. CL 379.
67. AD 97, 115.
68. Holroyd 605.
69. CH 106.
70. Delavenay, illustration 16.
71. Delavenay 242.
72. CL 388.
73. CL 399.
74. D. H. Lawrence: *Letters to Thomas & Adele Seltzer* (Santa Barbara: Black Sparrow Press, 1976), p. 157.
75. An exception was the poem "Resurrection," late in November (Hux 279).
76. CL 401.
77. CL 403.
78. CB I, 330–331.
79. CL 394–396.
80. CL 381–382, with additions from ms.
81. CB I, 331.
82. CL 396.
83. Bedford 61; MOM II, 80.
84. OM/BR, 10 November, 16 November.
85. Darroch 164.
86. Lacy 948.
87. M Russ 66.
88. ABR II, 62.

NOTES

89. CL 392, with additions from ms.
90. OM/BR, 2 and 6 December.
91. MOM II, 77.
92. CL 396.
93. Marwick 77.
94. Hux 284.
95. *Evening Standard,* December 10, 11, 1915.
96. CL 397.
97. Hux 478.
98. Lacy 957.
99. CL 403.
100. CL 389, 399, 397.
101. KML 56.
102. CL 401.
103. CL 393. Cf CL 180 for an earlier, less systematic discussion of the idea.
104. OM/BR, ?March/April 1916. Cf. OM/BR, "Monday" ?January 1916: "I suppose it *is* the difference that you live entirely mentally and not visually that makes me feel you tiring—sometimes I love just to *rest* from thinking and to take in sights and smells . . . by the senses . . . and that you *cannot* do can you?"
105. CL 395.
106. CL 394.
107. CL 394.
108. ABR II, 13.
109. Zyt. 61, CL 404, 403.
110. CL 404–405.
111. CL 405. For Lawrence's response to the General Strike of 1926 see "Return to Bestwood" in *Phoenix II.*
112. CL 405.

CHAPTER V

1. Hux 301.
2. Hux 333; CL 412.
3. CL 412, with additions from ms.
4. CL 409.
5. CB I, 346.
6. To Catherine Carswell, 31 December 1915; unpub., not in Lacy.
7. CB I, 346.
8. CL 405–406.
9. Zyt 62–63; CL 411.
10. CL 411; Zyt 85.
11. Lacy 981; Sunday [?7 January 1916].
12. CL 389.
13. FLM 198; this note was probably enclosed with Lawrence's letter to Russell of 13 January, in which he invited him to visit: M Russ 67.
14. CB I, 356; CL 416.
15. Hux 320.
16. Hux 315.
17. Interview with the author at Porthcothan, 10 June 1975. Mrs. Babb was born in 1904; her mother, she reported, died about 1921.
18. Hux 311.
19. CL 423.
20. Lon Mag II, 55.
21. CL 434.
22. PH/VS, 16 February 1916; unpub., BL.
23. CB I, 348.

24. Murry's novel *Still Life* was published by Constable late in 1916. Heseltine's description of "Goats and Compasses" would seem to settle a scholarly controversy about whether or not it was an early title for *Women in Love;* see DHLR 4, no. 3, and 6, no. 1.

25. Hux 320.

26. CL 434.

27. 29 February 1916; unpub.

28. Hux 333.

29. Lacy 1037 and 1052.

30. 11 February, unpub, not in Lacy; CL 413.

31. CL 412.

32. CL 412.

33. Zyt 68.

34. Se Keith Sagar, DHLR 6, no. 3.

35. CL 437.

36. MOM II, 93; OM/BR, 4 March 1916; unpub.

37. CB I, 582.

38. CL 411–412; M Russ 68.

39. CB I, 347.

40. CL 414, Lacy 989; Ottoline wrote on the letter: "Hurrah!"

41. 16 February 1916, unpub., BL. In chapter 3; Kouyoumdjian appears as "Michaelis," a slum boy from Dublin who has become a successful playwright. MOM II, 77.

42. Late January 1916; unpub., TxU.

43. OM/BR, late January.

44. PH/OM; 28 January 1916; unpub., TxU.

45. PH/BK; 14 December [1915]; unpub., BL.

46. CL 422, 427.

47. CL 427–428.

48. CL 437.

49. Heseltine's difficulties with conscription were the occasion of one of Lawrence's rare contacts with pacifist organizations: "I send you on these papers from No-Conscription league. I sent them another 2/6; they are worthy." Lacy 1029. Heseltine managed to stay out of the army for the duration, with the help of a "nervous stricture"—an inability to urinate in public? or a spastic colon?

50. CB I, 350, 351.

51. *Women in Love* (New York: privately printed, 1920), p. 70.

52. 27 May 1933; unpub., BL. "a certain girl": probably Dorothy Warren (see p. 171 above).

53. PL 256.

54. Lacy 1127 (misdated).

55. Among Lady Juliette Huxley's papers at the University of Texas is a soulful rejection of a suitor, who may have been Heseltine; see also MOM II, 86. She married Julian Huxley in 1919.

56. CB I, 351.

57. CL 427, 430.

58. CL 432–433.

59. 23 February 1916; unpub.

60. Hux 320.

61. Hux 332; To Catherine Carswell, 25 February 1916; not in Lacy; unpub.

62. Hux 333.

63. Hux 329.

64. Hux 333.

65. CL 433; CL 428.

NOTES

CHAPTER VI

1. Lacy 1060, 21 March.
2. Hux 339–341.
3. CL 439.
4. BTW 402.
5. CL 441–442; Lacy 1057.
6. Lacy 1058; Zyt 75.
7. JMM/OM, 26 March 1916; unpub., TxU.
8. MOM II, 84, 87.
9. CB I, 369.
10. BTW 403, CL 444, Zyt 78.
11. BTW 403.
12. FL/OM, early April 1916; unpub., TuX.
13. CL 444.
14. JMM/OM, 12 April 1916; unpub., TxU. "Monstrum, horrendum . . ." A horrible, deformed, huge monster: Vergil's description of Polyphemus in *Aeneid*, III.
15. FLM 425.
16. KM/SSK, 11 May 1916, RLC.
17. "Prologue to *Women in Love*", *Phoenix II*, 104–107.
18. BTW 409–412.
19. Hux 346–347; CL 451; Lacy 1086.
20. Hux 348–349.
21. Lacy 1086.
22. Chase, *The American Novel and its Tradition* (Garden City: Doubleday, 1957), p. 13.
23. CL 453.
24. CL 449.
25. CL 448.
26. 11 May, RLC.
27. KM/OM, ?17 May, TxU.
28. *Gossip*, 93–94.
29. LKM I, 316; KMJ 146.
30. LKM I, 68.
31. RDHL 78.
32. JMM/OM, 14 May, BRA.
33. CL 452.
34. BTW 417.
35. CL 455.
36. CL 565.
37. RDHL 17.
38. Lacy 1093.
39. CL 465.
40. CL 450–451.
41. CL 455.
42. CL 456; KM/OM, ?3 August 1916, TxU.
43. SFD 369.
44. CL 458.
45. Zyt 84.
46. CL 459–460.
47. FF 236.
48. CL 455.
49. TLS, 15 June 1916.
50. CL 463.
51. KMJ 158–159.
52. MGL 114, 115.
53. Zyt 86.

54. KM/SSK, ?24 June 1916, RLC.

55. Zyt 87, 92.

56. LKM I, 72 (misdated—should be 27 July 1916).

57. BTW 423; JMM/OM, ?28 July 1916, TxU.

58. BTW 421–422.

59. Lacy 1142.

60. CL 466.

61. CP 912, from the *Amores* version of "Dreams Old and Nascent." In 1928 Lawrence repudiated this text: "I have altered *Dreams Nascent,* that exceedingly funny and optimistic piece of rhymeless poetry which Ford Hueffer printed in the *English Review,* and which introduced me to the public. The public seemed to like it. The M. P. for school-teachers said I was an ornament to the educational system, whereupon I knew it must be the ordinary me which had made itself heard, and not the demon. Anyhow, I was always uneasy about it." (CP 852).

62. TLS, 20 August 1916.

63. CB I, 389.

64. CL 470.

65. CL 470.

66. MG/OM, 2 September 1916, TxU.

67. RDHL 95.

68. Zyt 91–92. "Androphobia": presumably a slip of the pen for "anthrophobia."

69. Hux 368.

70. CL 475–476.

71. CL 476.

72. Zyt 94.

73. JMM/OM, 28 July 1916, TxU; BTW 433.

74. Lea 54.

75. JMM/OM, c. 31 August 1916, TxU.

76. ABR II, 20.

77. FL/OM, ?10 September 1916, TxU.

78. CL 472.

79. FLM 204–206.

80. KM/OM, ?late October 1916, TxU.

81. SP 76.

82. CL 479.

83. SP 67–68.

84. SP 80, 82.

85. MGL 111, 108, 128.

86. John Woodeson, *Mark Gertler: Biography of a Painter, 1891–1939* (London: Sidgwick & Jackson, 1972), p. 228.

87. CL 477.

88. CL 477. "Kot's dog": Kot was known for his ability to howl so much like a dog as to deceive other dogs—a talent he had developed as a young man in Russia.

89. CL 478.

90. CL 478.

91. Zyt 97; the letter is dated "Monday 21 November," but 21 November was a Tuesday. For further details of the complex manuscript history of *Women in Love* see Ross and Kinkead-Weekes.

92. Printed by Ross in DHLR 8, no. 2, p. 205.

93. CL 480, Hux 378.

94. Lacy 1142, 6 November 1916.

95. Ibid.

96. Lacy 981, 1142.

97. CL 482, 483.

NOTES

CHAPTER VII

1. CL 483.
2. Hux 378.
3. CL 486.
4. CL 487.
5. CB I, 406.
6. CL 490, 491.
7. CL 493; CB I, 407.
8. CL 265, 491.
9. CB I, 409, 406.
10. CL 490.
11. DHL/CC, 21 November 1916, Yale.
12. Hux 380.
13. Hux 387, CL 497.
14. DHL/CC, 21 November 1916, Yale; CL 488.
15. Hux 383, CL 484.
16. OM/BR, 2 January 1917, BRA.
17. MOM II, 128.
18. DHL/CC, 15 January 1917, Yale.
19. MOM II, 128.
20. KM/OM, "Sunday night", ?7 or ?14 January 1917, TxU.
21. Hux 393, *Num. People* 231.
22. MOM II, 129.
23. CL 502.
24. AD 294.
25. Conversation with the author.
26. Darroch 201; OM/BR, 6 January 1917, BRA.
27. MOM II, 129; FLM 210.
28. CL 481.
29. CL 482.
30. Hux. 380.
31. CL 493.
32. DHLR 6, 255; Hux 389.
33. Lacy 1181, 1177.
34. SM 202, CL 423, SM 205.
35. Lacy 1178.
36. CL 497.
37. DHLR 6, 10; Hux 395.
38. Lacy 1194.
39. Lacy 1201.
40. Lacy 1203.
41. CL 501; DHL/CC, ?13 February 1917.
42. CL 486.
43. CL 498.
44. Hux 398.
45. CL 514.
46. Hux 401.
47. All quotations from "The Reality of Peace" are from the text in *Phoenix*.
48. Hux 403.
49. Zyt 112.
50. CL 512.
51. AD 294–296.
52. Lacy 1236, CL 511.
53. InH 231.
54. DHL/CC, ?13 February 1917, Yale.

55. Luhan, *Lorenzo in Taos* (New York: Knopf, 1932), 41–43.
56. Luhan 40, 51.
57. SP 92.
58. CL 513.
59. CL 562.
60. Hux 408.
61. CL 515.
62. RDHL 91.
63. CL 489–490.
64. DHLR 6, 266.
65. *Musical Chairs,* 126.
66. CL 523.
67. *Pioneer* 119.
68. CL 520.
69. CL 520.
70. *Pioneer* 119; CL 525.
71. CL 525–526.
72. CL 508.
73. Hux 414.
74. DHLR 6, 253.
75. On the revisions see Ross in DHLR 8, 206–208.
76. CL 519–520.
77. CL 525.
78. Included in SM, but not in SCAL.
79. Lacy 1113, CL 471.
80. CB I, 403.
81. *Pioneer* 119.
82. SP 95.
83. FLM 360, 327, 295.
84. From the early text in SM (revised in SCAL).
85. CB I, 501.
86. CB I, 436–437.
87. *My Life and Times: Octave Five 1915–1923* (London: Chatto & Windus, 1966), 167–168.
88. Lacy 1390. One should record Stanley Hocking's response, in 1967, to the suggestion that Lawrence might have been homosexual: "Not to my knowledge. I refuse to believe that Lawrence was homosexual. No, no! He already had a woman to dapple with." (DHLR 6, 250).
89. In June 1975 the author was informed by the Cornish police that the relevant "day-books"—records of police actions—have not survived.
90. *Musical Chairs,* 128.
91. Ibid., 127.
92. Ibid., 129–130.
93. Lacy 1255, CL 516.
94. CL 527.
95. Clark 301.

CHAPTER VIII

1. DHLR 6, 282.
2. AD 356; the poems were *Look! We Have Come Through!*
3. *The Autobiography of William Carlos Williams* (New York: New Directions, 1967), p. 69.
4. CL 288.
5. Unfortunately, all their early correspondence seems to have been lost.
6. CB I, 237.

7. CL 505.

8. Quotations from *Bid Me to Live* are from the Grove Press edition (New York, 1960).

9. CL 529.

10. H. D., *Tribute to Freud* (Boston: David R. Godine, 1974), p. xiv.

11. CL 532, with names supplied from ms.

12. CL 529.

13. CL 531.

14. *Musical Chairs,* 132.

15. Lacy 1300.

16. Hux 450.

17. CL 527. Cross did, however, pay Lawrence his fee; see their correspondence at Yale.

18. CB I, 447.

19. *Peter Warlock,* 168.

20. SP 101.

21. TLS, 22 November 1917.

22. CB I, 448.

23. AD 376.

24. Michael Hastings, *The Handsomest Young Man in England: Rupert Brooke* (London: Michael Joseph, 1967), p. 196.

25. AD 365; CB I, 400.

26. AD 361; Lacy 1296.

27. CB III, 98.

28. CB III, 96.

29. *In Flanders Fields* (New York: Ballantine, 1958), p. 198.

30. CL 528.

31. CL 539.

32. Lacy 1304.

33. CL 538.

34. CB I, 458; Lacy 1328.

35. Hux 432–433.

36. CL 538.

37. NIBW 92.

38. CL 539, FLM 462.

39. CB I, 455.

40. CB I, 463.

41. Conversation with the author.

42. CL 535.

43. MGL 157.

44. CL 542–543, 548.

45. CL 545–546.

46. Lacy 1354.

47. CL 542. George Lansbury: Labour Party leader and pacifist.

48. Zyt 134.

49. CL 545.

50. CL 514.

51. CL 543, 549.

52. AD 415–416.

53. Lacy 1339, CL 548.

54. AD 419, 424.

55. Zyt 155, CL 575.

56. CL 544.

57. CL 625, 617, 593.

58. Lacy 1382.

59. CB I, 465.

60. CL 547.

61. CL 550–551.

62. CL 551.

NOTES

CHAPTER IX

1. *Sons and Lovers,* chap. 7.
2. CL 552, 566.
3. CL 552, 555; CB I, 469.
4. Hux 446.
5. PL 453.
6. CL 560, 554.
7. CL 556.
8. Hux 446.
9. MGL 160, CL 559.
10. *The Evolution of an Intellectual* (London: Cobden-Sanderson, 1920), 70, 79.
11. AD 417.
12. AD 418.
13. CL 556.
14. DHL/LR, 14, 17 June 1918, RLF Archives.
15. RLF Archives.
16. CL 560, Zyt 144, CL 561.
17. CL 558, 559.
18. CL 550.
19. CB I, 471; CL 561.
20. *Phoenix* 80.
21. Hux 450.
22. CL 558.
23. CL 563.
24. MGL 162.
25. Zyt 149.
26. SP 110, Hux 452.
27. AD xviii.
28. CL 567.
29. Lacy 1417a.
30. Hux 453–455.
31. Zyt 146.
32. CL 563.
33. See Frank Kermode, "Lawrence and the Apocalyptic Types." *Critical Quarterly* 10 (1968), 14–38.
34. CL 563–564.
35. CL 563.
36. LKM I, 191.
37. Alpers 267.
38. MLM 135, BTW 490.
39. JMM/CC, 5 February 1933, TxU; KML 310; RDHL 93.
40. Lacy 1433. Balaam's ass recognized the angel of the Lord, though its master didn't.
41. LKM I, 193.
42. Lacy 1435.
43. SFD 483, 484.
44. ABR II, 35; *Goodbye to All That* (Garden City: Doubleday, 1957), p. 278.
45. FF 190–191.
46. KM/OM, ?14 November 1918, TxU.
47. FF 192.

INDEX

NOTE: Lawrence's works are listed under their published titles.

Index

Index

Index

Grant, Duncan, 49–50, 80, 86, 90, 276, 339, 384

Graves, Robert, 319, 384

Gray, Cecil, 198, 203, 248, 316–19, 380, 350, 354, 372; Frieda's affair with, 311, 331–33; friendship with, 299–300, 303; Lawrence to, on history, 368, 369; Lawrence to, on horror of Flanders, 342; Lawrence's expulsion and, 325; Lawrence's plan for Colombian community and, 334–36; on Lawrence's sexual potentialities, 313

Grenfell, Billie, 339

Grenfell, Ivo, 338–39

Grenfell, Julian, 339

Gross, Otto, 332

Haig, first Earl (Douglas Haig), 239

Hardy, G. H., 77–79

Hardy, Thomas, 9, 31, 35

Harrison, Austin, 288, 290, 293

Heartbreak House (G. B. Shaw), 381

Hegel, G. W. F., 118, 134

Heinemann, William, 8

Henderson, Arthur, 120

Henry, Nancy, 369

Henry, William, 279

Heraclitus, 118, 119, 121, 149, 190, 208, 288

Heseltine, Philip, 180, 185–87, 196, 197–202, 216–18, 298, 300, 316; break with, 204–5, 220, 234, 278; new Ranamin and, 168–72, 174; and putting together *Amores*, 195; and *The Rainbow Books and Music*, 192–94, 203; "The Reality of Peace" and, 337

Hewlett, Maurice, 17

History: views on, 368–69, 376–77

History (Lawrence), 368, 369, 371

Hitler, Adolf, 134

Hocking, Mabel, 279

Hocking, Mary, 279

Hocking, Mrs., 298

Hocking, Stanley, 279, 283, 298, 305, 325

Hocking, William Henry, 209–15, 325, 331, 334, 335, 355, 367

Hogarth (publisher), 378

Homosexuality: beetles as symbols of anal intercourse, 88–89; of F. Birrell, 87–89, 99, 313; blood-brotherhood and, 218, 222–29; 310–11, 314; conflict created by feelings of, 50; of Dickinson, 79; erotic feelings toward Murry, 223–24 (*see also* Murry, John Middleton); of Forster, 53–55; of D. Garnett, 50, 86–88; in "Goats and Compasses", 198; of Keynes, 50, 79–80, 82, 89, 225, 289, 313; Lawrence-

Hocking relationship, 309–15, 331, 367; in Prologue of *Women in Love*, 228; in "The Reality of Peace", 289; of Strachey, 24, 50, 86; unfulfilled social passion and, 53; in *Women in Love*, 198, 228

Hone, Joseph, 337

Hopkin, Enid, 362

Hopkin, Sallie, 29, 143, 292, 294, 362, 370

Hopkin, Willie, 29, 38, 70, 143, 292, 300, 356, 362, 374, 382

Horne (friend), 11, 96

"Horse-Dealer's Daughter" (The Miracle"; Lawrence), 285

Housman, A. E., 77

Huebsch, B. W. (and publishing house), 157, 167, 192

Humanity: contempt for, 150–51, 210–11; misanthropic attitude toward, 81–86; separation from, 245–50

Hunt, Violet, 100, 102, 103

Hutchinson, Mary, 348

Huxley, Aldous, 68, 92, 168, 172, 253

Individualism, 32–34

Industrialism: opposition to, 178; in *Study of Thomas Hardy*, 33–34; views on, 139

Jaffe, Edgar (brother-in-law), 32

Jaffe, Else von Richthofen (sister-in-law), 106

James, Henry, 6, 164, 166, 281

Jews, 260, 301–3, 308, 345

John, Augustus, 338, 339

Jones, Ernest, 237

Joyce, James, 16, 281, 337

Kangaroo (Lawrence), 7, 236, 280, 292, 298, 314, 334; Armistice Day in, 385; blood-brotherhood in, 310–11; Derby medical examination in, 375–76; expulsion from Cornwall described in, 325; Gray in, 300; harassment by authorities in, 317, 319; occultism in, 301; threat of conscription as central to, 18; war as seen in, 238

Keynes, J. M., 50, 77–83, 90, 96, 99, 225, 251, 289, 384, 386; D. Garnett and, 86, 87; homosexuality of, 50, 79–80, 82, 89, 225, 289, 313

Khroustchoff, Boris, 201

King, Emily (sister), 180, 292, 362

Kipling, Rudyard, 8

Koteliansky, Samuel Solomonovich (Kot), 11, 21, 26, 60, 68, 84, 197, 253, 268, 284,

(414)

Index

Index

Index

Index

Index

Index

DATE DUE

MAR 2 2 '85			
GAYLORD			PRINTED IN U.S.A